The Ecologies of Amateur Theatre

GW00673016

Helen Nicholson • Nadine Holdsworth
Jane Milling

The Ecologies of
Amateur Theatre

Helen Nicholson
Department of Drama, Theatre and
Dance
Royal Holloway, University of London
Egham, UK

Nadine Holdsworth
School of Theatre and Performance
Studies
University of Warwick
Coventry, UK

Jane Milling
Department of Drama
University of Exeter
Exeter, UK

ISBN 978-1-137-50809-6   ISBN 978-1-137-50810-2   (eBook)
https://doi.org/10.1057/978-1-137-50810-2

Library of Congress Control Number: 2018955707

Cover illustration: Kevin Mitchell in Collingwood RSC's *Puss in Boots* photo: Pam Johns

This Palgrave Macmillan imprint is published by the registered company Springer Nature
Limited
The registered company address is: The Campus, 4 Crinan Street, London, N1 9XW, United
Kingdom

Acknowledgements

This book has been, in many ways, a labour of love and we are indebted to numerous people who took time to share their insights and experience with us. Firstly, we would like to thank all the amateur theatre-makers who generously gave their time to talk to us, show us their theatres, open their archives and invited us to play readings, rehearsals and committee meetings, and who explained the challenges of set-building, lighting, prop and costume-making. We have felt warmly welcomed by many people in different amateur theatre companies, and their enthusiasm, dedication and creativity are recognised and acknowledged in the pages of this book.

We would particularly like to acknowledge the contribution to our research made by the national and international organisations whose work supports amateur theatre. Members of Voluntary Arts, The Little Theatre Guild, The Guild of Drama Adjudicators, the National Operatic and Dramatic Association, The All-England Festival and IATA/AITA offered wise advice and helpful encouragement.

We have appreciated the generosity of spirit shown by many people who work in the professional theatre, particularly The Royal Shakespeare Company, who spared time to be interviewed and shared their experiences of working with the amateur theatre sector. Our academic colleagues in theatre and performance studies and across the Arts and Humanities Research Council's Connected Communities Scheme have provided intellectual challenges as we developed our work, and we know the book is richer for their contributions.

And finally, we would like to acknowledge the immense contribution made to the research by Molly Flynn and Erin Walcon who, at different times, served as postdoctoral researchers on the two funded projects that informed this book. Cara Gray and Sarah Penny were inspiring doctoral researchers on the project, and we thank them for their enthusiasm, imagination and hard work.

This research was generously funded by two grants from the Arts and Humanities Research Council (AHRC): *Amateur Dramatics: Crafting Communities in Time and Space* REF: AH/K001922/1: *For Love or Money? Collaboration between Professional and amateur theatre*, REF: AH/N001567/1.

The AHRC recognises that the Arts and Humanities investigate the values and beliefs which underpin both who we are as individuals and how we undertake our responsibilities to our society and to humanity globally. We hope that this book contributes to that ambition.

Arts & Humanities
Research Council

CONTENTS

LIST OF FIGURES

CHAPTER 1

Ecologies of Amateur Theatre

July 2017. There is soft rain falling on an open-air production of *Twelfth Night* in the atmospheric gardens of Bowes Museum in Barnard Castle, in northeast England. The audience has come dressed for the weather, and hot pies will be served in the interval. This production of *Twelfth Night*, directed by Jill Cole, has a Victorian Steampunk theme, and the pre-show entertainment, aided by enthusiasts from the Teeside Steampunk Society, captures its playful mood. The play will begin in less than ten minutes, and anticipation is building. The company, The Castle Players, has a strong reputation for inventive and entertaining performances, which is strengthened by their collaboration with the Royal Shakespeare Company (RSC) as part of the latter's Open Stages Programme in which amateurs and professionals work together. Audiences for amateur companies are often sociable, even to people they have never met before, and I am quickly engaged in conversation by the couple sitting next to me. We look at the programme together and they tell me about people in the cast—one is a psychologist who works in the prison and another is a gardener. And Sir Andrew Aguecheek, they say, works in the sandwich shop. (Helen's Research Diary, July 2017)

October 2014. People of all ages are laughing and greeting each other warmly as they congregate in a large multi-purpose venue on HMS Collingwood, a naval base in the south of England, to begin the first of their twice-weekly rehearsals for *Dick Whittington*. In mid-October people are already struggling to get tickets for the five performances that will run 4–7th December. This is a popular group with a local reputation for putting on a

© The Author(s) 2018
H. Nicholson et al., *The Ecologies of Amateur Theatre*,
https://doi.org/10.1057/978-1-137-50810-2_1

good panto. I've been welcomed to watch proceedings and have been guided through the rigmarole of security having previously submitted my personal details and car registration. I learn that every audience member has to do this too and reminded that this is an odd place to see a show. The surprises keep coming. In the middle of a car park there is a dedicated storage and making facility where a group of women are chatting and busy assembling props: a giant three-tiered wedding cake, a large chest full of sparkly jewels and rat noses made from black feathers. Robin Sheppard, who is playing the pantomime dame whilst his teenage daughter is in the chorus, is trying on a host of garish costumes. He tells me about his personal collection of high heels and we have a conversation about the best places to buy 'big bras'! He is mischievous and makes a fabulous dame. (Nadine's Research Diary, October 2014)

February 2015. I am standing amidst racks of ornate costumes in the chilly wardrobe upstairs in Sidmouth Amateur Dramatic Society's purpose-built rehearsal space, as a small committee consults with director Gill Coley on casting the summer production, *Steel Magnolias*. During the evening auditions, different combinations of voices have offered glimpses of future comic performances, and Gill has gently guided work on the moment where M'Lynn talks of her daughter's death, the room quietened as we experience the play's emotional force. While the potential cast sips coffee expectantly downstairs, upstairs members pool their expertise to help Gill balance opportunities for individual performers against the needs of the play. They know *Steel Magnolias* will be popular with audiences, and that it needs the chemistry of a strong ensemble to do it justice and demonstrate SADS's ambition and prowess. More than that they need a hairdresser, prepared to coach the cast for free programme publicity. (Jane's Research Diary, February 2015)

Amateur theatre-makers are everywhere. Each week, year after year, people come together to make theatre. They rehearse in village halls, community centres, the backrooms of pubs, suburban sitting rooms, military bases and in beautiful atmospheric theatre-buildings owned and run by amateurs. Sheds and garages become workshops for set-building and prop-making, and bedrooms are crammed with half-finished costumes, rolls of fabric and boxes of ribbon. Memories are captured in old press cuttings and programmes stored in battered albums under beds and production photographs are proudly displayed in homes and on the walls of amateur theatres. Traces of amateur performances are archived in old shoe-boxes, productions replayed on scratched DVDs and the histories of amateur theatre companies carefully crafted into self-published books. Amateur theatre is part of the biographies of public buildings, integral to community-building and place-making, and central to the creative and cultural lives of those who, year after year, make theatre for the love of it.

Yet amateur theatre inhabits a paradoxical space. On the one hand, for its participants and audiences, amateur theatre is deeply enmeshed in life's rhythms, shaping the pattern of each year and marking life's changes as roles move from one generation to the next. For many communities, particularly those outside major cities and metropolitan centres, amateur theatre is simply *the theatre*, enabling audiences to discover new plays and enjoy old favourites, and to appreciate the liveness of theatre with the added delight of seeing familiar faces in different guises. On the other, amateur theatre is frequently unrecognised as part of the cultural ecology of contemporary theatre, largely invisible in the academy and, in professional theatre and popular culture, amateurs have been at best largely ignored and at worst derided. This book aims to open this paradox for critical scrutiny, to understand how the histories of amateur theatre illuminate the present, to analyse the contribution made by amateur theatre to the contemporary cultural economy and to shed light on its significance as a creative practice. *The Ecologies of Amateur Theatre* aims to address this form of cultural participation in its diversity and complexity, acknowledging its historical and social contingency.

So what is amateur theatre? Paying attention to amateur theatre reveals, of course, that it carries a multiplicity of meanings and includes a wide range of practices. The three snapshots with which we began the chapter hint at this spectrum; there is no one 'amateur theatre' any more than there is one professional theatre. The term 'amateur theatre' itself defies neat definition—for the purposes of our study we took it to refer to companies of people who make theatre in, with and for their local communities for love rather than money. Yet throughout our research we have found a porosity between different sectors, and the boundaries between the professional and amateur activity are rather more loosely drawn than is often understood. Professional musicians, choreographers, lighting technicians and electricians are regularly employed by amateurs, and playwrights, publishers and suppliers of stage lighting, costumes and sound equipment benefit from the amateur market. Some amateurs turn professional, but maintain links with the local amateur company that nurtured their talent. There is also a trend for professional theatre companies to invite unpaid 'volunteers' to join their productions, or to engage 'community casts' to widen access to the arts in which the authenticity of 'real people' on stage is valued as an aesthetic strategy (Holdsworth et al. 2017). Although we are alert to the iniquity of working practices where volunteers take the place of paid theatre workers, and recognise the opportunities offered to community casts by professional directors, our subject in this book is the work of amateur theatre *companies*, self-governing organisations whose primary focus is to make theatre. An amateur is very different from a volunteer; amateurs often sustain a life-long passion for their interest, whereas voluntary work suggests willing service, often to an organisation that is professionally managed. The distinction between head and heart is captured in the language; the word volunteer derives from the Latin voluntārius—of free will, whereas amateur famously stems from amātōr—to love.

This book takes place in the context of a contemporary amateur turn, and a renewed interest in the amateur in the twenty-first century. Reality TV shows have brought the amateur to public attention, with amateur bakers, amateur painters, amateur choirs, amateur potters, amateur dressmakers, amateur interior designers and many others displaying technical skill, creativity and passion for their craft in weekly competitions, often judged by leading professionals in their field. One such programme featured amateur theatre-makers; Sky Arts' *Stagestruck* in 2011 followed the fortunes of eight amateur theatre companies who competed to perform on a stage in London's West End. Nicolas Kent, the production company's creative director, recognised the communitarianism associated with amateur theatre: '*Stagestruck* is more than a talent show, it's a celebration of how amateur theatre can be a beating heart of communities across Britain'.[1] These programmes have all been aired on mainstream UK television, but global franchises repeat the format in many other countries, suggesting that amateur creativity is commercially successful as well as increasingly visible. Some amateurs forge careers that take advantage of their new-found status as TV celebrities, monetarising their wide appeal as 'ordinary' people who have honed their craft at home. The internet has brought a cultural revolution that supports a plethora of new forms of online creative participation—including bloggers, vloggers, film-makers,

---

[1] https://www.theguardian.com/stage/theatreblog/2011/may/11/am-dram-amateur-dramatics-professional. Accessed 15 June 2018.

critics, musicians, writers—who can easily and cheaply upload their work and distribute it through a wide range of websites and platforms. Digital technologies and interactive forms of performance have tested old distinctions between producers and consumers, promising new modes of participation. This new awareness of the power of the amateur led US art critic Ralph Rugoff to guest curate an exhibition, *Amateurs*, at the Wattis Institute for Contemporary Arts in San Francisco in 2008 that tested its cultural boundaries. In the accompanying publication, he declared that we are 'on the cusp of a cultural revolution', in which 'amateurs have returned with a vengeance' (2008: 9).

The primary motive for the research that informs this book was not, however, curiosity for the twenty-first century fashion for amateurs. Rather, it was inspired by a broader interest in how and why people make theatre in amateur companies that have arisen organically within local communities, and whose work was not initiated by professional theatremakers. Numerous studies of community theatre (Kershaw 1992; Jeffers and Moriarty 2017), socially engaged theatre (Bishop 2012; Jackson 2011; Cohen-Cruz 2010) and applied theatre (Nicholson 2014; Thompson 2009; Shaughnessy 2012) have highlighted the benefits of creative interventions by professional theatre-makers, where people in communities and institutions (schools, prisons, hospitals and so on) are encouraged to take part in different modes of artistic activity, activism and performance. There is, of course, an important place for this work within the cultural ecology, and it has taken its rightful place in the academy and in cultural policy alongside other forms of professional theatre-making. By contrast, however, there has been very little scholarly attention on amateur theatre (usually termed 'community' theatre in the United States). Insightful and important work on the history of amateur theatre and its close cousin, private theatricals, has been undertaken by David Coates (2017), Claire Cochrane (2001, 2011), Judith Hawley and Mary Isbell (2012) and Michael Dobson (2011), and John Lowerson's study of amateur operatics in 2005 addresses related territory. Arts consultant Francois Matarasso moved the debate into the twenty-first century with his close attention to a musical theatre company in the English town of West Bromwich in his volume *Where we Dream* (2012), and Ruth Finnegan's detailed study of amateur musicians, *The Hidden Musicians* (2007), captures a richness of musical culture in Milton Keynes, a modernist town about fifty miles north of London. Nicholas Ridout's book, *Passionate*

Amateurs: Theatre, Communism, and Love (2013) explores a very different set of concerns, focusing on an international account of theatre that
includes the work of Anton Chekhov, the Moscow Arts Theatre and
Augusto Boal as illustrative of 'romantic anti-capitalism' (2013: 6). It is
striking that the work of amateur theatre companies rarely features in academic debates about contemporary productions, nor are amateur theatre-
makers included in discussions about theatre and nationhood, place,
community, repertoire, heritage or identity and largely absent from discussions about theatre in community settings (Nicholson 2015). It is curious
that theatre and performance studies, a discipline that prides itself on its
egalitarianism, has been complicit in upholding a cultural hierarchy in
which amateur theatre has been largely disregarded. If Pierre Bourdieu's
(1992) claim that the academy legitimises particular tastes still holds
weight, this study of amateur theatre is not simply a response to an omis-
sion or oversight. It is also political, an act of cultural recognition.

   This introductory chapter frames debates that will be addressed in the
book, and defines the parameters of our study. By describing amateur theatre in ecological terms, we aim to explore its processes and practices as a
meshwork and multifaceted field of cultural production. An ecology of
practices recognises the shared knowledge and know-how that amateurs
possess, the friendships and informal networks that it inspires, the ways in
which it shapes lives, defines communities and contributes to place-
making. It does not aim to draw tight boundaries around fixed definitions,
rather, it aims to open questions, forge new connections and analyse principles of exclusion and inclusion. Further, our contention is that the amateur, when conceptualised as part of an ecology of theatre practices,
provides what Isabel Stengers calls a 'tool for thinking' about the dynamics of theatre as a whole (2005). Taking amateur theatre seriously as a
subject of inquiry presses us to re-think orthodoxies surrounding cultural
value, and to look at theatre from another perspective.

AMATEUR THEATRE AND CULTURAL VALUE

Even the most enthusiastic of amateur theatre-makers must acknowledge
that it is subject to stereotyping. Scarred by its association with the description of all kinds of poor quality practices as 'amateurish', the amateur sector is understandably resistant to the ways in which it is frequently cast in
popular culture and in the popular imagination. Arguably 'am-dram' suf-
fers more than other amateur practices from such derogatory caricatures,

perhaps in part because it involves the unpredictability of public performance. Furthermore, in contrast to more individualised forms of amateur craft, amateur theatre is dependent on social networks, friendship and shared histories, with companies often sustaining their own in-jokes, playfulness, rivalries and rituals over many years. As with all communities of interest, when seen from the outside, amateur theatre companies are sometimes vulnerable to charges of exclusion, however welcoming and inclusive they intend to be. One of the ambitions of this book is to focus on the cultural value of amateur theatre for its participants and audiences, a process that, following Geoffrey Crossick and Patrycja Kaszynska's excellent report, *Understanding the Arts and Cultural Value*, aims to 'reposition first-hand, individual experience of arts and culture at the heart of enquiry' (2016: 7).

Throughout the research that informs this book, we have benefitted from experiencing amateur theatre at first-hand, gaining unprecedented access to the processes and practices of amateur theatre-making. In Stephen Knott's elegant analysis of amateur craft, it is the processes of making, rather than the finished product, that defines the special qualities of amateur creativity. By describing amateur craft as an absorbing process and a dedicated practice, Knott neatly side-steps judgements of quality and taste that might otherwise be involved in assessing the products of amateur labour:

> [C]oncentration on processes of making rather than the final output leads to experiences of joy and play that are close to resembling the utopian dream of unalienated labour. So often overlooked, amateur craft is more complex, innovative, unexpected, roguish, humorous and elusive than its use as a cover-all term for inadequacy and shoddy work (amateurishness). (2015: xii)

Amateur theatre-makers may recognise themselves in this combination of roguish humour, playfulness and attention to detail; theatre-making involves many different forms of craft-knowledge, and the processes of set-building, prop-making and costume construction, for example, are often absorbing and creatively satisfying in themselves. Focussing attention on the practices of amateur crafts rather than definitions of amateurs themselves, as Knott recommends, has two important consequences. First, it challenges the idea, offered by sociologist Robert Stebbins, that amateurs can be categorised according to different types. Stebbins' taxonomy of amateurs delineates people according to their attitude and expertise, from novice and dabblers to participants and devotees. Stebbins books, *Amateurs: On the Margin between Work and Leisure* (1979), *Amateurs, Professionals and Serious Leisure* (1992) and *Serious Leisure* (2007) all recognise the significance of amateur activities to those involved. He notes that one way in which they are distinguished from other domestic tasks (he cites painting the house or laying a lawn) is that amateurs sustain their interest with commitment over time, whereas everyday jobs are simply a means to an end. But Stebbins' taxonomy has the effect of assessing amateurs according to the quality of their work, and his view of 'amateur thespians' conforms to familiar tropes. Second, by attending to the processes of making we hope to shed light on the spatio-temporal qualities of amateur creativity, and the expertise of amateur craftworkers. As Rugoff argues in his essay 'Other Experts', 'we are all amateurs' in some aspects of life, further suggesting that the boundaries between amateur and professional activities are not fixed, and that there are always 'networks of connection' between different cultural spheres (2008: 14).

In relation to amateur theatre, however, Knott's emphasis on amateur craft as process rather than product would be limiting. For amateur theatre-makers, the time-pressure of productions provides an important impetus for people with different forms of craft-knowledge to collaborate, and bringing a production together is part of the power of the experience and integral to its creative satisfaction. As such, throughout this book we are interested in how the repertoire and processes of making inform amateur productions, and in how performances are experienced by local communities. Our aim is not, however, to make judgements of taste nor to systematically assess the production values of performances we have witnessed. Rather, we seek to reposition the cultural value of amateur theatre by attending to both in the crafts of making theatre and the affective intensity of performance, recognising that both require collaboration, commitment and expertise. Part of our ambition in this book, therefore, is to challenge unthinking assumptions about 'am-dram', and reclaim the term 'amateur' as a mark of respect.

By focusing on amateur theatre *companies*, we are interested both in the agency of self-organising groups and in how they contribute to crafting their local communities. Professional theatre-makers have long been attracted to working in community settings, often to address what they perceive as a lack of creative opportunities, or, perhaps more accurately, to give local people the chance to participate in the kind of art-making that they value. Community theatre in Britain, as conceived by Ann Jellicoe and David Edgar in the 1960s and 1970s, tended to be project-based and led by paid professionals, often with a political agenda. For those on the political Left, the perceived conservatism of 'am-dram' was seen as an obstacle to the aspirations of community theatre. As Michael Mangan observed in relation to British culture, 'community theatre has an identity separate from that of am-dram: it is usually theatre with some kind of social agenda, often involving the celebration of a place or social group' (2010: 159). Community theatre has a long history of radical intervention, as Baz Kershaw famously argued, and throughout the mid and late twentieth century its disparate practices were united by a shared commitment to 'resistance to the dominant order... to egalitarianism and participatory democracy' (1992: 40). Jan Cohen-Cruz elegantly describes the radical vision of 1960s community-based performance in the United States in similar terms, as a contribution to participatory democracy (2005). Amateur theatre companies are usually less politically motivated, and tend to regard any social and personal benefit as a welcome by-product; their primary interest lies in the creative activity of putting on plays they find challenging and enjoyable to stage. In the same essay, Mangan associates 'am-dram' with artistic conservativism, but he is wrong in his claim that amateur theatre is 'seldom the home of the most cutting-edge or experimental theatre' (2010: 159). In an era when theatres in major cities are forging their own identities as innovative producing houses or reviving well-known plays and musicals that guarantee box office success, many new plays reach new audiences and are kept alive by amateur productions. Simon Stephen's *Pornography* (2007), Howard Brenton's *Anne Boleyn* (2010), Alecky Blythe's *London Road* (2011) and Jessica Swale's *Nell Gwynn* (2015) quickly became part of the amateur repertoire as soon as performing rights were released.

Twenty-first century community artists and policy-makers may have lost some of the spirit of counter-culturalism evident in the 1960s and 1970s, but there is a renewed interest encouraging widespread participation in the arts. Often framed as campaigns, initiatives such as the Fun Palaces began in 2014 to advocate for 'culture at the heart of every community', the BBC Arts Get Creative Campaign started in 2015 to 'boost creativity in the UK, as well as celebrate the millions of people already doing something artistic and creative every day', and in the same year 64 Million Artists initiated their national campaign to 'unlock the potential of

everyone in the UK through creativity'.[2] Fun Palaces emphasises community, whereas for 64 Million Artists, an organisation funded by Arts
Council England, creative activity is more individualised, as illustrated in
their mission:

> We believe passionately that everyone has the right to a creative life, that we
> are all instinctively creative but that often gets knocked out of us at school
> or work. With partners we are developing simple ways of helping people do
> stuff again, to just have a go without worrying about being good at some-
> thing or being an expert.[3]

The target of this campaign is neither amateurs nor amateur organisations, who are often skilled craftspeople who aspire to high standards and
are frequently interested in artistic complexity. Neither does it recognise
the creativity involved in quotidian life, which is not 'knocked out of us'
but, as anthropologists Tim Ingold and Elizabeth Hallam argue, is articulated in how we improvise, move and connect with the materials around
us (2007: 2–8). Furthermore, as Grayson Perry has observed, creativity is
expressed in the clothes we wear, in hairstyles, in our musical tastes, and
the aesthetics of home-making (Perry 2012). More significant for this
study is that such well-intentioned campaigns are largely built on a deficit
model—what organisers perceive to be lacking or missing in other people's lives. In many ways this new focus on creativity in adult life is much-
needed; arts organisations and funders have long encouraged young
people to join youth theatres, but there has been little support for those
who wish to continue to make theatre in adult life. But it is also noticeable, and perhaps significant, that some campaigns have missed opportunities to promote the creativity of the amateur sector as it already exists.

New terminology has arisen to describe creative activity in response to
the contemporary interest in cultural participation. Terms such as 'everyday creativity' and 'non-professional artists' have become widely used in
the cultural sector, with well-meaning ambitions to avoid, as one report
suggests, the 'belittling connotations' associated with the amateur and the

---

home-made.[4] But there are significant differences between 'everyday creativity' and amateur creativity. An analogy might illustrate the point. To be described as an 'everyday cook', for example, does not imply any specific skill-set nor sustained interest, whereas it might be reasonably expected that amateur cooks, amateur chefs or amateur bakers have acquired significant expertise and are committed to improve. Furthermore, distinguishing between professional and non-professional theatre-makers suggests distinctions of pay and training that are often less clear in practice than this terminology suggests. This misrepresentation extends to a national survey in the United Kingdom, *Taking Part*,[5] where participation in the arts and cultural activity is monitored and data officially collected. The results include information about 'voluntary work', which may be a euphemism for amateur participation, but it risks rendering amateur creativity invisible.

The term 'amateur' is only belittling if it is used pejoratively. Our contention is that there is still a need for the word in the lexicon, and that euphemisms or substitutes risk undermining the creativity of amateur participants and undervaluing an important part of cultural life. Our critical tendency throughout this book is to interrogate the cultural value ascribed to amateur practices, and this includes why the term amateur is circumvented, by whom, and what this avoidance does politically. Focusing further, we are interested in the specificity of amateur theatre rather than generalised ideas about amateur creativity and creative participation, although both impinge on this study. This responds to Crossick and Kaszynska's perception that cultural value is rooted in experience and practice:

> [T]hinking about cultural value needs to give far more attention to the way people experience their engagement with arts and culture, to be grounded in what it means to produce or consume them or, increasingly as digital technologies advance as part of people's lives, to do both at the same time. (2016: 7)

---

[4] See *Towards cultural democracy: promoting cultural capabilities for everyone*, 2017, Kings College London, p. 21. www.kcl.ac.uk/Cultural/-/Projects/Towards-cultural-democracy. aspx. Accessed 30 Dec 2017.

[5] See https://www.gov.uk/guidance/taking-part-survey. Accessed 31 Jan 2017.

Our research is driven by attention to what amateur theatre means to its many participants. We are interested in why people choose to take part in *theatre*, rather than seeking to explain the attraction of creative activity in general. What is special about the practices of amateur theatre that is different from other social art forms, such as singing in a choir or playing in a band or orchestra? Such questioning demands an expanded understanding of amateur theatre's multiple and changing practices, and an investigation of the enduring complexity of its affective power.

ECOLOGIES OF AMATEUR THEATRE: A TOOL FOR THINKING

In using the word 'ecologies' to describe this study of amateur theatre, we are invoking an analogy rather than considering the ecological implications of amateur theatre or its effect on the environment, however important this may be. The term 'ecologies' is intended to capture the ways in which amateur theatre is a situated practice, sited in places or communities, and rooted in its local environment. It also recognises that amateur theatre not only has its own networks and systems of support, and that it contributes to the wider ecosystem of theatre, whether this is described as professional theatre, community theatre or other forms of participatory performance. An ecology of theatre practices points to their fluidity and interdependence, and illuminates how their spheres of interest intersect and overlap, and where there is dissonance and difference. As Kershaw puts it: 'Theatre ecology is the ways theatres behave as ecosystems' (2007: 16).

Recognising that amateur theatre is integral to an ecology of theatre practices locates our research firmly within the disciplinary field of theatre and performance studies. In other words, this is not a sociological evaluation that measures the impact of amateur theatre on its participants, nor does it offer a detailed statistical analysis of members of amateur theatre companies, nor seek to make recommendations about what amateur theatre should or should not do in the future. Rather, we aimed to engage with the messiness of amateur theatre as a living practice, with a lens through which to think through the social, political and communitarian role of theatre. Isabel Stengers, writing about her philosophical encounters with science, suggests that this process is never neutral:

> What I call an ecology of practice is a tool for thinking through what is happening, and a tool is never neutral. A tool can be passed from hand to hand, but each time the gesture of taking it in hand will be a particular one. (2005: 185)

Stengers' 'tool for thinking' is an appealing image, not least because it invokes the materiality of theatre practices that we have encountered in our research. It also invites us to be open-handed about our own thinking tools. Although grounded in the study of theatre, *The Ecologies of Amateur Theatre* employs an interdisciplinary approach to think through questions relating to heritage, archive, labour and repertoire, and to analyse their relationships to place, community, identity and creativity.

The book is structured in eight chapters, each of which raises a different set of critical concerns. In Chapter 2, *Valuing Amateur Theatre*, we trace the evolution and complexity of the amateur theatre movement, and examine the role amateur theatre organisations have played in developing the cultural landscape of England and beyond. We trace how amateur theatre supported the place of adult cultural education and the institution of the National Theatre, and curated provision of regional theatre. Drawing on theories of diverse economies this chapter raises questions around the shifting perception of the value of amateur theatre and its relationship to cultural policy. Chapter 3, *Amateur Repertoires*, investigates the repertoires of amateur theatres and examines the place that amateur companies have in curating the national picture of live performance. In thinking about repertoires not as a fixed collection of play texts but as reiterative processes of 'repertoiring', the chapter reflects on the implications of amateur performance for playwrights, publishers, canons and new writing in the wider cultural ecology. In Chapter 4, *Amateur Theatre and Place-making*, we debate how amateur theatre contributes to the cultural health of a community. In this chapter we chart how amateur theatre thrived as part of a utopian vision, taking as case studies amateur theatre in Garden Cities and new towns, and noting its place amongst commuters who were sold a lifestyle in suburbia. Drawing on theories of place and place-making from cultural and creative geographies, this chapter raises questions about the role of amateur theatre in contemporary community life. Chapter 5, *Making Time for Amateur Theatre*, debates how participation in amateur theatre reflects changing patterns of work and leisure. The chapter investigates amateur theatre companies that arise from workplaces, and how they illuminate different forms of labour. It opens questions about what is meant by 'free time', and explores how amateur theatre companies respond to changing experiences of work and time.

In Chapter 6, *Making Amateur Theatre*, we turn our attention to making amateur theatre as craft and the creative processes that result in the swathe of amateur productions that populate village halls, community centres and little theatres every week. We argue that contrary to the stereotype of shoddy practice, that amateur theatre is often characterised by skilled labour and a desire to improve despite underlying material constraints. We also explore how amateur theatre, as a social and relational practice, helps to make and shape individuals and build communities, whilst also acknowledging how it can both reflect and challenge wider issues with access, inclusion and diversity in society. Drawing on theories of heritage and material culture, Chapter 7, *Amateur Theatre: Heritage and Invented Traditions*, considers how amateur theatre relates to questions of tangible and intangible heritage. We investigate how heritage-based projects, invented performance traditions and the digital realm have been put to work to capture histories and memories of theatre-making as a means of asserting the cultural value of this activity for people, companies and local communities.

In our conclusion, *Theatre and the Amateur Turn: New Ecologies*, we open questions about the place of amateur theatre in the future, drawing on the renewed and contemporary interest in amateur creativity.

Throughout this book we have sought to understand 'what is happening', to borrow Stengers' phrase, by setting clear parameters around the historical and geographical reach of our research. As this is the first major study of amateur theatre, we were keen to avoid unhelpful generalisations and so we have focused our attention on amateur theatre companies in England, though in so doing we recognise that amateur theatre is an international movement, and that the practices we discuss have long been shared across and within national borders. Our study is focused on and around companies that have theatre-making with and by adults as their primary purpose, but we are also aware that there is also much we have missed; amateur theatre happens in the Young Farmers, the Women's Institute, churches and many other community-based organisations, many of whom have a strong interest in charitable giving and voluntarism. To situate amateur theatre in an historical context, we have taken the long twentieth century as a starting point, a moment when amateur theatre became increasingly organised into societies, membership companies and national organisations. In so doing, we recognise that there is a longer and deeper history of different forms of amateur performance to which Cochrane, Hawley and Coates are contributing to in the UK context and which is being further investigated by theatre historians including Mary Isbell, Diego Pellecchia and Stacy Wolf in other parts of the world. The purpose of this book is not to construct a linear history of amateur theatre nor an archive of practices, but to understand its place in the contemporary ecosystem by historicising the present. By structuring the analysis to address some of the pressing issues that face theatre in many settings—the relationship between community, time, labour, repertoire, creativity and so on—the debates raised in *The Ecologies of Amateur Theatre* have resonance beyond the geographical and historical reach of our study. This conceptual framing, tested in the 'real' social contexts in which amateur theatre takes place, has relevance in other settings. The book aims to provide a tool for thinking seriously about amateur theatre as an ecology of practices in the twenty-first century, and how and why it has changed over time.

AMATEUR THEATRE RESEARCH AS FEELING-WORK

Amateur theatre-makers are enthusiasts by definition, and enthusiasm can be very infectious. One of the challenges we faced in undertaking this research was to find methodologies that enabled us to respond to the passion felt by amateur theatre-makers for their craft, and remain alert to new questions and modes of analysis. We also encountered many people for whom our funded research project brought a welcome visibility to amateur theatre and, understandably, this act of cultural recognition meant that they were keen for us to learn about their companies at their best. All narratives are selective, and we attended to questions arising from what we were told in interviews or read in archives, and listened to the gaps and silences in stories we heard. As oral historian Alessandro Portelli pointed out, 'memory is not a passive depository of facts, but an active process of creation of meanings' (1998: 69).

The research process intended to invite people involved in amateur theatre to reflect on their involvement, and articulate—sometimes for the first time—how they felt it shaped their lives. As researchers, we wanted to experience amateur theatre at first-hand, and we attended to the sensory and affective experiences of witnessing rehearsals, performances, committee meetings and other encounters. This form of ethnographic research as 'sensory participation' has been well theorised by anthropologists and cultural geographers, an approach elegantly summarised by Sarah Pink:

[I]t recognises the emplaced ethnographer as her or himself part of a social, sensory and material environment *and* acknowledges the political and ideological agendas and power relations integral to the contexts and circumstances of the ethnographic processes. (2009: 23)

Following Pink, this empathetic study of amateur theatre acknowledges our own feelings and emotional responses as well as seeking to understand its place in the cultural ecology. At each stage in the process, we developed research methods that aimed to capture the richness and texture of amateur theatre as a practice. We invited amateur theatre-makers to tell stories from evocative objects, to re-enact the scripts of old pantomimes and to respond to old photographs and documents we found in archives. In trying to understand the ecologies of amateur theatre we have attended auditions, rehearsals, costume-making groups and set-building weekends, competitive festivals, committee meetings and training workshops. We have visited archives in people's houses, in old broom cupboards in theatres, under stages in village halls and we have studied Facebook pages and trawled websites. We have seen a spectrum of productions in a plethora of settings: pantomimes in village halls and military bases, adaptations of TV favourites in community centres, revivals of plays in church halls, Shakespeare in stately home gardens, and contemporary plays, sometimes staged in atmospheric theatres lovingly maintained by members of the Little Theatre Guild. By engaging in a study that was open to the unexpected, we expected to learn about the everyday qualities of amateur theatre practice. Stengers summarises the generous intentions of this methodology:

Approaching a practice then means approaching it as it diverges, that is, feeling its borders, experimenting with the questions which practitioners may accept as relevant, even if they are not their own questions, rather than posing insulting questions that would lead them to mobilise and transform the border into a defence against their outside. (2005: 184)

Approaching the practice of amateur theatre 'as it diverges' meant that we found that amateur theatre-makers became increasingly involved in the research process, and, reciprocally, on many occasions we found ourselves emotionally moved by the work we witnessed. We have tried to capture something of the immediacy of our responses to meetings, rehearsals, productions and other events throughout this book by including extracts from our research diaries, which sit alongside recalled conversations and more formal interviews that listen to the voices of the many people who have taken the time to talk to us about making amateur theatre. As such, it might also be described, following Erin Hurley, as 'feeling-work' (2010).

The research was designed to enable us to experience a variety of different contexts in which amateur theatre takes place. Funded by two grants from the Arts and Humanities Research Council, we undertook a range of detailed case studies focusing first on amateur theatre in Garden Cities and suburbia, in the Royal Navy, in seaside towns and rural villages. Part of our aim in these case studies was to understand the contribution amateur theatre makes to the cultural economy outside major metropolitan centres. Alongside this, Erin Walcon, post-doctoral researcher on the project, engaged with companies in city centres, Acting Out, an LGBTQ company in Birmingham, and Philippine Theatre UK, a London-based company whose work is informed by the Filipino heritage of many of their members. Our case studies enabled us to work closely with different companies over time, undertaking detailed ethnographies of varying aspects of their work. As the project progressed, we extended our research to a wide range of companies across England and, with Molly Flynn the post-doctoral researcher on this part of the project, we turned our attention to the relationship between amateur and professional theatres with a particular focus on the RSC's *Open Stages* project, the first large-scale national intervention of a professional theatre company in the amateur theatre scene. As doctoral students, Sarah Penny has engaged in thorough archival research on amateur theatre and performance rituals on board ships in the Royal Navy, and Cara Gray's detailed ethnography of backstage work in amateur companies in Letchworth Garden City also informed this study.[6]

Throughout our research we have been overwhelmed by the generosity we have experienced from the amateur theatre-makers. Many amateur theatre companies and amateur organisations responded positively to our invitation to be part of the research, but it was also important to recognise where there was reluctance to participate. Some were concerned about intrusion, and we suspect that others simply saw academic research as irrelevant; it is perhaps sobering to be reminded that academics have a reputation for ivory-towered uselessness, perhaps particularly amongst those who have little experience of universities or who just want to get on with

---

[6] See Walcon and Nicholson (2017), Flynn (2017), Penny (2016) and Gray (2017).

the job at hand. Reciprocally, in discussing our research in universities we have occasionally encountered academics who, to our surprise, have mistakenly assumed that amateur theatre is undertaken only by people who are white and socially privileged. There is no one socio-economic group that dominates amateur theatre, and participants include people from a wide demographic, often working alongside each other in one company. We have not shied away from raising difficult questions about how few people who are black British, British Asian or other racialised minorities participate in amateur theatre, and this is a significant issue that some companies and the campaigning organisation Voluntary Arts are doing much to address. We wanted to ensure that a wide range of voices, practices and experiences were represented in our research, and, as we came more rooted in the amateur sector, we sometimes felt defensive when we have encountered prejudice against amateur theatre-makers, particularly when it came from those who enjoy the privilege of social and cultural capital with little first-hand knowledge of their work.

Describing our research as 'feeling-work' does not imply either a lack of critical engagement, nor that emotional responses have always been positive. Feelings can serve as a barometer of cultural value and political sensibilities, and sensitivity to our own and other's affective responses to amateur theatre illuminates the kind of deeply engrained attitudes and social practices Bourdieu described as *habitus*. Margaret Wetherell articulates the relationship between affect, emotion and social processes:

> How do social formations grab people? ... The advantage of affect is that it brings the dramatic and everyday back into social analysis. It draws attention to moments of resentment, kindness, grumpiness, ennui and feeling good, to the extremities of distress that can result from ill-use, and to the intensities of ecstasy. (2012: 2)

By embedding our research within the everyday practices of amateur theatre, we found that the affective enthusiasm and atmosphere of amateur theatre is often contagious, as Teresa Brennan promised. But we have also experienced moments of discomfort, felt in various degrees from mild awkwardness to more complicated feelings of unease. When attending a production alone, for example, we have found that the barrier of a research notebook is no protection against the discomfort of audience participation. Our feminist sensibilities were tested when we found that many people who lead amateur theatre companies are called chair*men*—an obsolete term in universities—and further surprised to find that this is often an accurate description.[7] Conversely, we have encountered many women directors in amateur theatre, and in numbers that puts the gender balance of professional theatre directors to shame. During our research we have encountered artistic tastes that we have not shared, and sometimes we have heard attitudes that we have found troublesome. Reflecting on our own affective responses to the research has been part of the feeling-work we have undertaken, particularly when feelings of ambivalence meant that we bumped up against our own values, leading us to undertake complicated emotional and strategic work. Sometimes we remained challenged, but at other times we learnt to see things differently. An example of backstage work might illustrate this kind of conundrum. On the one hand, a group of retired women making costumes in one room and older men making sets in a nearby workshop looks—and is—a clear division of labour along gender lines, raising questions about access, gate-keeping and so on. On the other, spending time with these groups revealed the deep connections people felt through working together, their shared histories and layers of mutual support. In fragile times, in which social isolation is increasingly evident amongst those who no longer work, it seemed misguided to disrupt this delicate ecology.

Capturing the affective power of research encounters we have experienced at first-hand is challenging in a book that is co-authored. The argument and analysis has been developed together and in collaboration, but we have each been the lead author for different chapters, with others adding examples as appropriate. Each time draft chapters passed 'from hand to hand', to repeat Stengers' suggestion, they changed a little, with 'the gesture of taking it in hand' adding to the texture of the analysis. Writing in this way has allowed, we hope, for the richness of the first-hand experience to be captured as far as the flatness and two-dimensionality of a book can allow. Our representation of amateur theatre, and amateur theatre-makers is inescapably partial and partisan, and inevitably there are as many omissions as there are inclusions. By engaging with the histories and practices of amateur theatre, however, it is their resilience, imagination and resourcefulness that lies at the heart of this book.

---

[7] We should also note that some inspirational women leaders in the amateur sector prefer the term chairman; Anne Gilmour, former Chairman of the Little Theatre Guild and secretary of International Amateur Theatres Association, observed that she would rather not be described as a 'piece of furniture'. Conversation Anne Gilmour with Helen Nicholson, Ealing, 25 October 2017.

References

Bishop, Claire. 2012. *Artificial Hells: Participatory Art and the Politics of Spectatorship*. London: Verso.

Coates, David. 2017. A Whistle-Stop Tour of Amateur Theatricals in Nineteenth Century Britain. www.youtube.com/watch?v=eRFMxKn5oR8. Accessed 27 Dec 2017.

Cochrane, Claire. 2001. 'The Pervasiveness of the Commonplace': The Historian and Amateur Theatre. *Theatre Research International* 26 (3): 233–242.

———. 2011. *Twentieth Century British Theatre Industry, Art and Empire*. Cambridge: Cambridge University Press.

Cohen-Cruz, Jan. 2005. *Local Acts: Community-Based Performance in the United States*. New Brunswick/London: Rutgers University Press.

———. 2010. *Engaging Performance: Theatre as Call and Response*. London: Routledge.

Crossick, Geoffrey, and Patrycja Kaszynska. 2016. *Understanding the Value of Arts and Culture: The AHRC Cultural Value Project*. London: Arts and Humanities Research Council.

Dobson, Michael. 2011. *Shakespeare and Amateur Performance: A Cultural History*. Cambridge: Cambridge University Press.

Finnegan, Ruth. 2007. *The Hidden Musicians: Music-Making in an English Town*. Middletown: Wesleyan University Press.

Flynn, Molly. 2017. Amateur Hour: Culture, Capital, and the Royal Shakespeare Company's Open Stages Initiative. *RiDE: The Journal of Applied Theatre and Performance* 22 (4): 482–499. https://doi.org/10.1080/13569783.2017.1358082.

Gray, Cara. 2017. *A Study of Amateur Theatre: Making and Making-Do*. Unpublished PhD Thesis, Royal Holloway, University of London.

Hawley, Judith, and Mary Isbell, eds. 2012. *Amateur Theatre Studies: Nineteenth Century Theatre and Film*. Manchester: Manchester University Press.

Holdsworth, Nadine, Jane Milling, and Helen Nicholson. 2017. Theatre, Performance, and the Amateur Turn. *Contemporary Theatre Review* 27 (1): 4–17. https://doi.org/10.1080/10486801.2017.1266229.

Hurley, Erin. 2010. *Theatre & Feeling*. Basingstoke: Palgrave Macmillan.

Ingold, Tim, and Elizabeth Hallam. 2007. *Creativity and Cultural Improvisation*. Oxford: Berg.

Jackson, Shannon. 2011. *Social Works: Performing Art, Supporting Publics*. London: Routledge.

Jeffers, Alison, and Gerri Moriarty. 2017. *Culture, Democracy and the Right to Make Art: The British Community Arts Movement*. London: Methuen.

Kershaw, Baz. 1992. *The Politics of Performance: Radical Theatre as Cultural Intervention*. London: Routledge.

————. 2007. *Theatre Ecologies: Environments and Performance Events.* Cambridge: Cambridge University Press.

Kings College London. 2017. Towards Cultural Democracy: Promoting Cultural Capabilities for Everyone. https://www.kcl.ac.uk/Cultural/-/Projects/Towards-cultural-democracy.aspx. Accessed 4 Aug 2017.

Knott, Stephen. 2015. *Amateur Craft: History and Theory.* London: Bloomsbury.

Lowerson, John. 2005. *Amateur Operatics: A Social and Cultural History.* Manchester: Manchester University Press.

Mangan, Michael. 2010. The Theatre in Modern British Culture. In *The Cambridge Companion to Modern British Culture*, ed. Michael Higgins, Clarissa Smith, and John Storey, 154–170. Cambridge: Cambridge University Press.

Matarasso, Francois. 2012. *Where We Dream: West Bromwich Operatic Society & the Fine Art of Musical Theatre.* West Bromwich: A Multistory Publication.

Nicholson, Helen. 2014. *Applied Drama: The Gift of Theatre.* Second ed. Basingstoke: Palgrave Macmillan.

————. 2015. Absent Amateurs. *RiDE: The Journal of Applied Theatre and Performance* 20 (3): 263–266. https://doi.org/10.1080/13569783.2015.1059262.

Pellecchia, Diego. 2017. Noh Creativity? The Role of Amateurs in Japanese Noh Theatre. *Contemporary Theatre Review* 27 (1): 34–45. https://doi.org/10.1080/10486801.2016.1262848.

Penny, Sarah. 2016. Crossing the Line. *Performance Research* 21 (2): 32–37. https://doi.org/10.1080/13528165.2016.1162524.

Perry, Grayson. 2012. All in the Best Possible Taste with Grayson Perry. Channel 4 TV, June 5.

Pink, Sarah. 2009. *Doing Sensory Ethnography.* London: Sage Publications.

Portelli, Alessandro. 1998. What Makes Oral History Different. In *The Oral History Reader*, ed. Robert Perks and Alistair Thomson, 63–74. London: Routledge.

Ridout, Nicholas. 2013. *Passionate Amateurs: Theatre, Communism, and Love.* Ann Arbour: The University of Michigan Press.

Rugoff, Ralph. 2008. Other Experts. In *Amateurs*, 9–14. California: California College of the Arts.

Shaughnessy, Nicola. 2012. *Applying Performance: Live Art, Socially Engaged Theatre and Affective Practice.* Basingstoke: Palgrave.

Stebbins, Robert A. 1979. *Amateurs: On the Margins Between Work and Leisure.* London: Sage.

————. 1992. *Amateurs, Professionals and Serious Leisure.* Montreal: McGill and Queen's University Press.

————. 2007. *Serious Leisure.* New Brunswick: Transaction Publishers.

Stengers, Isabel. 2005. Introductory Notes on an Ecology of Practices. *Cultural Studies Review* 11 (1): 183–196.

Thompson, James. 2009. *Performance Affects: Applied Theatre and the End of Effect*. Basingstoke: Palgrave Macmillan.

Walcon, Erin, and Helen Nicholson. 2017. The Sociable Aesthetics of Amateur Theatre. *Contemporary Theatre Review* 27 (1): 18–33. https://doi.org/10.10 80/10486801.2016.1262851.

Wetherell, Margaret. 2012. *Affect and Emotion*. London: Sage Publications.

Wolf, Stacy. 2017. 'The Hills Are Alive with the Sound of Music': Musical Theatre at Girls' Jewish Summer Camps in Maine, USA. *Contemporary Theatre Review* 27 (1): 46–60. https://doi.org/10.1080/10486801.2016.1262853.

CHAPTER 2

Valuing Amateur Theatre

Sitting in a regional theatre, built as a repertory stage in 1967 to enhance the cultural provision of a large regional town, I am in the audience for *The Play that Goes Wrong*, on tour in May 2017 after its sell-out West End run. The programme suggests I am in for *The Murder at Haversham Manor* staged by the Cornley Polytechnic Drama Society. The farce that unfolds is premised on a sharply mocking depiction of an amateur theatre company attempting to stage a period murder mystery. Many of the stereotypes of recent depictions of the amateur stage are referenced in the show—the ponderous welcome by the society's president is a catalogue of past disasters and misplaced ambition; the inadequate and hastily-constructed set of painted flats that decomposes as the play goes on; the forgotten lines, or moments where the cast become stuck in a loop of lines; the over-exaggerated physicality; the stage-struck delight of a novice performer who grins back at the audience laughter. There is sharp snobbery in the butt of the meta-theatrical jokes that extend beyond the amateur theatre. The fictional students have studied a conflated 'Meisner Method' acting and Michael Chekhov's techniques with pompous intensity, but cannot implement these lessons in their performances—an attack that mocks both professional theatre's 'naturalist' training and the play's amateur students who misunderstand it. The play is predicated upon a gauche amateurism that is compounded by the premise that this group is from Cornley Polytechnic—a defunct form of educational institution reincarnated since 1992 as a university. Regional theatres themselves are mocked, with their provincially inadequate audiences. Midway through the first act, the lead actor of the play within a play (also the amateur company's director and president) frenziedly hunts for a lost prop. A look to the audience cues our response—'It's under the chaise longue', we shout helpfully. Incensed the character lunges at us screaming 'What are you doing? You're the audience. You're not supposed to join in.' He berates us for our ignorance, 'Provincial blooming theatre! This isn't panto.'[1] The comic frame of the play pits the implied pedestrian, uncultivated educational achievement of these amateurs against the professional ambitions of the director and society president; this amateur company is to be his stepping stone to professional recognition and success.

The play is in a long line of meta-theatrical farces, sharing much with Aristophanes' *Frogs*, that enjoys the miserable failure to meet aesthetic standards. Here, as in many recent meta-theatrical British farces from Alan Ayckbourn's *A Chorus of Disapproval* (1984) to David McGillivray and Walter Zerlin Jr.'s series of *The Farndale Avenue Housing Estate Townswomen's Guild Dramatic Society* plays, the scene of failure to reach theatrical norms is the amateur. As discussed in more detail in the next chapter, these self-mocking depictions of amateurish misadventure have frequently been performed with gusto by amateur groups themselves. But what is so attractive or threatening about amateur theatricality and amateur theatre that has earned it such opprobrium in the contemporary cultural imagination? That question goes to the heart of the debate about the value of amateur theatre and the idea of cultural value itself.

Cultural Value and Amateur Creativity

Amateur theatre is a significant element in the diverse ways in which twenty-first century British theatrical life is organised and experienced. Emerging from a wider survey of amateur arts participation in England, Fiona Dodd and colleagues found over 1,113,000 people were members of amateur theatre groups, whose 92,000 performances reached audiences of over 21 million each year (2008: 32). Many amateur theatre companies are affiliated to the leading membership organisations today, the National Operatic and Dramatic Association (NODA), the Little Theatre Guild

---

[1] The third edition of *The Play that Goes Wrong*, printed to accompany the tour, has the simple instruction 'Vamps to cover' (Lewis et al. 2015: 30).

who, with the Drama Association of Wales and the Scottish Community Drama Association, form a network of support for affiliated companies across the United Kingdom. In England, there are more than 5380 amateur theatre companies regularly producing seasons of work, with many more youth and smaller-scale unaffiliated societies playing a vital role in offering opportunities to make and experience live theatre performance in all areas of the country (Dodd et al. 2008: 17). Amateur theatre groups also participate in the separate All-England Theatre Festival, a competitive one-act play organisation that holds regional, country-wide and national heats. These figures give an indication of the force and presence of amateur theatre in British culture today.

The amateur theatre membership organisations played a complex role in the history of British theatre and are key to understanding the evolution of the contemporary British theatrical landscape. The beginning of the twentieth century saw the appearance of the two largest amateur theatre organisations; the National Amateur Operatic and Dramatic Association (NAODA) was founded in 1899, and the British Drama League followed in 1919. The formation of these two membership organisations, preeminent amongst a number of smaller associations and guilds, marked the rise of the amateur theatre sector as a *movement*. This chapter sets out to look at the emergence and evolution of this movement of amateur theatre, the organisations that nurtured it and continue to coordinate companies and activities, bridging professional and non-professional cultural realms and providing advocacy for amateur theatre and theatre itself. The amateur theatre movement and its organisations have contributed to the establishment of a national theatre culture, had lasting impact on regional theatre provision, and on the idea of theatre as a participatory, creative practice. Although amateur theatre's contribution to the contemporary cultural landscape is evident, it has not been integrated into contemporary cultural policy and the pejorative stereotypes persist, as perpetuated in *The Play that Goes Wrong*. Running alongside the history of the evolving practices of amateur theatre has been a disjunctive representation of amateurs in the cultural imaginary. Thus, the history of the imbrication of amateur theatre in the cultural life of England raises some fascinating questions about the value and importance of culture in creating and sustaining a good life for individuals and communities.

How is the value of amateur creativity and amateur theatre understood in current public policy debates? In recent straitened times for public funding and public subsidy, contemporary cultural policy has been busy articulating the case for continuing public subsidy of culture and the arts, and part of that has been an extended discussion about the value of culture. 'Culture' as imagined by Arts Council England (ACE), the Department for Digital, Culture, Media and Sport (DCMS) and cultural economists has been rather narrowly defined, and cultural policy has largely neglected the rich seam of amateur culture, amateur creativity and the range of amateur theatre activity. Over the late twentieth century, with the rise of knowledge-based economies, culture has increasingly been understood as produced by the cultural industries and, since the 1990s, the creative industries, and cultural policy has focused attention on the production of economic value within the cultural realm. Much energy has been devoted to developing measures for the economic value of culture. Cultural economists Anheier and Isar (2008) and Bakhshi and Throsby (2010) have attempted to calculate an economic equivalence or proxy value for both the production of cultural artefacts and the consumption of cultural experience. Yet even David Throsby, one of the most significant figures in the movement for an economic defence of publicly funded culture, was circumspect, commenting that the experiential value of 'these cultural goods ... cannot be plausibly represented in monetary terms, no matter how they might be assessed' (2003: 279). Amateur theatre is a mode of cultural production in that performances are mounted, audiences sought and tickets sold. Amateur theatre companies operate as *companies*, providing entertainment, often sustaining the buildings in which they perform, and are linked in complex ways to local suppliers and businesses who offer support in kind or advertise in programmes to offset production costs. Indeed, Fiona Dodd's 2008 survey found the annual turnover for amateur theatre across England, including youth, schools and adult amateur theatre productions, was £122 million (2008: 46). Yet, because amateur theatre does not seek to provide a living for its makers, nor are amateur theatres primarily profit-making in constitution, the amateur sector lies outside prevailing understandings of the cultural economy predicated on profit-oriented, free market economics.

Part of the reason that amateur culture has been perceived as less culturally valuable may be precisely because it is not directly related to the cultural marketplace. John Holden, in his report *The Ecology of Culture* (2015), attempted to capture new understandings of cultural value by discussing cultural *ecology* rather than cultural *economy*. Holden's study of the cultural value of the arts discusses publicly funded, commercial and what he calls 'homemade' culture as the third leg of his cultural triad. Likewise Robert

Hewison's *Cultural Capital* (2014) looks at what he calls grassroots arts practices and culture and suggests that these practices have an 'essentially spontaneous and democratic nature' although 'much of this will be trivial and self-referential' (2014: 221). Whilst it is positive that Holden and Hewison see the amateur sphere as a key part of their account of cultural life, they cannot prevent a pejorative romanticism entering their rhetoric. It is difficult to define ways in which amateur theatre is 'essentially spontaneous', or of a more 'democratic nature' than publicly funded participatory work, for example. The characterisation 'homemade' casts the amateur as essentially domestic, local and the 'non-productive' cultural activity of an idealised 'home', and this cannot help but imply that it is less significant than subsidised and professional culture. From this perspective, amateur culture becomes a passive, private realm that might be activated on behalf of funded culture as part of 'building the holistic case for arts and culture', as the former Chair of ACE, Peter Bazalgette, suggested in his annual report *The Value of Arts and Culture to People and Society* (ACE 2014: 7). The rhetorical construction of amateur culture in these studies and reports implies the amateur sector is valuable primarily because it develops an appreciation of the arts, building an audience base for publicly subsidised cultural provision.

As Tim Edensor et al. have suggested, the challenge is to come to 'an understanding of vernacular and everyday landscapes of creativity [that] honours the non-economic values and outcomes produced by alternative, marginal, and quotidian creative practices' (2010: 1). Rather than consider amateur theatre as a non-economically-efficient part of the creative industries, it is more useful to think about amateur culture and amateur economies on their own terms, as part of the diverse economies that cultural geographers Gibson-Graham (2008) and Leyshon and Lee (2003, 2008) have suggested require more attention. Gibson-Graham argues for a much broader understanding of the economy, and they challenge the monolithic construction of 'the' economy. Rather, they emphasise that *diverse economies* are continually in play, and they note the many different ways that economic flows operate beyond simply market forces, including gifts and gifting, volunteer labour, barter, household flows, communal assets and in-kind donation. Throughout our research we have observed these diverse economies in play in different aspects of amateur theatre-making, such as the ways in which volunteers give time to serve on committees, props are sourced from local businesses and costumes are recycled. Gibson-Graham notes that these apparently '"marginal" economic practices and forms of enterprise are actually more prevalent, and account for more hours worked and/or more value produced, than the capitalist sector' (2008: 617). Within this broader understanding of the cultural economy, the value of amateur creativity and amateur aesthetic practices are not configured as marginal or outside the creative industries, but as a dynamic part of a cultural economy that enriches the cultural lives of communities. From this perspective, it is possible to understand that pejorative valuations of amateur theatre in the twenty-first century are produced in part by the commercialisation of the creative industries and in the defence of publicly subsidised arts. This has not always been the case, and a different evaluation of amateur theatre pertained in the early part of the twentieth century. Returning to this history reveals a complex story, in which the amateur sector was fundamental to the evolution of the theatrical ecology of the English regions and to the idea of a national cultural life.

The Amateur Theatre Movement

> It's a grey day in Peterborough, but it is lively in NODA's main office where Sue Cuthbert, Bronwen Stanway and Dale Freeman ply me with coffee and biscuits, generously answer my many questions and help me root through the archive room for back issues of *Noda Bulletin*, AGM minutes, and posters and programmes from shows. The phone rings constantly with queries around the summer school, safeguarding and young performers, fire certification, insurance, health and safety issues when setting up in unexpected halls, employment queries around cleaning staff contracts and holiday pay, raffle running and licensing rules, and the tax implications for successful shows or in-year losses. I talk to Tony Gibbs [then CEO of NODA], who reflects that now more information is accessible online, the value of NODA membership as an advisory service may diminish. Yet, 'amateur theatre is a hobby that has serious financial implications around its activities. There is a tension between the enjoyment of a hobby and the need for more business-like practices. You can't keep running what are in effect small businesses on the back of a fag packet. I suspect in the future, with the rising legal and financial constraints that surround amateur theatre, we may see fewer formally constituted groups'. (Jane's Research Diary, 9 March 2015)

It is precisely supporting individual groups through this complex nexus of financial and legal obligations that NODA articulates as its central aim, providing 'leadership and advice to enable the amateur theatre sector to tackle the challenges and opportunities of the 21st century'.[2] Managing the membership organisation of over 2000 groups and a turnover of almost a million pounds a year, NODA itself slimmed its staff team in the face of diminishing financial stability in 2016 and became a Charitable Incorporated Organisation with limited liabilities for trustees. The other leading umbrella organisation for amateur theatre operating today is the Little Theatre Guild (founded by existing building-based little theatres in 1946), which aims to 'co-ordinate the development of independent amateur theatres across the UK and beyond', representing a membership of just over 110 very active groups who stage over 900 productions annually.[3] As well as supporting their constituent members within the existing legal and financial frameworks, the Little Theatre Guild, and to a lesser extent NODA, also see advocacy on behalf of amateur theatre with arts and cultural policy-makers and government as a central plank of their organisational contribution. Some sense of the complexity of this engagement across a range of sectors and into advocacy is illustrated by the busy activities of the Little Theatre Guild Committee reported on at the Annual General Meeting.

I'm in the audience with 135 delegates at the Little Theatre Guild's 2016 70th Anniversary Annual General Meeting, hosted by The Crescent Theatre, Birmingham. It's been a hectic weekend with stand-up comedy, a chance to meet old friends and new, and I have managed to attend two of the varied workshops on offer. Martin Shaw's workshop on fundraising drew out many stories of successful collaborations with grant-funders, charities, and local authorities in piecing together sustainable improvements to the theatrical infrastructure that amateur theatre companies curate as cultural hubs for their regions. Helen Dyke, an employment law specialist at Irwin Mitchell Solicitors, offered a salutary look at the protection for employee and employer that companies need to have in place for any paid cleaning, technical, or administrative staff. Now, we're gathered back in the main auditorium, as the AGM welcomes new members, reminds groups about the Theatre's Trust Theatre Protection Fund, and Chair Andrew Lowrie reports on meetings with the Chair of the Culture, Media and Sport Committee at Westminster, and the LTG's submission to the Parliamentary Committee Enquiry, *Countries of Culture*. The LTG's recommendations to the

---

[2] https://www.noda.org.uk/about-us. Accessed 18 Dec 2017.
[3] http://littletheatreguild.org/. Accessed 18 Dec 2017.

Countries of Culture Enquiry call for the 'erosion of barriers between the professional and amateur sectors', for National Portfolio Organisations to be obliged to 'develop partnerships with community [amateur] theatres', and for increased funding for regional theatres and for community theatres where they 'represent the only viable cultural facility.' (Lowrie 2016: 3; Jane's Research Diary, 10 April 2016)

The management of an amateur theatre company at even the smallest scale requires at a minimum compliance with a range of current public-facing legislation, adequate insurance and the timely submission of accounts to the charity commission or Her Majesty's Revenue and Customs (HMRC). The burden of this commitment is often the reason societies give for closure, as Colbury and Ashurst Theatrical Society announced in 2013 after twenty years with the retirement of the chairman Stuart Ardern, 'We've run out of administrators … people to run the society' (Churchward 2013). Larger-scale groups and those that manage buildings or run a bar, have exponential levels of legal and financial responsibility. Beyond any cultural and artistic contribution that companies make in their local communities, amateur theatre offers a network of regional cultural hubs, opportunities for creative participation and wider social impacts. Organisations such as NODA and the Little Theatre Guild that coordinate these groups have a representative role to advocate on behalf of companies whose activity is vital part of cultural ecology, but who are currently less heeded than subsidised theatre organisations in cultural policy terms.

This is a strange disconnect because in contemporary cultural policy there has been the return of an anxiety about the passivity of cultural consumption and the implications of this for political citizenship. In part, the ongoing defence of subsidy for cultural and artistic provision is predicated on the principle that any citizen can, and indeed should, join in consuming 'great art for everyone' (O'Brien and Oakley 2015). The additional corollary of this cultural participation is that it models, or can stand in for, a politically engaged population, further defending the principle of democratic inclusion. What is interesting about this configuration is the focus on cultural *participation* not cultural consumption, where the value of arts participation is firmly linked to ideas of good citizenship and active civic participation. In the United Kingdom, Voluntary Arts is the Arts Council-funded organisation (founded 1991) with the task of supporting amateur or voluntary arts participation, promoting 'active participation in creative cultural activities across the UK and Republic of Ireland' and the pan-European articulation of this concern is evident in bodies such as Amateo (established in Slovenia 2008), the European Network for Amateur Participation in Cultural Activities.[4] Amateur theatre is an obvious example of a cultural participation that is neither passive, consumption-based, nor predicated solely on the idea of individual benefits such as personal well-being. The individuals and groups that we have talked to in amateur theatre do not produce in a vacuum, they most often imagine their creative output as connecting to others in their immediate social locale. As we observe in Chapter 4, amateur theatre makes a significant contribution to place-making, often conceived in local terms. This interest in the value of cultural participation extends to shared interest groups in regions, and to an imaginary of nationhood, as we argue in Chapter 7. Whilst individual theatre companies may not have a strong sense of cultural mission and contribution to the cultural ecology, the larger-scale organisations of amateur creativity frequently do, and have a sense of acting as cultural shapers, not just responders.

The separation of the amateur sector so firmly from the professional in cultural policy, and the value judgements implicit in that separation, did not pertain at the opening of the twentieth century. There were many small amateur theatre groups operating in the late nineteenth century, with enthusiasts emerging across urban centres alongside the private theatricals of grand houses or élite groups, as theatre historians Kate Newey (2005) and Judith Hawley and Mary Isbell (2012) have charted. Musical theatre and entertainments were part of garrison life and school culture, and multiple amateur operatic societies sprang up in the late Victorian era in the wake of extensive touring of Carl Rosa's company and the D'Oyly Carte Savoy companies, spreading the entertaining, achievable and politically-savvy Gilbert and Sullivan repertoire from 1875 (Lowerson 2005: 17). There were far fewer companies performing amateur *drama*, new or classical play texts, alongside reviews, musical comedy, operetta and concert party material, but things were to change. The turn of the nineteenth century was a remarkable time of social and technological evolution that produced an experience that 'modernity' had arrived across Europe and North America. Under pressure from the rising Independent Labour movement, a swathe of socially reformist legislation introduced by Liberal governments, notably Lloyd George's People's Budget of 1909, went some way towards

---

[4] https://www.voluntaryarts.org/why-were-here. Accessed 18 Dec 2017.

acknowledging the realities of economic inequality and the social and political threat that this might pose to national contentment (Lineham 2012: 18). The complex political and economic shifts that challenged social hierarchies, particularly the place of women, also prompted a rekindled interest in theatre itself, and the role that drama could play in remaking society. Multiple kinds of amateur theatre groups formed during the first years of the century—those that were politically-committed including in support of women's enfranchisement, those interested in avant-garde aesthetics, and those concerned with local theatrical provision, 'particularly significant in areas where metropolitan dominance and economic constraints had made the growth of an autonomous, home-grown, professional theatre culture difficult to sustain' (Cochrane 2011: 109). This was the moment of transition for amateur theatre, one that saw a sharp increase in the number of companies, and the concomitant emergence of organisations that gave shape to the burgeoning enthusiasm for amateur performance. The founding of the NAODA in 1899, as an act of 'mutual aid' between mainly northern groups who collaborated to tackle the expenses of producing large-scale musical and operetta, was a demonstration of the increased availability of non-work time for many in northern urban settings, a result of recent legislation impelled by early trade union pressure.[5] Whilst paid holidays were an undreamt-of luxury for most workers in England, and not enshrined in law until the Holidays with Pay Act (1938), there was an increase in non-work time for both working- and middle-class Edwardian populations employed outside the home. Civic élites conceded that activities such as music hall, spectator sports such as association football or the coming of cinema might operate as diversion, but historian David Powell notes that a new discourse of anxiety grew around the passivity of this popular commercial entertainment (1996: 37). One of the facilitating conditions for the emergence of so many amateur theatre companies during this period was the encouragement to the *active* use of organised leisure time for those in employment outside the home, including women who, Paul Thompson observes, made up about a third of the working population in 1911 (1992: 5). For women who worked within the home, organised 'leisure' of this sort was less obviously their right. However, non-paid working women might consider their involvement in

---

[5] John Lowerson notes that NAODA dropped 'Amateur' from their title, becoming NODA in 1925 (2005: 145).

early amateur theatre companies to be a form of civic-mindedness, a spirit echoed in the concomitant appearance of The Women's Institute movement (a Canadian initiative, established in the United Kingdom in 1915, to revitalise rural communities) and The Townswomen's Guild (founded 1929, after the introduction of the extended franchise in Britain, to educate women about good citizenship).

Today, one of the stereotypes of amateur theatre is that it is a middle-class pastime, but the appearance of many new amateur theatre companies at the start of the twentieth century was not simply a burgeoning of urban middle-class recreational life. Certainly, the Edwardian era saw an accelerated urbanisation: by the 1911 census 75% of England's population lived in towns, and a quarter of the country considered themselves middle-class. However, this emergent middle class was by no means homogenous, nor is it possible to identify a distinctively separate middle-class culture. As Lowerson suggests, the middle classes 'developed or adopted forms which were both class-specific and yet sufficiently amorphous to spread outside tightly social boundaries in limited circumstances which owed much to local community make-up' (1999: 197). Participation in amateur theatre was not necessarily seen as a 'respectable' pursuit by some tranche of the suburban middle class with its 'inflated social pretension' (Hammerton 1999: 294; Barrett 1999). This spirit is captured in fiction in the upwardly aspirational Pooter of Weedon and George Grossmith's *Diary of a Nobody* (1889), who is appalled when his feckless son, Lupin, takes up with amateur theatrical society the 'Holloway Comedians', a group of rowdy 'rather theatrical' young people (2010: 84).[6] Indeed, rather than a middle-class pursuit, it was in working-class communities that participation in play reading groups or amateur drama was more wholeheartedly engaged with, offering a new mode of cultural self-education. Although the powerful trope that education permitted social mobility both across classes and within classes was contested in the Edwardian era, with good reason,[7] there was a growing interest in cultural education within both working- and middle-

---

[6] The Grossmiths' gentle mockery of amateur theatre in this satire on middle-class anxiety may reflect more on their professional experience: George Grossmith originated twelve of the male leads for Gilbert and Sullivan operettas and Weedon, artist by training, professionally acted and wrote comic plays.

[7] 'Social mobility' was a phrase coined during this period by Pitirim Sorokin, Russian émigré of the failed provisional government, in his *Social Mobility* (New York: Harper Brothers, 1927). Andrew Miles (1999) argues that social mobility trended upwards over the period

class stratas of society and for women as much as men. The career of
J.R. Gregson, a cloth mill worker turned clerk, then journalist and playwright through his involvement with the amateur theatre movement,
illustrates this. His plays were staged at the Leeds Industrial Theatre, a
venue for many of the region's amateur factory groups. He described how
active participation in amateur drama might act as a resistance to patrician
control, and become an expression of a reclaimed working-class cultural
education:

> We were encouraged to think for ourselves and to follow our individual
> bent... Only in the drama did I find the fullest scope for this vital activity
> and in the service of the drama, as a by-product, what real knowledge I pos-
> sess and what real mental ability I exercise. (J.R. Gregson, cited in Rose
> 2001: 82)

That 'Culture' itself was not the preserve of the élite, but might be
accessed, enjoyed and actively participated in, as part of a self-cultivating
activity, underpinned the rising interest in theatre and amateur
theatre-making.

There is another strand to the history of amateur theatre, in which it was
harnessed to socialist ideals in circulation at the early part of the twentieth
century. The story of The People's Theatre, Newcastle illustrates this history of the emergent amateur theatre movement. At its inception, The
People's was primarily part of the progressive, socialist movement, as
People's historians Norman Veitch (1950) and Chris Goulding (1991) have
detailed. In 1911, the group staged Norman McKinnel's *The Bishop's
Candlesticks* (adapted from Hugo's *Les Miserables*) and Gertrude Robins'
village comedy *Pot Luck*, to raise money for the socialist cause. People's
Theatre archivist Martin Collins comments, 'they were just a bunch of local
socialists trying to make a few bob.'[8] After an initial success, the group for-
malised as a Clarion Club, thus a private member's club able to stage cen-
sored work such as George Bernard Shaw's banned *The Shewing up of Blanco
Posnet* (23 September 1911). Robert Blatchford, who founded the Clarion
movement, encouraged Drama clubs to spread across the country, and the

---

1839–1914, although he is sceptical of the overall impact of education on social mobility
over the longer period 1851–1970.

[8] Interview Jane Milling with Martin Collins, The People's Theatre, 24 May 2016.

National Association of Clarion Dramatic Clubs was formed in 1912. The Clarion Dramatic Clubs were just one of the ways that the Clarion movement mixed the benefits of political campaigning for the socialist cause with an attractive organised social life, and Blatchford's weekly newspaper *Clarion* (1891–1934) carried details of the multiple Clarion clubs for cycling, crafts, drama and choral singing, alongside the column 'Stage Land'. The success of the Newcastle Clarion Dramatic Club, which like other progressive theatres were staging Shaw, Synge, Ibsen and Galsworthy, led the early company to think of producing theatre as more than a social activity to raise political funds or for the 'the propaganda of socialism' (Goulding 1991: 14).

> I've been spending the day with the People's Theatre in Newcastle. Now based in leafy Jesmond, Sheila Cooper has taken me on a tour of their amazing rehearsal rooms and I've met the people who keep this huge project going – over 14 shows a year and the main auditorium seats as many as my regional theatre. In the thronging bar, after a funny, pitch-perfect perfor-

Fig. 2.1 Martin Collins, archivist for The People's Theatre, Newcastle-Upon-Tyne, 2016. (Photographer: Jane Milling)

mance of Jessica Swale's *Sense and Sensibility*, I'm talking to the theatre's archivist Martin Collins, who has brought down some of the early minute-books from the archive stores upstairs. Together, careful not to mark the pages, we read over the faithfully-notated, heated discussions of the 1920s about 'whether they should be a socialist organisation that does plays or a drama organisation that supports socialism.' (Jane's Research Diary, 24 May 2016)

The minute-book arguments encapsulate the conflict between principle and practice for the Clarion Dramatic Club, and in 1920 the club adopted the moniker The People's Theatre. It continued to stage theatre not on behalf of the Clarion cause, but rather to develop an aesthetic base that would house a socialist-leaning repertoire and become a beacon for local workers in their area, an instinct shared by other industrial urban amateur theatres such as the Leeds Civic Theatre (1925) and the Bradford Playhouse Company (1929). Raphael Samuel, Ewan MacColl and Stuart Cosgrove's classic study of workers' theatres of the Left traced the rise of politically activist leftist theatre that flourished in the 1920s and 1930s, inspired by Russian and German models, responding to a growing confidence prompted by the first Labour ministry in 1924 under Ramsay MacDonald (Samuel et al. 1985). The Unity Theatre, London (1936) and its many offshoots shared a pan-European socialist commitment as traced by theatre historian Colin Chambers, yet they were also happy to acknowledge their amateur status, and to be members of the British Drama League—Paul Robeson's performance in the Unity's *A Plant in the Sun* won the British Drama League Community Theatre Festival in 1939 (Chambers 1989: 159). The last Unity theatre still operating is the Everyman Theatre Cardiff (founded in 1942), a theatre that straddles the amateur and professional scene today. Other politically activist groups like the movement for women's franchise began to integrate drama, specifically self-authored drama, into their social and activist work. The Actresses Franchise League, initiated in 1908, staged hundreds of plays in diverse settings, as feminist historians Margaret Leask (2012) and Claire Hirschfield (1985) have outlined. These more radical modes of amateur theatre have been readily reclaimed by recent historians, as Claire Cochrane points out, as if they could be opposed to a residual 'ersatz bourgeois "am drama"' (2011: 110). However, such a simplistic binary by no means captures the prevailing situation in the early amateur theatre movement, where to differing degrees all parts of the amateur theatre movement saw themselves as progressive.

The need to revitalise and renew rural communities, and an emerging sense of democratic autonomy within village life itself, gave rise to another association of amateur theatre groups: the Village Drama Society. An unfairly maligned Liberal reform, the Local Government Act (1894) had created a new tranche of *elected*, rather than appointed, parish and district councils, which changed the organisational structures of local life, with 'between a third and a half of the seats won by farmers, a quarter won by craftsmen, and most of the rest by labourers', and about 200 women (Howkins 2003: 23). The Fabian Society celebrated, 'a charter for liberty which makes [the working folk who live in villages] citizens in their own parish and equal with the parson and the squire in its management' (Fabian Society 1894: 3). The spirit of this more democratic rural activity in villages and small towns was linked to the rise in amateur theatre-making, including the rise of 'pageantitis', often spearheaded by rural music theatre societies or amateur theatre companies like the Cotswold Players, some of whom were affiliated to NODA at the time. The Cotswold Players were inaugurated after the success of the Mid-Gloucestershire Pageant of Progress, 2–9 September, 1911 in Stroud. This Liberal-backed pageant, with 1100 local performers, had drawn crowds of over 12,000 as audience, as the company's historian Patrick Howell recounts (2016: 5). The enthusiasm of performers and audience led Constance Smedley to establish the Cotswold Players, and inspired the founding of smaller village groups in the area. Capitalising on the success of the pageant was in part down to Smedley's experience as a writer for amateur theatre companies, and her work with Geoffrey Whitworth, later founder of the British Drama League, in the rural amateur company, The Mummers (Smedley 1937: 6). This rural activity was by no means parochial or culturally isolated; Smedley and others from the company worked in London, her playwriting and direction for outdoor, platform stages consciously explored the rhythmic technique of Copeau's Vieux Colombier troupe (1913), and she and her husband left to teach in US universities during the First World War. The Village Drama Society, organised by Mary Kelly in 1918, brought together many equivalent village groups, and established a network of shared experience across rural communities north and south. Kelly herself noted that the First World War had allowed men to travel widely and they 'for the first time in their lives made the acquaintance of theatre in the shape of Lena Ashwell and other touring companies. The womenfolk had also... been well shuffled, and class distinction had seemed of little importance' (Kelly 1939: 142). As theatre scholar Mick Wallis identifies, Mary Kelly's championing of Women's Institute drama and village theatre societies shared an integrative spirit that 'signalled a modest commitment to democratic change' and displayed 'progressivist cultural innovation' (2000: 348).

All these elements that had impelled the busy amateur theatre-making activity of the Edwardian era had been accelerated by the outbreak of World War One. During the war, entertainment from ad hoc concert parties, Lena Ashwell's repertory tours, to prisoner-of-war revues, had attempted to maintain morale at home and at the fronts. In the immediate aftermath of World War One, there were multiple calls for national 'revitalisation', to re-connect with ideas of 'civilisation', and a series of initiatives for community-building emerged, including the literal building of a rash of Victory halls and spaces of congregation to enhance social life. As part of this revitalisation, Geoffrey Whitworth and friends formed the British Drama League in 1919, 'to assist the development of the art of the Theatre and to promote a right relation between Drama and the life of the community' as the inaugural edition of *Drama*, the national journal of the British Drama League announced (1919: 5) Reflecting on the experience of wartime theatrical activity, Eric J. Patterson declared:

> The first idea behind all concerts and theatrical performances had been to afford amusement for the men... gradually a new idea began to gain ground... To them it was not sufficient to be merely members of an audience, they wished to be members of a movement as well. They wished to learn the art of acting in order to express themselves... This war has not only been an age of destruction, it has also been an age of transition and reconstruction... Democracy has come into its own; therefore, the theatre of the future must be democratic in its outlook. True democracy implies the enrichment of the common life. (1919: 5)

Although this is in many ways a patrician spirit, there is strong articulation of the purposes of the British Drama League and the amateur theatre movement as improving the nation's common cultural life, advocating the educational benefit of theatrical participation, and suggesting that amateur participation might cultivate and console a nation recovering from a global war and social upheaval of an unprecedented kind. Amateur creativity is not viewed as culturally marginal, but as essential to the cultural ecology of reconstruction in post-First World War Britain.

The British Drama League gathered the very diverse range of amateur groups, and joined with the Village Drama Society to become, alongside NAODA, the dominant advocacy group for amateur theatre. It was the British Drama League as an organisation that was to pull the full force of amateur activity across the United Kingdom into focus, and channel the attention of its member groups on a series of key cultural goals to be achieved: the foundation of a national theatre, the awakening of all classes to the benefits of cultural education and the 'art of Acting, Drama and Theatre as forces in the Life of the Nation', including establishing 'a Faculty of Theatre at the Universities of the country' (British Drama League 1945). As Whitworth asserted, 'the Drama was par excellence the art of the people, and the Theatre everybody's business. It was therefore essential that the League should include representatives from every interest involved' (British Drama League 1945). Thus, alongside representatives from amateur groups, the British Drama League's Council included professionals such as actress-manager and activist Lena Ashwell, actress and activist Edith Craig, and Elsie Fogerty, founder of The Central School of Speech and Drama. It linked amateurs with experts from other walks of life alongside professional theatre workers, on its many sub-committees for Drama and Education, Professional Acting, Foreign Drama, Workshop and Bureau, Plays and Publications, Repertory Theatre, Library, Community Theatre Festival Central committee, as well as regional sub-committees. The dizzying scale of work also gives some indication of the ambition of British Drama League for amateur theatre, and for all theatre more widely. The British Drama League offices became located in the heart of Bloomsbury in Fitzroy Square, arguably once a centre of progressive modernism, where George Bernard Shaw, William Archer and Virginia Woolf had lived and artist Roger Fry, who served on the League's Plays and Publication Committee, ran his Omega workshops. The London-centred focus of the League caused some issues with regional groups, and the Scottish Community Drama Association (founded 1926) and the Drama Association of Wales (founded 1934) separated out from the British Drama League in part to champion a national cultural identity not linked back to this London centre.

One of the early activities of the British Drama League was to develop advocacy for theatre as cultural education for adults, as well as children, and they issued a report with the Board of Education, *Drama in Adult Education* (1926) (Emmet 2002). Mick Wallis traces the close relationship between the early spirit of amateur theatre and adult education, particularly the Workers' Educational Association founded in 1903 (2006: 109–115). There were other more radical 'from-below' approaches to adult cultural education. Ness Edwards was a Plebs League lecturer at the Central Labour College (1909–1929), and later a Labour MP, who advocated for a new theatre of facts that would educate the workers, avoiding bourgeois literary gloom (Samuel et al. 1985; Warden 2016). The British Drama League and NAODA approached the Carnegie UK Trust to underwrite a network of County Drama Committees who then employed County Drama Advisers from 1927, making the argument for participation in theatre as a vital element of cultural education (Emmet 2002). In Devon, for example, the County Drama Advisor was initially a full-time drama tutor employed through the Rural Extension Scheme of University College of the Southwest to promote amateur theatre through regional groups. After Carnegie funds ceased, County Advisors funded by Local Education Authorities or Rural Community Councils integrated amateur theatre into further education. The Devon County Committee of the British Drama League welcomed 'the additional resources placed at the disposal of all the voluntary bodies through the agency of the L.E.A.' (Rural Extension Scheme 1938: 68).

> Over coffee, I talk with Leon Winston about the shifting expectations and experience of a County Drama Advisor. A Devon County Drama Advisor from the 1980s, a lecturer at a further education College and occasional director with the Playgoers Society of Dartington, Leon Winston found the role offered 'real excitement, however many amateurs managed to turn out to the workshops. You knew you were leaving something that would help them think differently about their work.' As a multi-tasking Drama Advisor, Leon offered evening lectures, workshops and summer schools, adjudicated and critiqued performances, suggested repertoire, introduced relevant additional reading and training material to groups, and acted as a resource, sometime director, critic and advocate for groups aspiring to extend their abilities in amateur theatre-making. But he notes the shrinking of the role of County Advisor during the late 1980s, as his other work within Further Education came to demand more time, and as young people could study drama as a school subject and gain qualifications in it. (Jane's Research Diary, 10 November 2015)

Debates around the value of amateur theatre as educative or 'just' entertainment had been channelled by the 1949 Entertainment Tax that permitted exemptions for productions staged for non-profit, charitable or educational purposes. This clause might have implied that all amateur companies could escape the tax, but its application was extremely piecemeal and by no means logical: *Charley's Aunt* was considered educational, *Julius Caesar* was not.[9] Not all amateur companies wanted to claim the value of their work was educational, nor did they need to as the British Drama League's aim to see theatre established at the university level was coming to pass. In fact, during the second half of the twentieth century the shifting conception of the value of amateur drama has partly been produced by the development of theatre training and drama education within universities as an academic subject. Glynne Wickham, reflecting on the first drama degree programme at Bristol University in 1947, noted the impetus to university-level study 'had become established in terms of amateur dramatic societies on the perimeters of academic life before that war' (Wickham 1977: 121). Many of the leading figures of the pre-war amateur movement had been occasional university lecturers: Lawrence du Garde Peach taught at the University College of the South West before establishing the Village Players, Great Hucklow; Harley Granville Barker, Chair of the British Drama League, lectured at Cambridge, Oxford and Princeton; Francis Sladen-Smith at the University of Manchester. As Shepherd and Wallis note, drama was frequently figured as part of extramural studies, and the establishment of drama as a degree subject at provincial universities often came through the amateur-facing adult education departments, such as at Leeds in 1960 (2004: 12–14). Having laid the groundwork for the teaching of theatre at university level, the value of amateur theatre as a venue for adult cultural education was considerably changed. Amateur theatrical activity at the turn of the twentieth century was part of a broad-based renewal of interest, across social, political, educational and cultural spheres, in drama and theatre itself, and in what theatre might do in the world. Whether drama was used in presenting progressive subject matter on social issues, as a mode of creative education, as a collective activity in developing community bonds, as an artistic form of modernist innovation, amateur theatre and theatre-making became highly visible as a vibrant activity that might offer a range of people entertaining pleasures, educational opportunities and active, civic-minded involvement.

---

[9] Hansard records the House of Commons debate about this point as the tax was introduced on 6 July 1949: Exemption from Entertainments Duty of Amateur Entertainments, 1949, *Hansard* HC Deb vol 466 col 2192.

BUILDING THE REGIONAL THEATRE LANDSCAPE

Making and staging amateur performance is a key way in which geographical communities represent and celebrate their communal life in the places where they live. Contemporary subsidised regional theatres are tasked with creating 'destination' arts events, promoting tourism or acting as engines of regeneration in urban areas. Amateur theatres are largely freed from these imperatives, but contribute to the enduring, rich local 'structures of feeling', as Raymond Williams coins it—the meanings and values people attribute to their particular social and cultural experiences and relationships—that underpin the cultural life of places (Williams 1971: 64–5; Gilmore 2013: 87). The amateur theatre movement was from its origin predicated as much on a regional cultivation of networks as on a sense of a coherent national body. The importance of regionality was both economically pragmatic—spawned by the simple expediency of sharing resources, scenery, personnel or play sets in a locality—as well as ideological, developing a sense of local or regional cultural identity as riposte to metropolitan condescension and inaccessibility.

In the early twentieth century, a series of progressive legislative measures had enhanced local government's control and responsibilities: over town planning, over new housing provision through the 1911 rate reforms, over education, as the 1902 Education Act placed education under the oversight of county councils, not school boards. This enhanced responsibility of local government for the regional community as a whole marked a shift towards a more interventionist and collective spirit of local democracy, one that regions were enthusiastic to see extended to the cultural realm. Critic, journalist and translator William Archer's lectures on *The Old Drama and the New* (1923) identified the new dramatic turn, and the rise of interest in a new kind of theatre not as driven from the cultural centre of London, but rather drawing energy from a network, sometime competitive, of the large towns and the regions of Britain. For Archer the rise of civic pageants in the first decade of the twentieth century,

> were only the most conspicuous sign of a general hankering after dramatic expression. Village players and community players sprang up on every hand... It is by no mere chance that the pageant movement and repertory theatre movement came into being almost simultaneously. They were concurrent results of the same impulse towards dramatic expression; and in each case the desire to make money if it existed at all played quite a secondary part. (1923: 369)

Archer considered the most important aspect of this increased dramatic activity an introduction of a new kind of repertoire not seen in the provincial main houses or on the commercial touring circuits out of London. This new repertoire—Archer's own championing of Ibsen played a key role in the establishment of European realism in England (Postlewait 1986)—became part of the *raison d'être* of the repertory movement, Little Theatres, and many amateur theatre groups. Indeed the rise of the repertory theatre movement, built upon a burgeoning sense of regional identity, independence and pride, was one in which amateur theatre-makers were intimately connected. George Rowell and Anthony Jackson point out that the repertory theatre movement was driven by a desire for regional cultural provision distinct from the commercial or weakly written products of the stock companies housed in the Theatres Royal, and that this had an amateur impetus (1984: 7). The first repertory theatres, inspired by Annie Horniman's success with the amateur Irish Abbey experiment, grew to emphasise their professional credentials, but most evolved in close collaboration with amateur groups. The Stockport Garrick Society 'prepared the ground' for Horniman's Manchester Repertory Company at the Gaiety Theatre in 1908 (Cochrane 2011: 134). Edwin T. Heyes, who had been chairman of the amateur Stockport Garrick Society, went on to become business manager of the Playgoers' Theatre Company, which provided financial support for the trial season of Manchester Repertory theatre. Barry Jackson's Birmingham Repertory Theatre emerged from the amateur group the Pilgrim Players (Rowell and Jackson 1984: 48–51). The Birmingham Repertory Theatre's mission 'to serve an art instead of making that art serve a commercial purpose' chimes with that aspect of the serious amateur movement that looked, alongside the Independent theatre societies, to reinvigorate the range and ambition of the repertoire available to populations beyond London (D'Monte 2015: 49). As historian Allardyce Nicoll charted, 'almost all [repertory theatres] owed their being to preceding amateur effort', as the enduring enthusiasm of local amateur groups for initiating professional repertory theatres in their area, offering at very least financial support and an audience base (1973: 57). The initial repertory movement, modelled along the lines of the German municipal theatres but without their subsidy, found the economic environment challenging in the early decades of the century. In 1925 the British Drama League appealed to the Carnegie UK Trust that it could do 'a great deal to strengthen and stabilise the Repertory movement by means of quite small short-term subsidies to vigorous young societies, which had not yet secured adequate local recognition to become self-supporting'.[10] Alongside the professional repertory theatres, the first half of the century saw the springing up of multiple amateur repertory theatres, 'little camp-fires twinkling in a great darkness', as J.B. Priestley coined them in his excoriating tour of depression England, *English Journey* (1934). Priestley was speaking as president of the Bradford Civic Theatre, and his identifica-tion of the contribution of the amateur repertories to local communities is captured in his paean to the 'chain of such theatres, small intelligent reper-tory theatres organised on various lines, stretching across the country' as of 'immense social importance':

> To begin with, it is a genuine popular movement, not something fostered by a few rich cranks. The people who work for these theatres are not by any means people who want to kill time. They are generally hard-working men and women... In communities that have suffered the most from industrial depression, among younger people who frequently cannot see what is to become of their jobs and their lives, these theatres have opened little win-dows into a world of ideas, colour, fine movement, exquisite drama, have kept going a stir of thought and imagination for actors, helpers, audiences, have acted as outposts for the army of the citizens of tomorrow, demanding to live. (1934: 197–200)

In championing a new repertoire, the regional impetus of amateur the-atre leant its weight to the development of regional repertory theatres that offered cultural nourishment distinct from commercial touring. Alongside these repertory theatres developed regional amateur groups that offered the chance to see a better repertoire and the opportunity to participate in a cultural education that might mitigate the worst experiences of unem-ployment and regional economic decline during the hard interwar years.

Rather than seeing provincial theatre as the radiating spokes of London-based tours, the rise of the regional repertory theatre meant the providing of 'material that was more challenging as well as tailored to local audi-

---

[10] Carnegie UK Trust Minutes, 1 July 1925, p. 22. Carnegie UK Trust Twelfth Annual Report 1925, p. 116. The beneficiaries were Sheffield Repertory Theatre, the Liverpool Settlement Opera Company, and Mr. Fagan's Oxford Players were already in receipt of Carnegie funds, and the first set of repertory theatres to benefit from the British Drama League's reporting were St. Pancras People's Theatre, Leeds Civic Theatre, Leeds Art Theatre, Edinburgh Repertory Company, Southend Repertory Theatre and Bristol's Little Theatre, all amateur theatre groups.

ences' and thus to the idea of local cultural distinction (D'Monte 2015: 48). Literary scholar James Moran has noted the way in which regional modernism spread as inspiration amongst regions without reference to the culture of the capital. The influence of the amateur enterprise of the Abbey Theatre and of Yeats' playwriting on the English regions is evident in their early repertoire. Indeed, Barry Jackson's amateur Pilgrim Players took Yeats' *The Kings Threshold* (1909) in tandem with productions from the Abbey itself to the London Court Theatre in 1910, inverting the usual mechanisms for cultural dissemination (Moran 2013: 93). The influential critic and amateur theatre director C.B. Purdom also saw the Abbey as a model for theatre that represented a new form of cultural participation the early days of the Garden City Movement. This renewed interest in staging regional identity meant an increased encouragement through the initially amateur and the evolving network of regional repertory theatre companies to stage regional playwrights. Anne Horniman's creation of the Manchester Gaiety Theatre (1908) encouraged what has been dubbed the Manchester School of writers, including the work of Stanley Houghton whose *Hindle Wakes* (1912) was a favourite with amateur groups across Britain. The 1920s saw 'rich supply of rather formulaic one-act plays such as *T'Trip to Blackpool, Fooils and their Brass*, and *Anastasia and Nathaniel go Galivantin' to London*, mainly aimed at northern amateur groups' (Russell 2004: 154). In the context of more regional plays emerging from the repertory theatres with their new capacity to stage locally inspired work, as well as from the production of those plays finding a venue in the amateur little theatres, the need for the capture of regional accents emerged. The British Drama League gathered twenty-four dialect variants, 'typical examples of local speech' on gramophone records (British Drama League 1945). Akin to the activities of the English Folk Dance Society and the gathering of folk songs that Cecil Sharp undertook,[11] the collection of local dialects chimed with the romanticised yet valuable search for, and reinvention of, English national traditionalism as expressed through the local specificity of dialect, accent and culture.

With the outbreak of World War Two, the principles that had carried the amateur movement thus far—theatre-making as uplifting, consoling educative—were all at work in the regional touring work of Council for

---

[11] Indeed, Cecil Sharp was a member of the British Drama League Community Theatre Committee.

the Encouragement of Music and the Arts (CEMA). CEMA was initially happy to include 'those who are making music and acting plays for themselves, because [of] all this means to their own morale and, incidentally, to those people in their localities who can be entertained by their efforts', encouraging home-grown regional theatrical culture (Weingärtner 2012: 56). However, as state funding was increasingly directed at this effort, CEMA began to distinguish between professional provision and amateur facilitation and efforts, a distinction that pitted theatre's social or educative role against its value as 'Art': was CEMA to be an extension of the National Council of Social Services' work, or an Arts Council? CEMA's support for amateur work ceased in 1941. The following year in 1942, the British Drama League submitted *The Civic Theatre Scheme* to 'the Prime Minister, The President of the Board of Education' and CEMA (Heinrich 2010: 69). Mindful of the successful 'morale building' that amateur groups in theatre, music, dance and other arts had been doing through CEMA, the British Drama League argued that municipal authorities should be able to build and maintain civic theatres with local and national subsidy. A joint British Drama League and CEMA conference to promote the scheme was held in June 1943. The British Drama League looked forward to the post-war rebuilding of theatre, envisaging a closer relationship with civic authorities, who have 'grown drama-conscious', local government and the County Education Authorities. Although the British Drama League remained wary of central governmental control that 'in the name of social welfare, might spoil the integrity of the art... At the same time, one of our main preoccupations has always been the Theatre's claim to be recognized by the State' (British Drama League 1945). When it came, the state subsidy for the arts in the form of the Arts Council of Great Britain indeed offered to support regional theatre, although the Arts Council's focus on 'circulating metropolitan excellence' ran somewhat at odds with a second commitment to nationwide, regional provision in 'theatreless areas' (Cochrane 2011: 146–7). The shifting perception of the cultural value of amateur theatre was undoubtedly affected by the creation of the Arts Council of Great Britain. As Taryn Storey has argued, with the translation of CEMA into the Arts Council of Great Britain in 1946, existing commercial theatre managements had a surprisingly powerful effect on the Council and its disbursement of subsidy, and these commercial pressures began to entrench a language of artistic 'standards', 'risk taking' and innovation as the criterion for receipt of subsidy (Storey 2017). Multiple factors marked out amateur companies as ineligible for funding, but the insistence on a rhetoric of 'standards' as a criteria for receipt of public money has compounded pejorative post-war attitudes towards the amateur *as* amateur, and by rhetorical implication not meeting the 'standards' of subsidy.

By 1948, the local authority support for regional culture for which the British Drama League had campaigned was produced through the Local Government Act (1948). The Act permitted local authorities to levy up to sixpence in the rates for provision of entertainment in their locality. Yet in the period of post-war reconstruction, the building of civic theatres was a lesser priority for newly empowered local governments, and few were built until 1960s. A Conference on Civic Theatres in 1965, led by the Association of Municipal Corporations and the Theatres' Advisory Council, evidenced the contribution amateur theatre groups were making to sustaining civic theatres. For example, 'at Rotherham Civic Theatre the programme in 1964 included twenty-eight professional companies and eighteen amateur ones' (Taylor 1976: 75). Yet, a new era of separation between amateur and subsidised theatre was to be repeatedly produced by the rhetoric of the Arts Council: amateur theatricals 'may be short of high professional competence ... but they can certainly foster an interest in the arts and, within their accepted limits, they are a powerful auxiliary of diffusion' (Arts Council 1960: 11). This condescension reflects the accusation of provincialism levelled at regional art forms from the Arts Council. In part, amateur theatre's deep roots and long commitment to regional culture, and its widespread, enduring legacy of theatre-making throughout the country have contributed to this metropolitan disdain. Given the active engagement of the British Drama League in producing this Local Government legislation and civic theatre building, and the local support and fundraising amateur groups lent to these new civic theatres, the increased rhetorical distinction between the amateur and the subsidised in regional civic theatres was a profoundly ironic outcome to a policy that amateur theatre had helped to put in place.

Beyond the regional civic theatres, individual amateur theatre groups continued to contribute to their regional cultural ecology in sustaining the cultural infrastructure of neighbourhoods, villages, market towns and suburbs. Theatre groups hired rooms for rehearsals, sustained, renovated and built local structural assets such as small halls, meeting rooms, theatres and galleries. These cultural assets were frequently built using mixed income from diverse economies, from large-scale philanthropic trusts, local business sponsorship, membership donations, community-based fundraising activities, occasionally grants from local or regional councils, or Lottery funds. The Theatre Royal at Bury St Edmunds, one of the last remaining eighteenth-century auditoria in England, had fallen into disrepair and was used as a store by Greene King Brewery. Amateur theatre groups banded together led by Bury St Edmunds Amateur Operatic & Dramatic Society (BSEAODS) and drew in local civic, charity and central government money to restore the theatre into use in 1965. Now housing a company in receipt of ACE National Portfolio Organisation funding, its fabric is supported by the National Trust.[12] The Theatres Trust, the national advisory body on theatres in the United Kingdom, can tell many similar stories where amateur theatre companies have rescued and revitalised theatres and cinemas that commercial cultural interests can no longer sustain. Little Theatre Guild members today develop a relentless round of improvements, expansion and essential maintenance on the buildings for which they are responsible. Tony Childs of the People's Theatre talks me through the detailed drawings and plans for their expansion; at Bolton Little Theatre, Michael Shipley and I tested the disabled lifts put in with National Lottery Awards for All funding, and archivist Elizabeth Tatham showed me around their Heritage Lottery Funded archive that has been mined for images from performances that were turned into a huge decoupage mural in the refurbished bar (Shipley 2006); Janet Wild of the Progressive Theatre explained the complex funding they put in place for their refurbished foyer; Sidmouth Amateur Dramatics Society built their own rehearsal premises and wardrobe store, after long negotiations, on local council park land; Tom Williams talked me through the extensive funding package Chesil Theatre put together for an ambitious build next to listed properties; the list could go on. This capital expansion demonstrates a close working relationship with small-scale Arts Council capital funding, Heritage Lottery Funds, National Lottery funding, community arts projects, business sponsorship, business community engagement programmes, private sponsorship, local authority funding and charity funding sources. Indeed, in the context of retreating central or local government support for these spaces and activities, volunteers and amateurs feel that they are being asked to step into the breach in sustaining local cultural infrastructure once more.

---

[12] https://www.theatreroyal.org/a-labour-of-love/the-history-of-the-1965-reopening. Accessed 18 Dec 2017.

Fig. 2.2 Bolton Little Theatre: performances from the archive (funded by the Heritage Lottery Fund). (Photographer: Jane Milling)

In many places, amateur theatre companies remain an ongoing financial support for civic and regional theatres both in filling the stages with successful shows in terms of box office take, and in terms of audience-building for a venue. Chris Jaeger, Artistic Director of the Swan Theatre in Worcester, described the impact of amateur involvement on the subsidised professional Swan theatre, established by amateurs in 1965.

> It is an absolute fact that this theatre could not survive without them. Nearly a third of my year is an amateur hire. I get a good weekly rate, plus I get a cracking bar. The theatre would be insolvent if it wasn't for them.[13]

---

[13] Interview Erin Walcon with Chris Jaeger, Swan Theatre Worcester, 9 November 2014. All further quotations taken from this interview.

Understanding the economic contribution that amateur groups were making to the subsidised repertory's survival, Jaeger took a very different approach to the amateur groups, 'who are normally reviled and get very little help'. Jaeger attempted to develop a close relationship with these amateur groups:

> We reduced everybody's weekly rent by a thousand. We formed a Users Committee where everyone who hired the theatre had a twice-yearly meeting to discuss their problems... We used to do a yearly quiz night I'd do an arts quiz with lots of silly prizes. We did a cost price bar and put some food on for them – all the amateur groups put in a team. There was intense rivalry over that.

Most significantly, before the 2002 closure of the subsidised repertory company, all the amateur groups were programmed over the summer in 'a huge indigestible lump of amateur work' when the theatre was insufferably hot. When the theatre ceased working as a producing house, Jaeger programmed around the amateur groups. The theatre moved back into solvency, and even began producing its own work again. Jaeger concluded, 'It doesn't seem to be rocket science to me, they are customers. Who in retail wouldn't look after their customers?' Many regional theatres enjoy the benefits of amateur income, as Paul Jepson of the Northcott Theatre Exeter noted, in 2013, earnings came from thirteen visiting tours and five local amateur groups. At a smaller scale, the Manor Pavillions in Sidmouth mount a summer repertory season, but the tiny theatre is supported by the multiple amateur groups that use the venue,[14] and Postbridge Village Hall could undertake some refurbishments in 2016 with the profits from the one pantomime a year staged by Phyl's Follies. At all scales, there remains strong economic evidence of amateur theatre's continued involvement in regional cultural ecologies. With the demise of the British Drama League the overarching thrust of the development of theatre in the regions has become less urgent—in part because this part of the programme the British Drama League set for itself has been achieved. A recognition of regional strength and collaboration remains strong in the amateur movement—NODA organises its meetings and activities, including many

---

[14] Interview Jane Milling with Shirley Nelson, Sidmouth Amateur Dramatic Society, 26 January 2015.

regional specific competitions, by area, and the Little Theatre Guild is developing a new idea of regional hubs to reinvigorate a sense of collaboration and make additional local activities feasible for its member organisations. Amateur theatre remains a space where communities represent themselves back to local audiences, taking charge of their collective symbolic life. This communal act of making theatre involves amateur theatre-makers in a passionate engagement with a theatrical public sphere, where they are engaged with wider public debates and become part of what theatre scholar Christopher Balme calls 'the cultural body politic of a community' (2014: 45).

Making the National Theatre

Since the mid-nineteenth century leading theatre professionals had called for a national theatre in Britain that would demonstrate national cultural achievement and, through endowment or subsidy, be freed from commercial imperatives. Perhaps surprisingly, the amateur theatre movement was a central driving force for a professional National Theatre, the British Drama League's constitution enshrined the founding of a National Theatre as a leading aim (Emmet 1976). Geoffrey Whitworth, a founder member of the British Drama League, enticed the actor-manager Harley Granville Barker to become its Chair. Granville Barker, co-author of *A National Theatre: Schemes and Estimates* (1907), was a fellow supporter with Whitworth of the advocacy for a National Theatre. Whitworth and the British Drama League ran a competition for architectural designs for this potential national theatre through *Country Life* magazine in 1924.

> Henceforth the League became a kind of flying-buttress to the National Theatre Committee, to the mutual advantage of both bodies. (British Drama League 1945)

The ideal, imagined National Theatre was to embody much of the spirit of the amateur movement: the rediscovered importance of drama in culture, a space for exemplary, non-commercial, serious drama and a demonstration of theatre as social and public good. For Whitworth, a national theatre could be conceived of as 'no less than a Community Theatre writ large... the creation of a public consciously concerned with the practice of theatre art both for its own sake and as a major factor in the enjoyment of life' (1951: 149). In 1929, Whitworth and the British

Drama League hosted a conference attended by MPs and professionals as well as amateurs calling for public subsidy for a national theatre. It was the British Drama League that canvassed the 170 'leaders of British opinion' in support of the plans, as Granville Barker records in *A National Theatre* (1930). The House of Commons debates on the National Theatre Bill (1949) commended the energy of the Shakespeare Memorial National Theatre Committee (of which Whitworth was the honorary secretary), the British Drama League and the London County Council— 'private enterprise, municipal enterprise and State enterprise all working together'—for their advocacy (Rosenthal 2013: 35). Whitworth attended the ceremony to lay the foundation stone at the putative site of the National in 1951, just before his death.

However, this call for a National Theatre also reveals some of the limitations of the British Drama League as a representative organisation for the full range of amateur activity in England. As theatre scholar Loren Kruger argues, the hegemonic notion of a national culture is an imposition of a bourgeois ideal that inevitably occludes dissenting voices and the kind of social unrest epitomised by the 1926 General Strike (1987: 46). Indeed, many of the calls for a national theatre pejoratively commented on the 'masses', who were not imagined as the audience the national would invite. Kruger suggests that when the National Theatre was finally instituted in post-war Britain it was an attempt 'to reassert in the cultural sphere the supremacy lost by Britain in the political and economic spheres', as cultural consolation for 'post-imperial devolution' (1987: 35). This cultural supremacy was predicated on establishing a legitimacy for the theatre and for the best of British writing. The repertoire that most advocates for a national theatre wanted to see was that which might be taught on newly established English literature degrees, those authors—Shaw, Galsworthy, Ibsen—who had also formed the backbone of the early repertoire of the British Drama League theatres. However, this focus excluded a large segment of the amateur world since musical theatre, reviews, operetta, musicals—the repertoire of most members of NODA—were not to be considered appropriate material for the National stage, but rather were to remain the preserve of commercial managements. Given that an essential pre-requisite for the National's success was to be its appeal to a broad base of support, Harley Granville Barker valued the amateur movement primarily as audience-building, as 'breeding ... the audiences to which a National Theatre will appeal' (1930: 4). In this, as in much of the rhetoric around schemes for the National, the audience was conceived as passive, quite in contrast to the spirit of active creation that underpins amateur theatre-making. Essentially, in the move to legitimise theatre itself, the ideal of the National Theatre enshrined a particular range of dramatic literature, and by implication audience, as legitimate high culture. Sociologist Paul DiMaggio charts an equivalent trajectory in the United States, whereby social élites came to establish non-profit organisations as demarcated against commercial and popular activities. Although these 'systems of cultural classification present themselves as based on natural and enduring judgements of value, they are products of human action, continually subject to accretion and erosion, selection and change' (DiMaggio 1992: 43). Significantly, part of the process of legitimising the National Theatre project as of high cultural value, was a firm separation between the professional activity of the National and of all that the 'amateur' might represent, with little mention of the relentless role of advocacy that the British Drama League had played in the National Theatre's past.

International Networks and Influences

In the light and airy bar at the Crescent Theatre Birmingham, host to the 2016 Little Theatre Guild conference, I find a quiet corner with Anne Gilmour and Jo Matthews of The Questors Theatre. Anne has been the UK representative of IATA for many years. We're talking about how the international amateur organisations work and what happens at IATA conferences today. Attending the conferences over the years, Anne has seen a remarkable range of amateur theatre from a huge Icelandic mythic rock opera made by a village of 250 people, to young people's work from a school in Kenya, facilitated around Aids awareness by teaching staff. Anne reflects that while Belgium's amateur organisation Opendoek is funded by the Ministry of the Flemish Community, likewise the National Information and Consulting Centre for Culture (NIPOS) was established by the Czech Republic Ministry of Culture, and now hosts the IATA region's secretariat, the English amateur organisations receive no government support. The Drama Association of Wales had its small Arts Council Wales funding withdrawn in 2011. For the English theatre organisations, Anne reflects, 'unless you put in a huge amount of work to get funding through Europe, there is no infrastructural support'. Government funding can bring with it complex political difficulties of its own, of course. Anne notes that three recently affiliated Palestinian groups needed to be listed on the IATA Central European Committee website, but because NIPOS is a 'quasi-government organisation' and the Czech Republic does not formally recognise Palestine, listing the groups was difficult. 'An interesting by-product of seeing themselves as having government funding although they support amateur arts'. (Jane's Research Diary, 9 April 2016)

The British amateur theatre movement did not evolve in splendid isolation: a large-scale turn to participating in amateur theatre was paralleled in other nations like the United States, France and Holland. As in Britain, the amateur movements of European countries and in the United States were closely allied to the provision of regional theatrical culture, and often emerged from an interest in staging a new kind of repertoire in contrast to commercial offerings. Theatre historian Dorothy Chansky's study of the American Little Theatre Movement, which she dates 1912–1925, charts the multiple prongs of a movement that wanted a theatre of 'high artistic ideals' and to bring a European, and then American, modernist repertoire to theatres across the country. Much like its parallel British movement, the Little Theatre Movement was both a form of active resistance to commercial theatre offerings and an attempt to create 'a permanent audience class and a public belief in the importance of theatre in civic and personal life' (Chansky 2005: 8). This improving theatre of a European avant-garde contributed to a sense of theatre's rising cultural value, as Paul DiMaggio articulates (1992): that, and drama's appearance in university degrees at Harvard (1905), Yale School of Drama (1924) and Carnegie Institute of Technology (1914). Chansky is careful to note that despite the lofty intentions of the Little Theater Movement to bridge cultural difference, much of the material produced by white writers specifically for immigrant communities or dealing with black experience remained trapped in the racist attitudes of its day. Shannon Jackson interrogates the socially ameliorative impetus of the Hull-House Settlement, Chicago, and the role of amateur performance there in negotiating the competing demands of cultural assimilation and progressive social activism (Jackson 2001). The English movement experienced a healthy level of cross-fertilisation with other national amateur theatre movements across the globe through publications and journals, alongside the excitement about festivals and competitions, and the exchange and visits of key personnel in each movement. The search for a team to send from Britain to compete in American Little Theatre Movement's David Belasco Cup in New York, for one-act plays, was an impetus for the founding of the Scottish Community Drama Association. The British Drama League Annual General Meeting for 1937 recorded visitors from France, the United States, Belgium, Germany, Austria, Egypt, Latvia, China, Finland and Sweden through the year, and noted the success of Barry Jackson's Fourth Drama League Tour to the Moscow Theatre Festival. A British Drama League Foreign Drama Committee was formed, including professional and amateur representative groups that hosted the Societé Universelle du Théâtre at Stratford 25 June–2 July 1938, bringing the amateurs into contact with Firmin Gémier's Odeon theatre. There was also exchange at the level of the individual amateur groups. One popular mode, for the more financially stable companies, was participation in international amateur drama competitions. The small-scale organisation of visits and exchanges was supported on an ad hoc basis through personal connections between members of groups. The purview of *Drama*, the leading publication from the British Drama League, was relentlessly international. A special issue on *Foreign Drama* for 1937 reflected the cultural outworkings of the turbulent build-up to war in a report that noted the imposition of censorship and the physical threat to amateur and professional Jewish artists in Berlin. Marie Seton was disturbed by the political nature of the pageants and tableaux that accompanied the opening of the 1936 Olympic games (Seton 1937: 52). The same issue carried reports on the Soviet Circus and on an amateur Jewish theatre in Palestine. Exchanges and visits between international amateur groups and the British amateur scene were a route to cross-fertilisation and were organised at a national scale through the British Drama League.

The practices of self-entertainment and the value placed on group social activities, coupled with the argument for the beneficial, civilising effect of performing good drama, underpinned the remarkable endurance of amateur theatre groups in colonial settings. Michael Dobson has charted the way in which Shakespeare was welcomingly familiar with expatriate amateur groups and 'to perform Shakespeare in a distant land became the theatrical and social equivalent of planting a Union Jack there', although the practical outcomes of the performance were interestingly diverse (2011: 110). The close relationship between the military and bureaucracy—two institutions with long histories of amateur theatre production—produced a particular kind of colonial amateur theatre. For some it was a training ground: John Hughes, who was to become NODA Secretary, had been a member of 'Mountview Theatre in its embryonic days in Ceylon as Engineering Officer in Royal Navy' (Young 1999: 48). For others, amateur theatre had a more significant role to play. The indefatigable Geoffrey Whitworth was the representative for Drama on the British Council (established 1934), 'a body set up by the Foreign Office to promote artistic and cultural relations with other countries... at a time when the surface of international politics is ruffled with so many distrusts, the various European countries, both officially and popularly, have never been so ready to establish a friendship on the basis of common artistic interests', reported *Drama* (Whitworth 1937: 57). Indeed, the British Council was initially very open to the role that amateur theatre might play in the export of soft power through British culture to British dominions. In *A Handbook for the Amateur Theatre* (Cotes 1957), at a point when the deconstruction of the British Empire was almost complete, Peter Allnut reports on the ways in which the British Council had been supporting the building of small theatres for amateur groups in Kenya, Uganda, Northern and Southern Rhodesia, in defence of what Allnut characterised as 'the golden thread of British dramatic tradition' where 'European civilisation' lay in the hands of the amateur theatre groups (1957: 330). Held during the war for independence in Kenya, the incongruous nature of the British Council and British Drama League-sponsored amateur one-act drama festival of 1957 stands uncomfortably as part of the structure of the colonial dominant regimes. Biodun Jeyifo has noted part of the process of decolonisation of the idea of performance in nations in Africa has been to undo the colonial implications carried by amateur theatre practices (1990: 243). Jeyifo notes how histories of theatre in Africa have often used the 1932 British Drama League conference on Native African Drama and its report that determined 'that there is no indigenous drama', as a staging post in the African theatrical story (1990: 243). Rather than merely reject the colonialist approach for an afrocentric privileging of unbroken lines of indigenous, oral tradition untouched by colonialism, Jeyifo suggests that histories of African theatre might adopt a transcultural approach. This would involve an acknowledgement of 'the global relations of knowledge which make exchanges possible, but which also undergird the complex relations of unequal exchange between nations and the regions of the earth', global relations of knowledge in which amateur theatre has played a considerably cultural role (1990: 249).

In Commonwealth nations such as Australia, New Zealand and Canada, the formation of amateur theatre movements has frequently been considered both parallel to, and seeded by, the organisations of British amateur theatre. The rich complexity of the story of amateur theatre in Australia has been told by Veronica Kelly, Bill Dunstone and Harold Love, who observe the influence of the personnel and publications and the symbolic resonance of the British Drama League on the emerging Australian repertory movement, that was 'characteristically amateur' in resisting a commercial theatrical culture (Heckenberg and Parsons 1984: 131). Beyond the larrikin spirit, Australian amateur theatres' self-reliance was indeed an expression of provincial resistance to metropolitan decadence, but also to cultural exports from the 'mother country', and one that developed a distinctive cultural repertoire of Australian writing of a particular kind. The Australian amateur movement was predominantly Anglophone, despite the increased European influence from new arrivals in the 1950s, until the 1972 Whitlam government abolition of the White Australia Policy. In Canada, Anglo- and francophone amateur groups proliferated in the late nineteenth century and were formally identified as part of a shared amateur movement through structures such as the Dominion Drama Festival of 1932, thereafter an annual competition modelled on the festivals and competitions of the British Drama League and NODA. For some, the Canadian amateur theatre followed the British model as a way to distinguish a national theatrical 'repertoire' in resistance to the dominance of US money and repertoire, and because of the structures based on British culture put in place through the avid work of politician and writer Vincent Massey (Wagner 1999: 203). Yet, as Alan Filewod argues, a narrative of an 'evolutionary teleology of Canadian theatre from community-based amateur 'roots' to a professional theatre estate, in which 'amateur' means 'prenational',' does a categoric disservice to the amateur theatre *movements* of a Canadian state that embrace multiple language communities and First Nation cultures (2004: 108).

Given the complex multiplicity of national amateur theatre federations in different nations, and their knowledge of each other's work through journals, competitions and exchange visits, it is perhaps not surprising that the idea emerged for an international federation of amateur theatres linked across the globe. Founded in 1952, the International Amateur Theatres Association (IATA/AITA) came into being as the United Nations stepped in to the breach left by the collapse of the League of Nations and as UNESCO, the UN's cultural wing, sought to recalibrate a sense of humanist civilisation in post-holocaust Europe. Japan and East Germany were signatories with UNESCO in 1951, and both became early leading members of IATA. IATA worked closely with an international body of professional theatre practitioners, the International Theatre Institute (ITI) that had been established in 1948 in response to the call 'Enough narrow nationalism!' (Canning 2015: 167). Although concerned with professional theatre, ITI was closely linked to amateur, participatory imperatives:

its founders included J.B. Priestley, playwright and amateur-phile, and from the US Rosamond Gilder, editor of *Theatre Arts Magazine* and supporter of the Little Theatre Movement. Amateur and professional organisations IATA and ITI held joint congresses, shared offices in The Hague through the 1960s, and articulated the importance of theatrical participation beyond national boundaries. IATA was particularly keen to broach the political and cultural separation in Europe of the spheres of influence produced by the Cold War despite the pragmatic difficulties in exchanging personnel and of maintaining east-west dialogue (Canning 2015). Unlike a view of amateur theatre that configures it as a mode for exporting national soft power, IATA as a federation has cultivated an ethos of amateur theatre valued as a mode for transnational entente.

Re-evaluating Amateur Theatre

With much of the amateur theatre movement's initial programme for change achieved—from the establishment of a national theatre, the diverse regional provision of theatre performance spaces, the teaching of Drama as a subject at school and university, to the establishment of subsidy for theatre, the advocacy activities of the British Drama League for amateur theatre and for theatre more widely were no longer urgent. With the establishment of regional subsidised theatre and theatre within education at every level, many of the roles that the amateur theatre movement had played in the wider social fabric were taken on by professional organisations. The British Drama League became the British Theatre Association in 1972, which had a closer link to professional theatre and paid key officials. Financial strictures meant the British Theatre Association ceased operations in 1990, with the bulk of its extraordinary library moving to the still active Drama Association of Wales, and housed at the Royal Welsh College of Music and Drama. The British Drama League's role in coordinating groups and undertaking advocacy was increasingly taken up not by the British Theatre Association in its new formulation, but by the Central Council for Amateur Theatres (CCAT) which was formed in 1977 with professional staff. It was structured explicitly not as a membership organisation, but as an umbrella group for the rich complexity of amateur theatre organisations still operating in the second half of the twentieth century. The CCAT included GoDA, the Guild of Drama Adjudicators, founded in 1947 as an accreditation and training organisation for adjudicators for the multiple competitive speech and drama festivals, eisteddfods and amateur theatre festivals. Radius, the Religious Drama Society of Great Britain founded in 1929, was also a member. The CCAT articulated its role as a channel for sharing issues and concerns facing the amateur membership organisations, and as advocate and broker between amateur theatre and local and national government agencies. This commitment positioned it firmly in late twentieth-century bureaucracy as a leading member of what came to be termed the amateur arts 'sector'. One of the distinctive activities that accompanied this role as advocate was the need to gather 'evidence'. Part of the evaluative turn of late twentieth century cultural policy has been the increasing importance of gathering statistical data as part of the processes of 'accounting' to policy-makers and funders and, despite amateur theatre's disconnection from public subsidy, the CCAT saw considerable rhetorical value in establishing a 'state of play' for amateur theatre activity, commissioning surveys in 1979, 1981, 1989, 1990. Likewise, NODA has regularly surveyed its membership (2002, 2008 and 2012) and the Scottish Community Drama Association commissioned Greg Giesekam to review amateur activity in Scotland (2000). The largest government-sponsored survey from the Department for DCMS and ACE, supported by Voluntary Arts, *Our Creative Talent* (2008), focused specifically on amateur arts and participation, rather than the broader continuous DCMS household survey 'Taking Part' (The Office for National Statistics, n.d.). This desire for 'evidence' in order to talk to government remains part of the advocacy role. With the demise of the CCAT in 2011, the role of advocacy for amateur theatre societies has fallen to the two largest remaining membership organisations, the Little Theatre Guild and NODA.

A considerable part of the cultural landscape of Britain, from the provision of regional theatres producing regionally relevant and challenging repertoire, the establishment of drama within adult cultural education, to the founding of the National Theatre, has been generated and curated by the energy and advocacy of the amateur theatre movement working in concert with professional theatre and other expertise. As austerity has bitten in the new millennium, and local authority budgets and Arts Council funding have been increasingly squeezed, it is not support for amateur theatres that is being put under pressure, since the movement has worked as part of a parallel cultural economy beyond subsidy. However, the amateur and voluntary sector is increasingly being looked to in order to make up the shortfall in other areas, such as cultural and arts training or in the provision of communal space for hire by local groups. Yet, as Régis Cochefert of the Paul Hamlyn Foundation argued at a policy day around amateur theatre, there is only so far you can push the amateur sector in asking them to make up for the arts and culture that the centre will no longer fund.[15] In the context of a more straitened funding environment, cultural policy-makers and funders are turning to consider once more the benefits of a more widely encompassing definition of cultural participation, one that sees the benefits of active creative participation, rather than focusing on cultural consumption, as Chapter 1 has outlined. The amateur theatre organisations that have developed over the twentieth century and remain active today advocate for amateur theatre as a mode of active creative participation. They champion amateur theatre as an important independent space for collective creative expression that is part of a shared, social imaginary—'that common understanding that makes possible common practices and a widely shared sense of legitimacy'—of the theatrical public sphere (Taylor 2002: 105). The re-evaluation of the role of amateur theatre as part of a more broadly understood cultural ecology is the detailed study of the chapters that follow.

REFERENCES

Allnut, Peter. 1957. East and Central Africa. In *A Handbook for the Amateur Theatre*, ed. Peter Cotes, 329–335. London: Oldbourne Press.

Anheier, Helmut, and Yudhishthir Raj Isar, eds. 2008. *The Cultures and Globalization Series 2: The Cultural Economy*. London: SAGE.

Archer, William. 1923. *The Old Drama and the New*. London: W. Heinemann.

Archer, William, and Harley Granville Barker. 1907. *A National Theatre: Schemes and Estimates*. London: Duckworth.

Arts Council of Great Britain. 1960. *Fifteenth Annual Report 1959–1960*. London: Arts Council of Great Britain.

Bakhshi, Hasan, and David Throsby. 2010. *Culture of Innovation: An Economic Analysis of Innovation in Arts and Cultural Organisations*. London: NESTA.

Balme, Christopher B. 2014. *The Theatrical Public Sphere*. Cambridge: Cambridge University Press.

Barrett, Daniel. 1999. Play Publication, Readers, and the 'Decline' of Victorian Drama. *Book History* 2: 173–187.

Bazalgette, Peter. 2014. *The Value of Arts and Culture to People and Society*. London: Arts Council England.

---

[15] Amateur Theatre Research: A Symposium, Senate House, University of London, 23 January 2017.

British Drama League. 1945. *Twenty-Five Years of the British Drama League*. Oxford: Alden Press.

Canning, Charlotte. 2015. *On the Performance Front: US Theatre and Internationalism*. London: Palgrave Macmillan.

Chambers, Colin. 1989. *The Story of Unity Theatre*. Basingstoke: Macmillan.

Chansky, Dorothy. 2005. *Composing Ourselves: The Little Theatre Movement and the American Audience*. Carbondale: Southern Illinois University Press.

Churchward, Sally. 2013. Is It the Final Curtain for Amateur Theatre in Hampshire? *Southern Daily Echo*, August 12. http://www.dailyecho.co.uk/news/10605815.Is_it_the_final_curtain_for_amateur_theatre_in_Hampshire. Accessed 18 Dec 2017.

Cochrane, Claire. 2011. *Twentieth Century British Theatre Industry, Art and Empire*. Cambridge: Cambridge University Press.

Cotes, Peter. 1957. *A Handbook for the Amateur Theatre*. London: Oldbourne Press.

D'Monte, Rebecca. 2015. *British Theatre and Performance 1900–1950*. London: Bloomsbury.

DiMaggio, Paul. 1992. Cultural Boundaries and Structural Change: The Extension of the High Culture Model to Opera, Theater and Dance, 1900–1940. In *Cultivating Differences: Symbolic Boundaries and the Making of Inequality*, ed. Michèle Lamont and Marcel Fournier, 21–57. Chicago: University of Chicago Press.

Dobson, Michael. 2011. *Shakespeare and Amateur Performance: A Cultural History*. Cambridge: Cambridge University Press.

Dodd, Fiona, Andrew Graves, and Karen Taws. 2008. *Our Creative Talent: The Voluntary and Amateur Arts in England*. London: DCMS.

Edensor, Tim, Deborah Leslie, Steve Millington, and Norma M. Rantisi, eds. 2010. *Spaces of Vernacular Creativity: Rethinking the Cultural Economy*. Abingdon: Routledge.

Emmet, Alfred. 1976. The Long Prehistory of the National Theatre. *Theatre Quarterly* 6 (21): 55–62.

———. 2002. Amateur Theatre. In *The Continuum Companion to Twentieth-Century Theatre*, ed. Colin Chambers. London: Continuum.

Exemption from Entertainments Duty of Amateur Entertainments. 1949. *Hansard* HC Deb vol. 466 col. 2192. July, 6. http://hansard.millbanksystems.com/commons/1949/jul/06/new-clause-exemption-from-enter. Accessed 7 July 2017.

Filewod, Alan. 2004. Named in Passing: Canadian Theatre History. In *Writing and Re-writing National Theatre Histories*, ed. Stephen E. Wilmer, 106–126. Iowa City: University of Iowa Press.

Gibson-Graham, J.K. 2008. Diverse Economies: Performative Practices for 'Other Worlds'. *Progress in Human Geography* 32 (5): 613–632.

Giesekam, Greg. 2000. *Luvvies and Rude Mechanicals? Amateur and Community Theatre in Scotland*. Glasgow: Scottish Arts Council.

Gilmore, Abigail. 2013. Cold Spots, Crap Towns and Cultural Deserts: The Role of Place and Geography in Cultural Participation and Creative Placemaking. *Cultural Trends* 22 (2): 86–96.

Goulding, Chris. 1991. *The Story of the People's*. Newcastle: Newcastle upon Tyne City Libraries & Arts.

Granville Barker, Harley. 1930. *A National Theatre*. London: Simon Schuster.

Grossmith, George, and Weedon Grossmith. 2010. *Diary of a Nobody*. London: Vintage.

Hammerton, James. 1999. Pooterism or Partnership? Marriage and Masculine Identity in the Lower Middle Class, 1870–1920. *Journal of British Studies* 38 (3): 291–321.

Hawley, Judith, and Mary Isbell, eds. 2012. *Amateur Theatre Studies: Nineteenth Century Theatre and Film*. Manchester: Manchester University Press.

Heckenberg, Pamela, and Philip Parsons. 1984. The Struggle for an Australian Theatre. In *The Australian Stage*, ed. Harold Love, 118–134. Kensington: New South Wales University Press.

Heinrich, Anselm. 2010. Theatre in Britain During the Second World War. *New Theatre Quarterly* 26 (1): 61–70.

Hewison, Robert. 2014. *Cultural Capital: The Rise and Fall of Creative Britain*. London: Verso.

Hirschfield, Claire. 1985. The Actresses Franchise League and the Campaign for Women's Suffrage, 1908–1914. *Theatre Research International* 10: 129–151.

Holden, John. 2015. *The Ecology of Culture: A Report Commissioned by the Arts and Humanities Research Council's Cultural Value Project*. Swindon: AHRC.

Howell, Patrick. 2016. *Consistently Brilliant on a Breezy Hilltop: A History of the Cotswold Players: The First Hundred Years*. N.P: Quicksilver Publications.

Howkins, Alun. 2003. *The Death of Rural England: A Social History of the Countryside*. London: Routledge.

Jackson, Shannon. 2001. *Lines of Activity: Performance, Historiography, Hull-House Domesticity*. Ann Arbor: University of Michigan Press.

Jeyifo, Biodun. 1990. The Reinvention of Theatrical Tradition. In *The Dramatic Touch of Difference: Theatre, Own and Foreign*, ed. Erika Fischer-Lichte, Josephine Riley, and Michael Gissenwehrer, 239–252. Tübingen: Gunter Narr Verlag Tübingen.

Kelly, Mary. 1939. *Village Theatre*. London: Thomas Nelson.

Kruger, Loren. 1987. 'Our National House': The Ideology of the National Theatre of Great Britain. *Theatre Journal* 39 (1): 35–50.

Leask, Margaret. 2012. *Lena Ashwell: Actress, Patriot, Pioneer*. Hatfield: University of Hertfordshire Press.

Lewis, Henry, Jonathan Sayer, and Henry Shields. 2015. *The Play that Goes Wrong*. London: Bloomsbury.

Leyshon, Andrew, and Roger Lee. 2003. Introduction: Alternative Economic Geographies. In *Alternative Economic Spaces*, ed. Andrew Leyshon, Roger Lee, and Colin C. Williams, 1–26. London: SAGE.

———, eds. 2008. *The Sage Handbook of Economic Geography*. London: SAGE.

Lineham, Thomas. 2012. *Modernism and British Socialism*. London: Palgrave.

Lowerson, John. 1999. An Outbreak of Allodoxia? Amateur Operatics and Middleclass Musical Taste Between the Wars. In *Gender, Civic Culture and Consumption*, ed. Alan Kidd and David Nicholls, 196–211. Manchester: Manchester University Press.

———. 2005. *Amateur Operatics: A Social and Cultural History*. Manchester: Manchester University Press.

Lowrie, Andrew. 2016. Culture, Media and Sports Enquiry. *Little Theatre Guild Newsletter* 30 (2): 3 http://littletheatreguild.org/wp-content/uploads/2015/08/Aug-16-LTG-Newsletter.pdf. Accessed 18 Dec 2017.

Miles, Andrew. 1999. *Social Mobility in Nineteenth and Early Twentieth-Century England*. Basingstoke: Macmillan.

Moran, James. 2013. Pound, Yeats and the Regional Repertory Theatre. In *Regional Modernisms*, ed. James Moran and Neal Alexander, 83–103. Edinburgh: Edinburgh University Press.

Newey, Kate. 2005. *Women's Theatre Writing in Victorian Britain*. Basingstoke: Palgrave Macmillan.

Nicoll, Allardyce. 1973. *English Drama 1900–1930*. Cambridge: Cambridge University Press.

O'Brien, Dave, and Kate Oakley. 2015. *Cultural Value and Inequality: A Critical Literature Review*. London: Arts and Humanities Research Council.

Patterson, Eric J. 1919. Beginnings. *Drama* 1 (1): 5.

Postlewait, Thomas. 1986. *Prophet of the New Drama: William Archer and the Ibsen Campaign*. Westport: Greenwood Press.

Powell, David. 1996. *The Edwardian Crisis: Britain 1901–1914*. Basingstoke: Macmillan.

Priestley, J.B. 1934. *English Journey*. London: Victor Gollancz.

Rose, Jonathan. 2001. *The Intellectual Life of the British Working Classes*. New Haven: Yale University Press.

Rosenthal, Daniel. 2013. *The National Theatre Story*. London: Oberon.

Rowell, George, and Anthony Jackson. 1984. *The Repertory Movement: A History of Regional Theatre in Britain*. Cambridge: Cambridge University Press.

Rural Extension Scheme (Devon). 1938. *Drama* 16 (5): 68.

Russell, Dave. 2004. *Looking North: Northern England and the National Imagination*. Manchester: Manchester University Press.

Samuel, Raphael, Ewan MacColl, and Stuart Cosgrove. 1985. *Theatres of the Left 1880–1935 Workers' Theatre Movements in Britain and America*. London: Routledge Kegan Paul.

Seton, Marie. 1937. Theatre in Berlin. *Drama* 15 (4): 50–52.

Shepherd, Simon, and Mick Wallis. 2004. *Drama/Theatre/Performance*. London: Routledge.

Shipley, Michael. 2006. *Bolton Little Theatre: 75 Years of Drama*. Leeds: Millnet Financial Services.

Smedley, Constance. 1937. The Story of the Cotswold Players. *Drama* 16 (1): 4–6.

Storey, Taryn. 2017. 'Village Hall Work Can Never Be Theatre': Amateur Theatre and the Arts Council of Great Britain, 1945–56. *Contemporary Theatre Review* 27 (1): 76–91.

Taylor, George. 1976. *History of the Amateur Theatre*. Melksham: Colin Venton White Horse Library.

Taylor, Charles. 2002. Modern Social Imaginaries. *Public Culture* 14 (1): 91–124.

The Fabian Society. 1894. The Parish Council's Act: What it Is and how to Work it. In *Fabian Society Tract 53*. London: The Fabian Society.

The Office for National Statistics, Taking Part www.gov.uk/government/collections/sat%2D%2D2. Accessed 13 Oct 2016.

Thompson, Paul. 1992. *The Edwardians: The Remaking of British Society*. London: Routledge.

Throsby, David. 2003. Determining the Value of Cultural Goods: How Much (or How Little) Does Contingent Valuation Tell Us? *Journal of Cultural Economics* 27: 275–285.

Veitch, Norman. 1950. *The People's: Being a History of the People's Theatre, Newcastle upon Tyne, 1911–1939*. Gateshead upon Tyne: Northumberland Press.

Wagner, Anton. 1999. Becoming Actively Creative: Dr. Lawrence Mason the Globe's Critic 1924–1939. In *Establishing Our Boundaries: English-Canadian Theatre Criticism*, ed. Anton Wagner, 119–214. Toronto: University of Toronto Press.

Wallis, Mick. 2000. Unlocking the Secret Soul: Mary Kelly Pioneer of Village Theatre. *New Theatre Quarterly* 16 (4): 347–358.

———. 2006. Drama in the Villages: Three Pioneers. In *The English Countryside 1918–39: Regeneration or Decline?* ed. Paul Brassley, Jeremy Burchardt, and Lynne Thompson, 102–115. Woodbridge: Boydell and Brewer.

Warden, Claire. 2016. *Migrating Modernist Performance*. London: Palgrave Macmillan.

Weingärtner, Jörn. 2012. *Arts as a Weapon of War*. London: I.B. Tauris.

Whitworth, Geoffrey. 1919. The British Drama League. *Drama* 1 (1): 5.

————. 1937. The British Council. *Drama* 15 (4): 57.

————. 1951. *The Making of a National Theatre*. London: Faber and Faber.

Wickham, Glynne. 1977. A Revolution in Attitudes to the Dramatic Arts in British Universities 1880–1980. *Oxford Review of Education* 3 (2): 115–121.

Williams, Raymond. 1971. *The Long Revolution*. London: Penguin.

Young, John N. 1999. *A Century of Service: The Story of the National Operatic and Dramatic Association*. London: NODA.

CHAPTER 3

Amateur Repertoires

Amateur theatre makes a significant contribution to the British cultural economy in sustaining and creating the repertoires of live performance in Britain. As Fiona Dodd and colleagues calculated in their 2008 survey *Our Creative Talent*, there are almost 100,000 amateur performances staged each year in England and amateur theatre has been a dynamic shaper of the national repertoire alongside subsidised and commercial theatrical venues, educational institutions, publishing, criticism and cultural institutions (Dodd et al. 2008). At a local scale, the role of amateur theatre companies as 'a powerful auxiliary of diffusion' for national theatre culture was recognised by the Arts Council in 1960, acknowledging 'in many parts of the land [amateurs] will continue, except for the wireless, to provide the only possible kind of irrigation' (Arts Council 1960: 11). Underpinning the endurance of the amateur theatre companies has been the selection, curation and development of seasons of plays that tempt an audience out to enjoy a collective live theatrical experience. Thus the choices in repertoire made by these amateur theatre companies offer revealing insight into audiences for live performance across a wide swathe of England beyond metropolitan areas. Rather than see amateur theatre as separate from the commercial or subsidised provision of live performance, as the contemporary rhetoric of the Arts Council has tended to cast them, the accumulated wealth of amateur theatre performances inflects and contributes to the forming of a national theatrical repertoire in ways that have not been fully appreciated.

© The Author(s) 2018
H. Nicholson et al., *The Ecologies of Amateur Theatre*,
https://doi.org/10.1057/978-1-137-50810-2_3

Throughout the twentieth and twenty-first centuries, the central activity of amateur theatre-makers has been the staging of play texts. This is true both of affiliated theatre companies and small-scale groups unaffiliated to the organisations of the amateur theatre movement. Whilst amateur theatre companies tend to concentrate on staging existing play texts, they also devise or collaboratively create performance, most often today with amateur youth theatre groups as the entries for the 2015 All-England Theatre Festival reveal. Of the 214 one-act plays entered, the ten devised pieces were from youth groups.[1] New writing from amongst the amateur theatre membership is a dynamic element of theatre-making activity with multiple modes of encouragement for fledgling writers through competitions, play readings and amateur production. The choice of existing performance texts in the amateur sector encompasses both traditional play forms as well as providing a venue for cabaret, review, murder mystery or ad hoc events arranged outside a company's calendar of formal, large-scale productions. The material practices of the amateur companies' core activities in staging plays are closely imbricated with the wider commercial support structures of the theatre industry, drawing on costumiers, lighting, scenographic services and insurance agencies. Play publishers and performing rights holders have a particularly close relationship with the sector. Whilst commercial imperatives may not motivate or underpin the activity of the amateur theatre companies, an economic pragmatism is implicit in the decisions that companies make about their own choice of repertoire, and the amateur theatre sector overall is intimately involved in those material practices that produce the national picture of theatrical performance in Britain today.

There is not a uniquely amateur repertoire, although there are trends and emphases in the work of amateur companies that are distinctive in relation the subsidised and commercial sectors. Over the course of the twentieth century, theatre historians George Rowell and Anthony Jackson reflect that the amateur theatre movement was a vital support to the emergence of the repertory theatre movement, with whom they shared a commitment to producing serious new plays as an alternative to the offerings of the commercial theatres of their day. As the repertory theatre movement developed into the network of subsidised regional theatre provision in England, both repertory theatres and amateur theatres leavened their

---

[1] http://www.allenglandtheatrefestival.co.uk/about.htm Accessed 1 December 2017.

seasons with 'lighter comedies' and 'well-tried popular West End hits', suggesting a convergence of different repertoires (1984: 176). Conversely, cultural historian John Lowerson has charted the ways in which the amateur operatic group productions paralleled the rising popularity of commercial American musical theatre in the West End, replacing European operetta, after the 1940s. Yet, as Lowerson points out, the work of Gilbert and Sullivan has been almost entirely sustained in performance in recent years within the amateur sector.

> Choices made by the [amateur] movement may have been dependent on commercial products, but it has become the main arbiter of their availability and longevity ... crucial in the survivability of many composers' work. (2005: 106, 109)

The most recent survey of the *British Theatre Repertoire 2013*[2] reports that the amateur sector echoes the subsidised stage and regularly performs the second productions of new writing premiered in the subsidised sector, but of the '58 new plays presented by amateurs in our reporting theatres, 42 per cent were written by women, a much higher proportion than in the professional theatre' (Brownlee et al. 2015: 26). In terms of the choice of plays to stage, amateur theatre companies have paralleled many of the developments of the commercial and subsidised sectors, yet they have also sustained the distinctive tradition of Gilbert and Sullivan in their repertoire beyond its commercial viability, and are innovative in their production of new writing from women playwrights that is less regularly revived in the subsidised sector. However, rather than think about repertoires as simply a matter of the choice of play texts, it is useful to recognise that forming a repertoire is always a process of *repertoiring*, and this chapter will consider the processes of repertoiring in three ways: as an evaluative process of inclusion that stabilises through repetition particular kinds of plays and playwrights in performance; second, as the production of taste, a process of legitimation through performance that contributes to the production of local and national dramatic canons; and thirdly, as a process that generates familiarity and expertise in audiences, integrating popular

---

[2] The *British Theatre Repertoire 2013* report was commissioned by the British Theatre Consortium, UK Theatre and the Society of London Theatres, underwritten by Arts Council England, to build a 'statistical picture of what has been happening on British stages in the 21st century' (2013: 3).

or embodied repertoires. It is clear that a complex interplay of institutional, national, educational, commercial and economic imperatives is at work alongside and beyond aesthetic or artistic reasons that amateur theatre companies might have for particular play choices within their seasons of work. Amateur theatre production remains a key, if largely unrecognised, component of the repetition and reproduction of plays. It also supports playwrights as part of a process of forming the national repertoire, and this has economic benefits as well as cultural force for dramatists, theatres and audiences.

SHAPING A NATIONAL REPERTOIRE

The idea of a national theatrical repertoire lies between the idealism of a canon of revered texts and the pragmatic complexity of actual theatre in production at any given moment in England. As musicologist Joseph Kerman argued whilst trying to track modern operatic practices, 'a canon is an idea; a repertory is a program of action' (1983: 107). In the early twentieth century, the repertoire and programme of action for many companies in the amateur theatre movement was closely allied to the small-scale 'experimental' stage societies in producing Modern Drama—European drama in translation and those home-grown plays that offered progressive social commentary as in George Bernard Shaw's *Plays Pleasant or Unpleasant* (1898) and John Galsworthy's *Strife* (1909). Amateur theatre repertoire was also closely linked to the emerging repertory theatre movement that supported the development of regional voices and perspectives on work and social relationships as tackled by Stanley Houghton's *Hindle Wakes* (1912) or Githa Sowerby's *Rutherford & Son* (1912). Yet, equally regularly amateur groups performed musical revue, concert party shows, or versions of Oscar Asche's *Chu Chin Chow* (1916). This mixed economy of multiple kinds of performance within one company's season continued to be echoed in both amateur repertoires and those of the post-war subsidised theatres, as a series of Arts Council reviews reveal. The 1970 Arts Council report *The Theatre Today*, the 1986 Kenneth Cork report *Theatre IS for All* and the more recent *British Theatre Repertoire 2013*, demonstrate the practice of mixing serious drama and lighter comic or musical offerings characterises many of the mid-scale subsidised theatres. Ian Brown and Rob Brannen charted the increasingly mixed repertoire over the period 1970–1995 noting the decline of classic plays (20% down to 9%) and post-war drama (43% down to 22%) to be replaced by musicals, adaptations and new writing (1996: 381). Since the millennium, an increase in new writing on professional stages, underpinned by multiple new writing initiatives from the Arts Council, has meant that 'new plays constitute well over half of all productions' (Brownlee et al. 2015: 11). Again the experience of the large-scale amateur theatre groups is broadly comparable to the subsidised sector, as the *Repertoire* report found that 46% of amateur theatre produced in London and mainstream theatre venues was of new writing.

Imagining the British repertoire today, after the dominance of Shakespeare, much of what is valued as significant is serious drama that explicitly comments on political or social mores, from playwrights such as Samuel Beckett, Harold Pinter, Caryl Churchill and more recently David Greig, Simon Stephens, Lucy Prebble or debbie tucker green, as theatre scholars Kate Dorney (2013) and Vicky Angelaki (2013) note in their overviews of contemporary British theatre. A writer comes to be acknowledged as a significant, serious playwright through practices of selection and repertoire formation that are not only about the success of individual play texts, but about the development of a writer within a mesh of supporting mechanisms that carry their work to the stage. The amateur sector has played, and continues to play, a significant if hidden role in this interwoven texture of playwright support. Using Bourdieu's formulation of cultural capital, Yael Zarhy-Levo argues that far from intrinsic merit, there are multiple 'ways in which the artists and their work are constructed, championed, or judged by those who mediate their drama' beyond the artist's own endeavours in a network of competing forces and channels through which cultural capital is attributed to playwrights and theatremakers (2008: 5). Zarhy-Levo's analysis examines the routes by which particular playwrights or particular plays are legitimated and authorised, including by theatrical critics, play producers and directors, cultural funding organisations and educational institutions, but she misses the role of amateur theatre. Some of the works and playwrights that we now consider canonical have achieved that status in part because of their production and support within the amateur sector. One example is Harold Pinter and his first full-length play, *The Birthday Party*. Panned by critics when it was first produced in London on 19 May 1958, it closed five days later. The story of the play's resurrection is in part due to Stephen Joseph's support for a production in January 1959 in Birmingham and Leicester (Elsam 2010). However, the play's London resurrection came in May 1959 from the amateur Tower Theatre Company. Pinter was involved with the casting, with McCann played by David Jones who was 'later to become one of Pinter's best directorial interpreters' (Billington 1996: 184). Pinter was closely involved in the production, a former company member recounts, as he 'lived within easy reach … he would have wanted to observe rehearsals' (Elsam 2013: 78). The amateur Bolton Little Theatre staged *The Birthday Party*'s next outing in November 1959 and Pinter travelled up to oversee some rehearsals.[3] The Questors, Ealing staged a third production in December 1959 and again Pinter was involved in casting Peter Whelan, then an up-and-coming playwright, as Stanley. A significant part of the story of *The Birthday Party*'s eventual absorption into the modern repertoire is the series of amateur productions that Pinter worked with, and that were a mechanism whereby the play was enthusiastically received and established beyond professional production.

The amateur theatre has a long tradition of supporting professional playwrights, frequently in championing new plays from them, ensuring royalties and performance licences long after short professional runs of their work has ceased. This forms part of the economic infrastructure underpinning the possibility of writing as a full-time career for playwrights. Playwright and director Jessica Swale's original play *Blue Stockings* and her theatrical adaptations have been popular choices with amateur groups, and the amateur performance rights have been an influence in her writing career:

> As a percentage of my income it is not high but it's constant. It's psychological. If I create a piece of work which I know will have a life, that's a more attractive prospect. Not because I want to make money, but because you put your heart and soul into telling a story and if you only get to do it once, with one group of people, then it feels as if it falls a bit flat.[4]

Swale works across film and television where writers are better remunerated, but in her writing for the stage, the amateur performing rights for stage work 'more like £60–£70 per performance … is absolutely significant'. This combination of economic and aesthetic support from repeat productions in the amateur sector has also been part of the writing career

---

[3] Interview Jane Milling with Michel Shipley, Bolton Little Theatre, 29 June 2016.

[4] Interview Molly Flynn with Jessica Swale, 16 January 2017. All other quotations are taken from this interview.

of Amanda Whittington whose successful music-filled dramas like *Be My Baby* (1997), *Ladies Day* (2005), *Ladies Down Under* (2007) and *The Thrill of Love* (2013) tackle difficult subject matter with wit and many good roles for women. She was amongst the top ten most performed playwrights in the repertoires of Little Theatre Guild theatres in 2014, 2015 and 2016.

> I have a lot to thank amateur theatre for because my work is widely produced by that sector across the country, but that wasn't something I set out to do. What it's done is kept the plays alive. You get commissioned and a play goes on, in my case in a regional rep, for two or three weeks and if you're lucky it might tour a bit, but then that's it. Two to three years of work have gone into that short space of production time. The amateur market gives an ongoing and very healthy life to the work. So *Be My Baby* is now nearly twenty years old and that is being done a lot. *Ladies Day* is twelve years old and is done all the time, all over the place. What the amateur theatres are doing is keeping the work alive and out there and taking it to audiences I never imagined it would find.[5]

This sense of keeping the work of playwrights in circulation is multifaceted. It offers the playwright the experience of a wider audience with knowledge of their work as well as an ongoing life to their creative labour. This reproduction and repetition of the work in production also contributes to establishing a particular play in a national repertoire. Both Jessica Swale's *Blue Stockings* and Amanda Whittington's *Be My Baby* have moved onto school syllabi for example. Alongside this ideological work of production, the ongoing income from amateur performance rights can contribute to a playwright becoming a professional writer, that is, being able to sustain writing full-time. As Amanda Whittington articulates:

> the amateur circuit has given me a really good foundational income over the last ten years. It fluctuates year to year. If I had been relying only on commissions with no second productions in the professional or amateur theatres, I wouldn't have been able to sustain a career as a writer... Amateur productions are sustaining careers and keeping writers writing. If you look

---

[5] Interview Molly Flynn with Amanda Whittington, 23 November 2016. All other quotations are taken from this interview.

at the money and where the power lies in the industry, that's a sleeping lion. I don't think the sector realises how powerful it is in that way.

Far from operating outside the economic circulation of theatre play publishing and performance rights, amateurs are a significant force for sustaining a play in production over a far wider geographical range than would be possible through commercial or subsidised production. Moreover, amateurs' choice of playwrights' material can sustain plays in production for far longer than commercial mechanisms could support—however long a West End run, a regularly appearing play in the amateur sector will have a more enduring production history.

The licencing of the amateur performance rights has a long history. The separation of performance rights from publication copyright initially made possible under the 1842 Copyright Act, was refined by case law over the nineteenth century and applied equally to amateur or professional companies (Alexander 2010: 332). The D'Oyly Carte Company was one of the first to develop the widespread granting of performance rights for amateur groups, marking the rise of a popular movement of amateur theatre. Richard D'Oyly Carte released the regional amateur rights whilst the commercial Gilbert and Sullivan operetta was still performing the West End, producing a marked increase in the sales of the libretti (Joseph 1994: 163). This was a popular decision: in 1914 Howard Hadley, Secretary of National Amateur Operatic and Dramatic Association, estimated 20 of the 36 operatic societies in London, and 173 of the 312 provincial companies, mounted Gilbert and Sullivan shows and contemporaries considered the amateur societies to be 'a powerful adjunct and support to the culture of music and the drama' (Cellier and Bridgeman 1914: 395). For each show amateur companies paid 10% of the box office take, and additional income was earned from hire of the band parts and prompt books that had to be followed in every detail (Bradley 2005: 27). The commercial savvy of D'Oyly Carte and the Savoy operas extended to the illustrated postcards and posters designed to be overprinted with local production details, supplied by local printers such as Stafford & Co. of Nottingham, that the amateur societies were encouraged to use in advertising their productions. This maintained a sort of 'brand coherence' for the Savoy operas as they dispersed across the nation, and sustained for audiences a sense of the close connection between the Savoy original and the amateur version. Production rights for musical theatre and musicals, licenced by agents such as Josef Weinberger, operate in a broadly similar manner today, and amateur production rights continue not only to sustain individual play-wrights' careers, but also to support originating production companies, play publishers, agents and licencing companies.

The release of performing rights for play texts is not always straightfor-ward as agents and production companies may restrict the release of ama-teur performance rights if professional production is a possibility. Many of the amateur theatre companies we have spoken to as part of our research described the costs and timing of the release of performing rights as a major complication. Ian Guy of Exeter Drama Company recounted the difficulties with rights for Frank McGuinness' adaptation of *Rebecca* in 2005 that were denied:

> A professional version with Nigel Havers was being done in Plymouth, and obviously we were going to stop coachloads of people going down to Plymouth because we were doing it in a backstreet church hall. That is ridiculous.[6]

The difficulties of the variable release of performance rights were echoed by the two key play publishers, Samuel French Ltd.[7] and Nick Hern Books,[8] who today are licencing agents for many of the rights to popular plays, as Peter Smith, rights manager at Samuel French, explained 'We work on behalf of the agents, we don't restrict things ourselves, we'd love to license everything.'[9] Tamara von Werthern, performing rights manager at Nick Hern Books for twelve years, articulated the importance of rights income from amateur theatre production for playwrights and the intermediary role that the performing rights holder can play in the negotiations:

> It's heart-breaking when we have to say 'no'. There are always plays that [amateurs] are desperate to do and aren't available… We would much rather

[6] Interview Jane Milling with Ian Guy, Exeter Drama Company, 18 June 2016.

[7] Samuel French Ltd., formed in 1873 when Thomas Hailes Lacy sold his side of the US-Anglo French-Lacy collaboration, was the largest amateur performing rights licensor throughout the twentieth century.

[8] Nick Hern Books, founded 1988, has coupled play publishing with managing profes-sional and amateur performance rights since its inception.

[9] Interview Jane Milling with Peter Smith, Samuel French, 12 April 2016. All other quota-tions taken from this interview.

license it than not. I am quite active in having a dialogue with the agent or writers and producers. As soon as Jessica Swale's *Nell Gwynn* finishes in the West End it will be allowed for a window of time: we are able to licence it alongside the tour. The producers have said, 'Well, the tour is to a different area, so they can do it.' ... With Jessica Swale's *Blue Stockings*, the amateur rights were released when it was still at the Globe... It is really satisfying when a play is still hot and amateurs can do it when it is still on.[10]

The licencing of performing rights provides an additional income stream for publishers; Tamara von Werthern reflected that whilst the 2008 recession impacted script sales, performance rights income was unaffected or even increased. 'In times when there is not much money, amateur companies will not give up on putting on that play.' The release of amateur and educational performing rights adds to the long arc of a play's life beyond the initial performance and publication. The issues around the timing and geographical reach of amateur rights release reveal the conflicting economic paradigms that surround theatre-going: for the professional productions companies, regional touring is imagined as a zero-sum game, attracting audiences from a limited pool of the theatre-going demographic where a fragile profit must be defended from undercutting by a directly competing cultural offer nearby. By contrast, amateur theatre companies frequently report that they are serving a distinct audience demographic, one priced out by ticket costs or travel difficulties, a perspective supported by Arts Council England's 2016 *Analysis of Theatre in England* that concludes that 'proximity and ease of access to local cultural infrastructure play an important role in attendance levels' (Naylor et al. 2016: 29). Alongside this, the amateur theatre companies suggest they enjoy an enthusiastic audience grouping who will see both productions, amateur and professional, casting the amateur theatre-goer as a cultural omnivore, likely to participate in many types of entertainment and content, an approach that recent sociological analysis of theatre audiences by Chan and Goldthorpe would seem to support (2005: 193).

A recent example that crystallised the force of the amateur theatre sector in prolonging the production life for a play, generating simultaneous performances disseminated across many regions and illustrating the granular complexity of local cultural infrastructure for amateur theatre audiences, was the phenomenon of Tim Firth's *Calendar Girls*. Predominantly a writer of comedy, Tim Firth was familiar with the amateur theatre sector, 'the amateur world was very much part of my hopes and dreams. The proudest moment was seeing my first play in a Samuel French edition, because I thought somebody has viewed this and it might have a potential life.'[11] After the success of *Calendar Girls* as a film in 2003, Firth bought the stage rights from Disney and with producers David Pugh and Dafydd Rogers, developed a stage play that opened in Chichester in 2008, ran in the West End and toured nationally until 2012. Firth's motivation for writing a stage version was linked to the possibility of amateur as well as professional production:

> Part of the reason I came up with the idea of writing it for theatre was to potentially release it to the amateur market. I'd watched companies around me report the paucity of plays for women... Whereas the film will slavishly tend to follow the lead story, it was a chance to write a group comedy, where I'm happiest. A group comedy for women.

Once the amateur rights for the play were released on 1 September 2012, initially for a year, the play became the most produced in the United Kingdom. Peter Smith at Samuel French Ltd. who administered the amateur performing rights licences, recorded **666** productions of *Calendar Girls* during the extended eighteen-month rights release period. Part of the play's popularity was the range of leading roles for women, as the narrative follows the collaborative efforts of a Women's Institute group to raise money for a leukaemia charity by posing nude for calendar. The calendar's success and the media furore it creates complicates the relationships between the characters, and the second act explores the changes for each character brought about by the calendar's success. Although the play is a comedy, it tackles deeper themes around loss, grieving and aging. This, coupled with the theatrical challenge of the nude photography scene for amateur performers, in small-scale theatres where they are very likely to be known by audiences, produced a particularly intense rehearsal process for groups. As Tim Firth reflected, for amateur performers:

[11] Interview Molly Flynn with Tim Firth, 13 December 2016. All other quotations taken from this interview.

there was a certain accidental catharsis about the play over and above its success as a piece of art. There was something elemental about six to eight women spending a lot of time in each others' company rehearsing this play, which drove them to reach out to people who'd been through similar experience, which I think will never happen again in my career.

A percentage of each professional show's royalties went to the Leukemia and Lymphoma Research charity, now Bloodwise, and the amateur company forum hosted on Tim Firth's webpage details how many of the amateurs donated profits, sold their own calendars and held gala nights for cancer charities and local hospices. Groups who had performed the show met together for further fundraising, at an Afternoon Tea in Harrogate in 2104, and social media discussion forums connected companies internationally as amateur rights were released worldwide. Many professional theatre critics were nonplussed by the commercial success of *Calendar Girls*, wryly commenting on its focus on older women and its sentimentality. The play seeks to have an emotional impact on audiences. For example, in a moving *coup-de-théâtre* in the second act, as the pressures of the calendar's success threaten to alienate the characters from one other, letters flutter down onto the stage, symbolising the letters received by the original calendar-makers from women all over the world sharing their experiences of losing loved ones to cancer. Whilst *The Spectator* review dubbed the play 'dazzlingly funny, shamelessly sentimental',[12] its enthusiastic uptake by amateur groups suggests that amateurs recognised not sentimentality, but a 'commonality of feeling' with audiences, as Elaine Aston and Gerry Harris argue (2012: 16). The play's popularity with the amateur sector was indeed related to its commercially successful prior life as a film and West End show, its multiple large roles for older women performers, its accessible domestic comic form and the theatrical challenge of the nude scene. Yet, far more than this, *Calendar Girls* remarkable appearance in an amateur repertoire was linked to its meditation on loss and grief, and in its 666 productions across Britain and more beyond, it modelled with and for its audiences those qualities of empathetic action that 'a compassionate citizenry' might need (Aston and Harris 2012: 40). The fundraising and charitable activity that surrounded each production implied that

---

[12] Lloyd Evans' phrase from *The Spectator* review has become the strapline on Samuel French's publication of the play, Tim Firth, *Calendar Girls* (London: Samuel French, 2010).

the processes of 'repertoiring' were not solely a recognition of the inherent aesthetic qualities of the play. It also suggests that the play might be useful, through local audiences, to national concerns beyond the theatrical, and to thinking about what a national repertoire does beyond the realm of aesthetic representation.

In term of establishing a contemporary national repertoire, large-scale amateur theatre companies have echoed developments in the subsidised and commercial sectors particularly in staging an increasing number of new works. In the professional sector, the increased presence of new work has been hailed as one the successes of a reinvigorated national theatrical culture, produced as a ripple effect by the new writing development initiatives of the 1990s (Edgar et al. 2009). Amanda Whittington, past Chair of the Writers' Guild of Great Britain, reflects that the writing development culture of that era nurtured and supported many more new writers to the stage, but had some unintended consequences.

> Commissioning is king. Historically, the playwright has written their play and the agent sold it to a theatre. Now the theatre commissions the work, so the artistic director is involved from the seed of the idea through conversation with the playwright, to commissioning the first draft and giving feedback on every draft. The writers are much more supported but there's an element of ownership about that.[13]

A regional theatre that develops work in this way feels a strong sense of ownership over it, and other regional theatres are reluctant to offer that play a second production, wanting to nurture new work of their own. Whilst this enthusiasm for new writing offered many more initial opportunities for playwrights, Whittington observed that 'It became very unfashionable for a director to direct a second version of new work. In the sixties, Orton's play was done in London, and then Sheffield did it and then Leeds, and then Nottingham and Bristol, with the attitude "This is a really successful new play and now our audiences can see it." There was no snobbery about second productions and no sense of ownership.' This shift in focus within the subsidised professional theatre world, she suggests, has led to a significant shift in the role of amateur theatres.

---

[13] Interview Molly Flynn with Amanda Whittington, 23 November 2016. All other quotations taken from this interview.

The amateur companies stepped in with the attitude that the regional reps would have had in the sixties. They've seen this play in London, 'Now our audiences can see it'. That's where these new plays have gone and become part of the repertoire. Consciously or not the amateur companies have stepped in and taken that role as the keeper of the flame.

The amateur theatre sector's focus on a text-based repertoire has perhaps underpinned some of the creeping pejorative view of amateur work. Playwright David Edgar has repeatedly suggested this attitude to text-based repertoire is one shared by the subsidised sector, and he uses the Boyden report on regional theatre (2000) and subsequent Arts Council strategy *The Next Stage* (2000), to argue that physical, devised or experimental modes of performance have been characterised as innovative or cutting edge by cultural funders, at the expense of new writing (2013: 105). However, the actual production of new works in the national repertoire has greatly increased since the millennium, as Edgar discusses, and from the perspective of contemporary new playwrights, amateur theatres have to some extent stepped into the shoes of regional repertory theatres, as part of a process of 'repertoiring', in developing and sustaining this new writing into the national repertoire. Amateur theatres continue to offer a central contribution to the making of playwrights' reputations, to sustaining new plays in production, to supporting playwrights' professional careers and publishers and rights holders alongside the subsidised and commercial theatre industry. In the repetition and reproduction of particular play texts, amateur performance extends the life of a play geographically and temporally in ways that commercial or subsidised production could not sustain, ensuring that text's presence in a national repertoire.

CURATION, CANONS AND TASTES

As theatre historian Richard Schoch reminds us 'canons are functions not of texts, but of the institutions that safeguard and promote them', and the processes by which plays achieve canonical status are part of a complex critical framework with 'its attendants of knowledge, excellence and taste' (2016: 161, 226). At this point in the twenty-first century, the amateur theatre organisations are not regarded as taste-making institutions, and thus their impact on the performed canon is apparently less influential than that of the subsidised sector. In this the amateur theatre shares much with the commercial sector which is also seen as following popular taste, rather than taste-making, and thus as having less impact on an authorised dramatic canon. As Charles Altieri argues, 'canons are essentially strategic constructs by which societies maintain their own interests, since the canon allows control over the texts a culture takes seriously and the methods of interpretation that establish the meaning of "serious"' (1983: 38). As Chapter 2 explored, in the early twentieth century amateur theatre was acknowledged as significant force for taking play texts seriously and for generating a canon through production, but the understanding of this role of amateur theatre-makers has diminished. This comes, as John Guillory argues, from our readiness to reify an aesthetic canon in terms of its objects, rather than to understand it as a process of aesthetic evaluation. Amateur theatre companies are continually engaged in aesthetic evaluation, in generating local choices and judging or extending the tastes of local audiences. In this they form:

> imagined communities with real consequences for many people, but their 'local, temporary and conjunctural' acts of evaluation are the very cultural exhibits which prove the fact that values are never produced by an actual exclusive 'local' consensus but always emerge in a determinate relation to the entire culture which holds in conflictual interrelation every subcultural formation within it. (2013: 278–9)

The amateur theatre sector celebrates its distinction from the professional theatre, and amateur groups frequently articulate their knowledge of local cultures and the evaluative judgements their audiences are likely to make. In this they are indeed producing a local cultural canon, and at the same time as they are contributing to, and are in an inevitable relationship with, the ideal of a national theatrical canon.

The making of taste, and the assessment of audience taste, are not esoteric practices, but are firmly grounded in pragmatic realities. In this context, the way that amateur companies select, programme and curate a season for themselves reveals much about a company's self-construction, and how the group is thinking about the tastes and expectations of its regular and potential audiences. Early assertions of the role of amateur theatre were concerned with educational and cultivating aspects of drama for its audiences – 'the unprofessional players are not only becoming a recreational and education force in the community but are reviving the latent interest in the professional theatre', as G.W. Bishop observed (1929: xii). In the practice of building a programme, the pragmatic decision-making of each amateur theatre group reflects a complex mesh of diverse impetuses. In the early years of the twentieth century, aesthetic considerations in the choice of potential repertoire were tempered by the simple pragmatic issue of access to physical play texts. The dissemination of information about available plays and the lending library of acting playsets was one of the key functions of the British Drama League as an organisation (British Drama League 1945). Over the twentieth century, this role was taken on by local council libraries in their provision of playsets and performing arts collections.[14] The playsets were usually from one of the many presses that had sprung up during the nineteenth century, producing cheap, poor quality print, acting editions. These editions offered extensive production information, including 'the Stage-plot, or disposition of the characters… of incomparable value to provincial performers' as Oxberry's New English Drama claims (Barrett 1999: 177). Thomas Hailes Lacy, Kenyon-Deane, Samuel French, Garamond and the English Theatre Guild offered acting editions, aimed at repertory theatres and amateurs, which included notes from professional and commercial productions as 'virtual model books of the original production' (Rebellato 1999: 121). By the 1950s, new playwrights and theatre critics were increasingly dismissive of these production-based texts in which the 'riotous intermingling of sign systems was intolerable' (Rebellato 1999: 121), and sought a new kind of editorial approach focused on the 'dignity' of the play text as authored, rather than as performed. Whilst the published play texts might try to expunge the traces of their performance history, as Brian Corman reflects, 'the relationship between text and performance canons is symbiotic: critical evaluation leads to printing of the text; text availability leads to performance; performance validates choice of text' (1992: 317). The decision to publish texts and to encourage their production in the amateur sector through cheap editions contributed to stabilising a particular play within the performance repertoire, and this in turn implied a process that might lead to its location in a canon. This cyclical system of print and performance was inflected through most of the twentieth century by the presence of multiple amateur theatre groups, whose enthusiasm for a text as part of their local cultural canon then had an impact on the availability of that work in subsidised

---

[14] The British Drama League library is now housed by the Drama Association of Wales at the Royal Welsh College of Music and Drama, Cardiff.

or commercial venues and its visibility through scholarly critical interest into the national canon.

All the commercial play publishers produced booklets summarising the plot and production needs of each play, as did the British Drama League, whose *The Players' Library* was considered essential for many amateur groups in the first half of the twentieth century. Alerting companies to the range of new plays and productions in London theatres, and beyond, became an important component of the journals and magazines aimed at amateur companies from the outset of the movement, as in the case of *Drama,* the bi-monthly journal of the British Drama League, which also introduced examples of European innovation and technique. The *Amateur Theatre and Playwrights' Journal* (produced between 1934 and 38) took this role as play counsellor further, and was expressly addressed to the regional amateur companies, reviewing West End productions specifically with an eye to those that would transfer. Interleaved with interviews with leading players, advice from producers, the journal also published an example of new writing from the amateur sector each week—short one acts or serialised longer plays. Today the practice of identifying possible plays works in roughly equivalent ways. Both Samuel French and Nick Hern Books have an active relationship with amateur theatre groups. Tamara von Werthern's interaction with companies is multipronged:

> It's a supportive role. We have the opportunity to suggest things that might fit a group and we just want people to find the play they really love. It's not sinister [laughs] … it can be hard when you don't know what is out there. We have a playfinder on our website, where you can search for plays by the exact number of cast, theme, genre, good parts for older performers. And we have approval copies, we send out up to three a time for free.[15]

Peter Smith, rights manager for Samuel French Ltd. who hold many of the rights to more established plays, reflected on the relationship between the scale of the amateur groups he talks to and the kind of play choices they make: 'Village groups do Norman Robbins, David Tristram, an example is *Little Grimley do Strictly Sex Factor (on Ice)*… Bigger amateur companies that have a season in rep tend to do Coward, Rattigan, Pinter, Ayckbourn… Amateur societies in the UK know what they want to do.

---

[15] Interview Jane Milling with Tamara von Werthern, Nick Hern Books, 13 April 2016.

People have already planned far ahead.'[16] Companies keep in touch with both Samuel French and Nick Hern making phone enquiries about specific plays or looking for equivalent texts. From the other side, publishers frequently contact the larger-scale groups when performing rights for particularly popular new plays become available. This intimacy between publishers and amateur groups is one of the pragmatic processes by which local and national repertoires and canons are intertwined.

Curating a season from the range of possible plays available is a significant factor in each amateur theatre's calendar. Aesthetic considerations underpin the development of a season for an amateur group specifically the interests and passions of either individual directors, who often nominate plays they would like to tackle, or of a play-reading committee that considers plays that offer sufficient challenge and range to their membership. Tom Williams of Chesil Little Theatre outlined the way that their selection process developed:

> We have a small production committee – about 8 or 9 members, a mix of actors and directors and technical side, that change each year, but about half the committee stay on for continuity. They are tasked with finding six plays and to build a good season. Then they need to find six directors ready to produce the plays. It can be that a director is chosen and given a play, they may say 'Choose a play for me', or that a director says 'I'd like to do this one'. We are constantly asking membership 'What would you like the plays to be?'.[17]

In the Chesil context, the production committee choices are then approved by the executive committee who take 'more commercial decisions, making them with an eye to the audience and to the artistic elements' and oversee the balance of the season with sufficient challenge and roles for the gender and age make-up of the company, and in the light of the costuming and scenic demands. Other groups depend more fully on the desires of individual directors who pitch their proposed plays to the theatre group's committee as Shirley Nelson outlined happens at Sidmouth

---

Amateur Dramatic Society.[18] The need for an individual director's enthusiasm is also key to the Royal Navy Theatre Association (RNTA) groups, one of which, the Admirals' Players, have traditionally adopted a particularly democratic process by handing over decision-making to its entire membership. Potential directors pitch ideas for scripts, which are circulated to members to vote on using a single transferable system that determines the outcome. In recognition of Roger Mitchell's assertion that the process was 'probably too democratic', the company now insists that members who vote should be prepared to participate in the show in some capacity.[19] Everyone appreciates that the success, or not, of the overall production process is heavily determined by the strength of the director's vision and their willingness to devote time and energy to this demanding role. This can mean that key figures exert a powerful control over a company's repertoire. Chris Blatch-Gainey, a dominant presence in Collingwood random salad company (RSC), has, for example, successfully aligned the company to his passion for Sir Terry Pratchett's comic fantasy Discworld series. Since 2002, he has directed eleven adaptations of Pratchett's work for the company including *Mort* in 2003, *Wyrd Sisters* in 2010 and *Lords and Ladies* in 2016. In fact, Collingwood RSC's dedication to Pratchett's work led the company to develop a close relationship with Stephen Briggs, who adapts Pratchett's novels for the stage, to the extent that he accepted an invitation to adjudicate one of the RNTA's spring festivals.

Whatever mode companies use to gather interest and proposals for the constitution of a season, all must needs then balance it against expected audience enthusiasm.

Over coffee at the Little Theatre Guild Conference in 2016, I talk to Frances Percival of Southport Little Theatre and Maureen Hornby of Formby Little Theatre about the delicate relationship between programme choices and audience tastes. Formby Little Theatre stage four productions a year, running for ten nights each. Maureen calculates that they 'make between £4,000–5,000 on each production, but once you've taken out the running costs, insurance, royalties etc., it is difficult to break even. If it wasn't for our Friends – we have Friends that donate monthly as well – our accounts would probably show a loss.' The importance of season subscribers or friends as

---

[18] Interview Jane Milling with Shirley Nelson, Sidmouth Amateur Dramatic Society, 27 January 2015.

[19] Interview Nadine Holdsworth with Roger Mitchell, Admirals' Players, 24 April 2015.

regular audience members means that many programming committees have a pretty clear idea of the mores and expectations of a core audience base. [Jane's Research Diary, 9 April 2016]

For Frances Percival at Southport Little Theatre, the question is how to balance a mixed programme against subscriber tastes: 'We do productions down in the bar that can only seat 120. We've done something a bit more avant-garde that we couldn't put on the mainstage; we've done *Equus* there. On the mainstage half the subscribers would walk out and not rejoin.'[20] More than simply a balance between serving and guiding audience taste, the conversations with many members of amateur theatre companies has shown that there are distinctive tranches of audiences who will favour different kinds of repertoire, as well as loyal members who will come to everything. As with any theatre venue or company, the ongoing financial viability depends upon balancing the tastes and mores of the core audience—for many amateur theatre groups these can often be quantified as subscribers or members—with those attracted by more challenging material. Janet Wild, chair of the Progressive Players, Gateshead, reflected that the audience figures for their May 2015–2016 season demonstrated the interrelation of pragmatics and aspiration within the larger-scale amateur theatre's process of programming. Between watching rehearsals, talking with cast and production team, and two Progressive members writing a play they might offer for a later season, Janet outlined the decision to stage *Get Up and Tie Your Fingers* (1994) by Northumberland writer Ann Coburn about women in the herring industry. Coburn's play was a popular choice amongst the membership because of its challenging storyline and local vernacular, yet it was a less-well known title and had relatively poor houses, considerably less than the 85–100% capacity audiences that most of the company's shows attract. Balancing the books meant the company were prepared for this and did more comedy in that season, including Peter Blackmore's *Miranda*, a three-person vaudeville version of *The Hound of the Baskervilles*, Georgina Reid's *Ladies of Spirit*, Eric Chappell's *Heatstroke*, with better known drama such as Lee Hall's *The Pitman Painters*, Miller's *Death of a Salesman* and Swale's *Blue Stockings* to offset the expected losses. Amateur audiences' knowledge and tastes are not built

[20] Interview Jane Milling with Frances Percival, Southport Little Theatre, 9 April 2016.

in isolation, but are inflected by experiences of recent professional theatre productions, popular film or television connections, and the local influence of other amateur groups in their locality. The relationship between commercial or subsidised professional theatre production and amateur taste-making is complex. Many of the new play productions—second performances of professional premieres—are of far more challenging material than the stereotype of light comedy as traditional amateur fare. As Tamara von Werthern at Nick Hern Books reflected:

> We do have very challenging plays on our list and it amazes me what people are putting on their stages. *Wendy and Peter Pan*, the Ella Hickson show, has flying in it, and it is technically really complicated to do, but it's going like hot rolls because the rights are just released. A different kind of challenge is offered by *Jerusalem*, which for a long time was one of our top ten. All the Jez Butterworth plays, *The River, Mojo, Jerusalem* are popular – in the first four months of this year alone [2016], we have thirty productions that we've licensed.[21]

For unaffiliated and smaller-scale amateur theatre groups, who produce much less work, the decisions about production choices are less complex. Small-scale groups producing only one or two shows a year are more likely to embrace a more populist or accessible mode of performance, rather than structuring their work around an idea of the civic function of repertoire or a responsibility to build public taste. Yet, at whatever scale the groups are working, in their curation of repertoire they are acting as brokers of theatrical canons for a locally configured audience, and as taste-makers.

Popular and Embodied Repertoires

Theatre historian Tracy C. Davis has coined a working definition of repertoire that attempts to move beyond the reification of particular play texts in canons and towards an idea of a repertoire as a set of performance modes and genres that are practised and become embodied in culture. Davis draws on performance studies scholar Diana Taylor's idea of repertoire as a kind of performance work that is lived, embodied and passed

---

[21] Interview Jane Milling with Tamara von Werthern, Nick Hern Books, 13 April 2016.

from generation to generation as a form of cultural genealogy 'people participate in the production and reproduction of knowledge by "being there", being a part of the transmission' (2003: 20). Taylor configures this living and lived repertoire as a potentially more radical body of work, 'the repertoire allows for individual agency ... [that] both keeps and transforms choreographies of meaning' (20), as opposed to the idea of the archive, which she considers a product of a fixed, state sponsored idea of the text. Whilst Taylor's embodied repertoire is a living tradition passed directly from masters and pupils, historian Joseph Roach suggest a repertoire can be discontinuous, remade and re-imagined through collective, cultural remembering or 'surrogation' (1996). Tracy C. Davis synthesises Taylor and Roach's approaches emphasising the extent to which repertoire is a reliant upon cultural memory, audiences and reception. For her, a repertoire comprises:

> multiple circulating ... discourses of intelligibility that create a means by which audiences are habituated to understand combinations of performative tropes and then recognise and interpret others that are unfamiliar, so that the new may be incorporated into repertoire ... improvisation that sustains intelligibility. (2009: 7)

This rather broad idea of a performative repertoire allows us to acknowledge 'derivation, consistency and comparability' (2009: 23). Davis, writing in the context of theatre history, argues that this formulation allows us to look beyond the innovative, exceptional, or the canonical and rather to appreciate the cultural processes of familiarity that make an everyday repertoire, one that is frequently neglected in our documentation of theatre because so much of it was simply taken for granted, borrowed, derivative and consistent.

It is exactly in this third mode of repertoiring that the amateur theatre plays a key part. Much theatre history, as well as contemporary theatre criticism and commentary, is primarily concerned with the radical, noteworthy, career-making or innovative. The bedrock of theatre-making and theatre-going that draws on the commonly known, the consistent or the established is little regarded. A key part of what amateur theatre does, alongside the commercial and subsidised theatre, is to build audience familiarity and expertise in plays, performance texts and the habit of play-going. Through the repetition and endurance of kinds of repertoire, amateur theatres build audience knowledge and capacity, not just in terms of building audience numbers for live performance, but in building their expertise. Beyond the commitment to staging second productions of new works from playwrights, amateur theatre offers a palette of genres and modes of performance—comedy, musical theatre, farce, murder mystery, thriller, pageant, Shakespeare and classics, alongside twentieth-century stalwarts such as Beckett, Pinter, Orton—that is the enduring national repertoire (Dobson 2011). Davis has pointed out that we should not downgrade this aspect of the repertoire simply because it is familiar, since it is the means by which 'audiences are habituated to understand combinations of performative tropes' and thus to recognise and accept innovation (2009: 7). Indeed, this familiarity is the pre-condition for that innovation and the exceptional, as the cultural process of repertoiring in which audiences can appreciate borrowing, influence, allusion and novelty in live performance.

A central component in establishing the familiarity of an habituated repertoire comes through the relationship between repertoire and genre. Davis and cultural historian Christopher Balme invert the traditional mode of thinking about genre—that generic choice operates as a determining component of repertoire formation, in other words that only texts within genres such as tragedy or serious, realist drama are revered and preserved in both the canon and the repertoire. Instead, Davis and Balme argue that 'the subject matter and forms of theatre reflect social anxieties and influences (new caste stratifications, regional differences, market differentiation, language, migration, etc.) that circulate as repertoires and consolidate as genres' (2015: 405). Following literary theorist Gérard Genette, rather than see genres as pre-existing categories, they reflect on the force of 'spectatorial habits' which means that 'genres in particular need to be seen as processes of negotiation and calibration between production and reception, which in turn influence institutional frameworks as well as social functions' (2015: 416). A consideration of one of the most popular and enduring genres in amateur theatre reveals some of these processes of negotiation and recalibration. Pantomime has been a relatively late, post-war introduction to the regular output of amateur theatre companies, but for smaller societies and village-based groups, the panto is sometimes the only production that they stage—the whole amateur repertoire for that place. One of those groups is Phyl's Follies based in Postbridge, a tiny Dartmoor village of around 160 residents, spread out along the moor road.

In January 2016 I drive up over the moor in dense fog, I'm the only thing out apart from the sheep I swerve to avoid, sitting mid-road licking the salt spread because it is due to freeze. The lights of Postbridge Village Hall glow gently in the distance. The wood-framed village hall is full to capacity, with a high stage at one end cloaked by green curtains. The panto's prompter and musical accompanists are squeezed in at the front, in jackets clad in fairy lights. Tea orders for the interval are delivered to us in our seats from urns brewing on the shelf in the tiny porch. Up on stage it's Ben Crocker's *Beauty and the Beast* lightly adapted with local references by first time directors Annabel Caunter and Alison Geen. Kenny Watson's outrageous neon-clad Ma Wrinklefruit parades down the aisle sitting on local laps and harassing the burliest audience members. In his first role, eleven year old Rowan Munk is our narrator sheepdog Fly, chasing engagingly around us explaining everything. (Jane's Research Diary, 28 January 2016)

Sitting in the Warren House Inn a couple of weeks later with Annabel and Alison, we talk about why pantomime is the perfect genre for Phyl's Follies. Alison Geen explains the script changes she negotiated with Ben Crocker, 'Can we change the poodle to a border collie? Can I put references to local places? We have to mention Widecombe because they think they're better than us, very posh. Once we get a border collie involved we can talk about the local sheepdog man who's got to train the dog.'[22] Our conversation is punctuated by local residents popping by to greet them or reserve sausages from Annabel's business Postbridge Pork, Meat Dartmoor. These overlapping roles that individuals play in the local community is part of the challenge of staging the panto for Phyl's Follies. The performance group is drawn from a wide mix of people from the village and surrounding hamlets. Many of this year's actors were newcomers to the panto with no stage experience. Alison and Annabel evolved a mode of directing through questioning, because of the need to be 'diplomatic in how you put information across and how you direct or guide people'. Rather than an aesthetic choice, as Annabel reflected, the decision to stage a pantomime was about involving large numbers of the local residents as performers, backstage and audience. 'Your neighbour is your neighbour because you don't know when you'll need them up here… The panto brings the community together. It makes winter in a small place like this.

---

[22] Interview Jane Milling with Annabel Caunter and Alison Geen, Postbridge, 23 March 2016. All other quotations are taken from this interview.

You all have a common interest and you find out about people, and can think about going to knock on their door because of it.' Another village group who today perform only a pantomime is Moretonhampstead Variety Group, and the importance of panto as genre and the significance and force of the traditionally recognisable pantomime was brought home by the contrast between two recent productions. In 2014, the Moretonhampstead Variety Group staged *Alice* less as a pantomime than performance with installation. The group developed a steam-punk aesthetic, and the local art studio worked with villagers to create strange hybrid objects for the Museum of Improbable Objects. Some of these beautiful pieces—a bread and butter-fly pinned under glass in a belljar, or a delicate lightbox where the Cheshire Cat gradually appears through a series of Muybridge-style film stills—referenced a neo-Victorianism echoed in the costumes and the setting of the performance. Whilst the performances were very well attended, not everyone was keen to be involved in work that felt unusual and stylistically unexpected for a pantomime. The repercussions of this rumbled on through the village for months in the local newsletter, in pub discussions and conversations in the café.

> It's February 2015, and I'm steaming in the rammed village hall, as the opening moments of *Cinderella* unfold. The piano strikes the first chords. Suddenly a thunderous cheer goes up and the wooden floor reverberates with foot stamping, as uproarious laughter greets the arrival of the fairy godmother. In a remarkable coup de theatre, Andy, hairy-chested in a sparkling pink tutu descends from the flies on a diamante-crusted crescent moon, as Moretonhampstead celebrates the return of a 'traditional' pantomime. (Jane's Research Diary, 21 February 2015)

At the curtain call on the last night of the production, director Becky Baggett stepped forward to thank everybody and to acknowledge the return of a proper 'traditional' pantomime to the village. A final resounding cheer sends us out into the night. The value and importance of familiarity in tropes, conventions, and the broadly accessible populist genre had been explicitly recognised.

Yet, the early amateur theatre movement was keen to encourage its membership to experiment with genre and to engage with new theatre, as a form of embodied repertoire. The hundreds of advice books aimed at amateur groups published over the twentieth and twenty-first centuries link the amateur theatre to wider cultural movements and a broad repertoire beyond the British. The inspiration of modernist European theatre is evident in Harold Downs' epic two volume *Theatre and Stage* (1926), and in C.B. Purdom's *Producing Plays: a Handbook for Producers and Players* (1930). The idea of collaborative creation and the community crafted play and ensemble is developed in Mary Kelly's *Group Play-Making* (1948) and in Peter Cotes' *No Star Nonsense: A Challenging Declaration of Faith in the Essentials of Tomorrow's Theatre* (1949). Cotes calls for actors to play a range of roles as part of a 'long-term commitment to company working', in a company aiming at 'widening audience demographics by removing traditions that might alienate first time theatregoers' (1949: 84). Further aesthetic experimentation and innovation is suggested in Newton's 1967 *A Creative Approach to Amateur Theatre*, which catches some of the spirit of the new movement of experimental theatre-making in small groups of the late 1960s. The broader political context frames the manuals' representation of the value of amateur culture: in 1933 Francis Sladen-Smith jests that the perfect producer-director will 'take his rightful place among the world dictators who are so fashionable at the present moment' (1933: 14) whilst Cotes' *Handbook for the Amateur Theatre* (1957) reflects the shifting allegiances of ex-pat theatrical culture in 'Theatre in the British Commonwealth', following the development of politically radical work by an amateur theatre group in relatively newly-independent Pakistan. What distinguishes most of these books is their hands-on approach, all include advice on how to arrange a rehearsal schedule and how to work with your designer, wardrobe team and set-builders. All make address to the individual director—the ruling genii of the project—and the skills needed to managing a complex supporting cast of assistant roles. Yet more recent handbooks such as Michael McCaffery's *Directing a Play* (1988), Helen E. Sharman's *Directing Amateur Theatre* (2004) or Sarah Burton's *How to put on a Community Play* (2011), are aimed at the amateur market but also at educational contexts from university students to school productions, a phenomenon that marks the rise of drama and theatre studies training. What is noticeable in these recent handbooks is the absence of any reference to the framing context of a season's repertoire or to using a play text to build or sustain audiences for a season, nor do the books imagine the director as part of the company to the extent that they will be a prop-maker or take a minor role in the next show. In other words, by the late twentieth century the amateur advice books have become part of the self-help, self-skilling, proto-educational genre.

Fig. 3.1   Amateur Theatre Handbooks. (Photographer: Jane Milling)

One of the most infamous commentaries on this kind of advice book was Michael Green's *The Art of Coarse Acting* (1964). This handbook is a complex burlesque on the mode of handbook advice and on the difficulties of embodying a repertoire for amateur actors. Its delightful parody inspired a swathe of new writing from within the amateur community, new writing that played clever games with genre itself and explicitly reflected back on the amateur theatres engagement with repertoire. The perspective of the *Art of Corse Acting* is an insider's view, the book emerged from Michel Green's time with four amateur groups: The Crescent, Birmingham; The Northampton Players; Northampton Drama Club; and The Questors. Many of the difficulties that beset amateur troupes—reduced casts, unlearned lines, improvised scenery—are skewered in the volume. The coarse actor, exemplified by amateur thespian enthusiast Askew, undertakes a kind of sabotage of the amateur production since he can 'remember his lines, but not the order in which they come' (Green 1964: 16). The coarse actor has a personal repertoire—a fixed set of expressions, gestures and tights—for multiple roles. The book does not bemoan the inadequacies of the amateur theatre, but rather it offers advice to the aspiring coarse actor as a series of wheezes, specifically never to let your director know what you plan to do: 'many a promising Coarse Actor has had his tricks frustrated because he was foolish enough to introduce them at the dress rehearsal' (1964: 35). Surprise, innovation and improvisation are the Coarse Actor's stock in trade.

Coarse acting includes much interplay with questions of textual repertoire. The frame of reference for the book is commercial theatre, it expects its reader to be familiar with commercial producer Binkie Beaumont, actors Laurence Olivier, Ralph Richardson and Edith Evans, and a wide set of plays from the familiar: Shakespeare, Marston, Moliere, Sheridan; the popular: *Porgy and Bess, Goodbye Mr Chips, Bulldog Drummond*; the modern: *Journey's End, Noah, The Lady's Not for Burning*, and the more involved: James Saunders' *Double Double* and Ostrovsky's *Wolves and Sheep*. However, the repertoire as imagined by the book is not only about play texts, but also references an embodied understanding of repertoire as 'text performed'. Watkins, cousin of Askew, a restive coarse actor and sixth citizen in *Julius Caesar*, finds his moment in the sun by repeating the end of every line declaimed by Mark Anthony over the body of Caesar:

Mark Anthony: Friends, Romans, Countrymen, Lend me your ears,
    Coarse Actor: Ah, ears, ears, ears, (nodding and grimacing to the other citizens). (1964: 46)

The humour of this coarse acting intervention in text lies in the reader's multiple layers of recognition. The reader can recognise the actorly strategy of focus pulling; the generic confusion implied in the misplacement of 'comic peasant' stock acting in Anthony's great speech; a misunderstanding of the importance of homogeneity not individuation in acting in 'chorus' roles and, as the advice concedes, ill-applied technique: 'In fairness to Watkins, he was only adopting a technique much loved by the professional theatre, where the standard crowd noise is to repeat the last line of what the main character has said. One can hardly blame a mere amateur for copying the device' (47). In 1972, at the Ealing-based Questors Theatre, Green arranged the World Coarse Acting Championship. Modelled on the festival circuit of amateur theatre, the competition included teams from Rose Bruford Drama School, Latimer School, alongside a team from the RSC, featuring star actor Roger Rees, who came second to the Bunny

Langridge Players, a fantasy group from The Questors with an Agatha Christie spoof *The Vicar Did It; or, Streuth*, written by cast members. The following year, a second festival had teams from the National Theatre and Salisbury Playhouse—both subsidised theatres—as well as amateur sides. In 1977 The Questors took a version of the Coarse Acting Festival up to the Edinburgh Fringe to critical acclaim. The *Coarse Acting Show 2* went up to Edinburgh in 1978 with *Moby Dick, Dernier Appel Pour Petit Dejeuner, The Cherry Sisters* and *Henry the Tenth (Part Seven)*. Impresario Brian Rix's arranged a transfer to the Shaftesbury Theatre, West End for six weeks. Coarse Acting festivals and competitions continued at The Questors through to the new millennium—November 2017 saw the return of the Giant Coarse Acting Festival to The Questors, 'just when you thought it had gone away'.[23] In 2002 Michael Green's three coarse Shakespeare plays *All's Well that Ends As You Like It, Henry the Tenth (Part Seven), Julius and Cleopatra* (complete with the tragic death of the snake), were introduced onto the Oxford and Cambridge Board syllabus at GCSE level.

The titles of the plays from the Coarse Acting Festivals indicate the engagement with genre that underpins the idea of an amateur theatre's repertoire. All the parodies play with texts well-established on the commercial and subsidised stages, as well as in the larger building-based amateur theatres. The parody assumes shared complicity and competence in the audience not only for the texts themselves, but the playing styles and production ethos of these performances. In *A Collier's Tuesday Tea*, set in the Hepplethwaites cosy cottage in Slagton, a mining village vaguely reminiscent of D.H. Lawrence's oeuvre, pastiche dialect stands in for working-class northernness. But the aura of gritty realism disperses as one by one the legs fall off the kitchen table at which the family sit. The cast are frozen holding up the table unable to enact their rehearsed blocking, until improvisational inspiration arrives, 'Maybe they need some food and drink at the pit head', says Ida, and the table top and cast members shuffle skilfully off between the narrow flats. These parodic farces create a mythic version of amateur performance as catastrophically transgressing professional standards and norms. The texts play with the range of genres most popular in amateur theatre – French farce, murder mystery, realist northern

---

[23] The Giant Coarse Acting Festival. The Questors, London. 24–25 November 2017. http://www.questors.org.uk/event.aspx?id=694 Accessed 2 January 2018.

drama—and reframe that repertoire in a self-reflexive, farcical form. Yet of course, to stage these farces requires exceptional timing, deadpan performances and pitch perfect reproduction of generic cliché in order to work. As W.B. Worthen argues 'it is precisely the technologies of the repertoire that intervene, that enact the process of transmission, embodied practices such as editing, reading, memorization, movement, gesture, acting that produce both a sense of what the text is, and what we might be capable of saying with and through it in/as performance, what we want to make it signify' (2010: 68). At the very moment that they appear to most mock and undercut amateur theatre production, the Coarse Acting farces simultaneously celebrate the endlessly inventive, improvising, coarse actor wrestling with remaking an amateur repertoire.

Forging New Repertoires

The Coarse Acting plays are just one example of the considerable amount of completely new writing in the amateur sector that contributes to an expressly amateur repertoire, much of it generated by amateurs for amateurs, but occasionally the product of a commissioned work by a professional writer. Indeed the practice of amateur companies commissioning new plays was sufficiently widespread that Jonathan Meth prepared a guide, underwritten by the Arts Council, on *Commissioning New Work: A good practice guide for amateur theatre companies and playwrights* (2004) which lays out wise advice on timescales, pay rates and the developmental relationship between playwright and theatre company. One example of the commissioning relationship built between professional writer and amateur theatre company is that between the Playgoers Society of Dartington Hall and Nick Stimson, playwright and associate director of the nearby Plymouth Theatre Royal. The Playgoers commissioned Nick to develop a play to celebrate seventy years of the Playgoers at Dartington in 2016. *Inventing Utopia* (2016) grew from Stimson's historical knowledge and the experience of three creative team members from the company, Richard Clark, Jo Loosemore and Gordon Frow. Unusually, Stimson brokered the relationship with the Arts Council applying for funding for *Inventing Utopia*, after an earlier collaboration with the company writing the large-scale *Love and Fire: A Totnes Play* (2013), commissioned by the Playgoers from their own funds. *Love and Fire* (2013) had followed an episodic history of three feuding families through time, linked by a female gravedigger, Bertha Winchester. Nick Stimson reflected on the impact of that play:

The audience stayed behind every night and wanted to talk about what Totnes was, what it could become. You don't get that very often spontaneously. It was only on for six performances, but it was worth it.[24]

Working in a similar way on *Inventing Utopia* in 2016, the company held three full-company script workshops.

We had a good process. There was Richard the director who has a very strong practical theatre background – he trained at Dartington and taught in colleges for many years – Gordon, and Jo Loosemore who runs drama on the BBC [Radio Devon]. They had a script development process going on, where we met five or six times in the writing process to find out where we were and to build better ways of developing that script.

This developed the sense of ownership over the material for the performers and Society. *Inventing Utopia* followed the story of the Playgoers Society of Dartington itself. The first half presented the real personnel of the Elmhirsts' utopic experiment on the Dartington estates and original members of the Playgoers' Society. The second half connected Dartington and Maurice Browne's championing of R.C. Sheriff's *Journey's End* (1928), with contemporary experiences of post-traumatic stress in veterans. The play was sold out every night, and in the interval and afterwards audiences were eager to talk about the Dartington experiment, the way forward for the Dartington Trust and their own relation to the place. Stimson is equanimous about the investment of his labour in a show for a specific group, likely only to have one staging: 'Sometimes you can do a professional play and it is just another show. I have four new shows opening this year. But something that has real impact for a community is really exciting.'

The more usual mode through which new writing is introduced into the repertoires of amateur theatre is the wide range of writing from within companies themselves, developing new voices. This work has perhaps been neglected in part because it tends to have an emphasis on styles, genres and subject matter somewhat different to the work that came to be associated with the term 'new writing' in the subsidised sector at the turn of the millennium. Amateur new writing has been somewhat eclipsed, not

---

[24] Interview Jane Milling with Nick Stimson, 2 Dec 2016. All other quotations are taken from this interview.

because of questions about quality, but rather because of the remarkable rise of programmes supporting new writing within the subsidised sector. These subsidised programmes have grown to shoulder some of the burden of support for new writing that the amateur sector had provided, as outlined by theatre scholars on recent dramaturgy Cathy Turner and Synne Behrndt (2007), Jacqueline Bolton (2012) and Duska Radosavljević (2013). Not only new writing 'powerhouses', but the less financially secure small-scale professional theatre companies have offered increased opportunities for diverse writers and modes of writing (Tomlin 2015: 70). Prior to the recent increase in subsidised support for playwrights, the activities of the amateur theatre sector had provided a significant route to staging and publication for playwrights' work. In particular, through playwriting competitions and festivals, amateur theatre companies were a catalyst in starting new writing careers. Three striking examples from the 1950s and 1960s illustrate the varieties of journeys that were facilitated. David Campton started writing for amateur groups Leicester Drama Society and the Vaughan Players. In 1954 Campton won both the Leicestershire British Drama League one-act playwriting competition, and another one-act play, *The Laboratory*, won the international new writing prize run by the amateur Tower Theatre Company (Taylor 1976: 181). Campton's early work was dubbed comedy of menace, and he was published alongside Pinter by *Encore* magazine, and moved into professional writing through his work with Stephen Joseph's company, and his television writing. The amateur competitions offered space to acknowledge Campton's fresh voice and alternative subject matter, and gave his work a performance venue that led to a professional writing career. Likewise, James Saunders began his playwriting career at The Questors, Ealing. Saunders has been called an early exponent of theatre of the absurd, and The Questors staged both his competition winning short play, and his first full-length play, *Next Time I'll Sing to You*, which won The Questors' New Plays Festival in 1962.[25] The Questors had built a commitment to new writing into its policy for repertoire, staging a newly-authored premier each season from 1946. From 1960–1978 it ran an annual Festival of New Plays 'three new plays presented in repertoire with nightly discussions with

[25] Jim Irvin, Obituary, James Saunders, *The Guardian*, 5 February 2004. https://www.theguardian.com/news/2004/feb/05/guardianobituaries.artsobituaries Accessed 7 December 2017.

the audience and usually with the author' (Chambers 2002: 628). Caryl Churchill's first full-length play *Having a Wonderful Time* (1960) was staged under these auspices (Aston and Diamond 2009: xi; Churchill 1985: xi). In 1964 The Questors' staged a series of short one-off performances of plays under the title *Five Plays from Berlin*. 'One of these was *Guildenstern and Rosencrantz* by a young playwright called Tom Stoppard who directed the first version.'[26]

Alongside the imperative to discover and develop new playwrights whose voices were to be significant forces in extending national culture, the amateur theatre sector has used competitions and new writing initiatives to encourage new drama that addresses the needs and interests of specific companies in their location and communities. In 1925 the Village Drama Society started an annual playwrighting competition 'one of the first moves to find new plays' for the amateur movement 'but the writing of plays began almost as soon as the VDS was founded' (Wallis 2000: 352). Mary Kelly was disappointed in the existing fare available for the burgeoning groups in villages and under the auspices of the Women's Institutes, 'for the most part we get only… realistic comedies… that do not even dare to look the mirror squarely in the face' (Kelly 1939: 168). It was the Village Drama Society's offer of publication and the potential for a wider dissemination of play texts that drew out a large number of writers. The variety of forms and modes of new writing developed in this way is remarkable, from Kelly's own *The Mother* (1936), a sharply class-conscious two act drama that parallels the death of a young child with the futile losses of war. Clarice M. Wilson's *Every Woman* (1931) offers an expressionistic reflection, in the manner of Maeterlinck's *Blue Bird*, on the domestic pressures of women's daily lives and the articulation of that unpaid work as service to the entire community. Olive Popplewell's stirring play *The Pacifist* (1934) follows Mavis, who rejects the domestic comfort offered by her imminent marriage, in order to lead a pacifist meeting as a passionate orator and work for the international pacifist cause. The new writing prompted by the Village Drama Society produced a range of one-act plays for predominantly female casts, but in both their subject matter, form and address these plays developed a wider purview beyond what might be considered local or village concerns.

---

[26] http://archive.questors.org.uk/prods/1964/berlinplays/page.html Accessed 1 June 2016.

There remains a vibrant culture of new writing from amateurs them-selves, encouraged at a variety of scales, from one act or ten minute play competitions, rehearsed readings or evenings of short plays, workshops with youth groups, to writing opportunities that cross over into the sub-sided theatre. One-act plays have been a particularly significant form for amateur theatre, one of the most enduring national amateur writing opportunities, the Geoffrey Whitworth trophy (inaugurated in 1951), is presented for the best original play staged as part of the competitive inter-regional one-act festival run by the UK Community Drama Festivals Federation. For many years the magazine *Amateur Stage* ran a playwriting competition, and the *Amateur Theatre and Playwrights Magazine* offered to publish successful competition entrants (Saunders 2012: 74). There are regular festival competitions for short form new drama run by particular companies or regional associations such as the Norfolk One Act Playwriting Competition,[27] the Windsor Fringe Kenneth Branagh Award for New Drama Writing in its fifteenth year,[28] the Isles of Scilly One Act Play Festival,[29] the Congleton Players One-Act Playwriting competition,[30] or Chesil Theatre Winchester's 10x10 competition. Other occasional writing competitions might mark a special occasion, for example, the amateur Lace Market Theatre, Nottingham, ran a new writers competition for the 2014–2015 season to prompt new local writers, and to support Nottingham's bid as a UNESCO World Heritage Literature City.[31] Bolton Amateur Theatre Society ran a writing competition with the Bolton

---

[27] Sponsored by June Owen of Garboldisham Amateur Dramatic Society to promote play writing for the amateur theatre. https://www.noda.org.uk/regions/east/the-fourth-nor-folk-one-act-playwriting-competition Accessed 7 December 2017.

[28] The Windsor Fringe Drama Awards reiterate 'Only amateur playwrights are eligible and only one script per author will be accepted. Each script must be an original work by the entrant, and must not have been previously published or performed.' http://www.windsor-fringe.co.uk/drama-awards/ Accessed 7 December 2017.

[29] St Mary's Theatre Club annual one-act play (15–30 minutes) competition has run since 2010. In 2016, as part of the Isles of Scilly Festival, after rehearsed readings of shortlisted plays, the audience helped to choose the winner. https://www.facebook.com/stmarysthe-atreclubios Accessed 7 December 2017.

[30] http://www.congletonplayers.com/index.html Accessed 7 December 2017. All 400 entries in 2017, granted the Congleton Players free performing rights for their work.

[31] The resulting one-act comedy *One Act Play* by Matt Fox was staged in January 2015. https://lacemarkettheatre.co.uk/LaceMarketTheatre.dll/News?NewsItem=38 Accessed 7 December 2017.

Octagon, for a new full-length play from a local writer for production in 2015. The Little Theatre Guild collates a number of the new writing opportunities for amateurs, and the newsletter for November 2015 carried notes on The Questors' play reading of Effie Samara's new play *Sartre*, Ilkley Theatre's Walter Swan Playwriting awards, where the winning play (of 200 entries) was staged at the Playhouse Studio and the subsidised West Yorkshire Playhouse, Leeds. The Tower Theatre Company collaborated with a new venue in Dalston to produce smaller-scale new writing, and the New Venture Theatre, Brighton ran a ten minute play festival (Shipley 2015: 9). Alongside competitions, the amateur sector has a long history in teaching playwriting. The British Drama League supported training for playwrights through weekend intensives, correspondence courses and summer schools, and offered 'a full written criticism of full-length or one-act plays, for a small fee' (Gunn and Bingham 1957: 132). When Stephen Joseph was beginning his project to generate a new kind of theatre and thus was in need of a new kind of playwright, he ran 'ongoing intermittent short playwrighting courses ... under the auspices of the amateur British Drama League. Joseph's biggest catch via this route was surely David Campton, who would later join up as a company regular' (Elsam 2013: 72). The role of amateur theatre organisations was particularly significant in the earlier twentieth century before the appearance of theatre and drama as a university-level subject, and before responsibility for new writer development was more fully taken on by subsidised theatres.

One of the common characteristics in much of the writing for amateurs by amateurs today is the desire to write for and about local communities, and this often leads towards historical content and documentary or episodic writing that draws on regional or local culture and experience. Talking with Annette Cooper and Beverly Quinn, leading members of the Washington Theatre Group during the 1980s and early 1990s, Beverly details the history of new writing workshops run within the group that led to self-authored pantomimes and an off-shoot theatre-in-education group. One example of a local story staged by the group at the Washington Arts Centre and firmly directed to local audiences was *There was an Old Woman* (1985). The play about women and the decline of the coal industry, written by folk songwriter and junior school teacher Ed Pickford prior to the miner's strike, was repurposed and performed to packed auditoria in October 1985 after the March return to work, as the implications of pit closures were being profoundly felt in the area. More recently, South Devon Players' writer-director Laura Jay worked with local historian Nigel

Voisey in developing *Survivors of the Titanic* (2015) which used documentary sources from the Loss of the Titanic inquiry to retell the story from below decks. The story has local connections—the rescued crew limped home to Plymouth—but the play was concerned with the large-scale wider historical canvas. The South Devon Players, winners of the Voluntary Arts Epic Awards 2016, are an interesting example of an initially unaffiliated group who write all of their own material. Laura Jay, one of the group's instigators, explained the group formed because some members of Brixham Operatic and Dramatic Society wanted to tackle different kinds of material and extend the aesthetic possibilities of their work. For a very small group starting out, the cost of royalties for existing material was prohibitive. The company have developed a distinctive neo-historicism in their writing, reworking the king Arthur legend as *Mordred* (2016), local tale of smugglers outwitting the excise men in *The Ballad of Resurrection Bob* (2013), or staging their own adaptation of *Les Miserables* (2013). Several of their members are stage-fight trained, are keen Live Action Role Players, or play pirates for street performances at Brixham's pirate festival.

> In the rehearsal rooms the company rents from the local spiritualist church, high on a hill above Brixham, the storage cupboards are bursting with costumes and props from previous shows. Director Laura Jay and two performers are in long rehearsal skirts marking a scene from their new play *Survivors of the Titanic,* where the wives of lower decks stewards besiege the White Star Line Company gates for news of their husbands. Actors form groups and imagine their placement on the stage, the acting is presentational, groups concentrate on making sure the dialogue makes sense and that the purpose of the scene is clear. Between scenes, I ask group members, old and new, about what attracted them to South Devon Players and what ideas about acting they draw on as they act. (Jane's Research Diary 15 November 2015)

The episodic style of the play follows the ordinary families and the lower ranks of the ship's crew below decks, culminating with the sinking at the end of the first act. The second half stages a series of scenes from the public inquiry launched into the disaster, dwelling on the consequences and repercussions of the disaster for surviving passengers and crew. I saw the *Survivors of the Titanic* staged in a whitewashed wood-panelled Baptist church repurposed as a community centre, the nave of the room forming a narrow auditorium and the pulpit steps became the ship's bridge. The counterpointed episodes of the play laid bare the structural reasons for the disaster and charted the very different outcomes for wealthy and working-class passengers. This was a performance far from the romanticised retellings of the disaster found elsewhere in popular culture, and the episodic mode of writing, and presentational style, allowed the audience to follow the story in a wider historical context. For many amateur groups, different kinds of new writing from members are built into their repertoire, from rehearsed readings to full-blown production. If they stage a pantomime, almost all groups adapt the script to local contexts and many groups write their own—the genre offers a firm structure and familiar set of narratives to a new writer. Many new plays emerge as historical and documentary dramas on local stories or themes relevant to the communities for which they are written. This is a mode of new writing that is less concerned with linking to contemporary national or international aesthetic trends, and more concerned to forge links with audiences in particular places. It is a repertoire that represents strands of community history and experience back to those local audiences in a way that could not be made economically viable within the strictures of a commercial, or even a subsidised, theatre context. These are repertoires of community storying that would not exist were amateur theatre groups were not writing themselves.

The repertoiring practices of amateur theatre are closely interconnected with the subsidised and commercial theatre sectors and contribute to the cultural economy in ways that have facilitated a range of playwrights to the stage and sustained their works in performance. In extending the geographical range and longevity of plays in local repertoires, they have influenced the national dynamics of performing rights, publishing contexts and playwrights' earnings. The work of repertoiring in relation to play texts has built 'spectatorial habits' and developed audience expertise in a wide range of genres. This chapter has considered the processes of repertoiring around traditional play texts, as the root of most amateur theatre companies' raison d'être and what they imagine as their contribution to their local culture. There is a considerable amount of other kinds of new writing from amateurs—in revue, burlesque, interactive murder mysteries, reminiscence shows, writing or devising projects with amateur youth groups, performance poetry, films, heritage trails, for example, that is rarely recorded in the publicly facing presence of amateur theatre groups. Alongside the more obvious establishing of local canons, these other modes also contribute to the ways in which the processes of repertoiring have an effect beyond the aesthetic and into the wider social context in which amateur theatres work. In this, and in cultivating accessible, popular and familiar repertoire as part of their activity, amateur theatres participate in what theatre scholar Christopher Balme has called 'theatre's many public functions' and social roles, which he argues is an urgent imperative in the context of increased mediatisation of culture and the increased concentration on aesthetic innovation in contemporary subsidised theatre (2014: 27). The cultural value of amateur theatre lies in part in its contribution to the range, scope and sustainability of live theatre performance, mediating and reinvigorating our national theatrical repertoire, and in building a love of theatre and live performance in participants and audiences as part of our national cultural ecology.

REFERENCES

Alexander, Isabella. 2010. 'Neither Bolt nor Chain, Iron Safe Nor Watchman Can Prevent the Theft of Words': The Birth of the Performing Right in Britain. In . *Privilege and Property: Essays on the History of Copyright*, ed. Ronan Deazley, Martin Kretschmer, and Lionel Bently, 321–346. Cambridge: Open Book.

Altieri, Charles. 1983. An Idea and Ideal of a Literary Canon. *Critical Inquiry* 10: 37–60.

Angelaki, Vicky. 2013. *Contemporary British Theatre: Breaking New Ground*. London: Palgrave.

Arts Council England. 2000. *The Next Stage: Towards a National Policy for Theatre in England*. London: Arts Council England.

Arts Council of Great Britain. 1960. *Fifteenth Annual Report 1959–1960*. London: Arts Council of Great Britain.

———. 1970. *The Theatre Today in England and Wales*. London: Arts Council of Great Britain.

Aston, Elaine, and Elin Diamond, eds. 2009. *The Cambridge Companion to Caryl Churchill*. Cambridge: Cambridge University Press.

Aston, Elaine, and Geraldine Harris. 2012. *A Good Night Out for the Girls*. London: Palgrave.

Balme, Christopher B. 2014. *The Theatrical Public Sphere*. Cambridge: Cambridge University Press.

Barrett, Daniel. 1999. Play Publication, Readers, and the 'Decline' of Victorian Drama. *Book History* 2: 173–187.

Billington, Michael. 1996. *Harold Pinter*. London: Faber and Faber.

Bishop, George W., ed. 1929. *The Amateur Dramatic Yearbook and Community Theatre Handbook 1928–9*. London: A&C Black.

Bolton, Jacqueline. 2012. Capitalizing (on) New Writing: New Play Development in 1990s. *Studies in Theatre and Performance* 32 (2): 209–225.

Boyden, Peter. 2000. *Roles and Functions of the English Regional Producing Theatres: Final Report to the Arts Council England.* Bristol: Peter Boyden Associates.

Bradley, Ian. 2005. *Oh Joy! Oh Rapture! The Enduring Phenomenon of Gilbert and Sullivan.* New York: Oxford University Press.

British Drama League. 1945. *Twenty-Five Years of the British Drama League.* Oxford: Alden Press.

Brown, Ian, and Rob Brannen. 1996. When Theatre Was for All: The Cork Report, After Ten Years. *New Theatre Quarterly* 12: 367–387.

Brownlee, David, David Edgar, Wendy Haines, Clare Ollerhead, and Dan Rebellato. 2015. *British Theatre Repertoire 2013.* London: Arts Council England.

Burton, Sarah. 2011. *How to Put on a Community Play.* London: Aurora Metro.

Cellier, François, and Cunningham Bridgeman. 1914. *Gilbert and Sullivan and Their Operas.* Boston: Little, Brown and Company.

Chambers, Colin, ed. 2002. *The Continuum Companion to Twentieth-Century Theatre.* London: Continuum.

Chan, Tak Wing, and John H. Goldthorpe. 2005. The Social Stratification of Theatre, Dance and Cinema Attendance. *Cultural Trends* 14 (3): 193–212.

Churchill, Caryl. 1985. Introduction. In *Plays 1.* London: Methuen.

Cork, Kenneth. 1986. *Theatre IS for All: Report of the Inquiry into Professional Theatre in England Under the Chairmanship of Sir Kenneth Cork.* London: Arts Council of Great Britain.

Corman, Brian. 1992. What Is the Canon of English Drama, 1660–1737? *Eighteenth-Century Studies* 26 (2): 307–321.

Cotes, Peter. 1949. *No Star Nonsense: A Challenging Declaration of Faith in the Essentials of Tomorrow's Theatre.* London: Theatre Book Club.

———. 1957. *A Handbook for the Amateur Theatre.* London: Oldbourne Press.

Davis, Tracy C. 2009. Nineteenth Century Repertoires. *Nineteenth Century Theatre and Film* 36 (2): 6–28.

Davis, Tracy C., and Christopher B. Balme. 2015. A Cultural History of Theatre: A Prospectus. *Theatre Survey* 56 (3): 402–421.

Dobson, Michael. 2011. *Shakespeare and Amateur Performance: A Cultural History.* Cambridge: Cambridge University Press.

Dodd, Fiona, Andrew Graves, and Karen Taws. 2008. *Our Creative Talent: The Voluntary and Amateur Arts in England.* London: DCMS.

Dorney, Kate, ed. 2013. *Played in Britain: Modern Theatre in 100 Plays.* London: Methuen.

Downs, Harold. 1926. *Theatre and Stage.* London: Pitman.

Edgar, David. 2013. Playwriting Studies: Twenty Years On. *Contemporary Theatre Review* 23 (2): 99–106.

Edgar, David, Dan Rebellato, Janelle Reinelt, Steve Waters, and Julie Wilkinson. 2009. *Writ Large: New Writing on the English Stage 2003–09*. London: British Theatre Consortium.

Elsam, Paul. 2010. Harold Pinter's the Birthday Party: The 'Lost' Second Production. *Studies in Theatre and Performance* 30 (3): 257–266.

———. 2013. *Stephen Joseph, Theatre Pioneer and Provocateur*. London: Bloomsbury Methuen.

Green, Michael. 1964. *The Art of Coarse Acting*. London: Hutchinson.

Guillory, John. 2013. *Cultural Capital: The Problem of Literary Canon Formation*. Chicago: University of Chicago Press.

Gunn, John, and Barbara Bingham. 1957. *Acting for You*. London: Lutterworth Press.

Joseph, Tony. 1994. *D'Oyly Carte Opera Company, 1875–1982: An Unofficial History*. London: Bunthorne Books.

Kelly, Mary. 1939. *Village Theatre*. London: Thomas Nelson.

———. 1948. *Group Play-Making*. London: G.G. Harrap.

Kerman, Joseph. 1983. A Few Canonic Variations. *Critical Inquiry* 10: 107–125.

Lowerson, John. 2005. *Amateur Operatics: A Social and Cultural History*. Manchester: Manchester University Press.

McCaffery, Michael. 1988. *Directing a Play*. London: Phaidon.

Meth, Jonathan. 2004. *Commissioning New Work: A Good Practice Guide for Amateur Theatre Companies and Playwrights*. London: Arts Council England.

Naylor, Richard, Bethany Lewis, Caterina Branzanti, Graham Devlin, and Alan Dix. 2016. *Analysis of Theatre in England*. London: Arts Council England.

Newton, Robert. 1967. *A Creative Approach to Amateur Theatre*. London: J. Garnett Miller.

Purdom, C. B. 1930. *Producing Plays: A Handbook for Producers and Players*. New York: E.P. Dutton.

Radosavljević, Duska. 2013. *Theatre-Making: The Interplay between Text and Performance in the 21st Century*. Basingstoke: Palgrave Macmillan.

Rebellato, Dan. 1999. *1956 and All That*. London: Routledge.

Roach, Joseph. 1996. *Cities of the Dead*. New York: Columbia University Press.

Rowell, George, and Anthony Jackson. 1984. *The Repertory Movement: A History of Regional Theatre in Britain*. Cambridge: Cambridge University Press.

Saunders, Graham. 2012. Prizes for Modernity in the Provinces: The Arts Council's 1950–1951 Regional Playwriting Competition. *History Research* 2 (2): 73–109.

Schoch, Richard. 2016. *Writing the History of the British Stage*. Cambridge: Cambridge University Press.

Sharman, Helen E. 2004. *Directing Amateur Theatre*. London: A&C Black.

Shipley, Michael. 2015. New Writing. *Little Theatre Guild Newsletter*, November 9.

Sladen-Smith, Francis. 1933. *The Amateur Producer's Handbook*. London: Thomas Nelson.

Taylor, George. 1976. *History of the Amateur Theatre*. Melksham: Colin Venton White Horse Library.

Taylor, Diana. 2003. *The Archive and the Repertoire*. Durham: Duke University Press.

Tomlin, Liz. 2015. *British Theatre Companies 1995–2014*. London: Bloomsbury.

Turner, Cathy, and Synne Behrndt. 2007. *Dramaturgy and Performance*. Basingstoke: Palgrave.

Wallis, Mick. 2000. Unlocking the Secret Soul: Mary Kelly, Pioneer of Village Theatre. *New Theatre Quarterly* 16 (4): 347–358.

Worthen, William B. 2010. *Drama: Between Poetry and Performance*. Oxford: Wiley-Blackwell.

Zarhy-Levo, Yael. 2008. *Making of Theatrical Reputations*. Iowa City: Iowa University Press.

CHAPTER 4

Amateur Theatre, Place and Place-Making

In March 2016, the UK's Conservative government published the first White Paper on the Arts and Culture since Jennie Lee's *A Policy for the Arts: The First Steps* in 1965. Entitled *The Culture White Paper* and authorised by Ed Vaisey MP, Minister for Culture and the Digital Economy at the time, the document sets out a series of objectives for culture and cultural participation. The 'outcome' and 'output' indicators cover a range of social and economic measures, including improving subjective well-being, increasing the cultural participation of people from disadvantaged backgrounds and Black, Asian and Minority Ethnic (BAME) communities, reducing crime and improving the nation's soft power.[1] Despite an interest in extending cultural activity, there is no mention of amateur arts anywhere in *The Culture White Paper*. Fifty-one years earlier, the Labour politician Jennie Lee also hoped to increase cultural provision, but she also expressed an aspiration to break down barriers between amateurs and professionals, offering the very practical suggestion that they might use the same theatres to perform and share responsibility for venue management. The two White Papers neatly capture changing attitudes to amateur

---

[1] We are aware that BAME is a contested term on the grounds that it assumes a white norm. https://www.thetimes.co.uk/article/ethnicity-labels-are-divisive-says-phillips-qptswxk3l93. Accessed 25 June 2018. In this instance, it is used to refer to official data and documents, where the term is still regularly used.

© The Author(s) 2018
H. Nicholson et al., *The Ecologies of Amateur Theatre*,
https://doi.org/10.1057/978-1-137-50810-2_4

creativity in the minds of government officials, and signal attitudinal shifts towards amateurs in the cultural ecology.

There are many differences between the two White Papers, but it is important for this chapter to note that they both recognise that the arts and cultural organisations contribute to place and place-making, albeit from different political perspectives. Both White Papers seek to extend the benefits of cultural activity to a wider social demographic and geographical area, with both emphasising cultural provision for those living outside London. In 1965, Jennie Lee included the arts as part of her vision to cultivate a 'new social as well as artistic climate', particularly in new towns and Garden Cities (1965: 5). In 2016 Ed Vaisey favoured increased cultural activity across the country because of the contribution it makes to urban regeneration, well-being and economic prosperity. 'Cultural place-making can shape the fortunes of our regions, cities towns and villages,' it states, and goes on to outline how Hull was attracting tourism, new jobs and businesses to the city because it had been designated the 2017 UK City of Culture (2016: 30).[2] *The Culture White Paper* also launched a new Lottery-funded scheme, Great Places, designed to encourage different local organisations and stakeholders to work together to create places that are culturally rich.[3] The list of possible cultural sector partners comprises local government, universities, the police, local health and care commissioners. At the bottom of the list the report's authors suggest that 'the local voluntary and community sector, including trusts and foundations' might be included, but amateurs are conspicuously absent.

The distinction between local volunteers and amateur artists marks a difference between the two White Papers. In 1965, Jennie Lee's 'new social climate' included amateur arts, and she cited approvingly the contribution the Little Theatre Guild was making to local and regional cultural activity, describing Birmingham Local Authority as 'progressive' in its decision to offer the amateur Crescent Theatre an interest-free loan. By 2016, amateurs had ceased to be part of the vision, and financial generosity had waned. By contrast, however, *The Culture White Paper* was very keen on volunteering:

---

[2] https://www.gov.uk/government/uploads/system/uploads/attachment_data/file/510798/DCMS_The_Culture_White_Paper__3_.pdf, p. 30. Accessed 24 July 2016.

[3] Launched as a pilot in 2017, Great Place Scheme aims to meet 'local social and economic objectives'. https://www.greatplacescheme.org.uk/. Accessed 31 July 2016.

> Volunteering is a way for people of all ages and from all backgrounds and walks of life to get involved in cultural activities and support the work of cultural organisations. (2016: 27)

Getting 'involved in cultural activities' could include the kind of all-absorbing passion for local theatre-making that we have encountered in the amateur companies we have researched. Two sentences later, however, this interpretation seems less likely:

> We will work with Arts Council England, Historic England and other publicly-funded cultural organisations to encourage more volunteering opportunities in the cultural sectors. (2016: 27)

The Culture White Paper favours, it appears, volunteers who freely give their labour to support the professional cultural sector. The use of the word 'voluntary' implies generosity, but funding constraints also mean that cultural organisations are increasingly reliant on volunteer (unpaid) labour to function. The use of terminology in *The Culture White Paper* is significant; volunteers are valued for their contribution to extending cultural organisations' prosperity, and, in the process, it is expected that volunteers' well-being and employability will be enhanced. This mix of economic and social objectives surrounding voluntarism fails to recognise that many local amateurs are already creating and maintaining a sense of place, by making theatre for the love of it.

Yet running alongside and complementing policies that advocate voluntarism lies a renewed interest in creative and cultural participation, and a recognition that shared experiences of the arts contributes to feelings of belonging. The invitation in this chapter, therefore, is to consider amateur theatre as part of the ecology of place and place-making. Attending an amateur production often carries a special atmosphere, the responses of audiences underlining its localism. For members of Acting Out, an LGBTQ company in Birmingham, performing plays that reflect their identities in the tiny theatre of The Wellington pub creates feelings of mutual support. The pub is important to the company; the gay landlords provide the venue for free in anticipation of bar sales. Alex Wrightson, secretary of the company, describes a performance of coming out stories, and how this reflected the members' attachment to place:

The pub... are particularly vocal when they don't like a production we've put on, so I'm always quite shocked when they like something. They liked the first one we put on, with the tight leotard, because they got loads of money out of the bar, it was a big audience. We got commissioned last November to do SHOUT festival in Birmingham. We were asked for coming out stories... There were lots of different stories, which we amalgamated together. We have a writing group... they are all older homosexual gentlemen, and they were describing the public toilets that the police would arrest people outside. Someone laid roses outside when the toilets were knocked down... LGBTQ is first, and yet the amateur dramatics thing is secondary.[4]

For this company and their audiences, the performance celebrates LGBTQ experiences in Birmingham, marking places and memories in performative acts. Amateur theatre, for Acting Out, is a vehicle of cultural recognition and one way to create a sense of belonging to a place.

Many amateur theatre-makers take responsibility for crafting their local communities, and adding to the histories and recollections that distinguish one place from another. As we observed in Chapter 2, there is a utopianism and sense of hope that is embedded in the history of amateur theatre, and the case studies that I have chosen to discuss in relation to place echo this history. In this chapter I will situate place-making in an historical context to analyse how amateur theatre became integral to an international vision of social change in the twentieth century. I have chosen the Garden Cities and suburbia as case studies, focusing particularly on amateur theatre in establishing the cultural fabric of place. I will start by raising conceptual questions about place-making as a material practice, expanding on issues that we raised in Chapter 2 about the cultural value of amateur theatre. My suggestion is that amateur theatre has long made a significant contribution to place-making, encouraging an affective attachment to place, sustained over time and with emotional commitment.

PLACE, PLACE-MAKING AND CULTURAL VALUE

As *The Culture White Paper* testifies, the relationship between the arts and place-making has been subject to renewed attention in recent years. It is well documented that the cultural sector and the creative industries are

---

[4] Interview Alex Wrightson with Erin Walcon, Birmingham, 5 March 2015.

making a significant contribution to urban regeneration in the twenty-first century, and cultural quarters across the globe have re-fashioned post-industrial wastelands with the intention of raising local aspiration and boosting the creative economy. In many cities in Britain, a regenerated site has at its centre either a newly-built theatre (CAST, Doncaster), art gallery (Turner Contemporary, Margate) or music and concert venue (Sage Gateshead). Programmes vary, with many designed to attract those with metropolitan tastes, as well as providing opportunities for local people to participate in the arts and other cultural events with wide appeal. There are economic and social benefits to the surrounding area: Birmingham's Custard Factory is a good example of a post-industrial cultural quarter that offers space to incubate creative start-ups and Small and Medium Enterprises (SMEs), who are in turn served by pubs with craft beers, pop-up shops and independent coffee shops. Cities are regarded as the economic hub of the twenty-first century and, inspired by Charles Landry and Richard Florida, many have been re-visioned as 'creative cities' and their unique attributes re-branded to capture the highly competitive and mobile workforce deemed necessary for commercial success. Florida identifies 'talent, innovation and creativity' as the 'key economic factors' needed for global capitalism, and argues that cities that wish to attract and retain this 'creative class' will make appropriate cultural provision (2002: 9). The cultural organisations themselves, however, have been widely resistant to this elitism, and *The Culture White Paper* also appears to recognise the inherent inequality in this approach to place-making. Emphasis is placed on increasing the number of disadvantaged groups participating in the arts and their governance, including serving on the boards of cultural organisations.

Much attention has been paid to re-branding cities as cultural hotspots to attract the affluent creative class, and, at the other end of the spectrum, to regenerating areas of urban deprivation and providing cultural opportunities for the socially disadvantaged. Amateur theatre is not generally associated with either end of this spectrum and this may be another reason why it has tended to lie outside the gaze of many policy initiatives. Yet it is not just re-branded cities that carry cultural values; all places are inscribed with distinct social meanings but, as the human geographer Tim Cresswell has argued, such 'common sense ideas' are often 'quite vague when subject to critical reflection' (2004: 11). It is worth pausing, therefore, to reflect on how the specific term place-making has entered the contemporary political lexicon. One version of place-making is associated with the trend for re-developing urban spaces but, unlike the Creative City movement, place-making projects aim to improve city environments through local participation. This approach to place-making is currently influencing policy-makers, emphasising how communities can assist professional cultural and civic organisations to re-animate public spaces that have become under-used, unappealing or unsafe. Described by place-making pioneer Fred Kent as 'citizen-inspired design',[5] Kent's organisation, *Project for Public Spaces*, focuses on re-vitalising public spaces (parks, waterfronts, streets and markets) or public buildings (libraries, court houses, civic buildings). In this conceptualisation, place-making is explicitly interventionist and sometimes activist, and primarily focuses on the edginess of metropolitan urban life rather than suburban residential areas or small towns that might be considered more quotidian or mundane.

So where does this leave amateur theatre? Amateur theatre is often defined by its localism and is integral to many communities, not least because unlike some forms of amateur creativity, theatre-making depends upon collaboration and regular social interaction. Kevin Spence, former Chair of the Little Theatre Guild and a trustee of CAST, described how the repertoire and place are closely intertwined in his local area of South Yorkshire, and how he used this to his advantage when directing productions at Doncaster Little Theatre:

> You have to take work out, because we realised that's what you have to do in Doncaster... So we took out *Glee Club*, to village halls, community centres, working men's club. We took out *Blood Brothers*, *Kes*, a wonderful production of *Kes*. We took out stuff that they were going to come to see. It more important that they came to see it. We did *Brassed Off* with Dinnington Band and Hatfield band in combination... We took it to Hatfield Miners Welfare, and they abandoned the Bingo for us, and that was a big thing to do.[6]

In a post-show discussion with a retired miner and his wife in Hatfield, a village ten miles from Doncaster, Kevin Spence recounted that the couple had not visited the town for over thirty years, living in what he described as a 'totally self-contained community'. Although there are

[5] http://www.pps.org/reference/what_is_placemaking/. Accessed 12 August 2017.

[6] Interview Kevin Spence with Molly Flynn, Jane Milling and Helen Nicholson. Doncaster, 14 June 2016.

some lively amateur theatre companies in cities, it is perhaps most often associated with non-metropolitan places—towns, villages and suburbs—where professional arts provision is less regularly available nearby. The membership of affiliated societies would confirm this perception; the majority of member companies of the Little Theatre Guild in 2017 were situated outside major cities, and in NODA's London Region, for example, more affiliated companies were based in the suburbs or surrounding towns than in the city centre.[7]

For this analysis of amateur theatre's role in place-making, therefore, I will move beyond both interventionist definitions of place-making in urban public spaces and place-production in creative cities, whilst acknowledging that both are significant to twenty-first century cultural policy. All places are imbued with social meanings that enter the geographical imagination, often in quite subtle ways. In tracing the complex web of meanings associated with place, Cresswell observes how the distinct but related concepts of mobility and rootedness have become attached to specific cultural values:

> In contemporary social thought, words associated with mobility are unremittingly positive. If something can be said to be fluid, dynamic, in flux or simply mobile, then it is seen to be progressive, exciting and contemporary. If, on the other hand, something is said to be rooted, based on foundations, static, or bounded, then it is seen to be reactionary, dull, and of the past. (2006: 25)

If, as Loretta Lees (2004), Doreen Massey (2005) and others have suggested, cities are primarily perceived as networked and mobile, they are regarded as emancipated and progressive. By implication, places that are associated with stability and rootedness are considered backward-looking and uninspiring. Drawing on the work of anthropologist Liisa Malkki, Cresswell calls this perception of rootedness a 'metaphysics of sedentarism', a term he uses to describe how 'fixed, bounded and rooted conceptions of culture and identity' arrange human experience. On the one hand, he suggests, sedentarism offers an appealing image of home and belonging, a moral geography of place. On the other, it can be used to

---

[7] See   https://www.noda.org.uk/regions/london;   http://littletheatreguild.org/. Accessed 25 Aug 2017.

further prejudice, particularly against diasporic communities, migrants or refugees. This is not, however, a simple political binary between the Left and the Right; there are advocates of sedimentary metaphysics from both political perspectives—Cresswell cites the writing of socialists Raymond Williams and Richard Hoggart and conservative T.S. Eliot as 'united in their respect for roots and their use of metaphors of mobility to suggest threat' (2006: 36). Cresswell is careful to juxtapose this analysis of rootedness with its opposite, nomadic metaphysics, which exercises another kind of power. Nomadic metaphysics privileges mobility, and it is connected with alterity and social freedom, and also with the networked world of global capitalism—the kind of socially privileged, fast-paced, mobile and individualist society Zygmunt Bauman memorably described as 'liquid' (2003, 2005). As Cressell puts it, nomadic thought has 'little time for traditional kinds of "placey place"' (2006: 55).

Much amateur theatre happens in 'placey-places', where life-long membership and loyalty to local theatre companies are not unusual. As such, amateur theatre is inevitably caught up in the binaries Cresswell identifies. Writing in a similar vein about vernacular creativity, a term used to capture a range of amateur activity, Tim Edensor et al. argue that cultural hierarchies have been defined in spatial terms:

> A major constraint is the tendency to produce and maintain dichotomous understandings of creativity and space through the reproduction of binary spatial distinctions between global/ local, cool/ uncool, creative/ uncreative, fixed/ mobile, centre/ periphery and urban/ rural contexts. (2010: 11)

Edensor and his co-authors recognise that such spatial relations not only mark social inequalities, they also signify distinctions of taste. This signifies another layer of inequality, Edensor et al. argue, in which tastes deemed 'cool' or cutting-edge are allied to the social and cultural privilege associated with a cosmopolitan, mobile and urban workforce. By extension, the contemporary focus on the metropolitan creative city has meant that towns, suburbs and rural areas have become stereotyped as 'devoid of creativity' (2010: 12). In some ways this attitude is replicated in the academy, not least because most universities are city-based, and many have a role to play in the creative economy; in theatre studies itself there are numerous studies of theatre and the city but there is far less research on theatre that is both generated and performed outside metropolitan centres, particularly if it does not conform to the researchers' tastes or to perceptions of what is creatively innovative. This exclusion links the geographical imagination with cultural value, and it is also political.

All this suggests that amateur theatre is susceptible to cultural stereotyping, largely because in the popular imagination it is associated with the sedimentary metaphysics of towns, suburbia and rural life rather than the edginess and mobility of urban cool. Perhaps the most straightforward illustration of this caricaturing of amateur theatre is found in popular culture. In the BBC's long-running radio drama, *The Archers*, set in the fictional village of Ambridge in rural England, amateur theatre is organised (and controlled) by the irritatingly persuasive Lynda Snell, who corrals talentless and often reluctant locals into the annual village production. Unlike many of the other characters, Mrs. Snell does not have deep roots in Ambridge, and her theatrical interests symbolise her desire as a relative newcomer to throw herself into village life, albeit tinged with tastes acquired in the commuter village of Sunningdale where she had previously lived. The other fictional doyenne of amateur theatre is Margo Leadbetter from the 1970s BBC TV sit-com *The Good Life*, who is an icon of suburban living. Set in the London suburb of Surbiton, and memorably played by Penelope Keith, the pretentious Margo takes her roles in the local amateur operatic society very seriously, sometimes playing the lead wearing preposterous costumes. Neither characters have much of a sense of humour and this means that they, along with their theatrical interests, are often the butt of the joke. In many ways these stereotypes are linked to evaluative judgements about location, and these two examples show how, in popular culture, amateur theatre has become a trope for the apparent conservatism of rural and suburban life, representing the sedimentary metaphysics that Cresswell described. This way of thinking is not confined to British popular culture; the opening scene of the film *Revolutionary Road*, set in suburban Connecticut and based on the novel by Richard Yates, sees the couple Frank and April Wheeler arguing about April's role in an amateur play, described by Frank as 'crap'. What becomes clear, however, is that April's amateur production symbolises the boredom and repetitiveness of their suburban lives.

These fictional representations may be remote from lived experience; they are built on evaluative imaginaries of place rather than on the artistic or communitarian qualities of amateur theatre. For a more nuanced and accurate picture of amateur theatre's relationship to place, there is a need to find another way to conceptualise place beyond the value-laden binaries (urban/suburban; progressive/conservative; cool/uncool and so on) that haunt its depiction. Lucy Lippard's analysis of the lure of local offers a productive starting point for this analysis of place-making, not least because she acknowledges that although many people are attracted to the idea of the local it remains outside their experience, perhaps because 'they may not be willing to take the responsibility and study the local knowledge that distinguishes every place from every other place' (1997: 7). For Lippard, the local is connected to place, to shared memories and to its future potential:

> Inherent in the local is the concept of place – a proportion of land/town/ cityscape seen from the inside, the resonance of a specific location that is known and familiar. Most often place applies to our own 'local' – entwined with personal memory, known and unknown histories... A layered location replete with human histories and memories. It is about connections, what surrounds it, and what formed it, what happened there, what will happen there. (1997: 7)

This way of thinking about place-making as an on-going process of connecting memory and imagination chimes well with the different ways in which amateur theatre companies contribute to their local areas. This raises further questions about what kinds of places are imagined, and how amateur theatre has contributed to place-making as a creative act, and how, in the words of Cresswell, 'place provides the conditions of possibility for creative social practice' (2004: 39).

Amateur Theatre in Utopia: The Garden City Movement

The idea that place-making is a creative act may be newly described in the twenty-first century, but in terms of amateur theatre it is not a new concept. As Jennie Lee's White Paper testifies, amateur theatre thrived in many new communities, finding enthusiastic participants in Garden Cities, suburbia and the new towns constructed in the era following World War Two. In this section I shall chart how amateur theatre became embedded in England's first Garden Cities at the beginning of the twentieth century, a case study that enables me to explore the significance of amateur theatre in newly constructed neighbourhoods. The case study asks why amateur creativity became an integral part of the early settlers' social vision and cultural values. There is therefore much to learn from these early and mid-twentieth century social experiments, not least in how the architecture reflected the cultural values and technologies of the time, and how the spatiality of urban design ordered the everyday practices of labour and leisure. There is also renewed international interest in the Garden City Movement in the twenty-first century, where it is regarded as one response to the lack of affordable homes and a declining sense of community. Once housing is built, the challenge becomes how to create a sense of belonging in newly constructed communities. As John Lewis, the Chief Executive of Letchworth Garden City Heritage Foundation commented, 'town planning is relatively straightforward, but it is social activity that creates successful communities'.[8]

The Garden City Movement began as an egalitarian social experiment in England at the end of the nineteenth century, and its principles influenced newly-built settlements across the world throughout the twentieth century. Part of the contemporary appeal of Garden Cities is their long commitment to creating sustainable environments in which people might live and work; the first Garden City was conceived in response to the dirt and degradation evident in many cities when, towards the end of the nineteenth century, the long-term consequences of industrialisation were clear. Middle-class social reformists sought a range of measures to ameliorate its worst effects, including Samuel and Henrietta Barnett who established the Settlement House Movement in London's East End in 1884 to encourage working-class education, Octavia Hill who co-founded the National Trust in 1895 with the primary intention of protecting open spaces, and Margaret McMillan, whose pioneering work in Bradford and London's Deptford sought to improve the lives of children living in urban squalor in the early years of the twentieth century. Philanthropic industrialists contributed to this social movement, led by George Cadbury and W.H. Lever, whose model villages in Port Sunlight (1899) and Bournville (1893) aimed to create healthy living conditions for their factory workers. The buildings in their corporate communities were designed to invoke the stability of old English villages and adopted the vernacular architecture of the Arts and Crafts style, with gardens for horticulture and open spaces to encourage community life. In Bournville, for example, residents were

[8] Interview Helen Nicholson with John Lewis, Letchworth Garden City, 9 November 2015.

given front gardens but garden gates were not permitted because, Tristram Hunt notes, they might 'hinder the community spirit' (2004: 426). Many of these reforms were built on socialist principles, taking the work (and sometimes friendship) of William Morris as inspiration. Morris' practical socialism not only led to a revival of craft and renewed attention to the aesthetics of domestic interiors, it also connected the built environment with communitarianism, creating a moral geography of place that foreshadows the contemporary interest in well-being and sustainable living.

The first Garden City was formally established in 1903 in Letchworth, about thirty miles north of London. The pioneering visionary was Ebenezer Howard (1850–1928), whose book *Tomorrow: A Peaceful Path to Real Reform* was published in 1898, and reprinted in 1902 as *Garden Cities of Tomorrow*. This book outlined the principles for planning a whole new town, in which the best opportunities of urban life might be combined with the healthiness of country living. As David Matless suggests, the configuration of spatial design Howard sought was not only to reconstruct 'the build environment but also the very fabric of civilisation' (1998: 32). Despite its egalitarianism, the Garden City Movement had very little support from organisations of the Left; Hunt points out that the Independent Labour Party, the Co-operative Society and the trade unions offered no financial support and the Fabians were actively hostile. There was evidence of double-standards, Hunt observes, and George Bernard Shaw publicly ridiculed the idea before 'surreptitiously investing in a number of developments' (2004: 435). Undeterred, Howard's plan was to organise the city according to different zones, confining the industry to the area near the railway station to minimise pollution, and separating leafy residential areas from the 'well-watered gardens' and boulevards of the civic and commercial centre. Each zone was defined in terms of its relationship to urban and rural life, differentiating between town (industrial sites), country (residential areas) and the hybrid town-country (the civic and commercial centre). With these distinct zones, Howard aimed to 'raise the standard of health and comfort of all true workers of whatever grade', by assuring 'a healthy, natural, and economic combination of the town and country life' (1902: 2). His vision was social and political, declaring that 'Town and country must be married, and out of this joyous union will spring a new hope, a new life, a new civilisation' (1902: 48). Importantly, the Garden City movement was international in its ambition from its inception, intending that the reformist movement would spread widely across geopolitical boundaries.

As we have already observed in Chapter 2, amateur theatre was associated with progressive ideals and socialist politics in the early part of the twentieth century. These attitudes were in part synonymous with Howard's approach to place-making, which was informed by both practical economics and cultural values; *Garden Cities of Tomorrow* references William Blake, John Ruskin, Charles Dickens, Leo Tolstoy, Nathaniel Hawthorne and William Morris alongside leading politicians and economists of the day. This combination of cultural capital and manufacturing industry influenced Letchworth's city planning. On the one hand, the domestic buildings designed by architects Barry Parker (1867–1947) and Raymond Unwin (1863–1940) were in the Arts and Crafts style, reminiscent of pre-industrial rural cottages with rustic casement windows, and on the other, Letchworth depended on profitable local industry for its economic sustainability. From the beginning Letchworth was a magnet for manufacturers inspired by William Morris, and it attracted businesses with an element of craft. Publishers and printers were early occupants; J.M. Dent and the Temple Press, the Arden Press and W.H. Smith bookbinders took factory space, and the Garden Embroidery Works and St Edmunsbury Weavers were all in business by the end of 1910. It would be wrong, however, to associate Letchworth with quaint cottage industry; the Spirella corset factory was built between 1912 and 1920 by a large and profitable American company, whose co-founder William Wallace Kincaid was both sympathetic to the Garden City ideals and wealthy enough to fund factory buildings in tune with the Arts and Crafts architectural style. Other factories were involved in high-tech manufacturing—Phoenix Motors Ltd., for example, led the new motor car industry which was an economic feature of early Letchworth, and the Foster Instrument Company made sophisticated scientific measuring equipment. Culturally, however, as Standish Meacham argues, Letchworth was indebted to a myth of Englishness associated with pre-industrial rural life (1999: 1–3). This pastoral aesthetic was performative, articulated in pageants, folkdances and Ye Olde Maye Day celebrations; a photograph dated 1907 shows crowds of residents on the street in fancy dress, costumes that represented an Arcadian image of rural simplicity. Meacham attributes this idealisation of Englishness to nostalgic conservatism, but he misses the influence of William Morris and Robert Blatchford on the founders of Letchworth. William Morris' *News from Nowhere* (1890) was a Marxist utopia, and Blatchford's *Merrie England* (1894) was socialist polemic that attacked Adam Smith's economic vision. As we observed in Chapter 2, Blatchford, a Fabian, was an influential figure in the Clarion Club, and was closely allied with Morris' nostalgic image of socialist communities, to which he added his patriotic Englishness. In an oft quoted passage from *The Fortnightly Review* in 1907 he declared:

> English Socialism is not German: it is English. English Socialism is not Marxian; it is humanitarian. It does not depend upon any theory of "economic justice" but upon humanity and common sense. (1942: 106)

Letchworth's Englishness, though archaic in aesthetic form, was indebted to this communitarian approach to political radicalism. Yet as a new city, Letchworth lacked history and cultural memory, and they harnessed English folk performance, pageants and other outdoor events to invent a tradition and to animate their version of utopia. The passion for this kind of amateur performance, as Cathy Turner has noted, included masques and workers' processions that celebrated the city's artisan culture, but in the process any 'gesture towards revolutionary politics is stabilised by its dramaturgy' (2015: 70).

Amateur theatre held a pivotal role in Letchworth's place-making, and exemplifies how the Garden City ideals turned into practical action in the town's social and cultural life. Local theatre companies are often initiated and sustained by a catalyst, whether this is an individual enthusiast, a campaigning movement or an organisation. In Letchworth this fell to Charles B. Purdom (1883–1965), the city's first accountant who regarded theatre as a vital part of the new community's life. Purdom was a prolific author and editor of works that spanned theatre criticism, economics and town planning, but his life-long passion was theatre, becoming General Secretary of British Equity in 1939, and the first secretary of the Guild of Drama Adjudicators in 1947. In October 1906 he wrote to the Letchworth Magazine stating that 'of all places in the country, Garden City should be the one where the conditions would be altogether favourable'.[9] Anticipating The People's Theatre in Newcastle discussed in Chapter 2, Purdom was influenced by socialist principles, drawing inspiration from Tolstoy's *What is Art?* (1897). He founded the Letchworth Amateur Dramatic Society in 1907, and the society's first production was an adaptation of Tolstoy's *Ivan the Fool* in the same year. *The First Annual Report* (1907–1908),

---

[9] Cited in Brunt, A. W. (1942) *The Pageant of Letchworth*. Letchworth: Letchworth Printers p. 106. http://lgcs.org.uk/pageant/pagej06.htm. Accessed 28 Dec 2017.

written by Purdom and published by J.M. Dent & Sons, carries the influence of Tolstoy's egalitarian perception of art, and is also reminiscent of Matthew Arnold's view of culture:

> It is desired to prepare the way for a theatre that will express the best thought and feeling of those who are attracted to the new town, and worthily represent the new social movement of which Garden City is an embodiment. The Society therefore seeks to take advantage of the unique opportunity provided by the creation of a new community to make theatre a really active and potent part of the social and intellectual life of the people. (1908: 4)

The intention here is clear; amateur theatre would not only enrich the 'social and intellectual life' of Letchworth's new residents, it also represented a new social movement in which theatre—and specifically *amateur* theatre—would take a central place.

Purdom's interest in amateurs is articulated in his autobiography, *Life Over Again* (1951), where he reflected on the reasons for his commitment to amateur theatre in early Letchworth. For Purdom, amateurism represented a new kind of theatre that was anti-commercial and artistically innovative. In attempting to foster the 'distinctive value as art in the work of amateurs who worked for love, more value than in what the professional did who worked for a living', he actively promoted theatre-making that would be 'served by artists who also worked in the town's factories' (1951: 169–170). This is an interesting play on the word 'value', and indicates his social priorities; he considered acting to be more authentic when it was 'for love' and beyond monetary benefit, and suggested in egalitarian terms that everyone, including factory workers, might be considered artists. Purdom's professed dislike of the affectations of professional actors was matched only, however, by his disdain for what he described as the 'old-fashioned amateur' who resented training and was interested only in staging popular plays that, by his own admission, found favour with audiences. Looking back at his theatre work some years later, Purdom makes a persuasive case for amateur acting:

> In acting an amateur can express something of his inner life, his unconscious mind, in a way that can be done in no other way. Too much amateur acting is, it is true, mere exhibitionism, the desire of people to show off; but much of it is motivated by a need to express desires, thoughts, fears, ambitions, aims, and ideals that cannot otherwise be expressed. (1951: 180)

Purdom created his own disciplined rehearsal methods to aid this quest for self-expression and authenticity in an attempt to avoid 'mere exhibitionism'. In an illuminating passage, he describes his approach as 'no joke' and describes how those with experience of 'amateur theatricals would not stand my methods and abused me freely' (1951: 170). This resistance to theatrical experimentation from the amateur old guard not only resonates with some companies today, it also shows Purdom's commitment to creating a new kind of theatre that represented and extended the social and socialist values of the first Garden City.

The repertoire Purdom favoured was international and innovative, thus mirroring Ebenezer Howard's vision for Garden Cities as an international socialist movement. There was no pre-industrial pastoral aesthetic in Purdom's theatre; the repertoire was intentionally intellectually and socially challenging. Ibsen's *A Doll's House* was staged in 1908, an early production of George Bernard Shaw's play *The Shewing-up of Blanco Posnet* followed in 1912 when it was still banned by the censor, and other plays staged between 1908 and 1912 included work by contemporary Irish playwrights—Lady Gregory, W.B. Yeats and J.M. Synge; the Garden Cities were instrumental in establishing part of the innovative amateur repertoire that we discussed in Chapter 3. The cast lists are a roll-call of the intelligentsia of Letchworth, with regular appearances of the members of the Dent family (publishers), Percy Gossop (Vogue Magazine illustrator) and Purdom himself often 'producing' the play and playing the lead role. The 1907 production of *Ivan the Fool* may have satisfied their creative and political ambitions, but it was neither a crowd-pleaser nor a money-spinner, although with impressive tenacity it was reprised in 1909 and 1911, playing to similarly small houses. Purdom wrote repeatedly to the local paper, *The Citizen*, expressing his concern about the lack of enthusiasm shown by factory workers to his choice of repertoire. An outdoor production of Lady Gregory's play *Spreading the News*, with a plot that satirises village gossip and offers a moral lesson about neighbourliness, however, was better received in the summer of 1908.

Despite egalitarian aspirations, it was the middle-class pioneers who were the cultural leaders in the place-making project, many of whom might now be described as the creative class. They regularly performed leading roles in Purdom's plays, with some lending their professional expertise to productions; Percy Gossop designed and painted the set and his beautiful Arts and Crafts illustrations adorned marketing material and high-quality programmes published by J.M Dent & Sons on hand made paper. According to Purdom, there were also many 'painters, joiners, electricians, and just ordinary labourers' who worked backstage, though he seems unaware that this division of labour also maintained inequities of class. He also noted that amateur theatre invaded citizens' domestic spaces, whose homes were 'plundered for furniture, carpets, and all other kinds of properties' (1951: 174). There was, however, dissatisfaction with the venues in which they performed, and during his time in Letchworth, Purdom campaigned for a purpose-built theatre that would model the status and repertoire of the Abbey Theatre in Dublin. He lobbied high profile members of the arts community, including near neighbours George Bernard Shaw, Edith Craig and Edward Gordon Craig. Edith Craig became an enthusiastic supporter of amateur theatre as a leading member of the Little Theatre Guild and founder of the British Drama League, and although she contributed to founding a theatre at St Christopher's School in 1924, the theatre that Purdom imagined was never built.[10] Amateur theatre did thrive in the town, however, and several companies emerged between its foundation in 1903 and the outbreak of World War One in 1914, including one in the Spirella factory. The Spirella women showed their libertarianism when they performed a suffrage play for the company's American owners on their visit in 1913. The play, *When Eve Reigns*, was written especially for the occasion by E.L. Price and included spirited references to the gender inequalities of Letchworth life. On his death, Kincaid bequeathed money to The Settlement in Letchworth for a new hall, built in 1956 and fully equipped with a stage, which is still in regular use for amateur productions.

With Ebenezer Howard, Purdom moved from Letchworth to Welwyn where the second Garden City was established in 1920, and stayed there until his death in 1965. As one of its early residents, he quickly founded The Welwyn Garden City Theatre Society in 1921, and his first production was a reprise of Shaw's *The Shewing-up of Blanco Posnet*. Perhaps his most notable success was another collaboration with Charles Lee, with whom he had written pantomimes in Letchworth. Furious at achieving only second place in the first British Drama League Competition in 1926, Purdom took Charles Lee's one-act play *Mr Sampson* to the New York Little Theatre Tournament in 1927, where they won the coveted David

---

[10] For a more detailed account of Edith Craig's involvement with amateur theatre, see Cockin, Katharine *Edith Craig (1869–1847): Dramatic Lives* London: Cassell.

Belasco Cup. In his autobiography Purdom notes the satisfaction he felt in this achievement, observing that it was a measure of his confidence that he sent a telegram home with news of their success before the adjudication had been announced. Enthusiasm for competitive drama festivals led like-minded residents L.W.P. Barber, W.B. Johnson, J.C. Nairne, F.J. Osborn and the actress Flora Robson to form a committee in 1929 to establish the Welwyn Drama Festival. The festival continues to thrive, a legacy of Purdom's vision, and in 2017 The Barn Theatre hosted the 83rd festival and welcomed fourteen companies from across the United Kingdom. Perhaps less in tune with Purdom's vision is the parody of the Welwyn Garden City Festival Finals in *The Farndale Avenue Housing Estate Townswomen's Guild Dramatic Society Production of Macbeth* (1984), where events conspire against the hapless performers.

Amateur creativity flourished in the Garden City environment, and remains an important part of its heritage and sense of place. Letchworth quickly became known for its numerous societies (some accounts suggest as many as eighty or ninety by 1910), many of which met at the Skittles Inn, the non-alcoholic pub opened in 1907. This building remains an important part of Letchworth life today; the Skittles Inn is now known as The Settlement, home to the thriving amateur company The Settlement Players as well as many other amateur societies, social groups and adult education classes. Amateur theatre in the early Garden Cities was defined by its contemporary repertoire, with early settlers favouring scripted plays, often from other parts of Europe, that prompted social criticism. The paradox was, perhaps, that although the choice of plays was designed to encourage inclusivity and stimulate debate, their very intellectualism meant that they sometimes lacked popular appeal. This paradox also inhabits professional theatre, as Christopher Balme has observed, where the social efficacy of the theatrical public sphere depends on 'an almost irresolvable dichotomy between production and reception' (2014: 13).

The Spirit of the Place: Letchworth and Pantomime

Throughout our research, we have encountered amateur theatre companies that contribute to defining a sense of place, creating communities not only through the process of making, but also through their deep-rooted relationships with loyal audiences. This is often most evident in annual pantomimes, where scripts are either authored by members of the company or customised to include local references and in-jokes. It is here that the relationship between production and reception is perhaps most in harmony, where place is performed in ways that local audiences recognise. Twenty-first century pantomimes are immersed in this tradition, and we have seen this on numerous occasions, including a pantomime performed by the Royal Navy group the Admirals' Players that made jokes about submariners and a production of *Robin Hood* with town councillors from different political parties playing opposite each other as the benign Robin Hood and the evil Sherriff of Nottingham. This tradition for localism is long-held in English amateur theatre, and we have found joyful enthusiasm in amateur pantomimes that is often absent from their professional counterparts where tired celebrities are type-cast in expensive productions.

Letchworth Garden City offers an important illustration of how pantomimes contributed to creating a sense of place from its foundation. Community cohesion was dependent on shared commitment to a common ideal, and this was frequently referred to as 'the spirit of the place'. The spirit of the place is a phrase that recurred in Letchworth, articulating the ways in which many citizens were actively and creatively engaged in place-making. In early Letchworth, the spirit of the place was an aspiration as well as lived experience, part of the sensory texture of place that Lucy Lippard described as 'partial reality, partial dream' (1997: 7). Early amateur theatre-makers directly acknowledged this tension between reality and dream, perhaps most clearly theatricalised in the pantomimes of 1909, 1910 and 1911, all of which satirise the high-mindedness of the Garden City vision and, in the process, bear witness to the realities of living in the newly-built community. The pantomimes, written by Purdom with his musical collaborator Charles Lee, were staged in Howard Hall in the centre of Letchworth. The two published scripts for the 1910 and 1911 pantomimes offer a unique insight into the early settlers' representation of place.

The early pantomimes lampoon the eccentricities of Letchworth and its Garden City ideals. Letchworth had become known for its 'cranks' (variously described as vegetarian, sandal-wearing spiritualists who enjoyed dew bathing), which Charles Lee had enjoyed documenting.[11] In his autobiography Purdom describes how the first pantomime (January 1909) set the tone by satirising local politicians, food reformers, Lady Bountiful and

---

[11] For a more detailed discussion see Meacham (1999: 142–143).

Suffragettes. Demonstrating that Letchworth could laugh at itself, the two subsequent pantomimes in 1910 and 1911 continued in this tradition. The programme for the 1910 pantomime emphasises its localism, and states its objectives clearly:

> The Pantomime is first of all for Letchworth people and afterward for every-one else. It carries a guilty satirical record of local events and a more or less accurate representation of Letchworth characteristics. (Programme notes, The Second Garden City Pantomime, 1910)

'Letchworth characteristics' were the source of much comedy; the 1911 script contains a particularly good joke about the friendliness of Brussels sprouts to ridicule the vegetarianism advocated by many in the town. The plots of both pantomimes centre around rebellion; in 1910 the rebellion of children against conventional education was central to the plot, and in the Third Garden City Pantomime in 1911 rebellious women caused the Letchworth menfolk to undertake their own laundry. In this production the pomposity of Letchworth's (male) hierarchy was targeted, as they were encouraged to wear corsets by a particularly persuasive Spirella salesman. But the script cannot be read as an example of feminist utopianism; Purdom was reputedly anti-suffrage and social order is restored only when the women return to the laundry.

The Second Garden City Pantomime in 1910 is particularly illuminating as it is here that the spirit of the place was personified, played by a garlanded Percy Gossop. The plot revolves around the town's children, who rebel against the authority of the autocratic Keeper of Norton Common and take over the running of Letchworth, a process that requires the adults to regress to childhood. The play opens on May-Day, and the stage directions note (with a hint of irony) that local residents dance around the maypole 'and perform the dances they firmly believe their fathers to have danced long before their little town was built' (1910: 5). The adults struggle to come to terms with their enforced childishness, their Rousseauian Romanticisation of childhood challenged under the tyrannical rule of the children. The audacious children even dare to question the Spirit of the Place, whose opening speech reminds the audience of Letchworth's more eccentric practices and comments on the practical difficulties of living in the Arts and Crafts housing (a recurring theme in the play):

Fig. 4.1 Postcard of The Garden City Pantomime, 1910. (Garden City Collection)

I am the Spirit of the Place. I am only six years old… Under every red roof I dwell, though I have a special weakness for those with a loose tile or two. In every snug ingle-nook you will find me gently kippering myself. The letters in the Citizen are my principal diet. At dawn I bathe in your emerald water-butt; all day I tend the delicate young dandelions in your gardens; at night I sleep in sheers of the City magazine. Insomnia never troubles me. Whenever I cough a brand new Society springs up; whenever I sneeze the Estate office trembles in its shoes, and wishes it wore sandals. (1910: 12)

Gossop's speech neatly captures an image of Letchworth life that is somewhere between the real and the dream, both of which seem to be inherent in the spirit of the place. The play also serves as a cultural commentary on the town's relationship to English folk culture and high art. The May-Day festivities invoke an imaginary of Medieval England that, though treated with a hint of irony, offer the younger members of the cast opportunities to dance, but high art is more extensively satirised. Central to the plot is the Higher Arts Club, led by the poet Willie West (played by Purdom), with a composer (Harold Hall), painter (Hugh R. Dent) and, importantly, a 'converted hooligan' (A.H. Borwell) who had been reformed by the civilising power of art (the High Art Club had locked him in a padded room and forced him to listen to the poems of Shelley and Ella Wheeler Wilcox until he capitulated). The pompous Willie West describes their secret mission as 'spreading culture among the middle and lower classes', a task made easier by the fact that everyone is in disguise on the day of the popular folk pageant. They caricature themselves as humourless, and their intonation of The Chant of the Higher Art is accompanied by a 'mystic dance'. The chorus is as follows (1910: 19–20):

> *I* am an arty party,
> *He* is an arty party;
> *We* are an arty party,
> And our art is extremely high

It is not difficult to imagine the audience reception to this satirical representation of the Dramatic Society's aims and the comic potential of their mystic dance, and their earnestness remains a running gag throughout the script. At the beginning of the final act the Spirit of the Place finally reappears, and his opening speech is delivered as a direct address to the audience. The spirit is ailing under the children's rule, no one is wearing sandals or djibbahs, the vegetarians have been forcibly converted to meat-eaters and free-spirited local newspaper *The Citizen* has been suppressed. The only society that has survived the children's rule is the Dramatic Society, but they are prevented from staging Shaw or Galsworthy and are required to stage a new pantomime every week. Order is restored and the pantomime draws to a close, but not before some of the strongest principles in the Garden City had been subjected to ridicule; attachment to the English mythology of the folk tradition, the sanctity of childhood, vegetarianism, simple living and the moralising pretentions of those promoting high art. The town is saved when its citizens restore the ailing spirit of the place, who departs for Hitchin (the nearest town) to see if he can spread his spirit, no doubt furthering a local joke that in Hitchin they 'want me badly' (1910: 47).

There are many ways to interpret the localism of the early Letchworth pantomimes. In describing Purdom's pantomimes as 'placeful celebration', Cathy Tuner has argued that they 'offer a gentle reminder that too much complacency could lead to a stultifying atmosphere', whist also noting that they offer no real challenge to the 'imbalance of power between stakeholders' (2015: 65). Given that many cast members were Letchworth's cultural leaders who had previously imposed Tolstoy and Ibsen on reluctant citizens, any serious political challenge would seem unlikely. The pantomime shows Purdom's talent for self-mockery that is perhaps surprising, and it also affirms that part of the audience's pleasure for amateur shows is seeing people on stage who are well-known local characters. Purdom's seriousness about the social purpose of art was well-known from his many letters to *The Citizen*, and the Higher Arts Club would have been instantly recognisable to audiences. For Letchworth, a town barely six years old, this recognition was part of the process of place-making, not only clarifying its identity as a place with specific cultural values, but also having the confidence to lampoon them.

For all its foibles, the 'spirit of the place' represented a potent metaphor for Letchworth's early place-makers, and it was intriguing to know whether it still held resonance for Letchworth's amateur performers today. The script for the 1910 pantomime raised opportunities for research methodologies that were creative and participatory, and this seemed appropriate for an amateur theatre company. Reading the script for the Second Garden City Pantomime at a quiet desk in Cambridge University library, I began to wonder how today's pantomime cast would respond to it. I was searching for methodologies that would capture, as far as possible, the experiences of taking part in amateur theatre today and open questions about how participation related to place.

There's such a strong sense of the local in the script, might it be method-ologically interesting to see whether or not they relate to it now? Has Letchworth still got some of the 'spirit of the place', or is it just another Hertfordshire commuter town? Would reading the script stimulate discussion about what it means to live in a garden city today? Might this illuminate broader questions about what the role of amateur theatre is now – and might be in the future – in places where it is an important part of local heritage? (Helen's Research Diary, 12 February 2014)

Armed with copies of the pantomime script, doctoral student Cara Gray and I travelled to Letchworth one evening in July 2014. We had seen Letchworth's Christmas pantomime *Aladdin* earlier in the year, performed by St Paul's Amateur Dramatic Society (SPADS), a company that was founded in 1937.[12] In an era when many amateur companies are struggling to find young members, SPADS is a remarkably youthful and diverse society with a significant number of performers under thirty. On this evening in July 2014, however, long-serving SPADS members mixed with more recent recruits.

The company usually meet in St Paul's Church Hall, and we arranged to meet chairman Alan Reilly at 7.15 to put out the chairs. Alan has been a maths teacher, now semi-retired, and has been a long standing member of SPADS. I was very pleased to meet Peter Wright, well known locally as a successful electrician, whose family were early settlers in the garden city. Peter has played the dame for over twenty-five years, and I had heard about him from John Lewis, CEO of Letchworth Garden City Heritage Foundation. The plan was to spend the first half hour or so talking about their involvement in amateur theatre, and the second part workshopping the 1910 panto. I had chosen extracts from the script that particularly focused on the local, and wanted to know if it resonated with them today. (Helen's Research Diary, 11 July 2014)

One striking aspect of the discussion was that SPADs members regarded membership of local societies as one of the special attributes of Garden City life (there are still over 600 amateur societies in Letchworth, including

---

[12] SPADS have since been re-named as the Song, Pantomime and Drama Society, thereby maintaining their acronym, and loosening it from its Christian roots.

five theatre companies).[13] Amateur theatre-makers are 'doers' and it is not unusual to find members have multiple roles in their communities, joining choirs or serving as tree wardens for example. For long-standing SPADS members, the seasonality of amateur theatre enabled them to participate in multiple activities, including local history societies, craft groups and bird watching clubs. The younger members noted that participating in the annual pantomime gave them a sense of belonging to Letchworth and regarded it as both personally and socially beneficial, a way of 'giving entertainment' to the town. Some were university students, who found that taking part in the Christmas pantomime was a way to re-connect with Letchworth friends during the vacation. One member had a degree in applied theatre and was working locally as a teaching assistant, and regarded her participation in SPADS as an opportunity to maintain her creativity. SPADS members generously and politely shared their insights in discussion but, as a methodology, the interview seemed to lack the energy we have encountered in amateur theatre.

> The turning point in the evening came when we began to read the scripts. People were asked to read scenes in small groups so that we might get a sense of the arc of the piece. Peter read the Norton Common Keeper, a great character role. Another group read the scene with the High Art party, and a further group looked at a scene between the children and the Spirit of the Place. When it started, I felt I was making the group work, and I wasn't sure that they were particularly interested in an old panto script. But as they began to read laughter of recognition began to ripple through the hall, and the atmosphere lifted. Each group performed in turn, and I was surprised how funny the script still was. It was clear that it had stood the test of time, and Purdom's comedy writing was rather better than I'd expected. (Helen's Research diary, 11 July 2014)

The script prompted memories, with Peter Wright and some long-standing Letchworth citizens recalling how they were reprimanded by similarly autocratic Norton Common keepers in their youth. The actors were delighted that the geography of Letchworth was so accurately depicted in the play, and commented with some feeling that there were still problems maintaining the Arts and Craft houses, now protected as

[13] https://www.theguardian.com/society/2012/apr/03/why-government-sees-letchworth-model-community

part of Letchworth's architectural heritage. The *Song of the Spirit of the Place* in Act One was read with much amusement, prompting memories of cold winters and shaking casement windows (1910: 13):

> When the rain and sleet and the hailstones beat through every chink of the casement,
> And the plaster falls from the mouldy walls, and the damp wells up from the basement,
> Perhaps you reflect that your architect was a bit too Arts-and-Crafty,
> And you wish that your lot had been cast in a cot that wasn't quite so drafty.

These instances of cultural recognition in the workshop linked time and place, embodied as small moments of performance, in what Raphael Samuel might have called a theatre of memory (Samuel 1994).

The focus of this research workshop was not to find ways to re-enact a neglected part of theatre history, but to use the script to understand the present. The detailed references to local landmarks and some familiar tropes of Letchworth life resonated with SPADS members, but it was the depiction of the High Arts Club that stimulated the most heated debate, igniting discussions about the role and visibility of amateur arts in Letchworth's cultural policy. Plinston Hall, the company's long-standing performance venue, had been closed by the Letchworth Garden City Heritage Foundation in 2012 as it was under-used and unprofitable, but attachment to the hall ran deep. SPADS members were particularly struck by the ways in which the High Arts Club tried to convert citizens to their tastes, and felt aggrieved that the Heritage Foundation had invited international artists to Letchworth whilst ignoring, as they saw it, home-grown amateur talent. By reading the script they observed that the binary between high art and popular culture had a long history in local cultural policy. Despite a process of consultation, they felt excluded from the twenty-first century equivalent of Purdom's arty party and were surprised that similar debates were raging in 1910. When we explained that the early pantomimes were written by Purdom when he was city accountant, and that the High Art Club was performed by local people who were well-known for their cultural leadership, they commented that this level of involvement and self-mockery by city officials would be unlikely in the twenty-first century. As the discussion wore on, however, it became clear that it was not local history but place-making that concerned the cast, and specifically the uneasy relationship between Letchworth's official guardians of the Garden City's heritage and their own experiences as amateur theatre-makers. We had not predicted this response, and although it felt awkward as Letchworth Garden City Heritage Foundation had actively supported our research, it was a point of view that needed to be heard.

The pantomime script opened questions about how Letchworth's heritage might be interpreted, and how it relates to contemporary approaches to place-making and cultural policy. As the first of many Garden Cities across the world, there are pressures on Letchworth's 'institutionalised heritage', not least because the built environment serves as a constant and physical reminder of its Arts and Crafts legacy. Letchworth Garden City Heritage Foundation in the twenty-first century has, like Ebenezer Howard, an international perspective. The museum was redesigned with a new International Garden Cities Exhibition in 2013, shortly followed by establishing an International Garden Cities Institute that aims to 'bring together expertise to showcase Garden Cities from around the world as a solid model for new development'.[14] These initiatives respond to global interest in the utopian history of Garden Cities, as well as acknowledging that the Garden City model still inspires governments and town planners today. Both heritage and place-making are dynamic processes, and, as Laurajane Smith points out, 'heritage is not the historic monument, archaeological site, or museum artefact, but rather the activities that occur at and around these places and objects' as we will discuss in more detail in Chapter 7 (2011: 71). In Letchworth, 'urban practitioners' and professional place-makers Allies and Morrison had been employed by the Heritage Foundation to conduct a consultation process with local people, and their advice informed plans for a regenerated city-centre townscape drawn up in 2011.[15] Significantly, this included investment in a new cultural quarter to 'revitalise Letchworth Garden City and to provide an enhanced cultural offer'.[16] One aspect of this cultural provision includes converting part of

---

[14] www.gardencitiesinstitute.com. Accessed 12 June 2016.

[15] http://www.letchworth.com/sites/default/files/attachments/key_issues_report_part_two.pdf. Accessed 6 May 2017.

[16] http://cultureandsportplanningtoolkit.org.uk/case-studies-and-examples/case-studies/letchworth-garden-city-cultural-quarter.html; The development attracted a major Arts Council grant in 2014. http://www.letchworth.com/heritage-foundation/news/arts-council-awards-major-grant-for-new-arts-programme/. Accessed 10 May 2017.

the Art Deco Broadway Cinema into a receiving house theatre that opened in 2016, building on the popularity of live screenings from major professional theatres including the National Theatre, the Royal Opera House and the RSC. Plinstone Hall now houses a new 'studio school' that focuses on teaching creative subjects (art and design, dance, music, digital media, and performing and production arts) to fourteen to nineteen-year-old students, a strategy that aims to encourage creative entrepreneurship in Letchworth and surrounding areas. By 2013 the cultural quarter was already beginning to generate prosperity in an area that had become run-down, and the Town and Country Planning Association reported that it was attracting new business to previously vacant shops.[17] In common with many urban sites, cultural activity is central to Letchworth's plans for regeneration, and its identity as the first Garden City is a major place-making asset.

Amateur theatre remains a part of Letchworth's cultural ecology, although it is no longer central to the policy-makers vision for the twenty-first century Garden City in the way it was for Purdom and the early settlers. The innovative, international and outward-facing repertoire favoured by Purdom and his associates may not have been to every citizen's tastes, but it was very much in harmony with the experimental vision that shaped the town. Amateur theatre was exactly the kind of cultural activity that the town's pioneering leaders imagined, and it was their active involvement that ensured that amateurs staged cutting-edge contemporary theatre. Many companies started in this way continue to thrive, providing creative opportunities for local residents. In the twenty-first century, there is, of course, a delicate balance between creating sustainable communities and inequitable forms of gentrification. The Settlement, home to the Settlement Players, lies geographically outside the newly re-branded cultural quarter, but it remains a thriving community resource that is financed and maintained by Letchworth Garden City Heritage Foundation. SPADS' annual pantomime has settled into its new home at St Francis College School theatre. It is perhaps how amateur creativity and the international aspirations of Letchworth's place-makers are choreographed that defines the city's values, and, as the pantomimes attest, the dance between them is deeply rooted in the spirit of the place.

---

[17] http://www.cloa.org.uk/images/stories/Regenerating_places_and_communities_through_culture.pdf. Accessed 6 May 2017.

PLACES TO GATHER: ARCHITECTURES OF ENJOYMENT

Not all amateur theatre companies, however, were so closely and self-consciously allied to a social vision, even in newly constructed communities, as the early Garden Cities. In this section, I shall move away from Garden Cities where amateur theatre was harnessed to a utopian ideal, to consider the less structured contribution amateur theatre makes to place and place-making in suburbia and its near neighbours. Located on the outskirts of city centres, suburbia is often portrayed as drab and conservative, and parodied as a semi-private territory of low-key aspiration. For amateur theatre, the caricature is easy to conjure— amateur theatre is populated by a sea of Margo Leadbetters or real-life Abigails from *Abigail's Party*. A similar cultural stereotype in the United States might be drawn from the TV show *Desperate Housewives*. As Rupa Huq points out, 'the suburbs are places that are defined by the imagination as much as by geography' (2013: 29).

Yet amateur theatre thrives on the outskirts of cities, and suburban life is more complex and diverse than the stereotypes might allow. The Questors Theatre in Ealing is one of the largest and arguably the most successful amateur theatre in the country, founded in 1929 by Alfred Emmet and it still maintains the strong international connections he envisaged. Chads Theatre just outside Manchester was founded just after the First World War as Cheadle Hulme Amateur Dramatic Society and continues to offer a lively programme—both The Questors and Chads are members of the Little Theatre Guild and run their own theatres. I am interested here, however, in the smaller companies without permanent theatre buildings who operate in what might be described as 'commuter belts' and are kept alive by the enthusiasm and commitment of company members. The work of Henri Lefebvre is a useful touchstone for this debate, whose ideas extend debates about the relationship between place, pleasure and sociability. In his book *Toward an Architecture of Enjoyment* Lefebvre was critical of what he described as 'abstract utopias' conceived by technocrats, and suggested that places of enjoyment are defined not by architectural design, but by a 'theory of moments'. This is a phrase that he uses repeatedly in his work to suggest instances of emotional intensity that are found in everyday life. He suggests that 'the space of enjoyment cannot consist of a building, an assembly of rooms, places determined by their functions... Rather it will be ... moments, encounters, friendships, festivals ... play' (2014: 152).

Lefebvre's theory of place as 'moments, encounters, friendships, festivals and play' seems a particularly apt way to describe amateur theatre-making, particularly in companies who rehearse in a range of spaces and depend on enthusiasm to maintain members' commitment. If place is defined as much by activity as its geography, how might amateur theatre generate productive place-relations in suburbia? One way to trace the contribution amateur theatre makes to suburban life is to follow the Metropolitan line from central London to the towns of Watford and Amersham to the northwest of London, and chart the amateur theatre companies located along the train route. Branded as Metro-land by the Metropolitan Railway in 1915, the land was developed in the interwar period when new estates were built in Neasden, Wembley Park, Northwick Park, Eastcote, Rayners Lane, Ruislip, Hillingdon, Pinner, Rickmansworth and Amersham by Country Estates, a company set up by the Metropolitan Railway in 1919. Marketing for Metro-land echoed Letchworth's pre-industrial aesthetic, and black and white Tudorbethan houses were heavily promoted as part of a peaceful lifestyle. Unlike the Garden Cities, however, Metro-land was conceived not as an alternative vision of society but as a commercial enterprise, and its ambitions were towards privatised owner-occupation rather than communitarianism. In her feminist study of interwar literature, Alison Light notes that the period saw 'the increasing privatisation of social life', with the iconic suburban homes offering aspiration to a newly defined middle-class that, she argues, can be read as both a symbol of hope and oppressively stultifying (1991: 215–218). The interwar era also brought a new national identity after the jingoism and trauma of World War One, described by Light as conservative:

> [T]he 1920s and '30s saw a move away from formerly heroic and officially masculine public rhetorics of national identity... to an Englishness at once less imperial and more inward-looking, more domestic and private... In the ubiquitous appeal of civilian virtues and pleasures, from the picture of the "little man", the suburban husband pottering in his herbaceous borders... we can discover a sea-change in ideas of the national temperament. (1991: 8)

If Garden Cities were built on social vision, Metro-land sold a lifestyle. Metro-land capitalised on this dream, an ideal of Englishness that blended rural and urban life, and promised an arcadia within commuting distance of the city. From the beginning, amateur creativity flourished in Metro-land, with many amateur activities orientated towards home-making, such as gardening, DIY and domestic crafts—in his account of living in 1960s Berkhamsted, Richard Mabey describes his home as 'a Metroland theatre', a phrase he uses to suggest its self-consciously fabricated environment (2013: 31). As people flocked to suburbia, amateur theatre offered a sociable counter-balance to this new culture of individualism, and amateur dramatic societies were quickly established across the new suburbs.

Amateur theatre remains a popular pastime in areas once marketed as Metro-land. Of those still in existence, companies such as the Argosy Players in Ickenham, Belmont Theatre Company in Harrow, Hatton Musical Theatre, Harrow Light Opera and the Rickmansworth Players were all founded between 1944 and 1947 with repertoires of musical entertainment designed to lift post-war spirits (Hatton Musical Theatre was reputedly founded at a VE day party). The Ruislip Dramatic Society (1924) and the Pinner Players (1936) have been in existence longer, reflecting the interwar population growth of the area. Both companies have an unbroken history, and currently stage two or three well-supported productions each year. Their repertoire includes shows that are popular with amateurs: Tom Stoppard's *Arcadia* (Pinner 2014), Godber's *Bouncers* (Pinner 2016), Ayckbourn's *Season's Greetings* (Ruislip 2014) and the TV spin-off '*Allo 'Allo* (Ruislip 2016). On attending the performances, I found that they command local support and appeal to loyal audiences. Yet, how far their repertoire still represents an imaginary of Englishness, and what this means, is much in question. As Huq points out, west London suburbia has an increasingly culturally diverse population, with a rising black and Asian middle-class, a demographic that is reflected in neither the repertoire nor the casts. The 2011 Census figures for The London Borough of Harrow document that 71.9% (93,437) of Harrow's residents of working age were from black and minority ethnic groups, and the BAME population in Hillingdon rose to 47.8% in the same census. Both the Pinner Players in Harrow and the Ruislip Dramatic Society in Hillingdon are predominately white actors and directors, although it is noticeable that on the relatively rare occasions when black and Asian actors do perform, they are enthusiastically supported by friends and family in the audience. As we discuss further in Chapter 6, perhaps one of the barriers to participation from diverse communities lies in the wider social segregation in suburbia; most amateur theatre-makers become involved through word-of-mouth or a personal connection with a company member, and frequently participation depends on friendship and informal contacts outside the amateur theatre world. Drawing on friendship to cast productions is a well-known directorial tactic, and when AppEaling Theatre Company director Cathy Swift wanted to stage Ayub Khan-Din's play *Rafta Rafta* in 2018 at The Questors in suburban London, she persuaded her British Asian friends to audition. 'Amateur theatre' she observed, 'does not reflect the multicultural world in which we live. I would like to see this change.'[18] In other settings, however, and particularly outside major cities, amateur theatre makes social segregation visible.

If place is constructed through play, and the emotional intensity of what Lefebvre calls 'moments', place-making happens in the public spaces of theatre, in rehearsal and in the social activities associated with membership of a society. Few amateur theatre-makers in the Harrow and Hillingdon boroughs own their own building, and this means that many are dependent on spaces that have multiple uses, performing in church halls and community centres as well as larger civic spaces with purpose-built stages. For amateur theatre-makers, transforming a functional village hall or community centre into an atmospheric space is a regular challenge. In some ways the lack of fixed seating could present creative opportunities, as scenographer Pamela Howard suggests, '[t]he characteristic of a space has to be taken into consideration … Its atmosphere and quality deeply affect both audience and performers' (2009: 2). Most amateur theatre companies do not create site-specific performances, nor do they reconfigure their church hall or community centre to perform in the round or to use its existing characteristics to create intimate actor-audience relationships; they prefer an end-on proscenium arch for their repertoire of scripted plays. This requires theatre-makers to erase the building's habitual association with various toddler groups, adult education classes, keep-fit groups and wedding parties to create the kind of affective intensity and focus needed for a good performance. In turn, however, theatre becomes part of the narrative of these multiuse buildings, and the skilful crafting of story and atmosphere that overlays its other functions is often part of the process of making amateur theatre.

Harefield Amateur Dramatic Society (HADS) is located in the London Borough of Hillingdon and residents describe Harefield as the only village within the M25, the motorway that circumnavigates London. They would

[18] http://www.totalengagementconsulting.com/blog/tag/appealing-theatre-company/. Accessed 16 June 2018.

be reluctant to describe Harefield as suburbia, but it is within easy reach of London with Rickmansworth Station on the Metropolitan line just over three miles away. In common with other amateur theatres in the area, HADS was established in the post-war era, and since 1951 it has staged two productions each year as well as organising various other social events. Local historian Dave Twydell documented the first sixty years of the company in his book, *Mr Fothergill to Lark Rise: Harefield Amateur Dramatic Society 1951–2011*, where he recounts that it was initiated by Harefield newcomer Leslie Baxter and his landlady's son, Francis James. HADS was started as a way of raising local spirits in an era of post-war austerity, but Twydell also notes that some local people were initially suspicious of its political motives. The inaugural meeting was monitored by local members of the Conservative Party, who were concerned that such a gathering of creative people might attract Communists. Reassured, one Tory—Don Chapman—later became a member and, sixty years later in 2011 he was serving as the society's president. Communists were unwelcome in 1950s Harefield, and Twydell also seemed unimpressed by the presence of what he describes as the 'Ban the Bomb Brigade' who 'took advantage' of a production in 1961 about life after a nuclear war by protesting. Place identity can be prejudicial, as Tim Cresswell has made clear, it 'usually involves an us/them distinction in which the other is devalued' (2004: 27).

Whatever its political leanings may have been, HADS quickly established a local reputation for good entertainment. Twydell's account is selective and his tastes conventional (he suggests that it was 'fortunate' that Harefield was 'spared' their festival production of Ionesco's *The Lesson* in 1970), and his account stresses good reviews in the local press. The company gradually became more ambitious in its repertoire, moving from the one-act farces and comedies that were the mainstay of their early productions to John Osborne's *The Entertainer* in 1971 and *The Crucible* in 1979. The rehearsal methods for *The Crucible*, however, caused some consternation amongst the cast. Not only did rehearsals take place in a cold room in a house at the end of a muddy lane, but also the director was keen to experiment. Twydell's tone is unenthusiastic, describing her approach as 'method acting (being trees, etc.)' which was met with considerable resistance (2011: 25). What is clear from the history of HADS is that the company has been resilient in the face of a continual challenge to find performance spaces; over the course of its sixty-five-year history they have performed in many different venues around the village, including the school, Harefield Hospital Concert Hall, The British Legion Hall and a garden. Their sixtieth anniversary production in 2011 was *Lark Rise*, a choice that reaffirmed their identity as an English village, and included St Mary's Church Choir and the Village Band. Researching the work of HADS over a three-month period in 2015 I was able to observe their rehearsal methods, and to understand the company's relationship to place.

In Autumn 2015 the company were rehearsing for a production of *Journey's End* as part of Harefield's contribution to the centenary of World War One. The play had been suggested by Martin Davies, the local Anglican vicar, in part because the village has a historic association with Anzac forces; Australian soldiers from Gallipoli and the Western Front were treated at a hospital in Harefield, and there is consequently a military cemetery. The idiom of R.C. Sherriff's dialogue presented some difficulties for the cast, and the two directors, Tony Keyho and Dawn Davies (the vicar's wife), listened patiently to the cast, building their confidence. What was striking was the cast's commitment to telling the story of these young soldiers, and the seriousness with which they accepted the challenge. The company regularly performs in St Mary's Church Hall, but they struggle to find places to rehearse, sometimes using a small space in the local library or, on occasion, the houses of company members. My research journal captures one rehearsal in the home of one of the cast, and reflects on the relationship between the place and rehearsal's atmosphere.

> I arrived a bit late for the rehearsal having got lost in the dark, and I wasn't entirely sure that I was knocking on the door of the right bungalow. It was – the rehearsal had already begun and I was led to the conservatory. Wicker chairs had been pushed to the side of the room to clear a space, but it carried traces of its occupants' domestic life and other hobbies; family photographs and pictures of steam trains were displayed alongside pot plants and ornaments. The two directors followed their scripts intently, hardly looking up from the page as the young actor playing Stanhope struggled to remember his lines. I was surprised that there was no discussion about the play, nor debates about the roles they were playing. Other actors – many experienced HADS members – waited quietly in the wings, or rather on camping chairs by the cooker in the kitchen. The atmosphere was quiet, intent and purposeful. I felt humbled by their commitment, and wondered how many other amateur actors were similarly spending their evenings working on plays in people's houses. (Helen's Research Diary, 14 October 2015)

In this rehearsal three places were woven together; the domestic space of the rehearsal itself, the fictional world of the play and the imagined experience of actual soldiers in the trenches. This layering invokes Massey's view that place is made and re-made through interwoven stories, and that memory and story-telling is inherent to all placeful activity.

The performance took place to coincide with Remembrance Day on 11th November 2015. The set was designed to capture the oppressive qualities of life in a World War One front-line dug-out, and in performance its complexity and clarity drew the audience's attention away from the everyday ephemera of a twenty-first century church hall. There was a small exhibition in the foyer of relatives of the company who had fought—and died—in World War One, which drew the performance into the intimacy of family ties. The date lent the performance solemnity—the company provided tissues on the audience's seats in anticipation of an emotional response, and it concluded with everyone rising for the National Anthem, a gesture intended as a tribute to the war dead. The choice of the National Anthem reflected the actors' and directors' values rather than those articulated by play itself; the script illuminates the trauma of war but is notoriously non-committal about its justification or its heroism. Notwithstanding, it was the actors' emotional commitment that was striking about this production, an affective attachment to people and places both real and imagined, mutually entangled in the performance event, that stretched across time.

HADS is a generous spirited company, and it is testament to their open-handedness that they responded positively to my request to participate in our research. After the *Journey's End* run had come to an end, I was invited to attend a company meeting to talk to members about their experiences of participating in HADS. On a cold late November evening, an impressive twenty-four members turned out, representing a range of ages and social backgrounds, new members as well as those with long HADS service. We met in the small local library, and part of the evening was devoted to reading the review of *Journey's End* sent by the NODA representative. Eagerly anticipated, the company were aware of the reviewer's tastes and predilections (which they deemed rather conservative). Encouraged by his positive response, the company turned their attention to the research workshop.

One of activities I asked HADs members to do was to work in groups to put various statements about why they participated in HADs in order of priority. The statements ranged from the communitarian (I take part in HADS to

Fig. 4.2   Jordan Baker and Matt Smith in Harefield Amateur Dramatics Society's production of *Journey's End*, November 2015. (By kind permission of the photographer, Jan Scurr)

make a difference to Harefield) to the personal (HADS enables me to extend my own creativity). Each group was recorded, and the discussions shed light on their motivations and priorities. It was noticeable that every group prioritised the statement 'Amateur theatre brings people together and creates a sense of belonging'. Not all HADS members live in Harefield, and the pleasure of shared interests was regarded by many as more important than its contribution to Harefield as a village. (Helen's Research Diary, 24 November 2015)

It was by coming together as theatre-makers that they felt, as one member put it, 'in the right place'. Although everyone was generally quite happy to serve Harefield's audiences, their interest was not in Harefield as a 'placey-place', but in a more abstract sense of placefulness that arose from the emotional ties created when people work together to make theatre.

There are parallels here with Hilary Geoghegan's analysis of 'geographies of enthusiasm', a term she uses to describe how leisure pursuits turn into deeper emotional affiliation over time. In her study of the group of dedicated men who form in the UK's Telecommunications Heritage Group, Geoghegan argues that enthusiasm is an emotion that 'influences passions, performances and activities in space' (2013: 45). She makes a persuasive case for enthusiasm as integral to socio-spatial relations where a shared interest and expertise can bring people together and, at best, creates feelings of belonging:

> By recasting enthusiasm as an emotion... It is possible to reveals what it means to be in the company of kindred spirits, whether firmly rooted in place or imagined. (2013: 45)

As a material practice and an art-form, theatre is both 'firmly rooted in place' and imagined, and the final activity of the evening illustrated some of the emotional affiliation Geoghegan also found in the group of enthusiasts she studied.

In the final activity of the evening I asked people to write a postcard. They were invited to write anything they wanted about amateur theatre and their work with HADS. It need not be signed, but it would be read out. When everyone had finished writing, they put their postcards into the middle of the circle. Each person picked up a postcard randomly, and they were read out in turn. It was a moving experience, the messages making a strong testimony to the members' attachment to each other, their passion for theatre-making and their sense of pride in their own creativity. The responses varied. Some valued the social aspects of the group 'the banter and mickey-taking', whereas several others commented on the creative satisfaction it brought: 'it allows me to be creative and pushes me to develop ideas and new skills.' Perhaps the most touching contributions were those that showed how joining HADS marked a turning point in their lives, often at difficult times. As one active member put it: 'Joining HADS was something I did on my own. I took courage as I am basically a shy person.' The final contribution of the evening came from Richard Hollis, and seemed to summarise the sentiments in the room:

> HADS is an escape. Not an escape from stress, but into a different kind of stress, that makes you forget the original stress. It is an escape into a world that most people think has disappeared, but which still exists. A world where very different people can have a lot of fun doing something that feels worthwhile, even if it's not always done very well.

HADS members commented that the evening had given them the opportunity to articulate what they often think, but what they would otherwise find difficult to say. The postcard exercise produced a layer of protection that is not afforded in face-to-face interviews, and the comments were personal, intense and revealing. In each postcard that was read, it was the emotional strength of the theatrical experience—inhabiting place that is both safe and imagined—rather than attachment to their local area that was striking. This chimes well with Geoghegan's suggestion that emotional connections are found through passion for shared activity, interests shared with kindred spirits. John Suppiah, who is British Asian and a new member of HADS, wrote simply: 'I am in HADS because of the love I have for acting which is something that talks to my soul.'

Engaging in amateur theatre creates spaces of possibility, in Lefebvre's terms, that begins with shared enjoyment but also extends beyond the immediate emotional satisfaction of the performance. The feeling of being in the 'right place' that was articulated by HADS members did not underplay the antagonisms and frustrations associated with making theatre under pressure of time. Rather, it signified belonging on a deeper level, to places that are both imagined and embodied.

Affective Attachment to Place: Places of Performance

Theories of place that inform this chapter suggest that place is not a static location or inert piece of ground, but a process that is porous, embodied, dynamic and relational. The work of philosopher Edward Casey extends this debate, who makes a case for place as 'an event' that is continually changing and subject to re-definition. There is a performative quality to Casey's idea of place, and he suggests that its material qualities have 'gathering power':

> [P]laces gather things in their midst – where 'things' connote various animate and inanimate entities. Places also gather experiences and histories, even languages and thoughts. Think only of what it means to go back to a place you know, finding it full of memories and expectations, old things and new things, the familiar and the strange. (1996: 24)

This way of thinking focuses attention on the stories that gather in specific places, and how the 'eventness' of place creates opportunities for creativity and sociability. Doreen Massey's analysis of place might be usefully read alongside Casey's phenomenology; both suggest that place disrupts the linearity of past, present and future, suggesting that sensorial relationships with place scripts human subjectivity by shaping patterns of feeling and thought. Unlike Casey, however, Massey does not accept that it is ever possible to return to the 'same' place as both people and places are constantly evolving and changing, 'woven together out of on-going stories' (2005: 131). In other words, place is not an inert backdrop onto which ideas and experiences are projected, but place is created and perceived through the rhythms of the body, a sensory process that changes over time. Tim Cresswell summarises this neatly, suggesting that place is 'an embodied relationship with the world', and that places are constructed by 'people doing things and in this sense never "finished" but are constantly being performed' (2004: 37).

Applied to amateur theatre, the idea that places have 'gathering power' and that they are made by people 'doing things' opens new ways to think about how the physical and material practices of theatre—its creative activity—contribute to place-making. It suggests that there is a reciprocity between theatre as an event, and the theatre as a gathering place where stories are crafted. Of course, theatre and story are close allies, but one aspect of place-making is that friendship, memories and anecdotes are forged in the process of making. Some companies own their own theatres, working backstage as well as in performance, making it a regular gathering place for company members. Unlike many professional theatres where staff may come and go, many amateur theatre-makers have a life-long association with their theatres, and this lends the building a very special atmosphere. One such theatre is The Barn Theatre in Welwyn Garden City, which is situated opposite houses designed for the Daily Mail Model Home Village Exhibition in 1922. The Barn's charm lies partly in its architecture and the layers of memory that are etched in its fabric. It is not clear when Handside Barn was built—a piece of wood from the beams has been carbon dated to 1598—but it was a dairy farm in the nineteenth century until its closure in 1926, when it became a bottling factory for Welwyn Department Store until the 1930s. It was partially converted into a theatre in 1931, and The Barn Theatre gradually acquired adjoining store rooms and social spaces over time. It now has a fully equipped auditorium, a studio theatre in the old cow sheds, dressing rooms, extensive costume stores, workshops for set-building and a comfortable bar. Writing about The Settlement in Letchworth, Cara Gray describes how buildings have their own biographies, and their life-histories are particularly evocative for amateur theatre-makers who have long associations with a place. The Barn is similarly infused with memory, and also carries the material traces of its previous life as a cow shed and bottling plant in its architecture. A tiled floor where the milk churns once stood now forms the route to the costume store, and there are timber beams in the studio and auditorium.[19]

> There is a comfortable feeling to The Barn, and I am surprised how quickly I feel at home here. There is something about the warmth of the front-of-house areas that feels as it has been used for generations. There are photographs on the wall of past productions, and the area where costumes are made feels comfortable and industrious. (Helen's Research Diary, 24 April 2015)

The theatre is an evocative and historic building, but it hosts a contemporary programme of ten main house shows a year, a youth theatre production and various informal musical and comedy nights. The Barn serves as a major cultural hub for the community, presenting a diverse programme designed to appeal widely. In 2018, for example, it followed a sell-out run of Mike Packer's *tHe dYsFUnCKshOnalZ!* (billed as 'Unbelievably F*****g Offensive!'), with George Bernard Shaw's *Pygmalion*. The Barn Fringe introduces new acts and talents, and in June 2018, The Barn's first Open Mic Comedy Night was introduced, designed to attract new talent, tempt established stand-ups and cultivate aspiring comics. This initiative also tests the porosity of amateur-professional boundaries; usually for The Barn, entry is free, with the proceeds from a bucket collection distributed amongst the performers.[20]

There is considerable local loyalty to The Barn, and the high production values ensure that its productions play to good houses. The Barn has a history of theatrical experimentation, comparing itself favourably to

[19] Gray, Cara. 2017. *A Study of Amateur Theatre: Making and Making-Do*. Unpublished PhD Thesis. Royal Holloway, University of London. See also Penny, Sarah and Cara Gray 2017. The Materialities of Amateur Theatre. In *Contemporary Theatre Review*, 27, 1:104–123, DOI: https://doi.org/10.1080/10486801.2016.1262850

[20] http://www.barntheatre.co.uk/comedy-at-the-barn/event/202141. Accessed 16 June 2018.

professional theatre, as chairman Louis Davis observed in *The Drama News* in July 1965:

> We are amateurs can sometimes put on the experimental or the controversial which perhaps the professionals cannot afford to risk. (1965: 3)

Each Monday and Tuesday mornings a group of people gather at The Barn to build sets, make and mend costumes, order the archive and undertake many of the maintenance jobs that an old building requires. Many are long-serving members of The Barn, having taken multiple roles in its evolution as a theatre. Judith Claxton has maintained a long association with The Barn since she first came to Welwyn Garden City as a young bride in the 1960s. She found that she was initially 'a bit daunted' by the city as it was 'so organised – there are no cosy corners in the Garden City', but she also valued its 'good socialist principles'. Judith started as a leading actor, taking the role of Rose Trelawny in Trelawny of the Wells in 1969, and in an interview, she described how important it was to The Barn's 'ecosystem' to remain amateur, making theatre for love:

> Oh yes, there's a great affection for The Barn. We give our time and care.. but if someone is being paid, where does it stop? Amateurs like to be amateurs – we don't want to be told what to do by someone who's being paid. You give your time, and theatre's your love… Paying people to make costumes or build sets would disrupt the ecosystem. Once you get involved in something like drama, you make close friends. If you've put on a play, you've made a family. I don't want to act any more, but I do want to be involved in the theatre. There are some of us here have worked together over time in many different contexts, and that's The Barn. You can come in here, and just get lifted. Oh I couldn't do without The Barn. It's the heart of your life.[21]

This interview documents how life in Welwyn Garden City became more fulfilling for amateur theatre enthusiasts. Judith Claxton herself not only performed and made costumes, but she gave her organisational skills to the wider amateur theatre sector, serving as Secretary to GoDA for many years (following in the footsteps of Purdom), organising the Welwyn

---

[21] Interview Helen Nicholson with Judith Claxton, The Barn, Welwyn Garden City. 21 April 2015.

Drama Festival and acting as a member of The Barn Theatre council. Margaret Wallace is another member of the wardrobe team who meet on weekday mornings. She started to work backstage because her three sons became performers, and when she found that she was spending a lot of time transporting them she offered to help with costumes. At the time, she was delighted that her boys had chosen an activity that 'kept them out of trouble'. All three sons have since married, and they and their wives continue to make theatre at The Barn where they are affectionately known as 'The Wallace Collection'. One of Margaret's daughters-in-law, Lou Wallace who directs at The Barn, describes this shared interest across generations as 'wholesome'.[22]

For Judith Claxton and many of her contemporaries, the experience of taking different roles in the theatre has created an enduring attachment to the theatre as a place that influences how people feel about living in the town itself. Judith Claxton commented that the high cost of housing meant that members with young families no longer live in Welwyn itself, and it is testament to The Barn's gathering power that some members of all ages travel from the surrounding areas to take part in its productions. Whether The Barn's wandering actors will become the long-standing members in the next decades is unclear, but attachment grows over time and, as Massey suggests, a sense of place is created not through fixity, but through the layering of stories. Robert Gill, a leading member of The Barn, points out that 'the history of the Barn Theatre is really all about the history of the Garden City' and how Welwyn changes as a place will inevitably affect The Barn's future.[23] By coincidence Robert and Heather Gill now live in Purdom's Welwyn house, and Robert is leading a campaign for him to achieve civic recognition for his pioneering work in the Garden City Movement. At a commemoration of the fiftieth anniversary of his death in 2015 attended by Purdom's family, members of The Barn gave a rehearsed reading of Charles Lee's play, *Mr Sampson*, that had taken Purdom's cast to victory in New York. The performance captured the spirit of Purdom's theatre, illustrating how attachment to place and the narratives of theatre are interwoven.

[22] Interview Helen Nicholson with Lou Wallace, Hitchin. 15 May 2015.
[23] Interview Helen Nicholson with Robert Gill, The Barn. Welwyn Garden City 17 April 2016.

Every theatre has a ghost, and The Barn is no exception. He usually appears downstage left, quite late at night, when the stagehands and set-builders are the only people left in the building. Memory and performance are intimately connected, and theatre scholar Marvin Carlson suggests that this is one reason why there are so many theatrical ghosts; performers continually inhabit and re-inhabit roles that have already been performed, and theatre is concerned with the 're-enactment of events already enacted, and with re-experiencing already experienced' (2003: 3). Carlson calls this 'ghosting'—a term he uses to describe the ways in which memory operates in theatre—how each performance or actor is ghosted by performances or actors that have gone before:

> [g]hosting presents the identical thing they have encountered before, although now in a somewhat different context. Thus, a recognition not of similarity (as in genre), but of identity becomes part of the reception process. (2003: 7)

The 'things' Carlson describes might be the actors' bodies, the material stuff of theatre—props, set, costumes and so on—as well as the dramatic text (the play itself), that is recycled and re-imagined in performance. In amateur theatre, not only are props and costumes carefully and habitually recycled and reused, but also local people who have been 'encountered before' are recognised in a different context and with a new layer of identity. Pretending to be someone else, and being somewhere else, is part of the enjoyment of amateur theatre, both in production and reception. Not only does theatre-making engage and gather people together in ways that are memorable for the actors and audiences, its fictional qualities also create an imaginary world by performers who, in amateur theatre, have other quotidian roles.

COMMUNITY, PLACE AND PARTICIPATION

Throughout this chapter, I have argued that amateur theatre plays a significant role in place-making, fostering a sense of belonging and rootedness. At the same time, I have drawn on theories of place that recognise that the social meanings of place are fluid, and change over time. How far the repertoire and demographic of amateur theatre reflects social change in the twenty-first century is moot, but its place in local civic society is acknowledged by mayors who are frequently called upon to present prizes at festivals and attend performances wearing their mayoral chains. Despite considerable evidence that participation in amateur theatre crosses divisions of social class, the ambiguous place held by amateur theatre in national cultural policy, however, reflects its association with place as rooted, stable and bounded. This perception, and sometimes choice of repertoire, is perhaps one of the barriers to diverse participation.

Both place and community are marked by exclusions, as Cresswell and others have described. Historically, as we have shown, new communities sought to define themselves by both tackling challenging plays and by affirming local identities in humorous representations of their communities' ideals and daily lives. How far this link between egalitarianism and amateur theatre extends to local communities today is unclear, but it inspired The Common Lot, an amateur theatre collective in Norwich, to develop their play *Come Yew in: A Proud History of Strangers in Norwich* in Summer 2017. The Common Lot have a strong record of performances that tell local stories, inspired by the social and political ambitions of the community theatre movement. For *Come Yew in*, Simon Floyd, director and producer of the show, worked with company members and local people to research the history of new arrivals in Norwich which became a lively performance.

> It was a hot July day when I travelled to Norwich to see the performance, staged in the castle gardens. A band played, and we were welcomed to our seats. 'Come Yew in', we were told, was a greeting used by Norfolk people to welcome strangers. A caricature of an eccentric male professor narrated the show, bringing together fast-paced vignettes, sometimes in rhyming couplets and in song, about how new arrivals from different parts of the world had shaped the culture of Norwich. Dutch weavers in the reign of Elizabeth 1, Vikings and ice-cream making Italians made up the eclectic cultural mix, the dramatic atmosphere changing as each story unfolded. It was a fast-paced and slick affirmation of the cultural importance of migrants, and the polemic in Brexit Britain was well received. (Helen's Research Diary, 8 July 2017)

Perhaps the most poignant parts of the performance were those when a member of the diverse cast told his or her story, sometimes in the hesitant English of a recent arrival or refugee, and an NHS nurse from Eastern Europe wore her uniform for her performance. By charting the relationship between the past and present, the political message of the play was unambiguous, underlined in the chorus of the song *Come Yew In* which invited audience participation:

> We're going Norwich wide
> NR1 to NR5
> Muslim, Christian, Sikh or Jew
> And no religion too
> It you're gay or if you're straight
> Doesn't matter who you date
> Every girl and every boy and man
> Even if you're an Ipswich fan.

The audience participated enthusiastically and gave generously to the collection in aid of a local charity that supports refugees and asylum seekers. There appeared to be no dissenters, and the public expression of Norwich as an outward-looking and welcoming place seemed to resonate with its audience. Funded by The Norwich Town Close Estate Charity as part of their celebration of the 700th year of the city of Norwich, *Come Yew In* was designed to affirm the city's identity. The town crier symbolised the plays' civic role, and its message was spread to schools through a city-wide education programme. This suggests that the company recognised that there was a social intervention to be made around the subject of new arrivals, challenging the attitudes of those who did not share the liberal sentiments I witnessed in the audience on that sunny Saturday. An intervention that might be illuminated by sociologist Tariq Modood's notion of 'civic multiculturalism' (2013), which stresses the importance of opening up spaces to explore and experience inclusivity, which receives further attention in Chapter 6.

Throughout this chapter I have suggested that places are constructed by creative activity, and I have given many examples of the ways in which amateur theatre-makers contribute to that process. The Common Lot offers one example of an amateur theatre company that has taken on a political role in its community, working with local people to shape social and cultural values. Harriet Hawkins describes artistic activity as part of the creative geography of place, an embodied and material practice that shapes communities. But she also warns that it is not always the 'avowedly positive story that is often presented' (2017: 193), arguing that some interventions by professional artists can 'do damage to existing communities' by excluding and sideling 'the cultural characteristics of the location'

(2017: 193). Our contention is that amateur theatre companies have long histories in many villages, towns and cities, and that cultural policy-makers and professional artists who seek to contribute to place-making may well be advised to listen to their experience and attend to their expertise. Taking account of amateur theatre-makers, and working in partnership to increase the diversity of cultural participation, might be one way for artists to contribute to the delicate ecosystems of communities and the places they inhabit.

References

Balme, Christopher B. 2014. *The Theatrical Public Sphere*. Cambridge: Cambridge University Press.

Bauman, Zigmunt. 2003. *Liquid Love: On the Frailty of Human Bonds*. Cambridge: Polity Press.

———. 2005. *Liquid Life*. Cambridge: Polity Press.

Brunt, A.W. 1942. *The Pageant of Letchworth*. Letchworth: Letchworth Printers.

Casey, Edward. 1996. How to Get from Space to Place in a Fairly Short Stretch of Time. In *Senses of Place*, ed. S. Feld and K.H. Basso, 13–52. Santa Fe: School of American Research.

———. 1997. *The Fate of Place: A Philosophical History*. Berkeley: University of California Press.

Cockin, Katharine. 1998. *Edith Craig (1869–1847): Dramatic Lives*. London: Cassell.

Cresswell, Tim. 2004. *Place: A Short Introduction*. Oxford: Basil Blackwell.

———. 2006. *On the Move: Mobility in the Modern Western World*. London: Routledge.

DCMS. 2016. The Culture White Paper. https://www.gov.uk/government/uploads/system/uploads/attachment_data/file/510798/DCMS_The_Culture_White_Paper__3_.pdf. Accessed 12 Nov 2016.

Edensor, Tim, Deborah Leslie, Steve Millington, and Norma M. Rantisi, eds. 2010. *Spaces of Vernacular Creativity: Rethinking the Cultural Economy*. Abingdon: Routledge.

Florida, Richard. 2002. *The Rise of the Creative Class*. New York: Basic Books.

Geoghegan, Hilary. 2013. Emotional Geographies of Enthusiasm: Belonging to the Telecommunications Heritage Group. *Area* 45: 40–46. https://doi.org/10.1111/j.1475-4762.2012.01128.x.

Gray, Cara. 2017. *A Study of Amateur Theatre: Making and Making-Do*. Unpublished PhD Thesis, Royal Holloway, University of London.

Hawkins, Harriet. 2017. *Creativity*. London: Routledge.

Howard, Ebenezer. 1902. *Garden Cities of Tomorrow*. London: Sonnenschein & Co.

Howard, Pamela. 2009. *What Is Scenography?* 2nd ed. London: Routledge.

Hunt, Tristram. 2004. *Building Jerusalem: The Rise and Fall of the Victorian City*. London: Phoenix Paperback.

Huq, Rupa. 2013. *On the Edge: The Contested Cultures of English Suburbia*. London: Lawrence and Wishart.

Lee, Jennie. 1965. A Policy for the Arts: The First Steps. http://action.labour. org.uk/page/-/blog%20images/policy_for_the_arts.pdf. Accessed 14 Oct 2016.

Lees, Loretta, ed. 2004. *The Emancipatory City?* London: Sage Publications.

Lefebvre, Henri. 2014. *Toward an Architecture of Enjoyment*. Trans. R. Bononno. Minneapolis: Minneapolis University Press.

Light, Alison. 1991. *Forever England: Femininity, Literature and Conservativism Between the Wars*. London: Routledge.

Lippard, Lucy. 1997. *The Lure of the Local: Senses of Place in a Multicentred Society*. New York: The New Press.

Massey, Doreen. 2005. *For Space*. London: Sage.

Matless, David. 1998. *Landscape and Englishness*. London: Reaktion Books.

Meacham, Standish. 1999. *Regaining Paradise: Englishness and the Early Garden City Movement*. New Haven/London: Yale University Press.

Modood, Tariq. 2013. *Multiculturalism*. Cambridge: Polity Press.

Penny, Sarah, and Cara Gray. 2017. The Materialities of Amateur Theatre. *In Contemporary Theatre Review* 27 (1): 104–123. https://doi.org/10.1080/10 486801.2016.1262850.

Purdom, C.B. 1908. *Letchworth Dramatic Society: The First Annual Report (1907–1908)*. London: J.M. Dent.

———. 1951. *Life Over Again*. London: J.M. Dent and Sons.

Purdom, C.B., and Charles Lee. 1910. *The Second Garden City Pantomime*. Letchworth: Dent Publishers.

Samuel, Raphael. 1994. *Theatres of Memory Vol. 1 Past and Present in Contemporary Culture*. London: Verso.

Smith, Laurajane. 2011. The 'Doing' of Heritage: Heritage as Performance. In *Performing Heritage: Research, Practice and Innovation in Museum Theatre and Live Interpretation*, ed. Anthony Jackson and Jenny Kidd, 69–81. Manchester: Manchester University Press.

The Office for National Statistics, Taking Part. www.gov.uk/government/collections/sat%2D%2D2. Accessed 13 Oct 2016.

Turner, Cathy. 2015. *Dramaturgy and Architecture: Theatre, Utopia and the Built Environment*. London: Palgrave Macmillan.

Twydell, Dave. 2011. *Mr. Fothergill to Lark Rise: Harefield Amateur Dramatic Society 1951–2011*. Harefield: Harefield Amateur Dramatic Society.

CHAPTER 5

Making Time for Amateur Theatre: Work, Labour and Free Time

Patterns of labour are woven through the history of amateur theatre in England, with amateurism as a practice often defined in relation to paid work. Unlike voluntarism, however, which is widely regarded as part of the gift economy, amateur labour has been largely overlooked by political economists and consequently occupies an ambiguous space in the cultural ecology. For those on the Left, amateur labour has been perhaps most closely associated with the dilettantism of the idle aristocrat or the self-improvement of the aspirational middle class, available only to those with time and money to spare. For the eighteenth-century aristocrat, as Judith Hawley has pointed out, participating in amateur private theatricals without the need to become a paid professional was an important marker of status (Hawley 2012). Traces of this attitude exist today, as Glenn Adamson has observed, where amateurism is sometimes seen to 'reflect a culture of preposterous excess' in which 'the successful displacement of unused time into harmless leisure activities' unconsciously supports consumer capitalism (2007: 140). There are a generalised set of assumptions that connect the politics of labour with participating in amateur theatre, and may account, at least in part, for its marginalisation within theatre studies and cultural policy more widely.

There is, of course, a more nuanced way of understanding amateur labour that does not primarily depend on political or aesthetic judgements about how far amateur theatre-makers produce work that is recognised as counter-cultural or innovative, nor rest on presumptions about its

© The Author(s) 2018
H. Nicholson et al., *The Ecologies of Amateur Theatre*,
https://doi.org/10.1057/978-1-137-50810-2_5

'harmlessness' or artistic conservativism. As we noted in Chapter 2, the economy extends more widely than the market and, as a field of cultural practice, the labours of amateur theatre involve multiple forms of participation and different theatre crafts. Rather than unthinking or excessive consumption, as we point out in Chapter 6, craft-making in amateur theatre is often frugal, with costumes and materials for sets recycled many times. Yet divisions between labour and leisure are often complexly configured in amateur theatre, and binaries between paid and unpaid labour, and professional and amateur identities are increasingly porous, suggesting that temporal distinctions between work and 'free time' demand attention.

This chapter investigates how far time spent on amateur theatre reflects changing employment patterns, and asks how the everyday working lives of participants are refracted in amateur theatre. By tracing the rise of amateur theatre as popular workplace activity for employees in the twentieth century, we will consider the implications of different forms of labour both on individual amateur theatre-makers and the audiences they serve and the communities they represent. This takes on a particular urgency in the twenty-first century, where, as Zygmunt Bauman has argued, new patterns of work are affecting personal relationships, families and communities. He describes this fast-paced society as 'liquid', and characterises the fragile, temporary and disposable social bonds that he associates with it as 'liquid love' (Bauman 2003). Within the context of contemporary concerns about the speed and pace of life and anxiety about declining sense of community, it is perhaps surprising that so many people find – or make – time for amateur theatre. Working towards a production is time-consuming (if time can be consumed) as are the many other, less visible labours of committee work and financial management that are integral to the smooth-running of amateur theatre companies. The labours of amateur theatre carry their own temporal rhythms, and theatre works under the pressure of time; the rhythms of rehearsals define the week, and the annual cycle of auditions and productions often shape the calendar year. Furthermore, many amateurs sustain a life-long interest in theatre-making, and senior members of a company have often maintained loyalty to one company over a lifetime, their roles and mode of participation changing with age. The liveness of performance means that it is impossible to separate time from place, and re-thinking how and why time spent on amateur theatre contributes to community-building is part of the work of this chapter. The chapter explores the temporal dynamic of amateur theatre, opening questions about the space amateur labour occupies where, as Stephen Knott puts it, 'definitions of work, productivity, aesthetics, play and labour are continually negotiated' (2015: xvi).

This chapter takes up Knott's invitation to consider how work, play and labour are experienced in amateur theatre. Throughout the twentieth century amateur theatre was a regular part of life in the workplace—in factories, banks, shops, airlines, hospitals, railways, and found in London Transport, the Inns of Court, Mechanical Institutes, stockbroker firms and Young Farmers. Traces of this activity are still evident today, albeit diminished and adapted over time. This chapter draws attention to how changes to the temporal rhythms of work have influenced the ways in which people participate in amateur theatre, and how their lives as amateur theatre-makers relate to different work environments. My ambition is not, therefore, to define what amateurs or amateur labour might be, but to attend to its relational status both within and beyond other forms of labour and measures of time that might be called 'free'. I shall begin with a brief discussion of the history of ideas that influenced how distinctions between free time, paid labour and leisure activities have been understood in relation to amateurism, before moving to consider how a long tradition of amateur theatre in the workplace has shaped contemporary practice. By weaving a narrative that takes account of the historical relationship between amateur theatre, time and working lives, I hope to re-conceptualise amateur labour in ways that understand the cultural value of amateur theatre in an increasingly time-poor twenty-first century. Traversing thresholds between the different temporal registers of amateur theatre offers one way to conceptualise the material qualities of amateur theatre as a social practice, affective, live, embodied, precarious and sometimes utopian.

WORK AND FREE TIME: AMATEURS AND PRODUCTIVE LABOUR

I am in the archive at John Lewis Heritage Centre, surrounded by drawers of well-preserved fabric and leather-bound copies of *The Gazette*, the in-house magazine for John Lewis and Waitrose Partners, a term this profit-sharing retailer uses to describe its employees. One of the volunteers at the Heritage Centre, John, tells me that he was a leading member of the Peter Jones theatre company, a store in Sloane Square in London opposite the Royal Court Theatre. He performed in a Greek tragedy, he tells me, that involved making a severed head, accurately portraying his own features.

Every now and again he comes across it in his loft, where it can take him by surprise. (Helen's Research Diary, 10 July 2016)

John Lewis is a company that offers significant benefits to its partners, inspiring company loyalty and encouraging happy and productive employees. One aspect of this provision is cultural activity, and a range of choirs and theatre companies regularly perform, although this is often not visible to those outside the partnership. This chapter raises questions about work, free time and amateur theatre, asking how far this has sedimented a view of amateurs as socially privileged or affluent that is not borne out by experience or empirical research. In this section, I shall open conceptual questions about the relationship between work and free time, asking why they became interlinked in social theory and how they have shaped perceptions of amateurs in the popular imagination. Temporal distinctions between work and leisure are perhaps most often summed up by the phrase 'work-life balance', as if work and life were somehow separate entities.

The concept of 'free time' is one way to understand how amateur labour is differentiated from other working practices. 'Free time' is necessarily marked by its separation from work time, and in part this is a legacy of the working rhythms of the industrial revolution and new distinctions of class with which it was accompanied. E.P. Thompson traces this history in his essay 'Time, Work-Discipline and Industrial Capitalism' (1967), noting that 'time-discipline' became increasingly important during the nineteenth century, as workers shifted from agricultural labour that responded to daylight hours and the seasons to industrial labour that was governed by the clock. Theorists of 'free' or 'spare' time, including Thompson, generally invoke Karl Marx's concept of 'surplus labour' to understand how time was newly defined in the nineteenth century and became a marker of social inequality. Marx differentiated between 'necessary labour time' that was needed to support workers' livelihoods and 'surplus labour' that generated profit for capitalists. In Marx's political analysis, free time was only produced through exploitation of the time and labour-power of the working classes, and this in turn generated the uneven conditions under which only the affluent classes had 'time at its disposal for free development' (2007: 581). In an oft-quoted sentence, Marx summarises the quantitative link between spare time and work time:

> In capitalist society spare time is acquired for one class by converting the whole life-time of the masses into labour-time. (2007: 581)

This association between the exploitation of workers' time and surplus labour has shaped the ways in which free time has been understood. Marx's analysis of the working day, as Ridout points out, not only meant that work and leisure time were considered interdependent, but it also suggests that there is no such thing as time that is 'free', as all time is constrained by capitalism (2013: 37).

The association between spare time and social class, as described by Marx, has remained a powerful influence on theories of amateur labour. Writing in the 1950s, Hannah Arendt acknowledges Marx's analysis of the relationship between surplus time and work time, noting that in his classless utopia all forms of labour 'would be performed in a manner which very closely resembles the manner of hobby activities' (1989: 128). From her twentieth-century vantage point, however, she argues that Marx's view that free time would lead to emancipation was misguided. By 1955 Arendt observed a society dominated by mass consumerism, and she comments disparagingly that all activities outside work had been reduced to the trivial status of 'hobbies', serving only to shore up an economy built on excessive consumption (1989: 128). What is particularly significant about Arendt's theory of free time for amateur theatre is that she differentiates between two kinds of worker, each with distinct relationships to society. She separates *homo fabor*, whom she describes approvingly as the 'fabricator of the world' (1989: 126), and *animal laborans*, who uses leisure time only to satisfy their immediate needs. Following the tradition of John Ruskin and William Morris' idealisation of skilled craftworkers, Arendt's *homo fabor* uses craftsmanship and insight to build a society for the public good, whereas *animal laborans* is concerned with individual consumption, making the 'whole economy a waste economy' (1989: 134). Knott, who charts similar conceptual territory, addresses the implications of this position for amateur craft. He argues that Arendt's ideal of the craftworker (*homo faber*) has been used to marginalise amateur creativity:

> This elevation of the ideals of the *homo faber* that inherently marginalises the imperfect configurations of amateur labour that is largely dependent upon object analysis: whether the result of labour is considered an authentic addition to the material world or not... Yet the differential qualities of amateur space are elucidated in their full richness when analysis focuses not on the final object but on the process of making. (2015: 51)

Applied to theatre, in which the product is generally less durable than other forms of craft, there are further questions to raise about how the ephemeral liveness of theatrical experience is valued as a socially generative force. This not only raises questions about the relationship between the rehearsal process and production values, it also draws attention to the temporal qualities of theatre and its power to affect communities.

If the products of amateur craft are marginalised by Arendt's idealisation of the socially productive craftworker, the value of time spent on amateur activities is further challenged by Theodore Adorno's critique of the culture industry. Adorno makes explicit reference to amateur labour in his essay *Free Time* (1969), where he argues that hobbies have become the product of the commodified leisure industries. With traces of Coleridge's taxonomy of the imagination, Adorno suggests that amateur creativity is symptomatic of a society in which alienating conditions of labour have deprived people of their imaginations:

> At best what they then produce in free time is scarcely better than the ominous hobby – the imitation of poems or pictures which, given the almost irrevocable division of labour, others could do better than these amateurs (Freizeitler). What they create has something superfluous about it. (1991: 167)

This not only assumes, of course, that amateurs produce artwork that is inherently inferior in quality to that of professional artists, it also accepts that participating in hobbies is indicative of a society characterised by what he describes as 'senseless activity'. Both Adorno and Arendt, therefore, associate amateur labour with shoddy excess, symptomatic of an alienated workforce where people are limited by the horizons of their imaginations. This way of thinking resonates with two familiar tropes about amateur creativity—firstly that amateur labour produces poor craftsmanship and, secondly, that amateurs are inherently self-serving.

Arendt's socially productive craftworker not only marks hierarchical distinctions between process and product, as Knott observes, it also implies evaluative judgements about amateur theatre-makers themselves. Traces of this attitude can be witnessed today, albeit more sympathetically articulated. Of the few previous studies of amateur labour, Robert A. Stebbins' work *Amateurs: On the Margin Between Work and Leisure* seeks to address the work-leisure binary by providing a taxonomy of amateurs' identities. Although this shifts attention away from stereotypical views of the product of amateur creativity, his categorisation of six 'types' of amateurs on a scale according to commitment and their relationship to the professional world (as dabblers, post-professional participants or devotees, for example) serves only to further caricature the amateur 'thespians' he describes (1979: 66). More recently, Richard Sennett challenges Arendt's distinction between practical doing (*animal laborans*) and intellectual knowing (*homo faber*) in his widely-read book *The Craftsman*, arguing that 'both thinking and feeling are contained in the process of making' (2008: 7). Notwithstanding, Sennett accepts the purity of the craftworkers' skill in ways that mirrors Arendt's vision of the socially generative *homo faber* and thus maintains their professional privilege.

It is time to reassess amateur labour. The alignment between amateur labour and morally disciplined leisure time belongs to nineteenth-century industrial economies and unsympathetic assessments of amateur craft are indebted to mid-twentieth century sensibilities towards the emergent consumerist society. The twenty-first century has brought a new attentiveness to the dynamic between labour and time, and it has become commonplace to refer to the ways in which time has speeded up—how living with digital technologies is blurring boundaries between work and leisure, how a globalised economy is compressing space and time, and how the precarity of freelance labour and new flexible employment contracts have eroded the stability of regulated working hours. Amateur activity has been defined, in part at least, by its relationship to conventional temporal patterns of work, an idea that is rehearsed by Ridout in accepting that it 'accedes too readily to the distinction between work and leisure' (2013: 29–30). This not only fails to address new ways of working in which boundaries between amateur and professional labour are porous, it also misses the contribution of those with 'time on their hands' whether through retirement, unemployment or other factors.

Rather than situating amateur theatre within the disciplinary field of leisure studies that distinguishes between different kinds of amateurs, therefore, this chapter will invoke Sarah Sharma's idea of the temporal as 'lived time' to think through the labours of amateur theatre as both situated in the routines and rhythms of everyday life, and somehow also differentiated from them. Writing in the twenty-first century, Sharma's study of the cultural politics of time recognises the importance of Marx and E.P. Thompson in defining how capital controlled labour and free time. She further suggests, however, that in contemporary life time is not only segregated and regulated by the clock, temporality is also lived and experienced in very different ways. Her argument rests on the idea that, in the twenty-first century, 'differential time' is creating inequitable temporal relations, with people experiencing time in dissimilar ways (2014: 7). She argues that life continually negotiates a range of temporal registers, and that everyone's daily rhythms are inevitably entangled with other people's temporalities:

> Temporalities do not expect a uniform time but rather a time particular to the labor that produces them. Their experience of time depends on where they are positioned in a wider economy of temporal worth... The meaning... and experiences of time is in large part structured and controlled by both the institutional arrangements they inhabit, and the time of others – other temporalities. (2014: 8)

Sharma is interested in re-imagining time so that it is understood as a collective and relational experience, with the recognition that our own time always relates to other's temporal registers. This emphasis on relational time moves debates away from fixed binaries between labour and leisure, work and free time, process and product, and consequently challenges the moralising taxonomy between different kinds of craftworker and amateur labourer. Before returning to Sharma's concept of lived and differential time, however, I shall consider how this history of ideas relates to amateur theatre, and in practical terms how the temporal rhythms of working lives have influenced participation. In the next section we will investigate how amateur theatre became integrated into the industrial communities they served, where time spent on amateur theatre was supported by employers as part of factory communities and within a jobs-for-life economy.

MANAGING TIME: AMATEUR THEATRE IN INDUSTRIAL COMMUNITIES

As I observed in the previous chapter, amateur theatre has a long history of being allied to place-making and was regarded as particularly socially beneficial to residents in newly imagined communities. As a sociable activity, however, the success of amateur theatre also depends on making time to take part. Communities dominated by manufacturing industry had regulated shifts, which routinely meant that workers had free time together. In the north of England, holidays were synchronised when factories shut down for 'factory fortnight' or 'wakes week' long before holidays were enshrined in law in 1938. The significance of time to community-building has been under-estimated, perhaps, but the social bonds forged through shared interests can only thrive if there are opportunities to meet at regular times in the week. In the early part of the twentieth century, when amateur theatre was at the height of its popularity, the organisation of time according to the communal clock (or factory hooter) provided the temporal conditions in which amateur clubs and societies could particularly thrive in industrial communities. Regular hours and a stable workforce allowed people to share their leisure time, and although regulation of the working day accounted for only part of the temporal rhythm of everyday life, particularly for women, the routines it set up created structures that enabled collective social activities.

The twentieth century interest in amateur theatre in the workplace is appropriately read in the context of nineteenth century industrial relations. Victorian industrialists had demanded a disciplined workforce, and frivolous leisure activities were actively discouraged by puritanical Evangelists as well as factory owners. How workers spent their leisure time became a matter of moral concern, Thompson notes, and factory workers were increasingly monitored for their choice of 'respectable' leisure activities by factory owners or industrial managers, often members of the newly formed middle class (1967: 58). Belief in the civilising powers of the arts was widespread, and there was genuine public concern for the welfare of the urban poor, where the workers' rowdy and drunken behaviour gave cause for alarm. In the industrial towns in the north of England, as Jenny Hughes has observed, amateur theatre was an important part of workhouse life in the mid-nineteenth century and, in the same period, theatre was also integral to the religious and cultural life of Sunday schools and non-conformist chapels (2016: 40–59). Described as 'rational recreational activities', some forms of theatre were approved alongside Glee Clubs, choirs, hymn singing and temperance societies as acceptable activities. This meant that amateur theatre was allied to the protestant culture of self-help and self-improvement, raising it from charges of frivolity and giving it serious moral weight. As Hughes points out, one way to read the Victorian interest in 'rational recreation' is to regard it as a form of social control, a way of managing workers' time outside work as well as their long working hours. On the one hand, she suggests, 'sanctioned cultural activities can be understood as disciplinary impositions of middle-class respectability on the poor' (2016: 44). On the other, however, respectability gained through cultural activity was an important marker of self-worth for the urban poor, with economic benefits in times of low employment as job prospects were augmented. However understood, this history sets a precedent for amateur theatre in the long twentieth century, where amateur dramatic societies were often actively encouraged by employers and became integrated into the culture of the workplace and the communities they served.

The relationship between industrial labour, amateur theatre and social reform might be identified via the model villages founded by wealthy philanthropic industrialists, George Cadbury (Bournville 1898) William Hesketh Lever (Port Sunlight 1899) and Joseph Rowntree (New Earswick 1902). An inspiration for the Garden City Movement and its close contemporary, model villages were established to provide healthy living conditions for factory workforces. Bournville and Port Sunlight accommodated employees at Cadbury's and Lever Brothers respectively, whereas New Earswick served the nearby Rowntree Chocolate Works but was conceived as an integrated community where not all residents were Rowntree employees. Cadbury, W.H. Lever and Joseph Rowntree were all founding members of the Garden City Association in 1899, and influenced the building of Letchworth; Letchworth architects Barry Parker and architect Raymond Unwin designed Rowntree's New Earswick model village in 1902, with Unwin adding a theatre in 1935. All three men were governed by strong religious faith and believed in the importance of community and close-knit family ties; Cadbury and Rowntree were Quakers, W.H. Lever was a member of the Congregational church. By 1915, the heart of Bournville had been developed and the village green established as a centre for community life, with shops, a school, a school of arts and crafts, church hall and a Friends Meeting House. In each model village narratives of good living were deeply enmeshed with the temporal rhythms of labour and free time, and providing healthy and spiritually uplifting pastimes was central to their moral ambition. Amateur theatre was generally encouraged in these model villages; Port Sunlight and Bournville had amateur companies by 1910, and they were particularly well-supported by second Lord Lever, an enthusiast for private theatricals, and George Cadbury who organised events at his specially constructed theatre in the grounds of his Northfield Manor home.

In York, the Cocoa Works Dramatic Society was established in 1912 (now The Rowntree Players), and the theatre (The Joseph Rowntree Hall) was opened in 1935 by Seebohm Rowntree, son of Joseph Rowntree and

Chairman of the Rowntree & Co Limited. Seebohm Rowntree intended the theatre to enhance the lives of residents by 'providing a hall which may be a fitting centre for those recreational and educational activities which make for a full and happy life.'[1] It is too easy to suggest that this interest in theatre simply represents a patrician attempt to use the arts for the moral improvement of the urban poor. Rowntree's book, *Poverty: A Study of Town Life* had been published in 1901 and its account of the degradation of poverty had rocked the liberal establishment and led directly to reformist legislation. Perhaps most importantly for this study, the book challenged the conventional view that the poor were to blame for their own poverty and made a clear case for improved access to free education as a route out of poverty. Unusually for his time, Rowntree was particularly concerned with the plight of working-class women. 'No-one can fail to be struck by the monotony which characterises the life of most married women of the working class,' he writes, further suggesting that whilst husbands gain companionship with their workmates, the women's 'restricted education and a narrow circle of activities' led to their 'unconscious neglect' (1901: 77–78). Seen in this light, the theatre's contribution to a 'full and happy life' takes on wider social significance. By 1935 the Christmas edition of *Cocoa Works Magazine* (C.W.M) reported a wide range of cultural and sporting activities, including fell walking, classes for women in Greek and National Dancing and English Folk Dancing and the Rowntree Actors' Club. The description of the new theatre noted its state-of-the-art equipment—a cyclorama, lighting, curtains and the latest 'walkie-talkie apparatus'—with a view to enabling 'amateurs to produce plays at a modest cost' (1935: 7). The first season of The Rowntree Players in their new theatre included contemporary crowd-pleasers Walter Hackett's farce *Ambrose Applejohn's Adventure*, closely followed by Emlyn Williams' thriller *A Murder has been Arranged* in 1936. Perhaps most significant are the educational opportunities offered by the Cocoa Works to their amateur actors. Applications were invited for actors and potential actors to join a 'Dramatic Art Course' run by Hull University Extension scheme:

> The course is not a literary course for the aesthetic study of plays as a form of literature only, but a study of plays from the point of view of the actor or

---

[1] www.rowntreesociety.org.uk/joseph-rowntree-theatre/. Accessed 27 June 2017.

producer. It is a practical course in the kind of examination of a play which any actor should go through before proceeding to rehearsals on the stage. (1935: 15)

This university course was popular, and its subsidy by Rowntree's management represents their commitment to offering their workers educational opportunities that were both sociable and enjoyable. An article in the same issue of C.W.M., Seebohm Rowntree is reported to have commented on the reduction of working hours from fifty-four hours a week to forty-four, a move that allowed for 'the growing time of the human spirit' (1935: 6).

Enthusiasm for amateur theatre amongst factory workers was not confined to the philanthropic environment of the model villages. It was not unusual for most local people to be employed in one factory, coal mine or textiles mill throughout the industrial era and well into the twentieth century. As a direct consequence, social activities were necessarily tied up with workplace relations and time for amateur theatre rehearsals and performances was managed according to the working patterns of the major local employer. This placed amateur activity at the centre of community life. By 1945, amateur arts and local leisure activities were used to project an idealised image of community harmony; a British Council Education film about a textile town in the North of England promotes a picture of a community held together by happy nuclear families who work and play together.[2] *We of the West Riding* (1945) was written by the novelist Phyllis Bentley who was at the time president of the amateur company the Halifax Thespians. It tells the story of the Sykes family, largely played by members of the Halifax Thespians, and shows members of the family at work in the woollen mill, each taking responsibility for different stages in the production process—weaving, mending, pressing and packing worsted cloth to send to destinations overseas. Domestic labour was also defined by the factory, and women were depicted dutifully scrubbing clothes and doorsteps blackened by soot from the mill's chimneys. Members of the fictional Sykes family are shown happily involved in football clubs, brass bands, amateur dramatics, chapel choirs and cycling clubs where young people unite in song as they cycle across picturesque moorland. One scene shows

[2] http://www.anglotopia.net/british-history/video-west-riding-fascinating-look-life-yorkshire-1945. Accessed 12 May 2016.

a staged rehearsal and performance of *Jane Eyre,* which is particularly intriguing, not least because Phyllis Bentley was a notable Bronte biographer. The young woman playing Jane has clearly been encouraged to take elocution lessons to lose her Yorkshire accent, performing in stilted received pronunciation. This may have met the requirements of her role, but it also implies that participating in amateur theatre brings social mobility. The commentary defines amateur performance in terms of its localism: 'We're fairly typical of the West Riding... we'd all rather stand up and do a thing ourselves than pay to watch others.' The film ends with a rousing performance of Handel's Halleluiah Chorus which, we are told, 'is us through and through. Music we understand'. The message is clear: working for one local employer and participating in multiple amateur activities unites families and gives communities a sense of identity.

This promotional film implies that, when time is properly managed, both work and play contribute to social harmony. Perhaps this vision of community cohesion most closely resembles Adorno's sceptical analysis of free time as not 'freedom proper' but disciplined by capitalism (1991: 170). Bleached of its radical politics, this nostalgic vision of life in a textile town harnesses amateur creativity, not to emancipation nor extended educational opportunities, but to a highly constructed and conservative idea of working-class life in the austere years that followed World War Two. Yet it is easy to forget that working-class culture was neither widely acknowledged nor valued at the time; this is also the world described by the Left-wing critic Richard Hoggart, whose ground-breaking book *The Uses of Literacy* (1957) captured the neighbourliness of close-knit northern working-class communities during the same period. Hoggart's sociological account may be conventional, local, resistant to change and patriarchal, but it also places value on mundane activities of everyday existence. Seen in its historical context, the celebration of working-class life in the British Council film is perhaps less conservative than it appears today. Amateur participation in a range of activities (theatrical, sporting, musical) was portrayed as one of the distinct and special attributes of community life, and one that was active and socially engaged.

By the mid-twentieth century working patterns were changing cultural life, as Hoggart observed, and a more mobile society brought consequences for the amateur theatre. Rowntree's former Chocolate Works closed in 2005 following a take-over from Kraft, an American multinational company who had also bought Cadbury in 2010. Kraft moved confectionary production away from York in 2004, setting up factories in

Belgium, Sweden, Poland and Slovakia.[3] The social values of the early philanthropists were finally lost when Kraft-owned Cadbury dispensed with its free trade commitment in 2016. I was intrigued by the link between the early Garden Cities, university education and The Rowntree Players, and I set off for York to attend a heritage open day at the theatre. The freehold was at the time owned by York St John University, and the theatre has since been bought by the Board in 2017. Arriving at the theatre, it was clear that change was in the air, and this was reflected in the range of local people I met at Rowntree Theatre:

> There was a sense of local pride in the theatre, and in its communitarian history. I met local people who had heard stories of factory girls who would watch part of a film in their lunch hours, returning each day until they had seen the whole film. Others recounted the educational opportunities brought by the theatre, and described how it had served as a hub that raised the aspirations of factory workers. I was taken to see the immense cyclorama, the rig and backstage, each demonstrated by an expert amateur theatre technician. (Helen's Research Diary, 27 September 2016)

At the time of my visit, the old factory had been sold to property developers, and it now houses The Chocolate Works Care Village, a new residential centre for older adults and those living with dementia, as well as newly constructed family homes. Perhaps some of its residents will breathe new life into the theatre, and it will respond positively to the cultural changes of the twenty-first century.

AMATEUR THEATRE AND A JOBS-FOR-LIFE ECONOMY

One of the arguments in this chapter is that amateur theatre has been sustained by patterns of labour, and a relationship between employers and amateur theatre continued well into the second half of the twentieth century. In a jobs-for-life economy, Sports and Recreation Clubs subsidised by management were a regular feature of factory life, creating the sociable environment in which amateur theatre might flourish. As educational opportunities and living conditions improved following the 1944 Education Act and the National Health Service Act in 1946, the motives

---

[3] http://www.independent.co.uk/voices/cadbury-drops-fairtrade-scandal-business-i-watched-ethical-decline-from-inside-a7451906.html. Accessed 31 Dec 2017.

for supporting amateur activities in the workforce changed. Rather than ameliorating conditions for the urban poor, the focus of attention was on creating a loyal and contented labour force at all levels of the pay scale. In this section, I will explore the relationship between amateur theatre and the newly professionalised workplaces in the twentieth century.

The Edwardian era had seen the emergence of a new class of white-collar workers which, as Jonathan Rose suggests, were 'the political base of the national efficiency movement' (1986: 118). The Edwardians championed efficiency—a legacy of colonialism—and this created new kinds of employment for 'brain workers'. The professionalisation of teachers, bankers, engineers and so on and an expanded civic service grew alongside establishment occupations of law and medicine. Amateur theatre companies spread quickly in these new white-collar professions; Barclays Dramatic Society started in 1889 (now the Spread Eagle Players, invoking the bank's logo), for example, Sheffield Teachers Operatic Society (STOS) was established in 1901, and the Stock Exchange Dramatic and Operatic Society (Sedos) was founded in 1905 by senior members of the Stock Exchange. All three societies continue to thrive, although in common with many other workplace companies their ties with their respective professions have been loosened, although the Spread Eagle Players still acknowledge some financial support from Barclay's Bank and Sedos draws members from 'investment banks, law firms, brokers, the Exchanges and many other financial and city based firms'.[4] Sedos maintains a good reputation for their high production values, with a strong company of mainly young, university educated professionals. Perhaps the current RBS Theatre Company has the longest sustained history of engagement with the financial sector, their changing company name evidence of successive banking take-overs. Established in 1876 as The London and Westminster Amateurs, it became The Westminster Bank Dramatic and Operatic Society after the First World War and renamed The NatWest Theatre in the 1970s following a merger between the Westminster and National Provincial banks. Its current title, RBS Theatre Company, came about in 2003 as a result of NatWest's take-over by the Royal Bank of Scotland Group in 2000. It is no longer financially supported by the bank and has struggled financially, but its mission remains to provide 'all RBS Group staff, and their friends and family, with the opportunity to put

---

[4] https://sedos.co.uk/aboutus/index.htm. Accessed 14 June 2018.

on a production'.[5] It is no coincidence that many amateur theatre companies founded by white-collar workers tend to be located in cities; work continues to provide a focus for an urban social life, particularly if hours are long, and time spent commuting can restrict opportunities for place-based amateur activities near home.

Although each amateur theatre company established in the workplace has its own history, their relationships with changing employment allows for some common strands to be identified. One example is the town of Stevenage, which was the first New Town built as part of the 1944 Abercrombie Plan in 1946. It attracted a range of aeronautical and electronic industries within the first few years, capitalising on what Prime Minister Harold Wilson described as the 'white heat' of new technologies. As Anthony Alexander noted in his book, *Britain's New Towns: Garden Cities to Sustainable Communities*, the infrastructure of early Stevenage, together with the influx of a new class of professionals in high-tech factories, provided the conditions in which amateur theatre flourished (2009: 102). My father, Harvey Nicholson, was amongst the young professionals who took up employment in the electronics industry and the family relocated from Manchester in early 1959. There were few opportunities for social activity in the newly-built town, but he joined Stevenage's Lytton Players, an amateur theatre company that had been established in 1948. The family story is that he auditioned for an acting part, but was turned down because he had such an appalling singing voice. But he enjoyed theatre, and the director at the time suggested that might use his professional expertise as an electrical engineer in the lighting team. He relished the camaraderie of the lighting box, and particularly liked the mischievous power it gave him and his fellow technicians in their 1963 production of *The Tempest*. Designing complex lighting and sound effects for the opening scene was a creative challenge, and he and his fellow operators enjoyed the potential for playing tricks on the actors by including an unexpected thunder clap or flash of lightning. Long after he had given up amateur theatre, he would pay close attention to lighting design in professional productions he saw; creative experiences as amateurs often provides insights into the process of theatre-making that enhances their appreciation of professional theatre. Although this is not illustrative of company-supported leisure activities, it does mark a recurring trend in amateur

[5] www.rbstheatrecompany.co.uk. Accessed 12 Dec 2017.

theatre in which members' professional expertise benefits amateur productions. In my only performance in amateur theatre (playing Alice for
the Parkside Players in Ampthill when I was sixteen) my make-up was
expertly applied by the local dentist whose knowledge of the bone structure of the face informed his work. This remains the case today, particularly in backstage and committee work where, for example, professional
accountants can be found as treasurers, carpenters build sets and sound
engineers create the production's sound design. Rob Wallace at The Barn
Theatre in Welwyn Garden City described how his professional work as a
sound engineer informs his contribution to sound design, where he finds
creative satisfaction as he is 'free to experiment',[6] and illustrates how professional expertise and amateur creativity are often enmeshed.

The Barn Theatre remains indebted to young professionals employed
in high-tech factories in the 1960s and 1970s, many of whom have sustained a long-term commitment to the theatre. The expansion of Welwyn
in the post-war era provided new opportunities for high-tech industries of
the day, including Imperial Chemical Industries (ICI). ICI had been
established in Welwyn Garden City in 1938, but took full advantage of the
expanded post-war market for plastics and the expansion of Welwyn where
it located its UK headquarters. By the 1960s around 4000 people worked
on the sixty-five acre site, and in the 1960s and 1970s ICI not only
employed many local people on its production lines, it also attracted creative and talented professionals to work in Welwyn's plastics industry. Not
unusually for the day, ICI sponsored charitable work in the local community as well as supporting cultural, sporting and social activities for their
employees and their families. The ICI Recreation Club had its own amateur dramatic society, and amateur theatre took its place alongside other
activities such as golf, football and children's parties. In 1976 the ICI
newspaper, *Plastic News*, reviewed the drama society's production of
Hobson's Choice alongside news about swimming for the disabled and
Duke of Edinburgh Awards. ICI did not provide a theatre building for its
employees, and the Dramatic Society habitually used The Barn Theatre for
their performances, eventually merging into one company when ICI left
Welwyn in 1982. Heather Gill, a retired primary school teacher and now
archivist at The Barn, described how ICI was part of the social life of
young professionals in the town in the 1970s. She recalled that some ICI

---

[6] Interview Helen Nicholson with Rob Wallace, Hitchin. 15 May 2015.

employees were offered housing locally as their jobs involved frequent spells abroad, and they quickly became known as 'party houses'. ICI were keen to support their talented workforce, and providing housing and social activities were part of their retention policy. Heather's husband was at the time a member of ICI Dramatic Society, but she became a member of The Barn in her own right 'because you couldn't buy a drink at the bar if you weren't a member'.[7]

For some factory employees and their families, what had started as a lively social activity turned into a life-long interest in amateur theatre. Many long-standing members of The Barn Theatre were members of the ICI Dramatic Society, starting their involvement in the theatre in the 1970s. Derek Palmer, for example, took the role of Gerald Forbes in Priestley's *When We Are Married* at The Barn in 1970, adding set design, lighting and sound to his repertoire as an actor in subsequent decades. Along with many of his contemporaries, now retired, Derek continues to be involved in The Barn and is also Chairman of the National Drama Festivals Association. Norman Merry and Robert Gill were both members of the ICI Dramatic Society and remain an important part of The Barn's set-building team, with Robert Gill also serving on the National Executive of the Little Theatre Guild. Denise Duffy, now one of The Barn's archivists, described the long tradition of amateur theatre in Welwyn's factories, captured in my research diary.

> Denise had brought a signed photograph of Flora Robson, which had been given to her father. It was beautifully preserved, the signature clear and fresh. She told me that Flora Robson had worked in the Shredded Wheat Factory, a huge employer in the area from its opening in 1926. Flora Robson was employed in the personnel department at the company in 1927, and one of her roles was to encourage the dramatic society, which Denise told me, rehearsed in the dining hall. Robson quickly became active in Welwyn's amateur theatre culture, an interest that she maintained long after gaining success as a professional actor. After I had left The Barn, I drove round Welwyn to find The Shredded Wheat factory, an impressive design by architect Louis de Soissons. The listed building, owned by supermarket giant Tesco, looked forlorn and semi-derelict, a beautiful building without a purpose. (Helen's Research Diary, 4 March 2015)

---

[7] Interview Heather Gill with Helen Nicholson, The Barn Theatre, Welwyn Garden City. 17 June 2016.

Denise Duffy also remembered amateur theatre at Murphy Radio, another major employer in Welwyn. As a child, she recalled performing as the 'Murphollies' in the early 1950s, dressed in a turquoise outfit trimmed with cotton wool mock fur. She and her sisters rehearsed in the canteen and toured the Skaters waltz and other numbers around hospitals in the town.[8] Later, she followed her appearance as a child performer at Murphy Radio by painting sets for the ICI Dramatic Society. Robert Gill's involvement in The Barn began in 1971 when he offered to help the ICI Dramatic Society backstage, and he recalls that they would work until the early hours building sets at The Barn and go to work with very little sleep.

In the past, loyalty to one theatre perhaps mirrored loyalty to one employer, which was often the case in an industrial economy. Whether this shift reflects a wider social change from a jobs-for-life economy to more flexible and precarious employment patterns is unclear. By 2015 Robert Gill had observed a culture change in younger members' attitudes towards company membership, many of whom had drifted away from long-term commitment to one amateur theatre company:

> One thing which is very clear in the Barn these days, didn't use to be, but it is now – actors will come and act, and then when they've finished acting in our play, they'll go off somewhere else and act somewhere else. They don't hide that fact. They just go and do it. It's because they want to act. Whereas backstage people and the general support staff, they tend to stay. They only ever do stuff at The Barn. I think this is probably a common thing, wherever you go.[9]

With the demise of manufacturing industry, few factory-based amateur theatre companies survive intact, with exceptions being The Billingham Players that first formed as part of the ICI social club in Stockton-on-Tees and The Port Sunlight Players that still performs in the model village on the Wirral. Some children who joined their parents' companies in factories as children were inspired to continue in adult life; Denise Tricker, for example, began performing as a child at the Kodak Factory near London and is now a leading member of the British Airways Cabin Crew Entertainment Society (BACCES), playing the principal boy in the 2016

---

[8] Interview Denise Duffy with Helen Nicholson, The Barn Theatre, 28 April 2015.
[9] Robert Gill in conversation with John Davey, recorded at The Questors. 16 June 2015.

pantomime. In Worcester, the closure of the Kay's famous mail-order company in 2007 did not see the demise of Kays Theatre Group, who continue their unbroken tradition of performing an annual pantomime since 1954, now staged at the Worcester Swan Theatre. Whilst welcoming this amateur theatre company onto the professional stage, the artistic director of the Worcester Swan Chris Jaeger has observed that the pantomime attracts an increasingly elderly audience.[10] He believes that the pantomime is still associated with Kays as an employer, and predicts its demise as memories of the company it served begin to fade. Some cultural commentators, such as Zygmunt Bauman or Richard Sennett, might consider this lack of loyalty to be symptomatic of a socially damaging 'looseness of attachment' (Bauman 2005: 5) or as the weaker ties associated with new capitalism that Sennett regards as corrosive (1998).

Employers motivated by a mix of self-interest and philanthropy who hoped to maintain a long-term workforce are now thin on the ground, along with the paternalistic idea that they might create a sense of community for their employees and their families by providing satisfying social activities. This is still in evidence in The John Lewis Partnership Dramatic Society, which was founded in response to employee interest in the 1920s. Enthusiasm for amateur theatre spread across the partnership, with one-act play competitions between different department stores and branches of Waitrose popular in the 1960s and 1970s. Both Peter Jones in Sloane Square and John Lewis in Oxford Street had their own in-store theatres for use of partners, and although they no longer exist, The John Lewis Partnership Dramatic Society still performs annually at the Royal Academy of Dramatic Arts (RADA) and stages an open-air production at Odney in the summer, the private club for partners by the river Thames in Cookham. Although more flexible working hours introduced to suit longer opening hours for shoppers has curtailed time for rehearsal, aspects of the philanthropic tradition are still maintained. John Lewis offers significant loyalty benefits for its staff, including subsidised training, cheap holidays and heavily discounted theatre tickets. Other work-based theatre companies have been less fortunate. The London Transport Musical and Dramatic Society and the London Transport Players brought together amateur theatre enthusiasts from across the transport network, regularly playing at

[10] Interview of Erin Walcon with Chris Jaeger, Swan Theatre Worcester, 9 November 2014.

London's La Scala Theatre in the 1950s with an audience capacity of over 1000 seats. Neither company remains in operation. Increased privatisation, a precarious job market and a culture of twenty-four-hour work has significantly decreased time for amateur theatre, and employers' support for their own amateur theatre companies has waned. As Heather Gill commented wryly, 'it wouldn't happen in Tesco's'.

GIVING TIME: BRITISH AIRWAYS CABIN CREW ENTERTAINMENT SOCIETY

In twenty-first century service economies, the idea that homogenous workplace communities are constructed through activities developed in shared free time is diminishing. The shift from jobs-for-life industrial economies with their stable rhythms and routines to more flexible working patterns has not only changed the nature of the work that people do, it also means that life is fragmented and sometimes unpredictable producing, as Sharma points out, an 'uneven cultural politics of time... and inequitable temporal relations' (2014: 7). This has very practical consequences for amateur theatre, as a regular time commitment to attend rehearsals in local companies may be difficult if working patterns are no longer regulated by the communal clock.

Amateur theatre companies where employees share similar working conditions is one response to this conundrum, and the example I have chosen that illuminates the relationship between time and work in the service economy is the BACCES. BACCES grew spontaneously out of a highly successful and much publicised review staged by cabin crew in Chiswick Town Hall in 1970, and has been in existence since 1971. Its membership is confined to current or former British Airways Cabin Crew, many of whom are, of course, still flying and whose time off is therefore precious. Cabin crew have a very particular relationship with time; they regularly travel across time zones, affecting body clocks and interrupting sleep patterns. Airport delays and flight-times mean that working hours, and time off, can be unpredictable. Rehearsals accommodate cabin crews' lifestyles, and each winter BACCES stage a pantomime in a theatre within easy travelling distance to Heathrow Airport, playing not only to British Airways staff, but also attracting large and loyal audiences from the wider public. It is testament to the high production values of their show that BACCES play in professional theatre venues and, importantly for the company, box office sales make significant money for charity. Giving time to make high quality, family entertainment is both personally satisfying and generous, and their charitable work is part of the ethos of the company.

Members of BACCES are mindful that their work represents British Airways as a company and a national brand, and part of their commitment to high-quality production values is related to British Airway's reputation for high-quality customer service. Despite a history of poor industrial relations there is strong staff loyalty to British Airways amongst the company, with many cast members employed as cabin crew for long time (former president and cast member David Bowditch retired in 2017 after forty-eight years of flying). Dee Bull, one of the founder members of BACCES, was part of an elite and glamorous team of British Overseas Airways Corporation (BOAC) and British European Airways (BEA) air 'steward-esses' in the 1960s, where she recalls that most of the passengers were business men, sometimes travelling to parts of the world such as the former USSR that were inaccessible to other travellers. Dee Bull and Diane Goatcher, another long-standing BACCES member and choreographer, describe their continuing pride in the British Airways brand; they value the opportunity BACCES provides to stay in touch with the airline after their enforced early retirement at fifty-five years old.

> For Dee and I, we had to retire at 55 before the law changed which seemed very young. I would not have stopped flying, and it was a big shock. But because I was part of the entertainment society, that kept me with one foot in the door of British Airways, a place that I had spent 33 years, where I had met my husband and did a job I loved.[11]

Dee Bull and Diane Goatcher carry the cultural memory of the relationship between British Airways and BACCES, remembering times when BACCES' high profile and celebrity endorsement (Cliff Richard was a regular audience member in the 1970s) was regarded by British Airways Board members as very good publicity for the firm. From the 1970s to the turn of the millennium, management offered practical support to BACCES by arranging rosters to accommodate performances and providing rehearsal space and storage for costumes near Heathrow. This in-kind assistance was dramatically curtailed after 9/11 when a downturn in

---

[11] Interview with Helen Nicholson and Diane Goatcher, 12 July 2016.

passenger numbers led to cabin crew redundancies, and it was deemed no longer acceptable to offer generous arrangements for a pantomime in this economic climate. Notwithstanding the challenges they have faced as the culture of airline employment changed, BACCES members value the fact that it is the only society connected to British Airways that is officially permitted to carry its name.

I had become enchanted by the BACCES pantomime in 2014 when I sat at the back of a large auditorium to watch *Jack and the Beanstalk*. Truth to tell I was only going to stay for the first half; seeing panto on your own is a slightly odd experience, and I had seen the Admirals' Players panto the night before. But I was transfixed by the performance, and by Autumn 2015, I had secured agreement to attend rehearsals for their production of *Sleeping Beauty*, which was performed at Watford Palace Theatre in January 2016. Observing the rehearsal process not only illuminated their working methods as theatre-makers, it also demonstrated how their work as cabin crew affects their whole lifestyle and approach to life.

> The first time I attend a rehearsal in Waterside, and I managed to negotiate security at British Airways Head Office. We're in a large lecture theatre, and Jane as director is very much in change. Small groups of people have spilled out into the foyers to rehearse their scenes or perfect their dance steps. It's early in the process, and although there is an atmosphere of concentration it feels relaxed, and I am warmly welcomed. It is noticeable that many people are taking time to talk to me, to ask me what I am doing and share stories and memories. Dee has brought her photograph albums capturing over forty years of her involvement in BACCES, and invites me to take them home to read in more depth. I am touched by her generosity – these are Dee's precious memories, and she and I have never met before. (Helen's Research Diary, 11 October 2015)

This spirit of openness continued at each rehearsal, where the company's generosity to each other—and me—was palpable. Hospitality seemed deeply engrained in their social interaction, sharing food, making drinks for each other and, on one occasion in a particularly cold room, I was offered someone's warm jumper to wear. In his book *The Managed Heart*, Arlie Russell Hochschild argued that flight attendants are trained to empathise with passengers, and that their work involves a form of emotional labour that he calls 'deep acting' (2002: 111). Invoking Stanislavski, Hochschild suggests that everyday deep acting is acting 'as if', and using a 'trained imagination' to relate to others. Such feelings can be

commercialised, he suggests, and uses the example of Delta's flight attendants to argue that this ability to connect with passengers is a requirement
of airline management. Terry Hunt, BACCES script writer and lead author
of *Sleeping Beauty*, acknowledged that empathetic performance is part of
the job, describing their 'plastic smiles' at the end of a long-haul flight. In
part, the BACCES's hospitality was engrained habit; cast member Collette
Lucas, deprived of flying due to a shoulder injury, described with self-
deprecating humour that her friends recognised how much she was missing her work in the air because she kept pressing them to have more tea,
coffee and drinks whenever they came to her home. Terry Hunt observed
the similarities between their work as crew and rehearsals:

> It's almost like a continuation of our jobs in many respects, in our job you
> can work with someone and then not see them again for two or three years,
> and you pick up a relationship where you left off. That applies to both flying
> and the show that we do.[12]

There are points of connection between the emotional labour of life as
member of a cabin crew, the deep and lasting friendships made through
BACCES, and the cast's ability to connect with their audiences. There are
no longer stable crews on board flights, and this means that the job can be
lonely. Terry articulates the experience clearly:

> Every day at work you walk into a briefing and not know a soul. And every
> day you go to work you have that. So to be able to walk into a rehearsal
> room and see people that you know and you really get on with… we've had
> some fantastic friendships that have grown throughout the society. It's great
> having a party on stage, but you have to invite people to join you and that's
> what our cast are really good at.

There is a self-conscious awareness of how the demands of the job,
their training and their life as BACCES performers intermesh. Following
Hochschild, one reading would be that the gift-relationship offered by a
cabin crew is one way, and their emotional labour is sold to the commercial advantage of the airline. But participating in BACCES pantomimes, as
cast members repeatedly describe, offers an opportunity to do something

---

[12] Terry Hunt, in conversation with Helen Nicholson and other company members, 5 July
2016. All other quotations are taken from this event.

socially and emotionally significant. *Sleeping Beauty* director Jane Bowditch elegantly summarised this sentiment as 'feeling valued as people, and sharing with each other, audiences and charities something of what really matters in life: friendship, fun and care for others'.[13]

There are, of course, significant practical difficulties of rehearsing a pantomime when cast members are regularly undertaking long-haul flights and suitable places to rehearse are hard to find. Despite the obvious friendliness and sociability of the cast, rehearsals are characterised by focus on the job-in-hand, spending little time in gregarious banter or repartee. The twice-weekly rehearsals often run quite late, with cast members arriving directly from their shifts.

> It is nearly 11pm on a Monday evening in December, and I am sitting in a large room in a cold office block not far from Heathrow airport. I have been watching a rehearsal of *Sleeping Beauty* for over three hours, and my note book is getting full. On the back of my chair there is a white shirt and a smart BA uniform jacket with a name badge. Some of the cast have come straight from long haul flights, and although they are looking seriously tired, they are still working on their dance routine. Not for the first time, I wonder how they find the time and energy for rehearsals. (Helen's Research Diary, 5 December 2016)

The complexity of British Airways rosters means that it is rare for the entire cast to be assembled until the dress rehearsal, but there is an aesthetic beauty in watching dancers work on the choreography with their arms held out for their invisible partners. Cast members read in for each other, and adapt to absent actors in ways that other amateur theatre companies would be unlikely to accept. They also recount snatched rehearsals in hotel rooms and on the beach when on stopovers, and occasionally practising steps or learning lines in the aircraft's galley. There are, however, advantages to global travel; actor and costume-maker Steven Warner describes how he sources beautiful and inexpensive fabric for their elaborate head-dresses and costumes from trips to India and other parts of Asia.

The performance itself might be seen as an unashamed example of Glenn Adamson's 'preposterous excess' that defines the best pantomimes,

---

[13] Jane Bowditch in conversation with Helen Nicholson and other company members, 5 July 2016.

and the production values are extremely high. On closer inspection, however, there is also careful management and recycling of resources that ensures a generous donation to local charities. In one scene, the men wear their British Airways uniform trousers trimmed with stripes of sparkling ribbon and in another a much-loved and reused tree stump makes its annual appearance (affectionately named Mr. Stumpy by the cast). The script, always written by BACCES members, references their work as cabin crew, drawing gentle humour with in-jokes about pilots and British Airways' management that is appreciated by cabin crew in the audience. There is always a 'uniform number' in which the cast appear in full British Airways uniform, reminding the audience that they are both cabin crew and—for this moment—performers on stage. This aesthetic doubleness underlines their dual roles, and references to their in-flight work routines in performance allow the audience to witness a playful dialogue between the imaginary world of the play and their working lives. In the opening scene of *Sleeping Beauty*, for example, uniformed cabin crew pulled suitcases on wheels across the stage as the castle 'in the land of Nod' came to life behind them. In *Jack and the Beanstalk* (2014), the audience were welcomed aboard 'this British Airways flight to Cloudland' before their uniform number (in this case, a rendition of Pharrell Williams' *Happy*) at the end of which some of the cast exited using in-flight drinks trolleys as scooters. Work identities are foregrounded, and in lieu of the customary biographies in the programme for *Sleeping Beauty*, the cast give their tips for sleeping and beauty as 'two subjects very close to the hearts of cabin crew' (Programme notes, 2016). The invitation of the whole show is joyful, requiring not only the usual suspension of disbelief associated with the conventions and confections of pantomime, but also a playful awareness of the cast as working people who might resume service for British Airways the next day. In other words, once seen it is hard to look at cabin crew on flights in the same light again, whether or not they were actually members of the cast.

Reflecting on the relationship between their work as cabin crew and performers, BACCES members recognise that they have a practised ability to respond to different atmospheres and solve problems quickly. Jane Bowditch commented that, if things go wrong in performance, the cast will be able to deal with the unexpected efficiently and without people noticing. 'That's part of what we have to do in the air,' she observed. 'if you forget something, if things break down or you left something at the airport you can't just go back for it or phone someone up to fix it. You

Fig. 5.1 BACCES cast performing the 'uniform number' in *Sleeping Beauty*, Watford Palace Theatre, January 2016. (By kind permission of photographer, Amelia Brandao)

just have to find a way round it, and hopefully without passengers realising.'[14] For those who work in the service industries, for whom labour is immaterial and there is no obvious product, there is often particular satisfaction in making theatre, whether this is designing a set, making costumes or performing. Furthermore, as Collette Lucas describes, being visible and being heard on stage offers a welcome contrast to a work environment which requires unformed discipline:

> I love flying and being cabin crew is an amazing experience. But you are also a bit samey – we all look alike and there's not a lot of scope for being individuals when we're actually at work. Being in BACCES gives me the chance to be noticed and seen differently. It's a time to be free.[15]

---

[14] Conversation Jane Bowditch with Helen Nicholson and other company members, 5 July 2016. All other quotations are taken from this event.

[15] Collette Lucas, in conversation with Helen Nicholson and other company members, Egham. 5 July 2016.

Collette's re-description of 'free' time as an affective quality recognises the different temporal registers of her life, where her identity as a performer and cabin crew are not separate, but enmeshed and mutually embedded. For Terry Hunt, the ability to make things happen on stage has a deeper emotional significance. In conversation with cast members, he recalled a memorable experience when he had designed his first set as a teenager:

> I don't know how it came about, but just before the house opened I suggested to the director that the house tabs were left closed. I was self-conscious, but the director said, 'No, if that's what you want, we'll do it'. There was a flurry of activity as lighting cues were changed. But suddenly what I thought, how I felt, mattered. Someone was prepared to listen. That's something I won't forget.[16]

In common with other members of BACCES, Terry Hunt and Collette Lucas are affectively engaged in their work as crew and as performer and director. Both are integral to the narrative of life.

BACCES is a generous company, and its affective qualities are contagious. This is evident on stage, but there are other, less visible gift-relationships that have endured. Each year up to fifty members of the London Symphony Orchestra give their time at the weekend to record the backing tracks for the show. Bobbie Field, the professional Musical Director and conductor is joined by professional lighting designer Jonathan Haynes, who started his interest in lighting as a career when he accompanied his cabin crew mother to rehearsals as a teenager. The longevity of these relationships, and the time that is given freely, is part of the gift economy that supports BACCES in producing such high-quality work. But, in common with other industries, changed employment structures for new British Airways cabin crew are threatening BACCES' future. Mixed fleet contracts for crew at Heathrow airport, unlike previous contractual arrangements where crew worked either short or long flights, allow little time for other activities and recruiting new BACCES members has proved difficult as a result. Cast members are also expected to use annual leave for the week of the performance, which means that

---

[16] Terry Hunt, in conversation with Helen Nicholson and other company members, Egham. 5 July 2016.

Fig. 5.2   Collette Lucas
in *Sleeping Beauty*,
Watford Palace Theatre
2016. (By kind
permission
photographer, Amelia
Brandao)

participating costs them money. For those who relish their annual involvement in the BACCES pantomime, this potential loss is personally felt, but
it did not serve as a barrier to participation in 2017, where many new
members were welcomed. The significance of performing is perhaps best
summed up by long-term BACCES choreographer Diane Goatcher and
retired cabin crew, who says: 'each year I can dream'.[17]

---

[17] Diane Goatcher, in conversation with Helen Nicholson, Egham. 12 July 2016.

DIFFERENTIAL TIME, LIVED TIME AND CHANGING PATTERNS OF LABOUR

The annual rhythm of amateur theatre defines lives, and for those with a long-term commitment to amateur theatre, working lives are organised around the calendar of performances. Changing work patterns are redefining relationships with time, however, and social attitudes with which this is accompanied are influencing amateur theatre. For a generation that is accustomed to a culture of career mobilities, short-term contracts and self-employment, life-long membership of one amateur theatre company may seem similarly unfamiliar or unappealing. This is incomprehensible to some people who have remained involved in one company for much of their lives, perhaps taking on the burden of committee work in retirement, who regard moving between companies as lack of loyalty or a self-centred quest on the part of younger performers to seek the best roles. But it is part of a wider culture shift, and one that is unlikely to diminish. Perhaps this illustrates what Sharma describes as a 'larger biopolitical economy of time' in which life is increasingly structured and managed according to relationships with time (2014: 16–17).

Many cultural commentators have observed that the twenty-first century is eroding distinctions between work and leisure time, and this is particularly evident in the knowledge industries and the creative economy. This is not always unwelcome or perceived as undesirable; in their study of people with professional interests in the arts James Whiting and Kevin Hannam found that many pursued creative activities in similar or related mediums outside work, and usually for pleasure rather than as a route for employment. This is, as I have observed, not a new phenomenon in amateur theatre, where many members regularly use their professional expertise to build sets, compile accounts or make costumes. Whiting and Hannam make the case that some creative activities blur distinctions between work and leisure time and, for the participants in their research, this acts as a marker of identity:

> The performance of creative leisure also becomes a point of 'distinction' and group identity formation for the respondents in this research. (2015: 381)

Less optimistically, in her book *Work's Intimacy* Melissa Gregg observes that 'part-time precarity' has become a feature of the contemporary job market, particularly in the knowledge industries and the creative economy.

She suggests that freelance work involves 'living with constant uncertainty' about hours worked and levels of pay (2011: 154). Some members of amateur companies are professionally trained as actors, and find creative satisfaction in taking part without living the precarious life of a professional actor. Some work in creative jobs as drama teachers, musicians or as sound engineers for example, and those with salaried employment as dentists, nurses and accountants have more or less regular hours, but there are also many people who are not freelance creatives but self-employed in different trades, as electricians, plumbers, decorators and carpenters. Each of these roles and occupations has a different relationship to time, and to how time is differentiated.

Changing patterns of employment are affecting amateur theatre, and the shift from a working life based on routine and company loyalty to more flexible and precarious forms of labour is redefining social attitudes towards how time is spent. For many young people today, the idea that their entire working lives will be spent working for one employer in one place would be regarded as restrictive and even claustrophobic. Changing work patterns are impacting on amateur theatre, and this is one example of the challenges that face amateur theatre-makers as they embrace the twenty-first century. Writing at the end of the twentieth century, Sennett comments in pessimistic terms about the emotional impact of flexible and unstable employment patterns and laments the loss of 'bonds of trust and commitment' that he associates with jobs-for-life economies:

> The condition of time in the new capitalism have created a conflict between character and experience, the experience of disjointed time threatening the ability of people to form their characters into sustained narratives. (1998: 31)

Amateur companies require a loyal membership, particularly for the less glamorous jobs such as treasurer or box office, and some companies are closing because they are unable to find new people to fulfil these roles. But there is reason to be more optimistic; people are still seeking out opportunities to participate in amateur theatre and there is evidence that fickle actors turn into the company faithful over time (Walcon and Nicholson 2017). Perhaps amateur theatre is one place where such narrative stability might be found, however changing work patterns are understood, it is expected that amateur theatre will need to evolve if it is to thrive.

The central argument in this chapter is that amateur theatre reflects the ways in which time is experienced, and draws on Sharma's argument that time is always experienced in multiple ways, and in relation to others, as 'layers of temporal inter-dependence' (2014:148). Sharma describes this as 'differential time', in which there is an uneven political economy in that some people's time is regarded as more valued and valuable than others. Taking part in amateur theatre does not, of course, involve only those who are employed or go out to work, and includes those who are retirees, unemployed and those in caring roles for whom theatre-making can make a difference to feelings of self-worth. The idea of differential time challenges the idea that time is experienced autonomously, and rather than thinking about time as something to be managed to create more free time, Sharma aims to 'free time from this fixation' (2014: 150). Finding time for amateur theatre is often tied to feelings of self-confidence, where 'doing something for myself' also involves creating time for others.

REFERENCES

Adamson, Glenn. 2007. *Thinking Through Craft*. London: Berg Publishers.

Adorno, T.W. 1991. Free Time. In *The Culture Industry: Selected Essays on Mass Culture*, ed. The Culture, 162–170. London: Routledge [1969].

Arendt, Hannah. 1989. *The Human Condition*. Chicago/London: The University of Chicago Press [1958].

Bauman, Zigmunt. 2003. *Liquid Love: On the Frailty of Human Bonds*. Cambridge: Polity Press.

———. 2005. *Liquid Life*. Cambridge: Polity Press.

Cocoa Works Magazine. 1935. York: Rowntree.

Gregg, Melissa. 2011. *Work's Intimacy*. London: Polity Press.

Hawley, Judith. 2012. What Signifies a Theatre?': Private Theatricals and Amateur Dramatics in Britain and Abroad. Conference Paper, University of Notre Dame in London, July 7.

Hochschild, Arlie Russell. 2002. *The Managed Heart: Commercialization of Human Feeling*. Berkeley: University of California Press.

Hoggart, Richard. 1976. *The Uses of Literacy*. London: Pelican Books [1957].

Hughes, Jenny. 2016. A Pre-history of Applied Theatre: Work, House, Perform. In *Critical Perspectives on Applied Theatre*, ed. Jenny Hughes and Helen Nicholson, 40–60. Cambridge: Cambridge University Press.

Knott, Stephen. 2015. *Amateur Craft: History and Theory*. London: Bloomsbury.

Marx, Karl. 2007. *Capital: A Critique of Political Economy: The Process of Capitalist Production, Volume 1 Part 11*. New York: Cosimo Classics [1867].

Ridout, Nicholas. 2013. *Passionate Amateurs: Theatre, Communism, and Love.* Ann Arbor: University of Michigan Press.

Rose, Jonathan. 1986. *The Edwardian Temperament 1895–1919.* Ohio: Ohio University Press.

Rowntree, Seebohm. 1901. *Poverty: A Study of Town Life.* London: Macmillan Publishers.

Sennett, Richard. 1998. *The Corrosion of Character: The Personal Consequences of Work in the New Capitalism.* New York: Norton Books.

———. 2008. *The Craftsman.* London: Penguin Books.

Sharma, Sarah. 2014. *In the Meantime: Temporality and Cultural Politics.* London: Duke University Press.

Stebbins, Robert A. 1979. *Amateurs: On the Margin Between Work and Leisure.* London: Sage.

Thompson, E.P. 1967. Time, Work-Discipline and Industrial Capitalism. *Past & Present* 38: 56–97.

Walcon, Erin, and Helen Nicholson. 2017. The Sociable Aesthetics of Amateur Theatre. *Contemporary Theatre Review* 27 (1): 18–33. https://doi.org/10.10 80/10486801.2016.1262851.

Whiting, James, and Kevin Hannam. 2015. Creativity, Self-Expression and Leisure. *Leisure Studies* 34 (3): 372–384.

CHAPTER 6

Making Amateur Theatre

The first part of the twenty-first century has seen a 'contemporary renaissance' of craft and making and a renewed interest what it means to make and make together (Luckman 2015). This renaissance has led cultural historian Christopher Frayling to insist that 'craftsmanship is definitely in the ether, as an idea ripe to be "reclaimed", "re-evaluated" and "redefined"' (2011: 8). A question preoccupying many concerns the motivations driving this upsurge in craft practice. In *The Craftsman* sociologist Richard Sennett asks 'what the process of making concrete things reveals to us about ourselves' (2008: 8). In *Why We Make Things & Why It Matters*, furniture maker and craft theorist Peter Korn enquires, 'Why do we make things? Or, more specifically, why do we choose the spiritually, emotionally, and physically demanding work of bringing new objects into the world with creativity and skill?' (2013: 7). Much of this work builds on questions and ideas raised in the work of William Morris and John Ruskin during the nineteenth century, which, as we have discussed in relation to the Garden City Movement and amateur theatre in industrial model villages, was used by early twentieth century social reformists to elevate and idealise the importance of craft. Ruskin and Morris' conception of the skilled craft worker and the implications of craft was informed by the politics of work, concerns with the moral welfare of the worker and the associated health of society. For Ruskin, craft and creativity was a potent antidote to the condition of the contemporary workplace and exploitative

© The Author(s) 2018
H. Nicholson et al., *The Ecologies of Amateur Theatre*,
https://doi.org/10.1057/978-1-137-50810-2_6

capitalism, whereas Morris was driven by a conviction that making and sharing art and creative practice was crucial to a well-functioning society.

Recent scholarship has focused on the benefits of craft, creativity and making for the individual and the social, communitarian opportunities it provides. Psychologist Mihaly Csikszentmihalyi has famously theorised that the intrinsic pleasure of creative endeavour relates to the mental phenomena of 'flow' whereby the creative act becomes an all-encompassing activity. Korn refers to 'a centredness that touches upon the very essence of fulfilment' when he writes about the joy and empowering potential of aligning the mind, imagination and practical skill to produce craft objects (2013: 53). Sennett promotes a view of craftsmanship as doing work well for its own sake and the benefits that accrue from that, whilst the anthropologist Tim Ingold is concerned with 'the material flows and currents of sensory awareness in which images and objects reciprocally take shape' (2013: 20). In contrast to earlier conceptions of craft as something to be done with the hands rather than the head, Sennett, Ingold and craft scholar Glenn Adamson stress how thinking and making go hand in hand, where the creative process of making is a thoughtful and thought-through practice. Fundamental to all of these thinkers is the importance of craft and making as an embodied, material, sentient and sensory process. The proposition of this chapter is that amateur theatre-making can be approached in the same terms and that doing so complicates the dominant pejorative narrative that has become stubbornly aligned with it.

A parallel preoccupation, running alongside interest in individual benefits, is the cultural and social value of engaging in practices of creative-making. Nick Wilson, who researches the cultural and creative industries, has called for an understanding of 'social creativity' that shifts emphasis away from individualistic conceptions of creativity and the economic imperatives of the creative economy, towards the 'collective and relational nature of creative practice' (2010: 373), and in *Making is Connecting*, sociologist David Gauntlett writes extensively on the 'the power of making and connecting through creating' (2011: 1). In these formulations, the relational aspect of making and creative practice comes to the fore. For Wilson, attending to 'social creativity' invites a consideration of 'interaction across boundaries', in which the boundaries breached can be anything from disciplines to social groupings or nations (2010: 373). Key to Gauntlett's proposition is the idea that making requires individuals to come together in productive ways, a line of enquiry also central to Sennett's

Together (2013 [2012]). As cultural geographer Harriet Hawkins forwards in *Creativity*:

> One of the key dimensions of discussions around making and connecting has been an attention to how the actual practices of creative doing, and doing together, can come to form communities. (2017: 169)

Interestingly, there are two interrelated ideas of community that come into play here—the specific community of practice, the amateur theatre community, for example, brought together by cognate interests, but there is also the implication that these communities of practice have consequences for the wider community in terms of contributing to place-making as discussed in Chapter 4 or, as Sennett suggests, the facilitation of enhanced community relations—or, to put it bluntly, a *better* community.

The central connecting thread in this chapter is around ideas of making: making theatre and how making helps to shape subjectivities and build communities. I take inspiration from Ingold's conception of making 'as a process of growth' in terms of how people, things and groups come into being and evolve (2013: 21). In the first section I draw attention to amateur theatre's relationship to craft. Adamson has explored the old and much wrestled with tension over the status and legitimacy of craft and the distance presumed between it and the arts, which has a striking parallel with amateur theatre's relation to professional theatre (2007, 2013). He identifies how craft is primarily regarded as functional and supplemental and therefore in a subordinate relation to art as 'an autonomous field of practice' (2013 [2007]: 9). To say that craft is supplemental 'is to say that it is essential to the end in view, but in the process of achieving that end, it disappears' (2013 [2007]: 13). In a similar way, amateur theatre-makers are primarily judged on the theatrical outputs they produce, a focus that obscures the various craft practices and the craft of making that goes into realising it. Taking up the invitation posed by Ingold, this chapter resituates the critical gaze away from the outcome of the making process—the production—by bringing the skills, craft and practical processes particular to amateur theatre-making into view. As Stephen Knott implores in *Amateur Craft: History and Theory*:

> We must be alert to the characteristics of amateur labour – its idiosyncrasy, its uniqueness and how it stretches conventional notions of work. (2015: 51)

I also highlight amateur theatre-making as a social and relational practice reliant on cooperation, collaboration and participation in a shared space and address how these creative 'doings' have the potential to contribute to the construction and sculpting of dynamic communities. However, in the final section of the chapter I tackle the thorny issue of the demographics of amateur theatre. Particularly focusing on questions of race and ethnicity, I ask if 'making is connecting' as Gauntlett proposes, what issues arise when the connecting that takes place has a decidedly mono-cultural hue and reflects wider issues with access, inclusion and diversity in society. Drawing attention to some of the tensions and anxieties around this topic, I consider how amateur theatre companies have adopted proactive approaches to making convivial spaces for groups who aspire to represent and creatively contribute to the cultural life of diasporic communities.

Making: Craft, Skill and Creativity

Twenty ball-gowns; a wicked queen's black cape with stand-up red collar; several ornate masks for a masked ball; garlands made from flowers and shells; a tiara; a crown; fur stoles; a pink wig; a moth costume; a witch's black hat, cloak and broom; golden drapes; two thrones; a spirit of the forest costume; giant red flowers and leaves protruding from a rock; a fish outfit and two mermaid costumes. These were just some of the items and costumes assembled and made for a production of *The Enchanted Bird* (Ibong Adarna) by the amateur theatre company Philippine Theatre UK (PTUK) staged at the Chelsea Theatre in London 24th–28th September 2014. John Beglin, a professional chauffeur, acquired, altered or made all of the original costumes for this show. In 2015 we ran two Evocative Objects workshops, led by Erin Walcon, at The Questors Theatre, Ealing on 16th June 2015 and The Swan Theatre, Worcester on 27th June 2015 when we invited people to attend with objects that captured memories and stories of their experience of participating in amateur theatre. At The Questors Theatre, John Beglin wore one of his richly decorated costumes as he explained how at secondary school:

> I learned to do back stitch, I learned to do chain stitch, I learned to do draw stitch, I learned to knit. I learned an array of stitches … and all these boys

used to call me a sissy. But guess what came out of it in the end? Me ... it was something different, and it was something to do with who I am.[1]

Now in his late fifties, for John Beglin amateur theatre provides a creative outlet to maintain this aspect of his identity. His story is not unique. Many have spoken to us about amateur theatre as nourishment for a dimension of their personality that may not be fully realised in the professional or domestic arenas they inhabit. Emma Thomas, a former serving member of the Royal Navy, stated, 'I actually believe people have lots of different sides to them and [in the theatre] it's just a different side of me that doesn't normally come to the fore in my work environment.'[2] As such, making theatre plays a role in crystallising a sense of self in relation to others. Individuals become known as the one who does amateur theatre and it is common for people to get associated with and known for particular acting or backstage roles they re-perform. Robin Sheppard, introduced at the beginning of this book, is a garden designer by trade, but has a penchant for playing outrageous pantomime dames. Drawing on his quick wit, ability to spot a potential sexual innuendo at fifty paces and his easy rapport with an audience, he has played the dame in the past ten out of thirteen Collingwood RSC pantomimes. Through this repetition he has honed his act, he has a repertoire of looks, gestures and retorts to audience heckles crafted in rehearsal and through performance. At home he keeps the accoutrements that enhance his act: giant false eyelashes, patterned tights and a collection of high heels. Regular audience members are delighted by his hotly anticipated appearances, but he also relishes the opportunity to surprise his unsuspecting clients, to showcase another side of his character that may not come to the fore during garden design consultations and builds.[3]

For John Beglin, his identity is indelibly tied to his ability to tease an idea into being, to work out the practicalities of construction, select materials, sew costumes from scratch, embellish designs and repurpose

---

[1] Interview of John Beglin with Cara Gray, Evocative Objects workshop, Questors Theatre, 16 June 2015. All quotations taken from this interview.

[2] Interview Emma Thomas with Nadine Holdsworth, HMS Excellent, Whale Island, Portsmouth, 17 July 2015.

[3] Interview Robin Sheppard and Lucy Sheppard with Nadine Holdsworth, Southsea, 5 December 2014. When Robin Sheppard was not playing the dame, he directed the pantomime in 2008 and 2011.

Fig. 6.1   Robin Sheppard in Collingwood RSC's *Snow White*, 2009. (By kind permission of photographer, Pam Johns)

pre-existing items found in charity shops or donated by members. His capacity to take pleasure and pride from problem solving and finding creative solutions is palpable:

> How do you make a mermaid costume for crying out loud? So I sat and thought. And I got a piece of cardboard and I made a mermaid shape on the floor with a big tail on it and then I got another piece and I stapled the two together… Then I covered it with gold material, very, very fine criss-cross mesh material and you couldn't see the cardboard underneath it… It was amazing. I still can't believe I made these costumes.

Korn suggests that crafted objects become 'talismans that independently confirm their owners' central narratives of personal identity' and this is clearly the case for the costumes John Beglin makes (2013: 66). His passionate commitment to PTUK and his own craft practice compels him to supplement his meagre costume budget of £100 with his own funds and the costumes he creates are beautiful, as well as carefully crafted. Referencing ideas initially presented in Robert M. Pirsig's notable *Zen and the Art of Motorcycle Maintenance* (1974), Korn suggests that 'a good life may be found through craftsmanlike engagement with the actions, objects, and relationships of ordinary experience, through caring about what you do' (2013: 11). This view is further developed by Sennett's elevation of the creative fulfilment attached to doing a job well for its own sake by applying craftsmanship with care and skill. When John Beglin metaphorically refers to himself as 'the cat who gets the cream' it is because he has found a vehicle that enables him to enact a 'craftsmanlike' approach to costume design and, in turn, this contributes to the ongoing process of bringing himself into being through making.

Craft is not something that necessarily springs to mind when considering amateur theatre as the traditional stereotype casts it as synonymous with limited skill and shoddy production values—uninspiring direction, shaky sets, missed cues and unsubtle characterisation. A view epitomised by a recent Tweet from the playwright and Artistic Director of Tamasha Theatre Company, Fin Kennedy, whose suggested made-up theatre word of the day was '"amateurgy" (n.), poor quality dramaturgy from someone who doesn't really know what they're doing'.[4] It is assumed that amateurs

---

[4] Tweet, 3 August 2017. Fin Kennedy swiftly apologised for this tweet when challenged.

are playing around, 'dabbling' to use leisure theorist Robert Stebbins' oft-repeated phrase, for their own enjoyment and inevitably poor outcomes follow. Exploring political theorist Hannah Arendt's distinction between *homo faber* whom she applauded for using skilled craftsmanship to build a society for the public good, whilst deriding practical *animale laborans,* Knott explains that for her:

> Objects that result from amateur labour could not be considered genuine additions to the human artifice according to her schema, but were at best incidental, the unimportant detritus of an individual's cycle of perpetual consumption and production. (2015: 50–51)

The legacy of this thinking clearly persists, but many amateur theatre-makers are professionally trained or have honed their knowledge, skills and craft over years of dedicated practice. From carefully assembled box-set scale models of set designs, intricately constructed costumes and pieces of bespoke furniture made to satisfy the requirements of a production and space, there is evidence of craft understood as something made with the hands that requires skill and a thoughtful approach to design and making. Equally, amateur theatre-makers frequently demonstrate commitment to acting and directing as crafts that require the acquisition of skills and techniques. They do not necessarily have the benefit of knowledge accrued through years of professional training, although a surprising number do as scarce employment prospects and economic precarity drives an exodus from the professional to the amateur realm, but people *do* regularly seek opportunities to extend the tools at their disposal—to develop their craft. A trajectory Stebbins refers to in his account of 'serious leisure', whereby amateur pursuits rarely remain static, but instead adopt the mantle of increasing professionalisation derived from a refusal to remain a mere player, dabbler or novice in it (1992: 9). This desire to learn is in marked contrast to Adamson's identification of an assumed uncritical amateurism. He writes:

> If modern art, seen from a perspective like Adorno's, is grounded in searching self-awareness, then amateurism is a form of creativity that can never be integrated into this model. In the popular imagination, hobby crafts are on a par with such activities as stamp collecting and weekend sport – activities done in a spirit of self-gratification rather than critique. (2013 [2007]: 139)

But 'a spirit of self-gratification' does not necessarily equate to a lack of critical distance or a reduced capacity for self or collective critique. Part of the pleasure of amateur activity, the gratification, can be about learning to do things better, which chimes with Korn's insistence that 'the primary motive for doing creative work is self-transformation' and Stebbin's taxonomy of the 'durable benefits of amateur activity' including self-expression, feelings of accomplishment and enhanced self-image (Korn 2013: 102; Stebbins 1992: 7). Whilst the stereotype of 'self-congratulatory thespians' aggrandising their talents might be present in some quarters, there is equally a keen awareness of deficiencies, skills gaps and a strong impulse towards improvement through rehearsal processes, internal shadowing positions and informal systems of mentoring, as well as professionally led workshops.

In contrast to Adamson's observation that amateurs may be 'beneath the notice of the expert' (2013 [2007]: 141) and the assumption that the boundary between amateur and professional worlds needs to be rigorously policed in order to protect the professionalised 'field' the sociologist Pierre Bourdieu identifies, there is much evidence for porous boundaries and skills sharing. As cultural studies scholar Susan Luckman suggests, this boundary constantly shifts, often as a result of pressure from amateurs due to their scale and ambition (2015: 52). The drive within the amateur scene to learn and evolve has always created work for professionals and opportunities for organisations to marketise its expertise in innovative ways as David Coates has found in his fascinating research on amateur theatre and private theatricals in the long nineteenth century and this tradition continues (2018). In the contemporary context there is the RSC's Open Stages initiative and its Big Amateur Weekend, which has run since 2014 offering workshops on voice and text, acting, movement and stage combat, which was extended in May 2017 to incorporate the Big Backstage Weekend offering workshops on sound, lighting, set design and stage management for amateur practitioners. Whilst there is inevitably a sense in which activities such as these shore up the 'cultural capital' of an institution such as the RSC, there is also an opening up, a generosity of spirit that the RSC's former Artistic Director Michael Boyd presented as 'the straightforward redistribution of cultural wealth' when discussing Open Stages and amateurs have been keen to take every opportunity to benefit from this.[5]

For the past twenty years, several hundred amateur theatre-makers have signed up for the NODA Theatre Summer School, a week-long residential course that requires a significant investment of time and money. Many take a week of annual leave from work to attend and the residential fee for 2018 was £640. Described as 'the bubble', which captures something of the immersive experience it fosters, the Summer School provides an opportunity for partakers to share their passion with like-minded people, whilst receiving a training experience from professional practitioners that encourages them to take on board tips and techniques to enhance their and their company's practice. Many return year after year, with NODA Chairperson, Jacquie Stedman, estimating that only 33% were first-time attendees in 2016. Running in its current format since 1998, the summer 2017 programme was typical of the traditional provision with courses available on Musical Theatre in Rehearsal, Design for Theatre and Devising Drama, as well as new offerings including Directing Ayckbourn and Shakespeare. The former run by Richard Stacey, drawing on extensive experience working with Alan Ayckbourn at the Stephen Joseph Theatre in Scarborough and the latter co-taught by Michael Corbidge, a Senior Voice and Text Associate Practitioner with the RSC. Observing the Summer School during August 2016, I was struck by the common themes that emerged from participants around the importance of a safe environment to try out ideas, the acquisition of increased 'techniques, tools, confidence' and the aspiration for a professional ethos in their practice. During a rehearsal dedicated to the work of musical theatre composer, Jason Robert Brown, I noted:

> These are clearly people with a desire to learn. One by one they come up to sing solo in front of a group of twenty-three others sharing the same experience. It's daunting. The person running the session regularly stops them and gives them guidance to help them find their character and convey the narrative through song. They start again, they try to take on board the guidance they have received, they are stopped again and again. They keep going. The atmosphere in the room is warm and encouraging. The participants are all in the same boat. They are amateurs who want to improve their practice

---

[5] See https://www.contemporarytheatrereview.org/2017/molly-flynn-rsc-open-stages/ and RSC report. Accessed 31 Dec 2017.

and they support each other in this pursuit. (Nadine's Research Diary, 3 August 2016)

Importantly, the impetus to learn is not just fuelled by individual motives, but by a determination to raise standards more generally. When I asked Richard, a member of the Directing Drama course in 2016, about his experience he explained 'you can't do what professionals do, but if we use these techniques we can be so much better'. Blogging about her experience attending the Big Backstage Weekend in 2017, Rae Goodwin from Huntington Drama Club, concludes her post by writing 'I look forward to passing on what I have learnt to other club members as well as putting it into practice for future productions'.[6] So, there is a resolve to translate ideas gleaned to amateur rehearsal processes, to which I now turn.

In the theatre, making takes place in the rehearsal process, which theatre scholar Gay McAuley describes as 'the time when the multiple material elements that will constitute a unique work of art are progressively brought together' (2012: 5). Whilst on the surface it could be said that this is equally true of amateur as professional theatre, there are important differences to tease out. During a discussion with Ian Wainwright, the producer of Open Stages, the RSC's large-scale collaboration with amateur theatre companies, he referred to the fact that one of the challenges the RSC faced during this collaboration was that whilst the RSC comprised extremely experienced and proficient theatre-makers, they did not know 'how to make amateur theatre'.[7] An observation that begs the question—what is specific about making amateur theatre and how might that be evident through rehearsal? Amateur theatre companies create theatre within specific material constraints of limited time, limited resources and a reliance on good-will and volunteer labour, which all inevitably impact on the making process. Amateur theatre rehearsals happen in the free time (dependent on work patterns) designated for evenings and weekends, which means the stresses and strains of the working day and associated fatigue can seep into rehearsals. Temporal restrictions dictate that

---

[6] http://www.huntingdondramaclub.org.uk/wordpress/rsc-big-backstage-weekend/. Accessed 21 Oct 2017.

[7] Conversation Ian Wainwright with Molly Flynn, Nadine Holdsworth and Helen Nicholson, The Other Place, Stratford, 5 October 2016.

rehearsal time has to be focused and productive—there is no time to waste, which means the mainstays of professional theatre such as vocal and physical warm-ups or experimenting with different staging possibilities are regarded as luxuries to be accommodated if time permits. Rob Sloane, director at the amateur Rugby Theatre, described how working with the RSC had given him the confidence to use warm-ups and experiment in rehearsal:

> The RSC gave us good warm-ups for the time we had, we don't have an hour, so, what can we do in ten, fifteen minutes? It was massively helpful to me as a director... Everyone kind of jokes about the difference between amateur and professional is that amateurs love blocking, so they know what they are doing. And the professionals will scoff at that, saying no, you use these techniques to let it grow organically. And the amateurs will go, no, that's too waffly, we don't have time for that. We've only got two and a half hours so tell me what I'm doing... It was a challenge with amateur actors, but our productions were really good when we moved away from this...so people could see the benefits.[8]

The Tower Theatre Company, one of the amateur companies that collaborated with the RSC on *A Midsummer Night's Dream: A Play for Nation* in 2016, similarly noted in the programme for the show that one of the things they learned from working in a professional environment was 'to be open, searching and experimental in finding ways of reaching the essence of character and situation. At rehearsals we were encouraged to try different routes and not to get fixed on options too early'.[9] This learning was demonstrated vividly at the Big Amateur Weekend at Stratford-upon-Avon in November 2015, where returnees joined with first-time participants to watch the director Justin Audibert work with two experienced RSC actors:

> There is a large group watching the workshop, with all amateur participants concentrating on what they see. The actors are encouraged to try out ways of working, and offer suggestions for an approach to a role. Justin Audibert, the director, responds openly to all ideas, and the actors improvise different approaches. In the discussion afterwards, some of the first-time attendees

---

[8] Interview Rob Sloane with Molly Flynn, Rugby Theatre, 3 March 2016.
[9] Cited in programme for *A Midsummer Night's Dream: A Play for the Nation*, RSC.

are surprised that there is so much flexibility in his approach. So, one amateur director asks, don't you have a clear idea of what you want before the rehearsal? Previous attendees look askance at the question – they know what's coming – and Justin explains that nothing is ever locked down. The amateurs' learning is fast and evident – the RSC had to provide differentiated workshops for returning participants and newbies to satisfy demand for new approaches. (Helen's Research Diary, 21 November 2015)

Regardless of approach, the fact that participants invariably have different levels of experience and expertise means that a director often has to negotiate and accommodate assorted strengths, weaknesses and skill sets as part of the rehearsal process. Whilst many amateur companies audition for parts, several have an open-door policy epitomised by Kevin Fraser's account of Titchfield Festival Theatre:

> We've always said we would take anyone. That was always the ethos from the word go that if you want to act we would put you on the stage and it wouldn't just be a spear carrier, we would give you a part.[10]

This is all well and good in theory, but inevitably this inclusive approach has an impact on the making process. Equally, constrained availability and access to space means that the spaces for making spill out into other temporarily repurposed spaces such as bars, foyers and car parks, but most especially the home, which becomes a site for planning, rehearsal, sewing costumes and making props.[11] Limited resource demands a culture of creative problem solving, recycling and borrowing—the epitome of 'make do and mend'.

Making Theatre: Rehearsals at The Criterion, Coventry

Theatre and performance scholars have noted how rehearsal processes are notoriously under-researched in theatre studies (Harvie and Lavender 2010; McAuley 2012; Allain 2016). Yet, in order to write meaningfully

---

[10] Interview Kevin Fraser with Nadine Holdsworth, Titchfield Festival Theatre, 27th September 2016.

[11] This aspect of amateur creativity is discussed in depth by Cara Gray, in her unpublished thesis, *Amateur Theatre: Making and Making Do* (2017).

about the mechanics of making theatre it is vital to delve into the dark recesses of rehearsals, set building, costume and props making. To enhance my understanding of what it means to make amateur theatre, I began following the work of The Criterion Players in Coventry and during June 2017 observed rehearsals for its production of Alan Ayckbourn's comedy thriller *Communicating Doors* (1994) directed by John Ruscoe. In undertaking this research I was inspired by McAuley's ethnographic methods detailed in *Not Magic but Work: An ethnographic account of a rehearsal process*, which offers a model of how to open up 'the complex interpersonal relations, work practices and the collective creative process involved in rehearsal' that relies on being both 'enmeshed' in what is happening and sufficiently removed to be able to make observations and write notes on proceedings (2012: 4, 8). We might think of this as a form of 'feeling-work' outlined in the introduction, which is attentive to the social and material conditions and relations that underpin the creative process of making. Amateur theatre relies on people who often have long histories of attachment to theatres such as The Criterion, an affective relation built over time that inevitably contributes to their dynamics of engagement; so, wherever possible, I have tried to give an impression of the people involved, which is reliant on first-hand observation supplemented by conversations and interviews.

Hawkins proposes a critical geography of creativity and the need to 'put creativity in its place' by being attentive to the multiple sites and environments where creativity happens (2017: 2). Bearing this in mind, it is important to put The Criterion Theatre (The Criterion) in place. The Criterion Players formed in 1955 and it has built a reputation as one of the leading amateur theatres in the Midlands region. The Criterion is entirely run by volunteers with its current membership comprising close to two hundred company members and around 400 club members who support the work of the company through volunteer labour in the box office, bar and front-of-house. A member of the Little Theatre Guild, it runs its own theatre seating 120, which interrupts the flow of domestic houses in a small street in the centre of Earlsdon. It is an important part of the theatre ecology of the city, producing a repertoire of classic and contemporary plays in the midst of two professional venues, the Warwick Arts Centre and Belgrade Theatre, both within a three-mile radius, which many members of The Criterion never visit. A relatively affluent residential area that was incorporated into Coventry in 1890, Earlsdon grew up around the watch-making trade pursued in the city since the 1680s, a history marked by the presence of a clock on the roundabout that connects Earlsdon Avenue North and South. Earlsdon is a vibrant community, a 'placey place' with a central hub of shops (including an organic shop), pubs, cafes and a well-used library. It is popular with academics and students from the two local universities of Coventry and Warwick. The community spirit of the place is no better illustrated than by the annual Earlsdon Festival held on the first bank holiday in May since 1978. The original festival programme from 1978 offers insight into its galvanising impetus:

> This Festival may seem to be a celebration of what used to be; an attempt to capture the atmosphere of the village that Earlsdon once was. Perhaps it started out that way. But the enthusiasm with which everyone in Earlsdon responded to the idea showed that we are still very much a village community at heart ... let's hope that the enthusiasm for this Festival remains with us for a long time to come, helping us to maintain 'Earlsdon Village' as a vibrant and happy community in the city of Coventry. (Original 1978 programme reprinted in the 2017 festival brochure)

The Festival is still thriving and in 2017 took over the local streets and the public spaces of the library, churches and The Albany, a social club that offers dance classes, live music and quiz nights. With food stalls, fairground rides, craft activities, demonstrations of science projects, Tai Chi, Morris dancing, a steel band and numerous performances by singers, community choirs and local dance groups, the Festival encompasses an eclectic mix of interests. There were stalls for Friends of Palestine, Coventry Soroptomists and in the library, Abdul, a Syrian refugee to the city who works for Coventry Refugee and Migrant Centre and Sandip from Coventry City Council, encouraged intercultural exchanges by inviting people to have their names written in Arabic or Punjabi to highlight diversity in the city.[12] The Criterion, one of Earlsdon Festival's 2017 sponsors, was at the centre of proceedings with stalls and live entertainment.

The company website cites 'a deep sense of community ethos and identification with Coventry as our home' and claims that 'much time and effort has been invested in recent years to make the Criterion an important part of the local community of Earlsdon'.[13] The building itself, which is maintained by The Criterion Players, is part of the Earlsdon Heritage Trail

---

[12] http://www.earlsdonfestival.co.uk/. Accessed 27 Dec 2017.
[13] https://www.criteriontheatre.co.uk/about. Accessed 27 Dec 2017.

and a plaque outside the theatre asserts its history as a former Wesleyan Chapel (1884–1923) and Sunday School (1884–1960). Inside the theatre there are photographic displays of recent productions and other items proudly asserting the theatre's connection to professional practice. There is a stone plaque presented to the building on 30 June 1906 by Ellen Terry, who was born in Coventry in 1847, and a portrait of her as Queen Katharine in *The Vicar of Wakefield*. A framed letter from the professional actor Ron Cook dated 5 February 2004 announces his willingness to take up an invitation to become patron for this theatre where he played his first role as 'consumptive Little Willie in *East Lynne*' in 1963. The theatre is a community resource. It houses Saturday morning drama classes for 7–16-year olds, regular coffee mornings open to the public and is a popular venue for meetings by the Neighbourhood Association and social gatherings including the annual Christmas carol sing-a-long. Like many amateur companies it tries hard to promote a strong ethos of active citizenship, or what political theorist Chantal Mouffe refers to as 'embodied citizenship' (1992). Anne-marie Greene, a mother to two young children and a Professor of Work, Employment and Diversity at the University of Leicester, has volunteered behind the bar since 2004, helped out in wardrobe, acted, directed and taken on several committee roles prior to her current role as Vice-Chair and trustee of The Criterion. She explained during an interview that every member of the company is entered onto a cleaning rota and the display of commitment shown by cleaning the toilets and vacuuming the foyer earns rights so that 'there is a view that if you're going to be part of our company you should be part of our company. And there's also a general attitude that all things being equal, if you had two people auditioning and they could equally do the part well, you should pick the person who contributes to the company'.[14]

Before making proper can commence, the annual season has to be selected. The Criterion Players normally stage seven main house shows a year and two studio productions. The repertoire is varied, with mainstays of amateur theatre such as Alan Ayckbourn and Richard Bean's *One Man, Two Guvnors* (2011), sitting alongside more contemporary plays and unusual choices such as an atmospheric ensemble production of David

---

[14] Interview Anne-marie Greene with Nadine Holdsworth, The Criterion Theatre, Coventry, 26th September 2016. All other quotations from Anne-marie Greene are taken from this interview.

Almond's children's novel *Skellig* (1998), with a multigenerational cast ranging from eighteen to eighty staged during May 2017. The Artistic Director assembles the repertoire, assigns budgets and wields a certain degree of power in terms of political and aesthetic judgements based on their tastes and personal preferences. New ideas are introduced via a play reading group and avid theatre-goers who keep abreast of new productions and suggest things the group should consider as happened with Mark Hayhurst's *Taken at Midnight,* a play about a young Jewish lawyer and his mother who challenged Hitler's regime in the 1930s, which premiered at Chichester Festival Theatre in 2014 and received its amateur premier at The Criterion in March 2017 directed by Anne-marie Greene. Undertaking scripts newly released to amateurs can add layers of complexity to the making process though. When Anne-marie Greene directed *Let the Right One In* in 2016, she had to liaise with the owner of the rights to ensure they were happy with any proposed changes to the text and when the company secured the rights to stage *Rumplestiltskin,* which premiered at the Bath Theatre Royal in December 2014, as its Christmas show for 2016, Anne-marie Greene recalled:

> They [Bath Theatre Royal] wanted to see all the artwork, they asked for specific things ... a certain font size ... how we can use the music, what instruments we can have, all that kind of stuff. And we have to keep sending them things, they won't let us publish anything without having first okayed it.

Protectionism and 'gate-keeping' is fairly common when professionals deal with amateur companies, which speaks to some of the assumptions around standards and relative competence that are occasionally evident.

The final programme is arrived at in the interest of balance and in terms of the availability of amateur rights, which can be tricky to navigate in relation to rights being withdrawn or professional productions and tours taking place. The Criterion has established good relationships with staff at the publishers Samuel French and Nick Hern, which mean the company is notified of impending releases, which has enabled it to secure a number of national and regional amateur premieres. Securing rights plays a part in the dynamics of healthy rivalry with other local amateur companies based at The Loft in Leamington Spa and The Talisman in Kenilworth, as Anne-marie Greene put it with a smile, 'we really like it if we get a play before The Loft'. Yet, the material conditions governing amateur theatre mean that rivalry is tempered by cooperation and a willingness to share human and physical resources. It is not uncommon for a call to go out to other local groups to fulfil a particular casting need and costume and props are regularly borrowed and shared within the local amateur theatre ecosystem. In *The Rise of the Network Society* (2009 [1996]) the sociologist Manuel Castells proposes that rather than thinking of groups having non-porous boundaries, it is more fruitful to think that networks constitute the 'new social morphology' rooted in 'an ever-increasing multitude of connections and chains of relationality' (cited in Edensor et al. 2010: 15). Whilst people strongly identify with specific amateur groups, often based on geographical ties, there is an awareness of and adherence to a broader amateur theatre network regionally that facilitates some fluidity and exchange of people and goods, which also speaks to the kind of reciprocity central to political scientist Robert Putnam's conception of social capital. As sociologist Graham Day explains:

> The main proviso is that to do well networks must stretch out to connect with other networks or groupings that can deliver additional resources not available from amongst members themselves. As well as bonding, they need to 'bridge'. (2006: 218)

Amateur theatre, as a shared social structure rooted in common experience, invites mutuality or 'bridging' and, as Day suggests, 'when people are caught up in this close pattern of shared life, they are hard pressed to avoid sentiments of reciprocity; a favour done now must be returned later, although perhaps the timing and form of the exchange are left unspecified' (2006: 47). The material conditions of amateur theatre mean that its reliance on this exchange economy is a vital part of the making process. When, in 2015, The Criterion and The Loft both produced Lee Hall's *The Pitmen Painters* (2007) The Criterion lent out a beautiful Trade Union banner that a local artist had produced for them and they in turn borrowed a straightjacket from The Loft for a production of Anthony Horowitz's *Mindgame* (1999) in 2014. In addition to this exchange with other amateur groups, companies rely on and contribute to the local economy. Charity and junk shops are mined for bits of set, props and costumes. Printers produce programmes and flyers and local building merchants provide the bare materials for set building and decoration.

When I began observing the making process for *Communicating Doors*, a classic Ayckbourn play with clearly delineated characters within a plot combining murder mystery, comedy and time travel, I was told by several participants that there had been some teething problems. The production had been tricky to cast, one of the cast members dropped out, they had to rehearse at a company member's house for the first three weeks and rehearsals had been interrupted by holidays and illness. The cast and crew had six weeks to bring the production to fruition. Whereas professional companies might work on a show for six weeks full-time or much longer, The Criterion Players rehearse four nights a week for two and a half hours, which ratchets up to every night the week prior to the production, which takes place 24th June–1st July 2017. This punishing schedule is a reminder of the huge investment in time and labour required from those involved in amateur theatre. This cast will have only three nights off from 11th June to July 1st—they are troopers, who are driven by a love of theatre and the reciprocal bonds that tie them to each other and each project they undertake. Each time a new production is rehearsed and mounted at The Criterion it reinforces the site as a place of shared labour, creative investment and theatrical imagination, enacting in practice Hawkins' 'appreciation of how creative practices make place, how they produce and reproduce the sites and places of their production and consumption' (2017: 24). With every production, a shared community of practice, of making, is reinforced.

The technical production for *Communicating Doors,* occupied what McCauley calls 'a parallel universe', which is 'both spatially and temporally dispersed in relation to the actors' work' (2012: 131–132). Whilst the actors rehearsed in Anne-marie Greene's home for the first three weeks of rehearsals, the set team realised the design for a hotel suite produced by Simon Sharpe, for which he produced a carefully crafted and detailed miniature model, an intricate material object that spoke to its maker's creative investment. With the model as their physical guide, the set team constructed main flats with lurid pink and green striped wallpaper, hung four working doors, French windows and a double set of doors set in a small revolve stage crucial for the time-travelling aspect of the narrative. Upstage a bathroom space with toilet, sink, shower and bidet completes the picture. Les Rahilly, the props person, was responsible for gathering items to dress the set and facilitate the script. Les Rahilly has been involved with The Criterion for forty-five years and has spent the last thirty years doing props alongside her day job as a computer programmer for Massey Ferguson. She usually does props for two productions in a season and regularly helps out in the bar. She lives fours doors down from the theatre

Figs. 6.2 and 6.3 Box set and staging for The Criterion's production of *Communicating Doors*, 2017. (Photographer: Nadine Holdsworth)

and is known as 'the keeper of the keys' who can pop in for deliveries or emergencies. Now that she has retired she is in and out of the theatre all the time. She tells me she likes the challenge of getting a props list and working out how she will acquire everything given time, practical constraints and a budget of £200. This production presented two key challenges of acquiring a sofa and a laundry basket that could both conceal a five-foot, ten-inch male body. This entailed liaising with the set build team to construct a sofa frame, sourcing padding, fabric, and finding volunteers to upholster and make cushions. Ideally, John Ruscoe wanted a traditional wicker laundry basket on wheels but, having proved too costly, a compromise was reached of a painted MDF frame on wheels monogrammed with the fictitious hotel logo. In tune with Jen Harvie's observation of professional rehearsal processes 'each show is literally made by the conditions of its production – the dimensions and found furniture of rehearsal spaces, the limits of rehearsal time…' (2010: 13). Les Rahilly was present at every rehearsal I attended and it is clear that she takes her role and contribution to the making process seriously. She follows the script, makes notes of what and when things are needed and how they are used. She told me that this process is crucial to avert flaws in the final production as she sees things from an audience's perspective.

Even though Anne-marie Greene is not involved in this production she has given over a large 'music room' in her home to rehearsals four nights a week. This is a regular arrangement; she admits 'there are always people walking through and things going on and music and shouting and screaming and whatnot from the back of the house.' This is not the only evidence for domestic spaces of creativity or the home as a site of 'vernacular and amateur creative practices' (Hawkins 2017: 106). The director, John Ruscoe, planned his approach to the play and formulated rehearsal schedules from the comfort of his home; Maureen Liggins, described as a 'proper craftsperson', has sewn hotel monograms onto dressing gowns and the hotel security guard's jacket at home and Les Rahilly used her home computer to research and mock up a prop of an October 2001 newspaper. Knott acknowledges that amateur space is 'integral to and embedded in the experience of daily life' and that there are 'many examples of the tangential links between amateur space and various configurations of everyday socialized space' (2015: 45–46). Similarly Hawkins suggests that:

> To reflect on creativity in the home is not just to explore the home as a site of the creative economy, but also to consider how such creativities entwine with those of hobbies and of meeting practical everyday needs. (2017: 127)

The decision to contribute to making at home is often arrived at for practical reasons: access to a workable space (large enough to rehearse), resources (computer, sewing machine, tools) and a desire to fit amateur labour around the other demands or pleasures of daily life. Rehearsals take place in one part of a house whilst children embark on homework and bedtime rituals upstairs; curtains to dress a set can be hemmed or ironed whilst watching television and programmes can be designed as a washing machine cycle plays out. This overlaying of amateur creative labour and domestic routines/labour highlights the way that amateur theatre-makers negotiate 'creative practices within the time-spaces of the home' as Hawkins suggests, but also how some of the costs of these practices become embedded in the broader economies of the individual household (2017: 107).

When I visit rehearsals at The Criterion on Sunday 11th June, the cast have only been rehearsing on the stage since Wednesday when they completed a run of Act One and on Friday a run of Act Two. This Sunday rehearsal is spent tightening some of the weaker scenes and working on some complicated physical stage business that involves characters being thrown from and rescued from a balcony situated beyond the French windows. The cast are still relatively shaky on their lines and this slows proceedings down, but the atmosphere is simultaneously industrious and light-hearted. Group dynamics are very much in evidence, an easy banter exists between the actors and a considerable amount of humour is generated at the expense of Neil Vallance who cultivates an air of vague detachment from proceedings, asking at various times 'what are we doing?' After a five-minute break mid-way through the rehearsal Cathryn Bowler and Georgia Kelly re-enter the theatre laughingly exclaiming to the director, John Ruscoe, 'we just had to explain the plot to Neil, *again*!' which is met with good humoured eye-rolling. When the actors are not required on stage they retreat to the foyer to go over their lines or sit watching and prompting, present and part of the collaborative process.

> This is a working space where things are in process, coming into being. Ladders, lights, extension cables, a Henry hoover, a work bench, tubs of PVA glue, paint and half finished bits of set including a half-made sofa con-

sisting of a MDF frame and foam padding, which is waiting to be uphol-stered by a volunteer the next day. In the meantime four chairs from the foyer stand in for the sofa on stage. Les mills around as the actors rehearse waiting for opportune moments to dress the set with new additions and at one point she takes Neil aside to see if the laundry trunk he needs to be bundled into as a corpse will be more palatable with a duvet inside. (Nadine's Research Diary, 11 June 2017)

John Ruscoe brings a quiet expertise to the proceedings. He trained to be an actor for three years at the Drama Centre in the late 1960s and began acting in repertory theatres around the country before deciding that the precarious life of the professional actor was not for him and his young family. Having become a sales manager for a Building Society in Coventry, John has been involved in amateur theatres in the region for decades originally as an actor and, when he tired of this and found learning lines too taxing, he turned his hand to directing. He has directed numer-ous shows for The Criterion including, most recently, *One Man, Two Guvnors* in 2016 and a double-bill of Peter Shaffer's *Black Comedy* and Patrick Marber's *After Miss Julie* in 2015. During a conversation, he admitted that Alan Ayckbourn would not necessarily have been his first choice of production for 2017, but he was conscious that the company's repertoire this season had been 'a bit dark' and that there was a need for a lighter comedy aimed at the 'bread and butter audience'.[15]

Throughout rehearsals John Ruscoe sits listening and watching his actors intently. He intervenes by leaping up and onto the stage where he gives detailed and instructive notes. He is calm, reassuring and repeats the refrain 'try it' as a way of coaxing his actors to give new ideas a go. Writing about a professional production, McAuley notes:

Rehearsing a piece of text-based theatre is a creative process that consists of inventing, adjusting, and layering together minute details of gesture, into-nation, look and position in space in relation to words spoken. (2012: 78)

These concerns are evident in this amateur rehearsal process, but the temporal constraints mean that the time for exploration and decision-making is compressed. Whilst John Ruscoe encourages a 'try it' ethos,

[15] John Ruscoe in conversation with Nadine Holdsworth, Zafiri's Coffee Shop, Earlsdon, 1 June 2017.

there is a limit to how long things can be kept in play before being consolidated and fixed. Nonetheless, I am struck by the variety of directorial approaches he employs during this process. There is the usual blocking associated with amateur directing and working out how to overcome physical restrictions caused by furniture, limited backstage space and sightlines. With much hilarity, considerable time is spent working out how two women, Georgia Kelly and Cathryn Bowler, are going to lift and carry Neil Vallance, now a corpse, off set. Various options are tried, including Les Rahilly bringing in a rug to see if he could be slid off on that, but eventually another cast member, Pete Meredith, intervenes and explains to Georgia how she needs to engage her core and bend her knees to get maximum traction whilst locking her arms around Neil's chest. As such, there is an emphasis on working out through trial and error, which finds accord with Ingold's proposition regarding creativity as knowledge-building and 'the improvisatory creativity of labour that works things out as it goes along' (2013: 20). There is also evidence of creative agency exercised by the whole team—they are not looking to the director to 'solve' the problem, but finding it together through doing.

In contrast to the stereotype of wooden actors who exhibit minimal craft, these amateur rehearsals encompass traditional theatre-based approaches to physical characterisation and emotional through-lines and motivation, as well as interactions between characters. In terms of physical characterisations, Karen Evans is invited to consider how her character is 'a flamboyant lady so think about what your physical boundaries are' and Georgia Kelly is told that 'we need to see the sweat' as she plays hauling two people back over the balcony. John Ruscoe works sensitively with Georgia Kelly on her character's motivation during a scene when she is trying to hide the fact that she is upset. After advising that 'you're playing the obstacle, play to make her think everything's okay', he talks through various potential techniques for disguising and masking emotion whilst making the audience aware of what is going on. The note is specific, useful and fruitful as Georgia Kelly negotiates how she might play the scene with more purpose and emotional resonance and, importantly for John Ruscoe, to avoid a style that is 'a little bit too close up television'. At these moments I was acutely aware of how John Ruscoe translated knowledge and craft derived from his professional training to the current context of production.

John Ruscoe repeatedly stressed the importance of getting the right energy levels, pace and 'more drive', whether vocally or physically, to help a scene reach its potential. In one memorable moment he proposed that Karen Evans should play a scene as if she is suffering from diarrhoea and desperately needs to get off stage. In conversation after the rehearsal Karen Evans appreciated how this note brought home to her the urgency required for the scene and there was, indeed, a rapid injection of pace after he delivered his advice. Karen Evans is relatively new to The Criterion having worked on two previous productions, although she has been active in amateur theatre from an early age. She admitted she was finding the rehearsals for *Communicating Doors* the most challenging she had encountered and recalled times going home 'feeling crushed', but she was also finding it the most rewarding process. She felt that John Ruscoe pushes and challenges them to develop their characters, to discover new layers in performance, to refine rather than relying on their initial impulses. For her, this meant that she was being tested and growing as an actor.[16] Similarly Pete Meredith, who has ambitions to act professionally and recently auditioned for drama schools, disclosed during conversation that whilst he has learnt from all the directors he has worked with at The Criterion, John Ruscoe's expertise and many years' experience on the professional and amateur circuits, has been especially beneficial.

The easy group dynamics; the collision between domestic, work and amateur labour and John Ruscoe's ability to coax his actors to hone their characters and stagecraft was similarly evident during rehearsals a few days later:

John has his young daughter with him for the first hour of rehearsals. She is clearly comfortable in the environment and sits with her fidget spinner. John encourages her to take notes and a cast member laughs saying 'thank God we've got someone who knows what they're talking about'. Things have been added since I was last here—a towel in the bathroom, an old phone on the writing desk, a bin. The sofa is now half-upholstered, but John is not happy with it. It looks a bit scruffy for a high-end hotel and the front doesn't come down low enough to fully conceal the body that is hidden under it in Act Two. Neil is away for the weekend so John is rehearsing the scenes without him. Alan is struggling with his lines. He likes to go over his lines before rehearsals but he explains that he's been 'flat out' at work and hasn't had a chance. He's frustrated; he knows this makes the rehearsal less productive

---

[16] Karen Evans in conversation with Nadine Holdsworth, The Criterion Theatre Bar, 11 June 2017.

for him and others. John is never less than encouraging. After each scene John's notes are extensive encompassing physicality, intention, focus, volume, interaction, intensity, pacing and the need to avoid throwing away important lines. The cast listen, take things in and try to amend their performances accordingly. (Nadine's Research Diary, 16th June 2017)

By the first dress rehearsal held on Tuesday 20th June the space had been transformed from my visit four days previously. The bleacher seats fill the auditorium ready for the audience; the set has been further dressed with curtains, a light switch and the long awaited sofa (which is still causing problems). The dress rehearsal is run by the stage manager, Stella Gabriel, who sits at the front of the auditorium flanked by her sister Nikki Gabriel, who is the prompt alongside Karl Stafford and Dave Cornish, the lighting and sound designers, who sit at lighting and sound desks temporarily moved to enable communication and a close observation of how things are working on-the-ground. The rehearsal is conducted in a highly disciplined manner and I am struck by the refreshing gender and intergenerational dynamics at play here as a young woman runs and cues the rehearsal with respectful compliance from her more experienced and older male counterparts. The sense of shared serious endeavour, as well as conviviality, is evident after the rehearsal when everyone involved in the production congregates in the bar for notes on acting, sight lines, sound cues and malfunctioning bits of set until gone 11 pm.

The next afternoon I met up with Nancy Silvester, a member of the company, who is trying to salvage the sofa. She spent eight hours on Sunday 'sweating blood' on a pelmet to go round the bottom, complete with neatly crafted box pleats, but she is struggling to attach this to the frame. Her frustration is palpable, and this situation reveals something of the difficulties that can arise by doing things 'on the cheap'. The company accepted an offer of help with upholstery, but the job was not completed to satisfaction, 'it's lumpy bumpy' but they have neither the time nor the resources to start from scratch. The lack of resource also impacts on the ability to store furniture and props. There is a storage unit at the back of the theatre, but it leaks and the condensation turns everything mouldy. Defeated, because 'I can't put it right' Nancy Silvester decides to take a break and return in the evening. As she prepares to leave, Dave Cornish comes into the auditorium. He has been restocking the bar and cleaning the pumps, a job he undertakes in addition to his role as resident sound designer. His career designing electronics for GEC Telecommunications has furnished Dave Cornish with a certain degree of technical knowledge, but he is keen to stress, 'I'm no craftsperson, but I'm quite practical. I'm self-taught'. His first show for The Criterion was Alan Ayckbourn's *Absurd Person Singular* in 1977, which he proudly told me entailed seventy-five separate cues recorded individually on tape, cut with a razor blade and spliced together, which took him 'the full six weeks of rehearsal. I was up there every night while they rehearsed down here'.[17] Having overseen the gradual upgrade of sound equipment as new technologies have come on stream, Dave Cornish now works on a computer with sound files, software packages and enjoys experimenting with different channels and the possibilities of surround sound. The sound for *Communicating Doors* evolved through collaboration with John Ruscoe, who wanted to draw out the references to Alfred Hitchcock's thrillers he detected in the script. Deciding to use the stabbing sound from the shower scene in *Psycho* for the door revolve, Dave Cornish noted that this worked well because it was also reminiscent of a squeaky door if only the first bar was utilised and repeated. Again, I am struck by the care taken, the creative decision-making and the desire to do things as properly as possible. They may be amateurs, but the intent is purposeful and informed by years of unpaid creative labour.

My experience at The Criterion provided ample evidence for the idea that making together is a mode of building and shaping community (Hawkins 2017: 159). As we have pointed out in Chapter 4, this is all the more important given concerns with what Bauman characterises as a 'liquid society' in which relationships and communities are increasingly fragile due to the demands of twenty-first century life (2005). In his study of amateur theatre on the Gold Coast in Australia, Patrick Mitchell found that involvement provides 'opportunities to lead an expressive or creative life', but also that participants encountered 'an active social life, an experience of belonging and continuity' that ultimately brings 'deeper benefits beyond just being in the production' (2015: 197, 191). As people rehearse, build sets, design and make costumes and props together they build the foundations for and reinforce social bonds that can be understood in terms of Putnam's work on how engagement in community groups helps forge networks of reciprocal social relations or 'social capital' that help build trust, cooperation and solidarity with others that ultimately contributes to

---

[17] Dave Cornish in conversation with Nadine Holdsworth, The Criterion Theatre, 21 June 2017.

well-being (see Putnam 2000; Gauntlett 2011). All the people I speak to refer to the community ethos of the place, which is in no small measure attributable to the presence of the bar as a social space. When I emerge with the cast from the Friday night rehearsal the bar is already populated with members who come knowing they will meet familiar faces. A man sits with a pint at the bar; two elderly men sit in a quiet corner deep in conversation and a mixed group are laughing and greeting the cast members who join them. Here, I talk to Alan Fenn, a cast member, who admits he is an itinerant figure who finds it hard to settle. After ten years in the Royal Navy he moved around the country doing a range of jobs, some theatre-related, some not. He is currently working as a lorry driver as this gives him maximum flexibility to focus on theatre. He has settled in the Coventry area largely because of The Criterion where he has discovered a community of practice that take their theatre seriously whilst having a social side.[18] In amateur theatre social encounters are important and rehearsals are often constructed as social occasions with moments for shared food, chat, banter, gossip and fun, whether in the rehearsal itself or in the retreat to a bar afterwards. On one memorable occasion Pete Meredith deliberately withheld wearing the hilarious comb-over wig he had been given to signal the passing of time prior to his appearance with it during a rehearsal, which, as he knew it would, resulted in the cast having to stifle giggles and avoid corpsing altogether. After the shows the cast and crew join assembled friends and company members to share a drink and a chat. The night I attend the show on 26th June, Neil Vallance brought in a programme for an amateur theatre production he did in Oman in 1986 and much laughter emanated from the vision of him thirty years younger, but even more so by his uncanny resemblance to Pete Meredith. This is a group of people who clearly enjoy each other's company, who are at ease with each other and benefitting from the bonds of sociability the processes of making amateur theatre generate.

Participants often employ the rhetoric and emotional register of 'family' when they talk about their involvement in amateur theatre. Joe Allan, who writes, directs and performs with two Royal Navy groups, the Admirals' Players and Collingwood RSC, described how 'they become like a second family ... you build this family'; speaking about her involvement

---

[18] Alan Fenn in conversation with Nadine Holdsworth, The Criterion Theatre Bar, 16 June 2017.

with The Questors Theatre, Dorothy Lawson stated that 'I don't have any family, but Questors is like my family'; John Beglin referred to PTUK as 'my family' and many other interviewees have referred to their faux 'theatre family' as distinct from their immediate family rooted in ties of kinship, although there are numerous examples of extended family dynasties working with one company over decades.[19] The relationships within amateur companies often echo the complex interpersonal dynamics of extended family life—the hierarchies, varying roles, allegiances and squabbles—but, above all, the term 'family' used in this context suggests the often deep and lasting bonds forged as people make theatre together. Amateur theatre's ability to facilitate an active and supportive relational community or 'communities of care' has wider consequences for general well-being, as well as helping people navigate difficult pivotal moments in their lives that might include illness, redundancy, divorce or bereavement. In our conversation, Anne-marie Greene stressed the relational aspects that drive her participation: 'I think it's partly community … it is such a social environment for us. All our friends are here really, we have friends outside of Coventry but all of our Coventry friends are part of the theatre.' When she became critically ill in 2012 with a brain tumour this community came into its own, 'everyone just rallied around' with implicit emotional and explicit practical support such as child-care and hospital visits. Others have told us how engaging in rehearsals and the craft of making can be a retreat, an absorbing activity that serves as a temporary respite for those having a hard time in their personal lives. Care can be demonstrated through an invitation to make and do during costume mornings, set construction sessions and rehearsals so that the person under-going treatment for cancer or navigating the emotional turmoil of a relationship breakdown can occupy another field of making.

Making Diverse Communities: Creative Interventions

When people think about who constitutes the amateur theatre community, the prevailing stereotype is that it is predominantly populated by a traditional demographic of the white, middle-aged and middle-class. At

---

[19] Interview Joe Allan with Nadine Holdsworth, HMS Collingwood, 3 February 2014 and Dorothy Lawson interviewed by Maurice Newberry at an Evocative Objects workshop held at The Questors Theatre in Ealing, 16 June 2015.

The Criterion, there is a diverse demographic of ages and socio-economic backgrounds. The assembled team for *Communicating Doors* include a lorry driver, a stay-at-home mum, a call-centre worker, a Human Resources officer, someone currently unemployed, someone in property management and those retired from a variety of jobs and professions. This is positive and to be celebrated, but not without drawing attention to some more problematic omissions. What if the community being built and sustained is troublingly homogenous and fails to represent the diverse make-up in the vicinity? Hawkins suggests:

> As art forms evolve to be constituted by and through relations built between people time must be spent reflecting on the form and nature of these relations. Reflecting not only on how art might bring about social relations, but also whether or not these should be about bringing people together around things in common, or about raising uncomfortable and sometimes controversial issues. (2017: 179)

Anne-marie Greene touched on the difficulties that circulate around the issue of ethnic diversity when she acknowledged that given the demographic of the city 'diversity is a real problem … it's kind of a bit embarrassing really'. Drawing evidence from The Criterion's board meetings and her observation of a discussion held at a Little Theatre Guild annual conference a few years earlier, she cited problems with defensiveness and an insensitive use of language, which she characterised as a 'how can we get more of them?' rhetoric, motivated by the possibilities for an open choice of repertoire rather than any deep concern with creative interventions that contribute to representing and making resilient multicultural communities. She had also experienced negotiating discomfort with colour-blind casting when she cast a black actor in a production of David Auburn's *Proof* in 2015, which incorporated the theatre's first interracial kiss. After a couple of audience members walked out and an older member of the audience enquired pointedly 'were you supposed to cast a black actor in that part? Was that what was in the script?' she was left in no doubt that there is a residual problem around the cultural politics of race in her own and other amateur theatres.

One of the persistent challenges facing amateur theatre companies, and the organisations that support them, is how to address the paucity of participation of people of colour and racialised minorities. This problem is exacerbated in non-metropolitan areas with few residents who might be described as BAME where many amateur theatre companies are located, but equally, in parts of the country that are ethnically diverse NODA has urged its societies to 'ask themselves why none or few of their members are drawn from non-white communities, and be willing to take steps to remedy this'.[20] This is not an issue unique to amateur theatre. In November 2016 Voluntary Arts produced a report 'Open Conversations: Developing strong, effective connections to Black, Asian and Minority Ethnic communities', documenting the organisation's nascent strategy to tackle 'the relative lack of diversity in its staffing, governance and beneficiaries' by building relationships and dialogue to facilitate shared learning, rather than relying on formal consultations that asked questions about participation without ever listening to the implications of findings (2016: 1). Importantly, this document stresses the need to avoid a deficit model, which encourages under-represented communities to get involved in 'mainstream' cultural activity. Clearly, BAME communities are engaged in myriad creative activities and forms of cultural expression, but the report acknowledges that these are often divorced from the national support structures that might nurture them. This finding is depressingly reminiscent of cultural activist Naseem Khan's *The Arts Britain Ignores* from 1976, and it is important to ask what the barriers to participation in amateur theatre might be. David Bryan, who chaired the BAME Advisory Panel assembled by Voluntary Arts to tease out the complexities around this issue, stresses that 'all organisations form comfort zones and some aspects of diversity are outside that comfort zone' (2016: 18). Hence, organisations, including amateur theatre groups, have particular makeups, racial or otherwise, that are difficult to shift. People often come to it via word of mouth or friendship groups, which mean that cultural and racial homogeneity can sediment. Whilst many amateur theatre groups and members exhibit critical self-reflection, frustration and a profound awareness of the organisational failings that lead to a lack of progress in this area, in some conversations I have detected sympathy with Bryan's sense that 'some may say "if they [BAME communities] are not interested in what we have to offer, why should we make extra effort?"' (2016: 3).

---

[20] NODA factsheet 'It Isn't Always Black and White' http://www.NODA.org.uk/writeable/editor_uploads/files/NODAfacts/It%20isn't%20always%20black%20and%20white%20V4%20July%202013.pdf. Accessed 16 May 2017. All other quotations are taken from this source.

What this means is that a classic Catch 22 logic presides—if members of BAME communities do not make themselves available, they are not represented then they are not seen and this creates a perpetual cycle of non-representation and non-participation. Problematically this attitude also places the burden of responsibility onto BAME communities rather than shining a light on recruitment practices and cultures that signal exclusivity, or worse, a profound lack of sensitivity to racial politics.

The difficulties that circulate around this issue are brought starkly into focus by ongoing debates around the highly controversial practice of 'blacking up' in amateur theatre productions. 'Blacking up', whereby white actors don make-up to play characters from different ethnic groups, has its origins in the minstrelsy tradition associated with the early English folk traditions of mumming as well as the blackface minstrelsy evident in the popular performance forms of vaudeville and music hall in the nineteenth century. There has been a widespread recognition that material and discursive practices such as 'blacking up' are part of the armoury of colonial discourse, which relies on a nexus of repeated images that bypass the real lives and experiences of BAME communities and individuals in favour of a fiction inscribed with meaning from the dominant white culture that further instils their power. As theatre scholar Eric Lott makes clear, minstrelsy's fundamental consequence for black culture is 'the dispossession and control by whites of black forms', whilst also 'articulating precisely a certain structure of racial feeling' (1995: 115). In professional theatre 'blacking up' has long been debunked as an unethical racially pejorative practice that relies on a form of racial caricaturing rooted in regimes of representation that demean black subjectivity. To re-perform the practice of 'blacking up' invokes a long history of slavery, the denigration of cultural *others* and racial stereotyping.

Yet, in amateur theatre the practice, whilst limited, 'blacking up' has occurred in the twenty-first century leading to intense scrutiny by audiences, the media and local authorities. In April 2016 Westwood Musical Society caused controversy when it decided to 'black-up' one of its performers to play an impersonator of the actor Mr. T in its production of *The Wedding Singer* at The Key Theatre in Peterborough. Leitina Reuben-Travers, a member of another local group, Peterborough Operatic and Dramatic Society (PODS) expressed her incredulity at what she had witnessed:

I was gobsmacked. You could hear an intake of breath from the audience when he came out. I could not believe I was in 2016, I was appalled. As a black woman, I was offended to see someone blacked up. At PODS we rehearse for six months, and I can't believe no one at Westwood would have raised it as an issue. Last year we ran a campaign to try and encourage more people from minorities to join up, and I think this sends out the wrong message.[21]

In December 2016 an actor with Chelmsford Theatre Workshop posted a picture of himself in blackface on Facebook with the caption 'now I can finally play Othello'. After receiving complaints, the actor and theatre group issued apologies and insisted that no offence was meant, but many felt the wider implications of this, with one respondent despairing that 'it is the actions of a minority like this that see Chelmsford and wider Essex branded with the stereotype of provincial bigotry'.[22] In 2012 four performers withdrew from Yeovil Amateur Operatic Society's production of *South Pacific* when their objections to the director's choice of 'mahogany brown' make-up were dismissed. In 2007 Grange and District Amateur Operatic Society based in Cumbria withdrew its production of *Show Boat,* with its planned use of 'blacking up', following a local outcry that reached national attention after the actors' union Equity warned the production would cause offence and the National Assembly Against Racism coordinator, Milena Buyun, was reported stating 'We find that offensive. It's a throwback of an era where minstrels were used. It is dehumanising to black people. It is racist'.[23]

All these examples prompted online discussion threads that reveal something of the ongoing legacy of imperialist cultural imaginaries often manifest in anti-political correctness rhetoric. Leitina Reuben-Travers faced a barrage of discriminatory abuse and was accused of being ridiculous and hysterical, with one post claiming 'offended by someone blacking up. Seems like your (sic) ashamed of being black or something missy, get a life!'. Similarly the Chelmsford Theatre Workshop story provoked calls

---

[21] Stephen Briggs 'Row after man 'blacked up' for show', *Peterborough Telegraph,* 25 April 2016.

[22] http://www.dailymail.co.uk/news/article-4001094/Amateur-dramatics-society-race-row-blacked-Othello.html. Accessed 15 May 2017.

[23] http://www.dailymail.co.uk/news/article-462270/Drama-group-race-row-blacking-amateur-production.html. Accessed 15 May 2017.

of 'grow up snowflakes' and 'this political correctness has gone far enough'. In her stout defence of political correctness, theatre scholar Janelle Reinelt insists how 'the rhetorical juxtaposition of "political correctness" and "free expression" sets up a binary which can prejudice a nuanced analysis of complex cultural negotiations in and around particular theatrical performances' (2011: 134). The decision to draw attention to language or practices that ignite sensitivities is often maligned and dismissed as an over-reaction that masks the knotty source of concern and suppresses meaningful debate through what Reinelt terms 'cognitive assent or social pressure' (2011: 134). Equally, the call for political correctness might be understood in relation to feminist thinker and writer Sara Ahmed's appeal in *Willful Subjects* (2014) for a politics of wilful disobedience that adamantly refuses to obscure or acquiesce to social consensus that persists in delimiting feminist, queer and anti-racist histories, subjectivities and politics. My interest here, however, is in how the practice of 'blacking up' and the rhetorical riposte of 'political correctness gone mad' undermines amateur theatre's potential to contribute to making dynamic communities and the proactive strategies that some companies have embarked on to address limitations in this area.

The astonishing persistence of 'blacking up' as a representational strategy in amateur theatre practice has given rise to a number of disputes between theatre groups, their local communities and local councils. In 2000 Rotherham Borough Council initiated proceedings to issue a ban on 'blacking up' in all its venues following a dispute over Parkgate Amateur Operatic Society's production of *South Pacific* in 1999. A compromise was reached that banned the use of make-up that perpetuated derogatory stereotyping, followed up with revised terms and conditions for hiring Rotherham Civic Theatre. When Redditch Borough Council prevented Studley Operatic Society from presenting *Show Boat* at the council's Palace Theatre, the coverage in the local and national press provoked the licencing agent, Josef Weinberger, at the behest of the Rogers and Hammerstein organisation, to issue a strongly worded casting policy that stressed the 'racial specificity' of the cast. Concerns over 'blacking up' also prompted NODA to issue a factsheet 'It Isn't Always Black and White' to advise societies and local authorities on the issue, which by 2013 had been re-issued four times in revised versions.[24]

Admitting many NODA members 'do not believe the practice of "blacking up" to be offensive', the document touches on the history of the slave trade, the performance of minstrelsy and the perpetuation of racial stereotypes before stressing that concerns with blacking up are 'a genuine, heartfelt reaction that affiliated societies must take account of when deciding how to respond to the complex and sensitive issue'. The factsheet also highlights the statutory duty of local authorities to promote equality of opportunity, good race relations and to avoid unlawful discrimination. Yet, a troubling caveat states:

> It is interesting to note that the Licensing Act 2003 dictates that conditions cannot be attached to premises licences covering the performance of a play as a licensable activity which attempt in any way to censor or modify the content of plays. Societies may be able to use this clause to prevent local authorities from imposing a ban on any production that relies on 'blacking up'.

The vast majority of amateur companies refuse to go down this route or to acquiesce to the perception that amateur theatre is an enclave or retreat from the realities of contemporary multiculturalism. In *After Empire: Melancholia or Convivial Culture?*, the sociologist Paul Gilroy stresses the importance of social practices that bring different ethnicities and cultures into contact and highlights how regular interaction has the potential to breed conviviality, which Gilroy understands as 'the processes of cohabitation and interaction that have made multi-culture an ordinary feature of social life in Britain's urban areas' (Gilroy 2004: xi). Whilst Gilroy focuses on Britain's urban areas, I want to suggest that the promise of conviviality whereby 'people slowly discover the histories and mores of their fellow human beings' through everyday life and social practice so that 'the *toleration* of difference becomes *good-natured confidence* around difference' might also be found in non-urban areas and via the social practice of amateur theatre-making where people of different ethnicities can mix and co-create (Williams 2013: 51).

[24] NODA factsheet 'It Isn't Always Black and White' http://www.NODA.org.uk/write-able/editor_uploads/files/NODAfacts/It%20isn't%20always%20black%20and%20white%20V4%20July%202013.pdf. Accessed 16 May 2017.

When in 2012 Milton Musical Society, based in New Milton, a rural area in Hampshire, elected to stage *Ragtime!*, a musical about immigration and racial prejudice in New York at the turn of the twentieth century, and in 2015 when Mad Cow Productions, based in Shrewsbury, decided to stage *Hairspray*, which is set in the 1960s civil rights era in America to present a narrative about fighting discrimination in all its forms and demanding racial equality; both had to confront the fact they had no black participants amongst their membership. Both of these geographical areas have low numbers of BAME residents, with Shrewsbury based in Shropshire, a county where the 2011 census confirmed that 98% of the population is classified as being in a 'white' ethnic group in comparison to the 85.9% average for England and Wales.[25] In these circumstances the choice of repertoire is an interesting one, but at a time of heightened anxiety over migration to the United Kingdom, coupled with the rise of populist far-right rhetoric coming from a then buoyant UK Independence Party, it was an ideologically loaded one. Having committed to the shows and their promotion of racial tolerance and openness, both companies refused to accept that their composition was fixed and put in motion energetic recruitment drives to facilitate renewed communities of practice. During an interview, Alex Hinton, the co-Artistic Director of Mad Cow Productions, articulated a need to counter the representational deficit that meant potential black participants would 'have had a lifetime of watching musical theatre and plays that are white dominated', which underscored the impression that amateur theatre was not a space open to diverse participation.[26] She knew that she would have to disrupt this narrative, as she explained:

> When we put the open audition flyer out for *Hairspray* the artwork was 1% white and 99% black so it was about trying to sow the psychological seed and it was literally stopping people in the street saying 'Do you sing? Do you dance?'... I talked to everyone I could find who might be in travelling distance of here. I talked to sixth forms. I talked to schools and just positive discrimination throughout.

---

[25] https://www.shropshire.gov.uk/census-2011/census-2011-shropshires-profile/. Accessed 28 Dec 2017.

[26] Interview of Alex Hinton with Nadine Holdsworth, Severn Theatre, Shrewsbury, 17 November 2016. All other quotations from Alex Hinton are taken from this interview.

Members of Milton Musical Society similarly approached people at work or out shopping and, after failing to recruit and postponing the show in 2012, assembled six new black members to enable the show to go ahead in 2013. Mad Cow's campaign secured eight new participants including Yvonne Morris, who was recruited to play the role of Motor-Mouth Maybelle whilst getting her hair done. 'Trying to think outside the box, the one place we visited was Weavelicous, a hair salon in Frankwell special-ising in European and Afro Caribbean hair, where the owner, the lovely Silvie Veglio, allowed us to approach her clients.'[27] Despite the fact that Yvonne Morris lived in Llanidloes in Mid-Wales, she agreed to audition, was given the role and her husband drove the three-hour round trip twice a week so that she could attend rehearsals. Importantly, Yvonne Morris has stayed with Mad Cow Productions. She played a number of small roles in its 2016 production of *Spamalot* and has painted sets, helped out with costume and handed-out flyers.

Now, of course, there is something politically and socially awkward about ethnically white members of an amateur theatre group approaching strangers, presumably identified by their visual markers of difference, to enquire about their interest in singing and acting. In *Strange Encounters: Embodied Others in Post-Coloniality*, Ahmed points out that 'Through strange encounters, the figure of the "stranger" is produced, not as that which we fail to recognise, but as that which we have already recognised as "a stranger"' and clearly the black and Asian members recruited to Milton Musical Society and Mad Cow conform in some sense to the fetishisation of the stranger Ahmed discusses (2000: 3). Yet, there is some-thing else happening here. Ahmed also suggests that 'multiculturalism involves stranger festishism: the act of welcoming 'the stranger' as the origin of difference produces the very figure of 'the stranger' as the one who can be taken in' (2000: 97). By simultaneously recognising the stranger as such and soliciting their participation, 'as one who can be taken in' these groups resisted the disavowal of the *other* and their objectification implied by 'blacking up' and replaced it with a desire to put in play moments of encounter of bringing 'the stranger' into proximity that have the potential to facilitate newly constituted relationships and understand-ings on both sides or a convivial culture in Gilroy's formulation.

---

[27] http://www.shrewsburytoday.co.uk/hair-today-star-tomorrow-shrewsbury-theatre-group-finds-new-star-town-salon/. Accessed 15 May 2017.

Fig. 6.4 Marlyn Mabukela, Poppy Dhansingani and Ahmed Hamed in Mad Cow's production of *Hairspray*, 2015. (By kind permission of photographer, Guy Clarke)

Operating in parallel with amateur theatre companies who have tried to widen their membership, are companies formed to cater for specific cultural groups or diasporic communities. In 2002, Ramon Teñoso and his partner Maurice Newbery, along with fifteen founding members largely from the Filipino community, established PTUK with a remit to produce original plays about the life and experiences of Filipinos in the Philippines and abroad.[28] This London-based company emerged in the context of widespread transnational labour migration to the United Kingdom since the 1970s as migrant labour became crucial to maintaining the functionality of the NHS, hotel and catering industries, clothing manufacturers and social care. Many of PTUK's members arrived in the United Kingdom as economic migrants during this period. Having graduated with a degree in psychology from the University of the Philippines and worked as a researcher for a Philippine children's television programme *Batibot*, and as an administrative officer for Philippine Airlines, Ramon Teñoso came to the United Kingdom in 1987 and secured work in the healthcare sector. In the late 1990s he became involved with the now defunct Bayanihang Filipino UK, for whom he adapted and directed the Filipino classic novel, *El Filibusterismo* (1891), which was commissioned and performed as part of the centennial celebration of Philippine Independence in 1998. Since 2002, PTUK has been a vehicle for producing Ramon Teñoso's original plays and adaptations funded by donations from its members, their families and fellow Filipinos from across the United Kingdom.

In her study *Making Home in Diasporic Communities: Transnational Belonging among Filipina Migrants*, Diane Sabenacio Nititham suggests that: 'whether diasporans seek to return home or not, they orientate their motivations, practices and cultural products towards the homeland' and this impulse is very much in evidence in PTUK's repertoire (2017: 40). Many of Ramon Teñoso's plays tackle and take a stand on socio-political issues that are happening in the homeland such as *Pater Noster* (2006), a play about Filipino seafarers. Equally, they confront the migrant experience, feelings of dislocation, questions of belonging, as well as a strong felt attachment to the narratives and experiences of home. Ramon Teñoso's *Migrants* (2012) staged 14–15th December 2012 at Theatro Technis in London as part of the theatre company's tenth anniversary celebration, deals with the homecoming narratives and representations of the balik-bayan, a term used to denote a Filipino returning home after an extended period living overseas. Set both in the homeland and abroad, the play

[28] We are grateful to Sherwin Mapanoo for alerting me to the work of PTUK whilst undertaking the MA in International Performance Research at the University of Warwick.

represents a number of characters that share a common ground of situating themselves within and navigating the complex territory between the homeland and host country, the national and transnational. As such, *Migrants* can be characterised in relation to cultural theorist James Clifford's ascription of a specific mode of 'diaspora consciousness' whereby 'dwelling *here* assumes a solidarity and connection *there*' (1994: 322). This sense of double consciousness and affiliation is sharply present in one PTUK performer, Chelo Cruz's assessment of the *Migrants* project:

> We, here in the UK specifically, we haven't forgotten home, we are very much attached to it, that's why we're doing this project so that we get people knowing what's happening here, we get people involved here. What's really the situation for the migrant worker here.[29]

The connection between the homeland and host country is further enunciated in other outputs and initiatives. In addition to original plays, the company has also produced Ramon Teñoso's adaptations of traditional Filipino stories and folktales such as *Ibong Adarna* (*Enchanted Bird*) produced by the company in 2004 and again in 2014. These outputs are part of a commitment to keeping Filipino cultural heritage alive for diasporic communities and younger generations. PTUK often stage their performances in accordance with official Philippine holidays such as Independence Day and National Heroes Day. They also regularly engage in charity fundraising, especially for Philippine causes and have raised money for Street Orphans in Manila and the Helen Thompson Foundation following Hurricane Haiyan in 2013.

Diane Sabenacio Nititham found that Filipino migrants 'actively sought a sense of community, relying heavily on social networks and social practices to provide important support' (2017: 49). PTUK can be understood as one of the ways in which Filipinos negotiate their role as part of a diasporic community unified by shared bonds of national identity, ethnicity and culture and often a shared experience of alienation in their host country. PTUK enables members to be part of the common space of theatre-making through which they construct a home from home, where they can feel at home, as well as maintaining connections with and navigating their

---

[29] See https://www.youtube.com/watch?v=KGg7kQeQO0w, accessed 24 August 2017.

complex relations with their home and homeland. Drawing on sociologist George Simmel's ideas on sociability, Erin Walcon and Helen Nicholson have highlighted the 'aesthetics of sociability' that defines PTUK's working practices via the rituals of welcome, sharing food and relational encounters that mesh with rehearsals (2017: 22–23). This slippage is in evidence across all aspects of PTUK's activity. A film uploaded onto YouTube of a public reading/audition for *Migrants* held on 8th July 2012 at the Philippine Embassy in London captures an intergenerational group squeezed into a room with people intently following the script, getting up to read parts, sharing food, singing Filipino songs from the play, discussing and promoting the work of PTUK. When I attended a production of *The Enchanted Bird* at Chelsea Theatre on 28 September 2014 this same atmosphere was evident. As the predominately Filipino audience assembled, the mood was one of a social club where people greeted each other, hugged and laughed and after the show a social gathering ensued.

PTUK is a vital part of a wider social network of organisations and activities designed to bring Filipino migrants together. It participates in community cultural events such as exhibitions, beauty pageants, festivals, seminars and other recreational activities that are organised by Filipino migrants in London. The company involves itself in community events organised by the Philippine Embassy in London and is a member of the Kanlungan Filipino Consortium, an alliance of Filipino community organisations including the Campaign for Human Rights in the Philippines, Filipino Domestic Workers Association and the Bahay Kubo Housing Association, which aims to help Filipino migrants living in the United Kingdom. Yet, it is important to stress that PTUK is not an exclusive group as it invites cross-community involvement and co-creation. Whilst the majority of PTUK's members are Filipinos, there are British members and other nationalities participating too. The company operates an open-door policy with Ramon Teñoso keen to welcome members regardless of their ethnicity or theatre experience. A position reiterated in materials such as the programme for *The Enchanted Bird,* which stresses the company is 'open to all believers in theatre from any race, colour, creed or background'. The sense of an open invitation to join PTUK or see its outputs is apparent in many aspects of its approach to making and marketing the theatre they create. One of the marketing strategies for the 2016 production of *Aswang (The Birth of Malum)* involved filming and distributing via YouTube several voxpop videos from members of the company. The tone of these is overwhelmingly one of invitation with calls of 'come and join us', 'see you there' and 'we are inviting you all'. So, like Milton Musical Society and Mad Cow Productions discussed earlier, it is possible to see how PTUK is opening up another version of the convivial spaces for productive exchange Gilroy proposes. But, perhaps more importantly, all of these interventions contribute to sociologist Tariq Modood's notion of civic multiculturalism, which relies on 'creating new attitudes of inclusivity as well as rethinking national identities in a context of post-immigration "difference"' (Modood 2013: 166).

CONCLUSION

Throughout this chapter I have suggested that the significance and cultural value of making amateur theatre stretches far beyond what is produced on stage. Shifting the gaze from an often unfairly derided product to the processes and wider contextual parameters of making, as a social as well a creative practice, is crucial in appreciating the multiple benefits accrued to individual participants and communities. Taking the making process seriously reveals that people give not only their time and energy, but invest in honing their skills and craft; taking pride in doing the best job they can with the temporal, human and material resources at their disposal. As a consequence, our research has led us to see many excellent amateur productions that have exhibited high production values, innovative set designs, carefully nuanced acting, beautifully crafted costumes and thoughtful direction. Not always, but then we would say the same about professional productions too—there are some excellent amateur productions and some poor professional productions and everything else in between. Yet, there is strong affective power in watching people, many of whom have completed a day's labour, turning out to rehearse and perform on-stage and backstage, for the love of it. An affective power heightened by the presence of other company members and members of local communities who loyally turn up to support them as audience members or helping out front-of-house. There is a generosity at play in amateur theatre that can be moving to witness.

This research has found that making amateur theatre does contribute to shaping subjectivities through the opportunities it affords to live a creative life and nurture craft skills, but also by providing a vehicle through which people can volunteer, help out and feel needed in their immediate environment. As a situated practice rooted in place it helps build dynamic communities through the process of making, as well as the occasions it creates for social gatherings of makers, company members and audience. Contrary to the dominant stereotype, amateur theatre is often populated by a broad social demographic and one of the most striking aspects is its intergenerational constituency. It is common to find young people making with and alongside elderly members of the community and to see them trade skills and knowledge in productive ways. At the same time, to pick up on the idea of 'feeling-work' outlined in the introduction, we have all felt profound unease at times with amateur theatre's lack of diversity. Being in rehearsal rooms, watching productions, sifting through archival materials, attending committee meetings, festivals and events run by national organisations such as NODA, LTG and GoDA, it is evident that work needs to be done to open up amateur theatre as a convivial space that represents what it means to live in a culturally diverse society. It is also important that we acknowledge that amateur theatre is not alone in addressing this complex issue; anyone attending the annual conferences for TaPRA (the UK's Theatre and Performance Research Association) would observe that delegates are overwhelmingly ethnically white. We would hope that greater integration in youth theatres and schools will soon create the conditions in which both amateur theatre and university drama departments become more representative of the diverse society in which we live, but it is unlikely that this will happen without careful intervention and encouragement. This chapter has explored some examples of this opening up in metropolitan and non-metropolitan areas, which might galvanise other companies to actively breach the barriers that foster exclusion.

References

Adamson, Glenn. 2013. *The Invention of Craft*. London: Bloomsbury Academic.
———. 2013 [2007]. *Thinking Through Craft*. London: Bloomsbury Academic.
Ahmed, Sara. 2000. *Strange Encounters: Embodied Others in Post-coloniality*. London: Routledge.
———. 2014. *Willful Subjects*. Durham/London: Duke University Press.
Allain, Paul. 2016. Thick Description/Thin Lines: Writing About Contemporary Performance. *Contemporary Theatre Review* 26 (4): 485–495.
Bauman, Zigmunt. 2005. *Liquid Life*. Cambridge: Polity Press.
Castells, Manuel. 2009 [1996]. *The Rise of the Network Society*. 2nd revised ed. Oxford: Wiley Blackwell.
Clifford, James. 1994. Diasporas. *Cultural Anthropology* 9 (3): 302–338.

Coates, David. 2018. *The Development of Amateur Theatre in Britain in the Long Nineteenth Century 1789–1914.* Unpublished PhD thesis, University of Warwick.

Day, Graham. 2006. *Community and Everyday Life.* Abingdon: Routledge.

Edensor, Tim, Deborah Leslie, Steve Millington, and Norma M. Rantisi. 2010. *Spaces of Vernacular Creativity: Rethinking the Cultural Economy.* Abingdon: Routledge.

Frayling, Christopher. 2011. *On Craftsmanship.* London: Oberon Books.

Gauntlett, David. 2011. *Making Is Connecting: The Social Meaning of Creativity, Form DIY and Knitting to YouTube and Web 2.0.* Cambridge: Polity Press.

Gilroy, Paul. 2004. *After Empire: Melancholia or Convivial Culture?* Abingdon: Routledge.

Harvie, Jen, and Andy Lavender, eds. 2010. *Making Contemporary Theatre: International Rehearsal Processes.* Manchester: Manchester University Press.

Hawkins, Harriet. 2017. *Creativity.* Abingdon: Routledge.

Ingold, Tim. 2013. *Making: Anthropology, Archaeology.* Abingdon: Routledge.

Khan, Naseem. 1976. *The Arts Britain Ignores: The Arts of Ethnic Minorities in Britain.* London: Community Relations Commission.

Knott, Stephen. 2015. *Amateur Craft: History and Theory.* London: Bloomsbury.

Korn, Peter. 2013. *Why We Make Things & Why It Matters: The Education of a Craftsman.* London: Vintage.

Luckman, Susan. 2015. *Craft and the Creative Economy.* Basingstoke: Palgrave Macmillan.

Modood, Tariq. 2013. *Multiculturalism.* 2nd ed. Cambridge: Polity Press.

McAuley, Gay. 2012. *Not Magic but Work: An Ethnographic Account of a Rehearsal Process.* Manchester: Manchester University Press.

Mouffe, Chantal, ed. 1992. *Dimensions of Radical Democracy.* London: Verso.

National Operatic and Dramatic Association. 2013. It Isn't Always Black and White, 4th Version, http://www.NODA.org.uk/writeable/editor_uploads/files/NODAfacts/It%20isn't%20always%20black%20and%20white%20V4%20July%202013.pdf. Accessed 16 May 2017.

Nititham, Diane Sabenacio. 2017. *Making Home in Diasporic Communities: Transnational Belonging Amongst Filipina Migrants.* London: Routledge.

Pirsig, Robert M. 1974. *Zen and the Art of Motorcycle Maintenance.* New York: Quill Publications.

Putnam, Robert. 2000. *Bowling Alone: The Collapse and Revival of American Community.* New York: Simon and Schuster.

Reinelt, Janelle. 2011. The Performance of Political Correctness. *Theatre Research International* 36 (2): 134–147. https://doi.org/10.1017/S0307883311000216.

Sennett, Richard. 2008. *The Craftsman.* London: Penguin.

————. 2013 [2012]. *Together: The Rituals, Pleasures and Politics of Cooperation.* London: Penguin.

Stebbins, Robert A. 1992. *Amateurs, Professionals and Serious Leisure.* Montreal: McGill and Queen's University Press.

Voluntary Arts. 2016. *Open Conversations: Developing Strong, Effective Connections to Black, Asian and Minority Ethnic Communities.* https://www.voluntaryarts. org/Handlers/Download.ashx?IDMF=03810465-0337-4f49-a1d6-5ac97b06b349. Accessed 9 May 2017.

Walcon, Erin, and Helen Nicholson. 2017. The Sociable Aesthetics of Amateur Theatre. *Contemporary Theatre Review* 27 (1): 18–33. https://doi.org/10.10 80/10486801.2016.1262851.

Williams, Paul. 2013. *Paul Gilroy.* Abingdon: Routledge.

Wilson, Nick. 2010. Social Creativity: Re-qualifying the Creative Economy. *International Journal of Cultural Policy* 16 (3): 367–381. https://doi. org/10.1080/10286630903111621.

Amateur Theatre: Heritage and Invented Traditions

In 2015 the consultancy group BritainThinks released the findings of its research into the public's attitude towards UK heritage. Commissioned in 2013, the study marked twenty years and £6 billion of investment in the UK's heritage by the Heritage Lottery Fund, which spends money raised from the National Lottery to help protect, preserve and encourage engagement with the nation's heritage. Focused on twelve towns and cities across the UK, the study employed exploratory interviews and workshops with residents and local stakeholders to tease out their relationship with key heritage sites including museums and galleries; churches and cathedrals; libraries; heritage centres and trails; historic buildings, parks and woodlands. The results confirmed that heritage brings transactional economic benefits to areas through job creation, improved tourism and leisure opportunities, but that it also ignites an affective response through a sense of pride, belonging and identity that contributes positively to people's relationship with their community and their quality of life.[1] The heritage sector, encompassing tangible, intangible and digital heritage, is a vital part of the UK's economy and its cultural and creative ecosystem and, as such, is supported through the central government. Part of the Department for Digital, Culture, Media and Sport (DCMS) remit is to protect and

---

[1] See '20 Years in 12 places: Improving heritage, improving places, improving lives', https://www.hlf.org.uk/about-us/research-evaluation/20-years-heritage. Accessed 31 March 2017.

© The Author(s) 2018
H. Nicholson et al., *The Ecologies of Amateur Theatre*,
https://doi.org/10.1057/978-1-137-50810-2_7

237

promote artistic and cultural heritage and The National Trust and English Heritage, amongst other organisations, exists to preserve, sustain, support, manage and promote heritage in the UK. The UK's Arts and Humanities Research Council identified heritage as one of its three priority areas for research in its The Human World 2013–2018 strategy. Whilst in 2016, The Heritage Alliance, established in 2002 to bring together a coalition of heritage organisations advocating for the cultural and societal value of heritage to government and cultural policy-makers, launched the Heritage 2020 consultation to identify priority areas for the future.

As this brief overview indicates, there is no doubting the commitment and resources dedicated to the support and maintenance of UK heritage in the twenty-first century, but questions can be asked about what constitutes heritage, and what types of heritage are recognised and valued and what is ignored? Heritage theorist Laurajane Smith refers to 'authorised heritage discourse' to highlight how heritage relies on the classification and promotion of particular sites, artefacts and activities as worth selecting and preserving as heritage (2006). Writing with Emma Waterton, Smith argues that heritage can work to 'legitimise and de-legitimise a range of cultural and social values' and cultural activity (2009: 291). This idea is further evident in Rodney Harrison's *Heritage: Critical Approaches,* which argues that the promotion of authorised heritage discourse 'works to normalise a range of assumptions about the nature and meaning of heritage and to privilege particular practices, especially those of heritage professionals and the state' (2013: 11). All this suggests that heritage becomes the preserve of institutions and experts who adhere to a certain set of values that largely exclude popular practices such as amateur theatre. In the UK, the history and heritage of amateur theatre has traditionally been absent from national museums and archives; for instance, the Victoria and Albert Museum Theatre and Performance collection privileges the professional sector, which serves to obscure amateur practice. It can be found preserved in official local collections where there is particular interest in amateur creativity; the Letchworth Garden City Heritage Foundation maintains an archive that is a rich resource of amateur theatre in the city, but this is relatively unusual. In other countries amateur theatre receives better treatment in national archives; there is a Museum of Czech Amateur Theatre; the Cyprus Theatre Museum includes amateur activity in its remit and the organisation Het Firmament is dedicated to the cultural heritage of performing arts in Flanders, including amateur practice.

In the UK, collections and archives relating to amateur theatre, if they exist at all, are dispersed in local museums and libraries or maintained by amateur companies or by individuals who keep selected items. Making theatre leaves a tangible residue and more often than not, artefacts of amateur theatre—programmes, posters, designs, prompt copies, old props and bits of costume are kept in people's homes—displayed on walls, stored in spare rooms, under beds, in lofts, garages and cupboards, in what could be rather loftily termed private collections. They are kept as part of a compendium of lived moments, traces of performances that are long gone but held in the memory of participants. Without a coordinated impulse to collect and archive the material traces of amateur theatre vital material is inevitably lost or dispersed, which has the knock-on effect of creating discontinuous histories. This situation highlights the precarious and marginalised place of the amateur in relation to 'authorised' heritage, as well as the failure to recognise and value amateur theatre as part of a wider ecosystem of cultural practice. This is not a problem unique to theatre, but one that blights vernacular creativity in general as the art critic Jonathan Jones highlighted during his review of Tate Britain's 2014 British Folk Arts exhibition, which for him underscored the fact that 'there lies a whole other cultural history that is barely acknowledged by major galleries' or evidenced from the collections held in most museums (2014). This view chimes with cultural and media critic Patricia Holland's assertion:

> [T]here are other histories to be written, embedded in the old, interpreting, reconstructing, making sense of events in less dominant ways. Against a folkloric 'people's history' which leaves the power politics of official histories untouched is the recognition of politics of another form, working itself out through the detail of everyday life and reclaimed from records, like snapshots, which are outside the authority of legitimised knowledge. (1991: 14)

Largely ignored, as part of authorised national heritage, we have found there is plenty of evidence that amateur theatre makes a distinct and valuable contribution to local cultural heritage and that people regularly sift through the records to create alternative histories as Holland proposes. Endorsing the cultural heritage of amateur theatre and amateur theatre as cultural heritage might be understood in relation to Smith's assertion that 'heritage may also be a resource that is used to challenge and redefine received values and identities by a range of subaltern groups' (2006: 4).

The labour embarked on by individuals and amateur groups keen to capture and preserve their heritage is part of an active process of ascribing value to their amateur creativity. The results of this endeavour also find accord with Harrison's idea of *unofficial* as opposed to *official* heritage:

> [M]ay manifest in the rather conventional form of buildings or objects that have significance to individuals or communities but are not recognised by the state as heritage through legislative protection, or may manifest in less tangible ways as sets of social practices that surround more tangible forms of both official and unofficial heritage. (2013: 15)

Harrison's reference to the intangible heritage of social practice is crucial when considering amateur theatre. Part of the argument driving this chapter is that amateur theatre's heritage is as evident in the craft of making, conversations and cultural processes as it is in the tangible heritage projects amateur theatre companies embark on.

Drawing inspiration from Smith and Waterton, who are interested in 'the social and cultural "affect" of heritage and the intangible, but no less "real" or material, social and political consequences that heritage has in validating individual and collective senses of place, identity and collective memory', this chapter is concerned with the heritage work taking place around amateur theatre (2009: 292). I begin by looking at the various ways that amateur theatre companies contribute to sustaining local cultural heritage through the custodianship of buildings and the dissemination of local narratives. I highlight the attentiveness and care companies have shown to recording their histories through tangible heritage projects of archiving, exhibitions and publications and consider how these outputs are put to work. Drawing on theories of material culture I consider how material traces of performance evoke memories and are part of the intangible folklore and heritage of a company and how they become caught up in the life histories and personal narratives of those who keep and treasure them. I then discuss the invention of traditions and performance rituals such as festivals and awards ceremonies that contribute to the ongoing maintenance and preservation of amateur theatre heritage. To conclude, I consider how amateur theatre-makers are increasingly employing the digital realm and the ramifications of this for the proliferation of materials and memories in this expanded field. Above all, the chapter raises questions about the productive and creative role of amateur theatre heritage and cultural traditions that have blossomed around these local and often culturally marginal activities.

HERITAGE MATTERS: THE TANGIBLE AND INTANGIBLE HERITAGE OF AMATEUR THEATRE

Amateur theatre-makers are often heavily invested in what they do and where they do it and, as a result, have proved remarkably adept as custodians of important theatre buildings, that have, in turn, become local landmarks. Titchfield Festival Theatre in Hampshire currently maintains one of Europe's largest surviving medieval Great Barns as a multipurpose venue and in 1993 the Newcastle Players proved instrumental in securing Grade II Listed Building status for the Newcastle Players Theatre Workshop in Stoke-on-Trent, where they had been based since 1969. Founded at a meeting in the Church Coffee Tavern on 24 October 1901, the Stockport Garrick Society has a blue plaque to celebrate its status as England's oldest Little Theatre and in 2006 Ilkley Playhouse, home of The Ilkley Players, received a blue plaque when the building was incorporated into the town's tourist trail. Amateur theatre companies also play a role in disseminating and celebrating local narratives, histories, industrial cultural heritage or cultural figures via their traditions and repertoire. When The Lace Market Theatre in Nottingham had a tradition of doing small-scale productions in the bar area for first time directors to 'cut their teeth', these productions became known as '"fents" – a name taken from the off-cuts of lace sold at bargain prices … [which] paid homage to the area in which the theatre was situated'.[2] The Questors Theatre, based in Ealing in west London, runs a reminiscence project known as PlayBack, which entails going out to interview members of the local community on topics of local interest that have included Brentford Football Club, work at Ealing Studios and the laundry centre Acton's Soapsud Island. After, this verbatim material is shaped into a play by a professional playwright, which the company tour to local voluntary and community groups in Ealing and beyond. These practices have resonance with Jerome de Groot's argument in *Consuming History* that local initiatives offer 'a way of engaging with history at a micro-level, validating the individual experience instead of simply eliding the local in thrall to the more narrative-driven national history' (2009: 66).

[2] http://lacemarkettheatre.co.uk/LaceMarketTheatre.dll/UserDefined?PageName=0&SubPageName=2. Accessed 30 August 2016.

Most notable is the labour many amateur theatre companies invest to preserve, narrate and transmit their histories and cultural heritage through events and material culture. They maintain fulsome archives, as well as the creation of cultural documents including published histories, oral histories, films, websites and picture galleries that document production histories, but also memories, anecdotes, moments of encounter, interaction and exchange. These ventures are frequently galvanised by an anniversary such as *A History of Winchester Dramatic Society* published in 2014 as part of the company's 150th Anniversary celebrations and when Bolton Little Theatre, with support from a Heritage Lottery Fund grant of £47,100, produced a booklet celebrating its 75th anniversary year in 2006.[3] Combining narratives of production histories alongside the mundane, trivial and anecdotal, these publications honour the particularity of a company's character and social practices. According to de Groot, this impetus is part of a wider emancipatory trend of amateur historians keen to discover, research and narrate personal and local social history:

> The popularity of local history, as testified by the expansion of publishing, the increasing demand on local archives and the various Heritage Initiative projects, demonstrate a keen amateur desire to invest time and energy in investigating the past. It also illustrates a direct engagement with the tools of historical work, and emphasises the value of the individual's research and direct understanding of locale, geography and artefacts, rather than the imposition of historical meaning by cultural and institutional gatekeepers of one kind or another. (2009: 64)

As de Groot suggests, a significant feature of this activity is a do-it-yourself mentality, a desire to uncover and tell a story that would otherwise be lost and which recognises the value and importance of local knowledge and understanding. A perspective that often leads to oral history interviews with past members to ensure that their voices, memories and anecdotes, which Rebecca Schneider refers to as 'embodied archives', are not lost to the historical record (2001). What distinguishes these local historians is their attachment to 'a sense of place, and a desire to understand the narrative of that place', which includes the various micro-histories that

---

[3] Winchester Dramatic Society, *A History of the Winchester Dramatic Society*. Winchester: Sarsen Press, 2014, and Michael Shipley, *Bolton Little Theatre: 75 Years of Drama*, Leeds: Millnet Financial Services, 2006.

reside in place through its topography, buildings, societies and people (de Groot 2009: 63).

A typical example of a sustained impulse to capture amateur theatre practice as significant cultural heritage can be found in Market Harborough Drama Society (MHDS) based in the market town of Market Harborough in Leicestershire. With a population in the region of 23,000 this is an attractive and thriving place that secured the number one spot in *The Times and Sunday Times* 2016 list of the top twenty market towns in Britain and a commissioned report by ERS Research and Consultancy identified it as 'the town to which other market towns in Leicestershire aspire' (19).[4] Situated around the River Welland and part of the Grand Union Canal network, the town hosts a number of national and independent shops and has many markers of a vibrant community. It is a regular participant and winner in Britain in Bloom competitions; it is one of twelve places in the UK funded by the Big Lottery Fund's Communities Living Sustainably Programme and it holds a regular carnival and other events. Every September since 2002 it has staged Arts Fresco, the largest street theatre festival in the Midlands, founded by the late George Kitson, a former principal of The Central School of Speech and Drama, and his fellow MHDS members. It has been my home for nearly twenty years and I feel a keen attachment to what it has to offer as a place to live.

With its origins in a small drama club initiated by the Workers Educational Association in the early 1930s, MHDS has been active for over eighty years and I was informed by its treasurer, Arthur Aldrich, that it currently has over three hundred members and two hundred regular volunteers.[5] Producing seven plays a year, the society prides itself on a varied repertoire, which in the 2016/2017 season included standard amateur fare Oscar Wilde's *The Importance of Being Earnest* and Agatha Christie's *Go Back for Murder,* as well as an amateur premiere of *Pink Mist* by Owen Sheers. With the nearest professional theatre taking place fifteen miles away in Leicester or Northampton, the society is very well-supported locally, with the majority of shows playing to over 90% capacity and many selling out. A member of the Little Theatre Guild (LTG) network, the company

[4] https://www.llep.org.uk/wp-content/uploads/2016/08/Market-Towns-Study-August-2016.pdf. Accessed 6 September 2017.
[5] Interview Arthur Aldrich with Nadine Holdsworth, Market Harborough Theatre, 29 September 2016. All other quotations are taken from this interview.

is based in the Harborough Theatre, which occupies a prominent place in the town's topography, adjacent to the imposing Saint Dionysus parish church and the iconic grade one listed Old Grammar School dating from 1614, which was built on stilts to facilitate the butter market below. Resembling an Elizabethan merchant's house with its thick stone walls, mullioned windows and leaded lights, the theatre is described on MHDS's website as '[a]n early example of "heritage architecture"'.[6] Contrary to its grand external appearance, it was actually constructed in 1935 as a cycle-shed and store for Symington's Corset Factory, now the impressive premises of Harborough District Council, the library and museum. Apparently the factory's then Managing Director had an office that overlooked Church Square and he insisted on an attractive frontage that disguised the building's prosaic function. MHDS initially hired the first-floor hall as a performance space and subsequently arranged a lease to secure it as a permanent base prior to purchasing the freehold in 1969 following a local fund-raising campaign. Whilst the building's frontage has been maintained, the space behind the threshold has been re-modelled several times and now houses a 118-seat auditorium, lighting box, bar area, kitchen and dressing room; whilst the purchase of an adjacent building has facilitated the creation of a costume store and small meeting/rehearsal room.

Akin to many LTG theatres across England, the building is a vital creative hub within the local community and a valuable asset, which Arthur Aldrich confirmed raises in the region of £25,000 in annual lettings. Parsnips Youth Theatre runs after school classes there three nights a week and Octagon Films screens a cross-section of films as well as showing live broadcasts from the National Theatre, The Royal Shakespeare Company, the Royal Opera House and Bolshoi Ballet. In addition, historical and arts societies book the space and local schools and charities run fund-raising events on Saturday mornings. Coffee mornings are held for MHDS members every Tuesday when the bar area is full of people attending to administrative tasks, sewing, chatting, planning and reminiscing.

Like many other amateur companies that maintain their own theatres, the building itself has become a means to mark and celebrate MHDS's heritage. Immediately evident is the way the visual display showcases their diverse production histories to members and audiences. A gallery of high quality production photographs adorn the walls of the public areas, whilst

---

[6] See http://harboroughtheatre.com/building/. Accessed 27 March 2017.

in the foyer a digital display screen presents a rolling loop of very recent or upcoming productions. Visual culture theorist Elizabeth Roberts notes that 'photographs, the taking and display of, are always in-place, of a place and making a place' and this photographic display is an excellent example of this as the selection of images as 'a form of prosthetic memory operate at the juncture between personal and collective memory in the way they [the productions] are remembered, storied and inherited' (2012: 91/97). The photographs capture the malleability of the space and the skills of the design team who have enabled the small stage to transform into the working-class domestic environment of Stanley Houghton's *Hindle Wakes* (1912), the Lake District of Tim Firth's *Neville's Island* (1992) or the Tudor court of Howard Brenton's *Anne Boleyn* (2010). As Roberts suggests, 'Photographs and stories are performances in which the physicality or materiality of a memoried place is strengthened and brought into focus as a distinct and shared place' (2012: 99).

To celebrate MHDS's sixtieth anniversary in 1993, long-standing company member Arthur Jones published a history of the society called *Stage by Stage*, which was subsequently updated in 2008 by another member, Matt Howling, for the company's 75th anniversary. Adopting heritage discourse and the language of place-making, Howling asserts that the aim 'is to promote and showcase what the society does, as well as capture and preserve, in writing, its important place within the town's history' such as in 1985 when the society accepted an invitation from the local council to stage Shakespeare's *Richard III* on Bosworth Field as part of its programme to celebrate the 500th anniversary of the Battle of Bosworth Field that ended the War of the Roses (2008: ix). Both Arthur Jones and Matt Howling fulfil theatre historian Jacky Bratton's notion of the 'tribal scribe' who has been personally involved in the story they tell (2003). Both stress the collaborative nature of their endeavour, reliant on members sharing stories and memories to trace the story of the society 'as a collective body' (Jones 2008: xi). As such, the process adheres to Bratton's idea of scribal history as an 'accumulating account', which attempts 'to link events, creating some sort of reflexive chain or set of relationships' (2003: 19–20).

Drawing on the material traces of photographs, programme notes, cast lists, minutes from meetings and newspaper reviews, *Stage by Stage* charts the origins, distinct phases and mixed fortunes of the society as it has evolved and expanded. It teases out shifting audience expectations, judgements of taste and tensions regarding the repertoire as when T.S. Eliot's

Murder in the Cathedral was deemed unsuitable for 'these critical and anxious times' when produced at the outbreak of the Second World War in 1939 (2008: 4). It brings to life the constraints waged by poor physical resources and the various campaigns to expand the building's footprint. It celebrates numerous incidences of individual enterprise and effort, as well as collective fund-raising campaigns that have revived the society's fortunes and physical infrastructure. One memorable section recounts a period of substantial redevelopment in the 1970s, which is supplemented by the tale of one member, Bill Kent, who:

> [C]ame forward with the offer of a thousand hours of work. His diary, which survives, lists the range of jobs he undertook and the hours spent on them – plastering, carpentry, painting, cleaning up, working on the toilets, the stairs and the kitchen. Then, as his thousandth hour ticked away he said with a grin, 'time's up', downed tools and went. (Jones 2008: 30)

As Bratton stresses, 'the "chronological digest" is substantiated – often doubled or trebled in extent – by the addition of anecdote' (2003: 21). There is one thing to have the history of the company documented through a chronological account of production histories suggested by the title *Stage by Stage*, but what brings the rich life of the company alive are the anecdotes that provide glimpses of the interpersonal relationships and people that gives the company its distinctiveness.

The research processes that unearth these anecdotes, as well as the resulting artefacts, serve as what Smith refers to as 'prompts for recalling and authenticating cultural and social experiences', that are valuable for individuals, societies and a sense of a locality's heritage (2011: 69). Significantly, *Stage by Stage* was made possible by the existence of the company's archive, which consists of several large scrapbooks containing programmes, photographs, press cuttings and miscellaneous memorabilia that document every production by the group since 1933. The assemblage of materials has been reliant on the labour of individual members who have informally, yet purposefully, passed the baton down over the years. Bert Webb, a theatre manager and photographer, began the archive and the current custodian is Vivien Window, a regular member of MHDS since the 1970s and currently its President. For the past twenty years she has invested time to archive the company's productions and to add other items as they become available, most commonly when a former member of the group has died and their next of kin discover boxes of theatre-related ephemera.

For Vivien Window, who comes from Market Harborough, and her Australian husband Alan, who served in the Australian Air Force before moving to England and becoming a painter and decorator, the theatre has been their 'main hobby'. It has endured over fifty years of marriage, the raising of four children and years of offering foster care to children with special needs. For them, the theatre is an extension of that rich family life and talking with them invites stories of involving generations of children in shows, rehearsals and costume-making in their home. The couple contribute space in a spare room and their loft to the archive. It sits there as a record of a life lived and significant social relations in much the same way as the gallery of family photos that adorn the walls and every available surface in their home. However, whilst the space of the archive may be domestic, the approach to the task at hand is serious and professional. Advice has been taken on how best to preserve materials and the scrapbooks are kept flat in a dedicated closable cabinet to keep out the dust. Vivien Window proudly declared during an interview that 'the local museum said they couldn't do better'; in fact, she rejected an approach from the Harborough Museum for the archive to be re-located there, as she could not imagine restricted access and having to 'make an appointment'.[7] The domestic site of the archive was brought tellingly home during a visit I made to look at the archive:

> After following Vivien's ascent up the stairs on her Stannah stair-lift, I feel guilty as Alan has to lie on the floor to access the scrapbooks. I offer to help, but the offer is politely declined. I'm ushered into Vivien and Alan's bedroom where we'll be 'more comfortable'. Here, sitting on their bed, Vivien talks through the shows and the personalities involved. I hear about society stalwarts Ian and Queenie Parry, Ian Joule and Alec Riddett. I'm introduced to the various family dynasties and friendships. I hear about the only time the whole family – Vivien, Alan and their four children – appeared together in *Toad of Toad Hall*. It's a fascinating couple of hours when I'm reminded once again of the dedication and investment shown by amateur theatre makers. I'm left wondering what will happen to the archive after Vivien has had enough, who will take it on and will they give it house room as well as the same care and attention she has? (Nadine's Research Diary, 19 September 2016)

---

[7] Interview Vivien Window with Nadine Holdsworth, Market Harborough, 11 January 2016. All other quotations are taken from this interview.

The archive is clearly a spur for reminiscence and it is not surprising to learn how relatives have used it to gain knowledge and access stories about a loved one's leisure pursuits after they have died. Smith writes about heritage being inextricably tied to memory and that 'often its "preservation" occurred through the performance of passing on memories and family histories' which is facilitated by material culture such as this (2011: 78).

The archive offers insight into far more than MHDS's history of production and reception by the local press. For a start, the archive is interesting for the way it reveals broad societal shifts. Discussing the Women's Institute Jubilee Scrapbooks of 1965, Rosemary Shirley draws attention to how these materials are redolent of the way that the localised and the particular are intricately woven together and networked with large-scale technological, cultural and social developments (2015). This intersection between small-scale amateur practice and large-scale societal change also holds true here. The written and visual material articulates the progress of the company through time, captured through the documentation of changing repertoires, design innovations, new printing technologies and shifts from black and white to colour photography. The appearance of adverts in the programmes vividly illustrates an increasingly entrepreneurial approach to fund-raising, as well as shifting consumer aspirations. Equally, the more recent withdrawal of adverts is indicative of the current reluctance amongst company members to ask local companies for sponsorship. Turning the abundant pages of the archive, it is strikingly clear how the MHDS is attentive to and marks its cultural heritage. There is a card signed by the entire cast and crew of Derek Benfield's 1960s farce *Post Horn Gallop* to celebrate the society's 100th post-war production in 1965 and a programme note detailing the decision to re-stage *Candida*, the society's first production in 1933, to mark the society's 60th Jubilee Season in 1993. Additionally, the archive is frequently put to work to enhance the society's connection to its cultural heritage. Vivien Window keenly situates current productions within a long tradition of practice and consults the archive to identify earlier examples of a particular repertoire or playwright being performed so that she can write about these examples of cultural continuity in the society's journal *Backstage*. When *Blithe Spirit* was produced in December 2015 she notified members that:

> Unbelievably, this will be the fifth time we have brought "Blithe Spirit" to Harborough! In 1946 Margaret Gray produced it in the Co-op Hall. The famous Ian Joule gave us his interpretation in 1964... In 1991 Jeanne

Moore directed it, with Pauline Moore a lovely elusive Elvira floating around the stage. Jeanne's daughter Ruth … played Edith the maid, in the year 2000, with Anne Hepworth directing. Ruth has returned fifteen years later, to reprise her hilarious Edith for Sarah Clarke.[8]

This extract neatly captures something of the closely intertwined theatrical and familial histories that often characterise societies like MHDS, which can only be brought to life by those intimately engaged in its operations.

The fact that the archive exists at all is significant. In *The Archive and the Repertoire*, Diana Taylor states that even though the 'value, relevance or meaning of the archive, how the items it contains get interpreted, even embodied' may change over space and time, its very existence signals importance and its availability to be accessed and studied (2003: 19). A view endorsed by Vivien Window who referred to the importance of 'keeping memories going', 'remembering our past' and the duty she felt to preserve and maintain the archive for future generations. This perspective has currency with Holland's work on family photograph albums, which she refers to as 'an act of faith in the future' and that 'looking back at these modest records, made precious with and mysterious with age, is an act of recognition of the past' (1991: 1). The MHDS archive can be read in the same way, its curation imagines a future use value as well as acknowledging the past as culturally significant and, even though she would never think of it as such, what Vivien Window does for MHDS is an act of 'heritage management' (Smith 2006: 46).

The investment in the archive in terms of the time and labour taken to generate and maintain it, or the physical effort required to transport and display the archive at events, can be illuminated with reference to cultural critic Robert Hewison's understanding of the way in which heritage attains immaterial rather than material value:

The objects that hold these values are a source of aesthetic pleasure, emotional response, historical knowledge, but above all, of cultural meaning. That is why although they are not displayed to be sold, and cannot in any way be possessed by the viewer, such objects are some of the most valuable a society can own. They represent a society's significance, and as such they are priceless. (1987: 85)

---

[8] *Backstage, the Journal of the Market Harborough Drama Society,* January–February 2016, pp. 5–6.

Clearly Hewison is writing about society in the broad collective sense, but if this is substituted with the idea of a specific amateur dramatic company then the meaning still holds. These scrapbooks deny the etymology of redundancy suggested by the word 'scrap' by being displayed as productive objects of pride and prestige. The archive is marshalled for MHDS's annual Open Evening to market the work of the society to prospective members, casual helpers and audiences, because as artefacts they suggest, amongst other things, qualities of longevity, sustained creativity, inheritance and, as such, they are active narrative tools for propagating cultural value. When I visited the Open Evening held on 3rd November 2015 I was acutely aware of this wider significance and by chance witnessed Vivien Window's delight when a member of the local community walked in to donate a handful of posters advertising productions by the Apollo Players, a short-lived avant-garde splinter group from the late 1940s and early 1950s, under-represented in the archive, that produced 'the kind of plays which amateurs do not commonly risk' such as Sophocles' *Antigone* (Jones 2008: 9).

During this Open Evening the tangible heritage of the theatre building, archive and production artefacts, but also the intangible knowledge and skills that underpin the social practice of amateur theatre-making were on display. The event can be understood in terms of heritage theorists Rodney Harrison and Deborah Rose's description of intangible heritage 'as the non-material aspects of culture that help societies to remember the past and their traditions, to build a sense of identity, community and locality' (2010: 240). When I arrived with my son, who is a member of Parsnips Youth Theatre and very familiar with the building, we were welcomed warmly and accepted an invitation for a tour of the theatre. The tour evoked stories of great shows as well as missed cues, forgotten props and of how the performers struggle to cope with the almost non-existent wing space and the enforced intimacy and occasional embarrassment this necessitates during quick costumes changes. I had already heard about the theatre's infamous resident ghost, rumoured to be a murdered patron of The Green Dragon, an inn that once occupied the same site, but was delighted to see my son hearing this for the first time. These stories are part of the theatre's lived heritage and their repetition helps to sustain a narrative of the place and its inhabitants over the years. The evening provided an active illustration of Smith and Waterton's view that heritage is a 'cultural tool' that 'cannot be defined by its materiality or non-materiality, but rather by what is done with it' (2009: 292). As the members of MHDS exhibited artefacts, toured the building and talked to each other as well as visitors they demonstrated that 'heritage work' is not just about specific sites, records and materiality, it is about 'being in place, renewing memories and associations, sharing experiences'. It is 'a process of engagement' rooted in sociability, creative processes of remembering and storytelling, acts of meaning making and passing on knowledge that does work in the present as much as it functions to preserve a past (Smith 2006: 1). Something of these qualities are captured in my research diary from the evening:

> Marked by distinctly gendered patterns of labour, a group of men sat huddled around a painstakingly constructed miniature model of a set that was also represented through a photographic record of the production hung on the wall behind them. Referring to both artefacts, the men spoke of their craft with enthusiastic good humour as they tried to entice new recruits to the labour of designing, building and painting scenery. 'If you can hold a paintbrush, you're in!' Alongside the men, a group of women wore some of the 1920s costumes they had made and adorned with intricate patterns of beads as they sat sewing or doing guided tours of the newly catalogued costume store. In the costume store three women were steadfastly refusing to be interviewed by a journalist who had come from a local radio station. When he (and his microphone) had gone the women were more than happy to talk at length about the costumes they had acquired, made and re-purposed over the years. We laughed at the tiny, tiny waists of some of the period dresses and at how they had become adept at taking out and adding panels to accommodate their female performers. (Nadine's Research Diary, 2 November 2015)

Many costume designers and makers for amateur theatre companies talk through the various processes of unpicking, re-stitching, adding panels, shortening, lengthening, taking in, taking out, changing buttons and adding epaulettes that consistently preoccupies their role as a limited number of costumes are re-used and recycled. In turn, these items become another valuable part of the heritage of amateur theatre societies because they, like their wearers, have a story to tell. This quality was wonderfully captured by Jon Manley from TOADS Theatre in Torquay when he introduced us to a pair of checked trousers from the 1970s, which although he humorously declared 'burning is probably too good for them', he had worn for six out of the past seven shows produced by the company. Regardless of whether Jon Manley had played a villainous or heroic figure, the two-sizes too big trousers had remained a constant fixture. He explained:

I wryly consider them the epitome of am-dram. They illustrate all that we have to cobble together, whether it be props that are constructed from blue tac and string or ladies ankle boots made from socks with a cut out heel. The trousers shout 'I have no money!' or certainly very little money – they perform a task, whether good or not is debatable, but they do.[9]

These old-fashioned trousers are indicative of social-cultural anthropologist Arjun Appadurai's notion of the 'social life of things', which details how material objects acquire meaning through their use in any given context (1986). These trousers, like the costumes in MHDS's store, reveal something of the economic precarity of amateur theatre-making—of having to literally make do and mend. Equally, these material traces can be suggestive of the creative ingenuity prompted by such limited resources as discussed in Chapter 6.

Writing about the 'biography of things', anthropologist Igor Kopytoff draws attention to the ways in which, like humans, objects have life histories or their own unique biographies where things may change their use over time (1986). When Harriet Parsonage told us about a leather doctor's bag used by The Questors Theatre, she explained that it had originally been used by her paternal grandfather and gone with him on his travels in East Asia and Africa. When she inherited it from her late father in 2002, 'its theatrical potential became apparent' and subsequently that bag has:

> Graced Questors stages in both playing spaces many times, including *Hedda Gabler, Tis Pity She's a Whore, Great Expectations, The Importance of Being Earnest, Charley's Aunt, Travesties, Bloody Poetry*. It has been in numerous plays varying from 1600–early 1900s... I am delighted it has come into its own after decades of disuse... It has of course seen better days as a cursory inspection will reveal. I suspect it will expire in the service of Questors.[10]

The stories of Jon Manley's trousers and Harriet Parsonage's bag came to light during two workshops at The Questors Theatre, Ealing on 16th June 2015 and the Swan Theatre, Worcester on 27th June 2015. Inspired by social psychologist Sherry Turkle's collection *Evocative Objects*, which

[9] Jon Manley talking at the Evocative Objects Workshop, Worcester Swan Theatre, 27 June 2015.
[10] Harriet Parsonage talking at the Evocative Objects Workshop, The Questors Theatre, Ealing, 16 June 2015.

explores how objects are indelibly connected to who we are, how we understand ourselves and serve as valuable 'provocations to thought', we invited people to attend armed with objects that captured memories and stories of their experience participating in amateur theatre (2007: 5). As the above examples indicate, this research method gleaned many unique and, indeed, evocative tales of people's engagement and insight into how people think through material culture. A growing body of work in studies of material culture addresses how individuals and things co-produce each other in a complex web of interdependence that anthropologist Ian Hodder refers to as 'entanglement' (2012). For many thinkers this is due to how objects, things and ephemera are powerfully entwined with notions of the self, due to their ability to trigger memories, stories and emotion.

At the Evocative Objects workshop in Worcester I met Sabine Hoffman, a quiet and self-contained woman who had been a German teacher and translator prior to her retirement. She had been involved in amateur theatre all her life, most recently as a prompt for a number of companies in Birmingham. She arrived wearing a long service NODA medal that had belonged to her stepfather, Jack Myers, and the white bow tie worn by him in his capacity as a Musical Director for several companies in Birmingham. He was principally associated with Bournville Light Opera, part of Bournville Musical Society based at Cadbury's Factory in Birmingham, where he served for thirty-eight years. She also carried an aging, battered and highly annotated prompt copy of *The Desert Song* libretto. *The Desert Song*, a musical in three acts, was originally produced in 1926 and proved immensely popular in the mid-twentieth century with three film versions made by Warner Brothers in 1929, 1943 and 1953. It was Sabine Hoffman's stepfather's favourite show as it connected, according to her, to his experience as a British army officer in Tobruk in Libya during World War Two. Turkle writes about 'the things that matter' and these items clearly meant a great deal. Following her stepfather's death in 2002 he left a lot of scores which Sabine Hoffman gave to 'various folk who would appreciate them', but she 'could not bear to part with' the Desert Song libretto, which took on a special significance. This is reminiscent of John Horton and Peter Kraftl's understanding of how 'memories and emotions are frequently attached to specific objects', particularly at heightened moments such as bereavement (2012: 28).[11] Introducing the

[11] Interview Sabine Hoffman with Nadine Holdsworth, Evocative Objects Workshop, Worcester Swan Theatre, 27 June 2015. All other quotations are taken from this interview.

libretto, Sabine Hoffman drew attention to the multifaceted biography of the object itself and its entanglement with her family's history, as well as her sense of self and her relationship with others. Through the artefact, Sabine Hoffman exposed a history of use and re-use familiar to amateur theatre processes, as she said, 'The libretto is very worn and full of sello-tape. The red underlining is my mum's, she too did the show several times, and the blue is my own. So that libretto tells its own story', a palimpsest of the successive roles played in the musical by three different members of the same family, traced back in living memory to the history of the pioneering spirit of philanthropic factory owners discussed in Chapter 3.

As a material trace, the libretto has acquired symbolic value by becom-ing emblematic of the years and years of family engagement in amateur theatre, and the ways that it permeated the domestic space of the home, familial relations and ideas of inheritance.

> In the years when I was growing up, my dad did all the popular Gilbert and Sullivan's like *Iolanthe*, *Gondoliers*, *Mikado* and so on. We used to go to the dress rehearsals, and at home there was always a record on of whatever was current. I knew that one day I would join in… I did my first show when I was 23, in my first year of teaching. I started with *Trial by Jury* and *H.M.S. Pinafore*, a Novello show and *Bless the Bride*, which I really loved. I had a small part in that and could hardly believe it when I got flowers on the stage on the last night. Me – with flowers on the stage! Then we did *White Horse Inn* and *Carousel*. When I came back from three years in Germany, I did another twelve shows with my dad at Bournville before he finished there, sadly owing to deafness. We had got on very well with our common interest in amateur theatre.

Using her objects as prompts, Sabine Hoffman became increasingly emotionally invested in the stories her objects were evoking, her pride for a lost stepfather, the rituals of performance and the labour of amateur theatre practice that had deep resonance for her narration and perfor-mance of selfhood. During these workshops and through numerous con-versations we have been made aware of how the material traces of amateur theatre carry and transmit ideas, narratives of participation and memories that serve to connect people to their amateur participation and production processes. This represents rich social relations of shared labour, creative endeavour and cherished relationships amateur theatre produces, and which are part of its intangible heritage.

Inventing Traditions: Symbols, Rituals and Traditions

In addition to heritage work involving archive maintenance and publishing histories, amateur theatre groups and organisations invent and maintain cultures of practice, symbols, traditions and rituals. Founded in 1842 and claiming to be 'the oldest surviving amateur dramatic society in the world', The Old Stagers has maintained an unbroken tradition of performing annually during Canterbury Cricket Week apart from interruptions necessitated by the First and Second World Wars, which is documented in an extensive archive.[12] During this week company members are easily identified by their adherence to The Old Stagers colours of red, gold and black that adorn striped blazers, sashes and rosettes, as well as company banners that form a backdrop to the annual 'Epilogue' portrait. Besides the performance of a play, for the final two nights of the production run, the company traditionally produces an Epilogue, a satirical musical revue written in verse. Embracing subjects as diverse as war, the suffragette cause, Britain's relationship with Europe and Anti-Social Behaviour Orders, it 'has provided a political and social commentary on every year since 1842' and its familiar format prompted *The Times* to assert in 1934 that 'the *Epilogue* is not a *revue,* but a ritual' (Ritchie 2015: 285, 289).

This section of the chapter is concerned with how and why performance traditions become embedded in a company's culture and repertoire. I argue that they can be illuminated with reference to Marxist historian Eric Hobsbawm's discussion of invented traditions as 'a set of practices, normally governed by overtly or tacitly accepted rules and of a ritual or symbolic nature, which seek to inculcate certain values and norms of behaviour by repetition, which automatically implies continuity with the past' (1983: 1). Importantly, Hobsbawm highlighted the fact that many cultural practices perceived as traditions are, in fact, constructed and made to serve particular social, cultural and ideological purposes in the present. For him, 'It is the contrast between the constant change and innovation of the modern world and the attempt to structure at least some parts of social life within it as unchanging and invariant, that makes the "invention of tradition" so interesting' (Hobsbawm 1983: 2). On one

---

[12] www.oldstagers.com. Accessed 12 April 2016. For a discussion of the Old Stagers see David Coates 'The Development of Amateur Theatre in Britain in the Long Nineteenth Century', unpublished PhD thesis, University of Warwick, 2018.

level, amateur theatre companies employ the tradition and practice of designing and using names, acronyms and logos that become a short hand for a whole company and are marshalled to suggest unity over time and an association with place, culture and identity. So, the Stamford Bridge Players from Yorkshire, who regularly perform in Stamford Bridge Village Hall, stress their place within a geographical community; whilst The Infirmary Dramatic Operatic and Literary Society (The IDOLS), which brings doctors, nurses, administrators and maintenance staff together from Leicester Royal Infirmary, highlights their workplace connection. Whilst company names are a significant marker of cultural continuity, things can change to reflect shifts in taste, expectations and a target demographic as when the Skipton and District Amateur Operatic and Dramatic Society, in existence since 1924, changed its name to Skipton Musical Theatre Company in 2012 to better reflect its repertoire and encourage younger people to participate. Logos also have the potential to generate powerful symbolic associations through text and imagery such as the ancient white rose of Yorkshire symbol central to the Allerton Players from Northallerton's logo. These symbolic markers provide a way of differentiating amateur companies from each other and are suggestive of cultural continuity as all productions, regardless of the participants, are incorporated under unified branding that appears on websites, posters and programmes. Companies also traditionally invest in show t-shirts and sweatshirts, which are practically designed to market shows but serve a wider symbolic function of performing group identity through the prominent feature of names and company logos that literally adorn people's bodies.

The culture, practice and annual cycles of competitive festivals that feature heavily in amateur theatre traditions offer a further example of Hobsbawm's understanding of how invented traditions entail 'a process of formalization and ritualization, characterised by reference to the past, if only by imposing repetition' (1983: 4). From the All-England Theatre Festival (AETF), a six-month long festival of one-act plays in England, which began in 1919 under the auspices of the British Drama league, to the National Drama Festival Association (NDFA), founded in 1964, as an association of now nearly forty independent amateur drama festivals, which culminates in a week-long British All Winners Festival, competitive festivals are central to the amateur theatre calendar. They establish a sense of continuity with the past through their annual cycle, but also through the bestowal of specific awards including the Geoffrey Whitworth Trophy, presented in memory of the man who founded the All England Festival and the George Taylor Memorial Award, which since 1979 has honoured the founder of *Amateur Stage* whilst recognising the achievements of a playwright who has produced a new one-act play performed at a NDFA member festival. These festivals create systems to foster friendly competition and the recognition of achievement, but they also contribute to community and consensus building by helping to construct and formalise shared values, traditions and rituals within the amateur theatre community. Festivals underscore the fact that individual amateur groups and societies are part of a much wider nexus of activity, they get to share their work and, as discussed in *The Festivalization of Culture*:

> Festivals may allow organizations within communities to be fostered, generate opportunities to work together for a discursively constructed "common good", negotiate shared cultural values, shape and/or remake a community, and function as the basis for community formation and amalgamation beyond the constraints of a specific locality. (Bennett et al. 2014: 4)

In *Festivals and the Cultural Public Sphere*, sociologist Gerard Delanty argues that 'festivals have always been sites of cultural reproduction and renewal' (2011: 1). In particular, festivals establish the habitus, the public culture of amateur theatre, not least the culture and ritual of putting creative practice under scrutiny and judgement via competitive processes designed to acknowledge talent and raise artistic standards, which connects to the ethos of improvement discussed in the previous chapter. Throughout the AETF, entrants compete against each other in preliminary, quarter and semi-final rounds in one of four regional heats prior to the AETF Final and ultimately the chance to compete in the British All Winners Final. These one-act play festivals are highly managed with strict eligibility criteria and pre-determined categories for nomination, with the competitive element to proceedings undertaken via a professional adjudication system administered by the Guild of Drama Adjudicators (GoDA) that applies a common marking scheme to evaluate stage presentation, acting, directing and overall dramatic achievement. 'Stage presentation' is an archaic term, used only in amateur theatre, but it is well understood in this context. By 2016, the AETF Newsletter was reporting mixed fortunes; some regional heats had been cancelled and others had struggled to attract entrants or received poor box office takings. Nonetheless, and more optimistically for the organisers, there was an enthusiastic response in many areas, and youth groups were well-represented in the regional heats, thus bolstering numbers. The Newsletter notes the following statistics:

> There were 137 performing sessions which took place at 39 venues across the country. 330 groups took part using a combined cast and crew of 2,897. These productions were watched by a total audience of 6,950 who brought us an income of £52,000. (2016: 8)[13]

Maidenhead Drama Festival is particularly well-supported by youth groups, and the event takes over the local theatre, Norden Farm, for a full week, staging sixteen entries in 2016. The 2016 AETF were also held at Norden Farm, which Helen attended.

> The finals was my sixth experience of attending AETF events, and I felt I knew what to expect. The foyer was resplendent with silverware, an array of presentational cups and platters on display for audiences and actors to admire. I was greeted by an elderly gentleman who was wearing a dinner jacket and bow tie for his work as an usher. There was an atmosphere of quiet expectation, and there was a civic quality to the event, as the Mayor was in attendance wearing her ceremonial chains. I noticed, with some discomfort, that she was the only non-white person in the theatre. I wondered what she made of it all. Keen to use my twitter feed to publicise the event, I asked the gentleman usher if there was a hashtag, but he had no idea what I meant. It felt like going back in time. (Helen's Research Diary, 4 June 2016)

The theatre itself was a lively mixture of styles, including *RIP Mr Shakespeare*, a play devised and directed by Bev Clark for Hand-in-Hand Theatre Company that had been inspired by their work on the RSC Open Stages programme. The British All Winners Festival organised by The National Drama Festivals Association (NDFA) followed shortly afterwards, adjudicated by Jan Palmer Sayer, a member of GoDA and regular director at The Barn Theatre in Welwyn Garden City and hosted by her husband, Derek Palmer, the NDFA chairman. Shakespeare was well-represented; Hand-in-Hand's *RIP Mr Shakespeare* was reprieved for the event, and Rebekah Fortune directed an extract of *Comedy of Errors*. Both directors, Bev Clark and Rebekah Fortune, have worked professionally in

---

[13] www.allenglandtheatrefestival.co.uk/index_htm_files/NLJan17b.pdf. Accessed 29 December 2017.

the arts and their contribution to the festival demonstrates the blurred boundaries between the two sectors.

> It was good to meet up with people I had come to know and respect during the research. Colin Dolley, GoDA adjudicator offers characteristically wise insights into the week, telling me that I had missed some marvellous work by only arriving for the final two days. His top tip was a one-hander, *Scaramouche Jones* produced by White Cobra Productions in Northampton. Over lunch, Roger and Jean Cunnington, both on the Executive committee of AETF, discuss their concerns about the lack of BAME participants in amateur theatre, and express their frustration at the slowness of change. We wonder whether encouraging some of the BAME young people involved in youth theatre to become apprentice adjudicators might help. (Helen's Research Diary, 31 July 2016)

Invited to impart feedback for festival participants and festival audiences alike, adjudicators are an important and distinctive part of the amateur theatre ecology. Appointed for their expertise in theatre and drama, largely gained in educational or professional theatre contexts, they inevitably acquire significant cultural capital within the amateur theatre circuit, with the most sought-after adjudicators travelling extensively around the country to provide judgements on festival entries. People become GoDA adjudicators after an initial training day followed by a two-day selection weekend during which applicants are tested on their general theatre knowledge, their adjudication skills and ability to give effective verbal and written feedback. Understandably, adjudicators are selected for their ability to align their judgements with pre-existing models and experienced adjudicators, as a high degree of parity is desirable owing to the number of regional heats that take place. Hence, the adjudication process plays a significant role in establishing particular judgements of taste in the repertoire and craft of amateur theatre-making, as was evident when I attended a training day for individuals contemplating becoming adjudicators at the Worcester Swan Theatre on 7th February 2016. A diverse range of people assembled for this event including the former Chief Executive of NODA; a voice coach and a former BBC producer, but regardless of the different areas of expertise present, the important thing was establishing consensus on what constituted good or bad performance.

> Prior to our attendance we had all been given a copy of *Moving On*, a one-act play by amateur playwright and director David Titchener, to read. Part

of the day was spent watching a local amateur group perform the play on the Swan's main stage. Armed with notepads and pens, we were invited to take notes on strengths and weaknesses as we saw it under the headings of stage presentation, acting, directing and overall dramatic achievement. After the piece had finished we gathered in huddles to share our thoughts on pacing, characterisation, use of space and vocal range with a view to reaching consensus on where the piece fell within the marking scheme. The experienced adjudicators were clear that the objective was to encourage, evaluate and constructively criticise. It was no good saying something was great when it wasn't. Being cruel to be kind was the order of the day. (Nadine's Research Diary, 7 February 2016)

The adjudication process itself proceeds through a series of established rituals such as the invitation to tour facilities and the provision of a lit table in the auditorium from which to watch the show and take notes. Feedback sessions immediately after shows are keenly anticipated with company members eager to ascertain the nuance of the adjudicator's assessment; that said amateur companies and individuals do not always behave well. Companies have been known to shift entire box sets to accommodate the angle from which the adjudicator is viewing their show and on one memorable occasion at the Felixstowe Drama Festival in 1989, a young man who had taken on too much writing, acting in and directing *The House of Frankenstein*, took exception to Colin Dolley's adjudication and leapt onto the stage, swearing and cursing, before running out and throwing himself into the sea (Dolley 1989: 23). During our interview, experienced adjudicator Arthur Aldrich also somewhat debunked the ideal of community formation and learning from each other:

The biggest benefit should be, it isn't always, to see what other teams are doing, how they're doing it, compare yourself against them. Unfortunately, in practice, at the festivals most groups when they've finished acting disappear into the bar just waiting on what the adjudicator's going to say at the end of the evening. I'm not in favour of that personally but it's what often happens.

Performing Rituals and Symbols: The Royal Navy Theatre Association

Running alongside the national and regional festival circuit are a number of non-affiliated festivals including the Royal Navy Theatre Association (RNTA) festival, to which I will now turn. The RNTA and its constituent groups provide a case study for this discussion, and have invented traditions that function as systems with particular applications and meanings that contribute to the ongoing process of establishing historical continuity, sustaining cultural heritage and asserting a sense of cultural legitimacy. The RNTA was established in 1985 as an umbrella group for amateur theatre companies active on naval bases that involve naval personnel (serving and retired), Ministry of Defence staff, their family, friends and local members of the community. The RNTA annual calendar commences with a competitive spring festival before a summer production, which from 2012 to 2016 involved outdoor productions of Shakespeare staged as part of the RSC's Open Stages programme and culminates in a pantomime season in late November-early December.

Members are able to participate in these activities without paying a subsidy due to Royal Navy support. The individual theatre companies that fall under the auspices of the RNTA are named to situate them on particular naval establishments where they rehearse and perform; so, the Sultan Theatre Group is based at HMS Sultan, Collingwood RSC is based at HMS Collingwood and the Victory Players was so named because it comprised members of the Royal Navy and civil servants who predominately worked and performed in the Victory Building, which overlooked HMS Victory. However, as departments and staff began to move locations members of the Victory Players were increasingly based at HMS Excellent on Whale Island, where the Fisher Hall became a regular venue.

As Tim Stoneman, a former RNTA secretary and member of Admirals' Players explained:

> We then decided that, with the direct link to 'Victory' gone, a 'rebranding' (although we didn't call it that!) was in order. Because of the number of admirals with offices on the Island, the current name [The Admirals' Players] came into being – hence the location of the apostrophe… Scurrilously, when the Navy was much larger, Portsmouth was sometimes referred to as 'A mudflat surrounded by admirals'![14]

The RNTA logo combines the classic tragedy and comedy mask, which symbolises theatre, with an anchor. Inspired by the work of Clifford Geertz in *The Interpretation of Culture,* historian Byron King Plant proposes that 'what is relevant about symbols is not their ontological status,

---

[14] Tim Stoneman email correspondence with Nadine Holdsworth, 29 April 2017.

Fig. 7.1 Costume for the Admirals' Players *Little Panto on the Prairie* hanging in Fisher Hall, HMS Excellent, Whale Island. (Photographer: Nadine Holdsworth)

but rather, what their meaning is when such symbols are operationalized in a cultural context' (2008: 189). This logo appears on posters, programmes, official letters, tiepins and it is etched onto glasses presented to winners of awards at the annual RNTA festival. In each instance, the logo is deployed to mark distinctiveness by highlighting the combination of maritime allegiance and theatrical practice. Often placed adjacent to or visually aligned with the logo of the Royal Navy, which suggests a clear intent to draw attention to the Royal Navy as the unifying element that defines the groups socially, culturally and ideologically. In much the same way, the companies embark on fund-raising through ticket sales, the sale of programmes and soliciting donations for a number of service-related charities including the Royal Navy and Royal Marines Charity and the Defence Medical Rehabilitation Centre.

The intertwined relation between the Royal Navy and RNTA activities is evident in a number of other traditions and performative gestures embedded within the performance culture and repertoire that are arguably 'used to construct, reconstruct and negotiate a range of identities and social and cultural values and meanings in the present' (Smith 2006: 3). Acknowledging and underpinning the hierarchical chain of command central to the ethos and operational processes of the Royal Navy, it is notable that a senior figure traditionally serves as the President and figurehead of the RNTA. Equally, it is common practice to formally recognise the support of the establishment's Commanding Officer in programmes and announcements prior to the commencement of shows. Carrying on a tradition phased out in British theatres during the late 1960s, the RNTA groups still invite their audiences to stand or 'respectfully sit' for the National Anthem, an indication of the Royal Navy's sovereign association and allegiance to the monarchy, which audiences are temporarily invited to inhabit through what Michael Billig refers to in *Banal Nationalism* as a 'universal sign of particularity' (1995: 86). As I noted during a visit to see Collingwood RSC's pantomime *Dick Whittington* in 2014:

This is such an interesting experience as the clash of formal and informal collides at every turn. As an audience member you have to come onto the naval base past barbed wire fences, your name is checked off at the gate for security purposes and uniformed navy recruits direct and welcome people at the entrance ... the audience is packed with families and there are lots of young children – there is the general hubbub of a panto crowd with many sporting Christmas jumpers. People are here for a good time. Before the production commences the National Anthem is played and everybody stands, with some half-hearted attempts to join in whilst children are urged not to fidget. I'm reminded once again what an odd experience this is and one that is heightened by the military overtures of the mise en scene. (Nadine's Research Diary, 5 December 2014)

The same four RNTA theatre groups have competed against each other during the spring festival in recent years and the format is maintained year on year with an appointed adjudicator seeing every production, providing oral feedback immediately after shows, written reports and the selection of nominees and winners for the RNTA's annual Awards' Night. The festival is approached in a spirit of what Robin Sheppard referred to as 'friendly rivalry' that can take on its own theatricality as when several members of Collingwood RSC turned up wearing t-shirts promoting their production of Sir Terry Pratchett's *Lords and Ladies* to see *Murder by the Book* performed by the Admirals' Players, one of their rivals for the RNTA awards in March 2016. During an interview Chris Blatch-Gainey insisted that the competitive ethos of the festival is a significant motivator, which in his view connected with values commensurate with the Royal Navy.

> It's not just for the individual, it's for the group of people around you, and then you have this competition where you're trying to do a good show that beats the next establishment and the other and the other and the other, so you're trying to promote the best of the best, which is really the Navy ethos, trying to produce the best team to do the best job at all times.[15]

After the shows, feedback from the adjudicator is keenly anticipated and, as the then Chairperson of the RNTA, put it in an email, 'there is definitely a sense of occasion about the whole thing'.[16] I served as the RNTA's festival adjudicator in 2016 and felt at first hand the high stakes that accompanies this role:

> From my biog that appears in all the programmes, to the lit table in the plum place in the auditorium it feels like I'm on show as much as the production. Arriving at HMS Sultan I'm flanked by the Chairperson, Jules, and Edward, Secretary of the RNTA and we have a drink before I'm escorted to my seat. I joke about how I think they could at least muster me a uniform – with epaulettes! The person who welcomes the audience announces my presence and role before the show begins – *Honk!* The show is amateur theatre at its best with a cast ranging from young children to retired members, lots of ensemble work, set pieces and a very creative set made with limited resources. The audience are absolutely 'on-side' willing the performers to do well. After the show I'm steered to a meeting space where there is

[15] Interview Chris Blatch-Gainey with Nadine Holdsworth, HMS Collingwood, 3 February 2014.

[16] Commander Jules Philo email correspondence with Nadine Holdsworth, 5 April 2016.

a lavish buffet laid out and the large cast assemble to eat, share a drink and listen to my feedback. It's 20 minutes since the show finished, I have pages and pages of scrawled notes and everyone looks at me attentively. It's a daunting task – they've been working on the show for months and months and they want to know what I think of the show and, more importantly, their performances. (Nadine's Research Diary, 19th April 2016)

For individuals and companies, participation and success in the festival offers a chance to assert their distinction. During an interview Emma Thomas, a member of the Admirals' Players, spoke of it as 'an opportunity for people to be recognised for their skills in comparison with their peers and that fulfils something for them'.[17] She equally valued the chance to benchmark her acting asserting that 'it gives you a feeling of satisfaction that something you think of as quite good and entertaining actually is in a wider sphere'. This supports the view forwarded by Bennett et al. that festivals facilitate 'access to cultural capital, an opportunity to perform identity and a way to negotiate and secure individual and collective meaning and belonging' (2014: 2).

The RNTA festival culminates in an Awards' Evening, a black-tie social event combining food, drink, extracts from Festival entries, the formal announcement of the nominees and winners of various awards and a disco. The different theatre groups gather in packs to celebrate *their* nominees and winners, whilst at the same time acknowledging and applauding their rivals for a range of accolades from Best Actress, Best Director, Best Make-Up, Costume and Wigs to the most coveted of all, the Best Overall Production. Extending a tradition that stretches back to ancient Greek theatre when playwrights were awarded laurel crowns in recognition of their work, the professional theatre industry in Britain is replete with awards ceremonies including the Olivier Awards, the UK Theatre Awards and the Stage Awards, which all confer distinction and status on their recipients. It is no surprise, therefore, that the amateur theatre world has mirrored this tradition as, according to James F. English in *The Economy of Prestige*, 'prizes have always been of fundamental importance to the *institutional* machinery of cultural legitimacy and authority' (2005: 37). Echoing Bruno S. Frey's suggestion that there are higher demands for

---

[17] Interview Emma Thomas with Nadine Holdsworth, HMS Excellent, 17 July 2015. All other quotations are taken from this interview.

awards if an individual or group's 'position in society is uncertain' (2006: 380), English argues that:

> By creating awards for themselves, usually but not always under the auspices of a more or less formal professional association ... practitioners of a new, neglected, minor or otherwise less than fully legitimate artistic form assert their desire for wider recognition, for a better place on the cultural field as a whole. (2005: 63)

The RNTA Awards Night is a celebration of achievement, but it also legitimates and asserts cultural status via the performance rituals that underpin the awards process. Part of the evening's ritual involves the formal presentation of certificates, engraved glasses and cups issued as a permanent record of achievement, with the moment of presentation photographically documented. Significantly, senior ranking officers are invited to present awards and the President of the RNTA, most recently Commodore Steven Dainton (2015), attends the evening. The Navy personnel who are present in this capacity attend in full dress uniform, which heightens the sense of occasion and ceremony. These senior figures are invited to bear witness to the seriousness with which the groups attend to their theatre practice and this is clearly part of the validating apparatus, as is the presence of the adjudicator who duly performs their expertise for this extended audience. These invented traditions and the ritualised processes involved in the symbolic giving of awards can be illuminated by Victor Turner's work on social drama. This unfolding social drama helps constitute the social order and reinforce the power relations in play, not least through the spatialised ordering of the event whereby the amateur theatre-makers are distanced from the senior ranking officers and the adjudicator through the provision of a VIP table as my notes on the evening indicate:

> The annual AGM [Annual General Meeting] is still in process when I arrive at the Warrant Officers' and Senior Rates' Mess at HMS Collingwood, which is decked out in balloons. Entering the room it is clear that members of the different theatre groups have congregated together in readiness for the Awards' Evening. I'm ushered to the bar and presented with a pile of certificates that I have to sign. I feel a bit awkward – I'm in an uncharacteristically 'posh' frock – but everyone one else has made an effort and adhered to the dress code. I'm reminded, once again, that dress codes are very important in the Navy. I feel the weight of having to be present as my judgements are read out. After opening the

event with an appraisal of the festival I sit back down at the VIP table with Commodore Dainton and others. This seems to be both a neutral space and one heavy with meaning as I marvel at the display of stripes and medals. As the nominations are read out and the winners announced, the space erupt in whoops, cheers and rhythmic banging on the tables ... after the presentations a mum tells me that she's spoken to her son who wasn't there to collect his award. Apparently he is delighted and she thanks me for helping to boost his confidence. (Nadine's Research Diary, 6 May 2016)

The awards themselves furnish the recipients with symbolic cultural capital, but they also offer an opportunity to recognise and honour others with a long association with the organisation. For instance, the Doug Craig Award for best cameo performance was instituted in 2009 by Doug Craig, a former Chairperson and Patron of the RNTA and, in what English describes as a 'memorial gesture', the RNTA recently renamed their best actress award the Barbara Clayden Trophy in recognition of her significant contribution to Navy drama in her lifetime (2005: 109).

Running alongside the tradition of competitive festivals are a growing number of awards ceremonies and associated prizes devoted to the amateur theatre field. NODA runs an extensive awards process to celebrate the work of its membership in its twelve designated regional districts and there are a number connected to local professional theatres or newspapers such as Derby Theatre's Eagle Awards or the annual Rose Bowl awards. Initiated in 1963 by Walter Hawkins, the then Chairperson of the *Bristol Evening Post*, and John Coe, a journalist and drama critic, the Rose Bowl Awards were designed 'to recognise the huge talent often hidden away in the many amateur theatrical groups in the region'.[18] So, the awards were started as a means of countering a sense of deficit, a feeling that amateur work was being overlooked and needed the legitimation and cultural status afforded by an awards process that functions via '*cultural* economics' that rely on 'systems of non-monetary, cultural and symbolic transaction' (English 2005: 4). Today, the Rose Bowl Awards, given in nineteen categories, are highly prized by amateur theatre companies in the southwest region with sixty theatre companies paying the sixty pounds entry fee for the 2015–2016 awards. The south of England is served by the *Southern Evening Echo's* Curtain Call Awards and in January 2016, thirty members

---

[18] www.rosebowlawards.org.uk. Accessed 10 September 2016.

of the RNTA attended the Curtain Call Awards' Night, described as their version of the Oscars, to see Jane Blatch-Gainey win in the category of Best Supporting Actress in a Shakespeare Play for her portrayal of Banquo during the RNTA's summer production of *Macbeth* in July 2015. The evening is documented with 276 photographs on the Curtain Call website and Collingwood RSC's Facebook announcement prompted several impromptu and informal comments such as 'Woo Hoo!!' and 'Yah! Well done guys', which arguably contributes to the sustenance of a mutually supportive community through the very articulation and performance of that support via a public forum such as Facebook. In fact, the digital realm is increasingly a site through which amateur companies are engaging with and recording their histories, heritage and memories.

Digital Memories

Prior to the rise of the digital, amateur theatre companies communicated with their members via newsletters and bulletin boards announcing auditions and forthcoming productions. Now, companies are increasingly adept at using the digital realm—websites, social networking sites, email, blogs, YouTube and Twitter feeds—as a way of recruiting new members, marketing events, organising rehearsals, celebrating achievements, discussing working processes and disseminating outputs to potentially wider audiences. Many amateur theatre groups use Facebook, described by media and memory theorist Joanne Garde-Hansen as the 'sine qua non of digital memory-making and personal archive building', which has a capacious community-building capacity that 'allows users to share and consolidate personal memories into collective memories in order to shore up familial, social and even national allegiance' (2009: 144–145). Companies often run two Facebook sites with one internally focused as a conversational apparatus existing beyond the period of time spent making theatre and another outward facing to post posters, photos, reviews and announcements of shows. Garde-Hansen et al. explore how 'a shifting mediatised social scape, or, rather, digital media ecology' is having a profound impact on the way people 'embody, create and are emplaced within digital memories' (2009: 1–4). In this section I am interested in how this 'digital media ecology' effects the way that amateur theatre companies disseminate histories, commemorate heritage and store memories of production processes and creative outputs as part of the project of acknowledging the cultural value of amateur creativity. Referring to this significant societal shift as the generation of a 'social network memory', sociologist Andrew Hoskins suggests that this is 'social not only through its potential for forging and sustaining communal relationships and activities, but in illuminating the "well-travelled popular practices of others"' such as amateur theatre activity (2009: 30). As such, I explore some of the ramifications of the digital realm for the proliferation of amateur theatre materials and memories that may now linger long after the performance event has taken place. I also consider how the expanded field of the digital has the potential to open up the space of amateur practice to an increasingly globally networked audience.

A vast number of amateur theatre companies design and maintain websites that include 'history' or 'archive' in their drop-down menu options, which includes narratives charting the evolution of companies and a space to create online archives of scanned artefacts including posters, programmes, reviews and production photographs. The Talisman Theatre in Kenilworth even includes converted cine film footage of the company from the 1950s on its archive section. De Groot refers to these online repositories as 'community archives' due to the fact they are 'local, small, individual projects interested in keeping a record of a particular group' and, as he points out '[a]rchives do not simply relate to particular social identities but accrue around areas, institutions, hobbies' (2009: 100). Importantly, de Groot draws attention to the democratic potential of such initiatives:

> Community archives can also preserve unofficial history, and provide communities with spaces for reflection, consideration, self-definition and identity formation. They give people the chance to claim their past back from official versions of events, to preserve fading ways of life, and to dissent from mainstream historical narratives. (2009: 100)

The Northamptonshire based Thrapston Amateur Dramatic Society's (TADS) website is typical of the way companies are deploying the digital realm for ease of storing and disseminating information and creating repositories for capturing the past and the present, which contributes to the creation of company narratives and community-building, as well as individual and collective memory formation. This website contains information about forthcoming productions, it lists shows from 1927 to the present and contains a section on news and events, which, dating back to 2008 chronologically archives numerous activities including auditions, play readings, shows, social events, details of awards received, requests for volunteers and more ad hoc items such as the write-up from the Fifty Plus Northants Adventure Club about a murder mystery event the society ran in 2014. As such, the multidimensional history and current life of the society, the shape of its annual calendar and its production repertoire is freely available to all.[19]

The website also includes a history section, which comprises an article by TADS member Stan Hayes, detailing the group's origins as the Corn Exchange Players formed in 1913 and its re-emergence as TADS in 1927 after twenty-four vice-presidents, mostly consisting of the 'local landed gentry' subscribed ten shillings and sixpence and eighty-seven ordinary members handed over two-and-six to make it financially viable. Hayes documents how the group has kept going until the present day despite constant pressures as rehearsal and performance spaces including local hotels and the canteen of the local foundry, the Smith and Grace Screw Boss Pulley Company, were closed and demolished. It informs its audience that the local community resource of the Corn Exchange became an auction house, the Smith and Grace foundry became a housing development and that the company has since settled in the town's former cinema, now the Plaza Centre, which is owned by the local District Council. In this example, which mirrors many across the country, the resilience of the amateur company maps onto changing patterns of class, labour and leisure and its longevity is implicitly set against the relative transience of other buildings, businesses and creative industries, which have fallen by the wayside in the locality. The article also recalls how, during a period of particular financial restraint, it avoided the cost of room hire in a local school by enrolling itself as an evening class, with the director acting as tutor and being paid. These historical nuggets become part of the folklore and identity of a society and new technologies are helping to facilitate the preservation and dissemination of this important, locally significant heritage.

The digital also potentially offers a way in which the difficulties of being marginalised or culturally invisible can be challenged and complicated, not least, as Gauntlett recognises, because the web has made it 'easier for everyday people to share the fruits of their creativity with others' (2011: 5). Recognised as 'a platform for vernacular creativity', there are now numerous examples of amateur theatre companies uploading anything

[19] http://tadsthrapston.org.uk/. Accessed 15 December 2017.

from full productions to short extracts of productions on YouTube (Burgess and Green 2009: 6). This is an intriguing phenomenon as what was once an ephemeral activity, designed to primarily attract a locally net-worked audience, now has the capacity to be recorded and disseminated far and wide. Most uploaded material from amateur theatre societies are getting views in the hundreds, but this should not diminish the capacity to reach large audiences that the decision to upload sets in motion, more-over, there are examples of significant dissemination. Bexhill Amateur Theatrical Society's outdoor productions of *Hamlet* from July 2011 and *Much Ado About Nothing* from July 2013, which had audiences in the hundreds when they were first produced, have, at the time of writing, had 284,530 and 39,034 views respectively on YouTube. The comment func-tion available indicates that this extended digital audience has been inter-national in composition (as at 4 September 2017).

These uploaded videos also have ramifications for the way in which amateur theatre is remembered. As video artist and digital culture aca-demic Shaun Wilson points out:

> [f]rom a phenomenological perspective, the issues that emerge here play out a significant role in both how accounts of the past are recalled from a con-textual point of view and how they are then changed and re-experienced through the endless reproduction of digital narrativity. (2009: 185)

The Bexhill Amateur Theatrical Society's *Much Ado About Nothing* cast are no longer reliant on highly fallible human memory that recalls a ver-sion of events that gets muddied through time; they have access to a digi-tal memory, a permanent record of an event that ultimately works to augment the embodied memory of performance. In addition, researchers in the creative and digital industries, Jean Burgess and Joshua Green, stress that 'practices of audiencehood – quoting, favoriting, commenting, responding, sharing, and viewing – all leave traces' that are significant (2009: 57). In fact, they go as far as to characterise YouTube as a demo-cratic form of cultural archive that it has the capacity to expand notions of what constitutes cultural heritage:

> The idea of YouTube as an archive has significance for the prospect of wide-spread popular co-creation of cultural heritage, supplementing the more specifically purposeful and highly specialized practices of state-based cultural archiving institutions like public libraries and museums; or media companies and broadcasters. (Burgess and Green 2009: 88)

Arguably, digital media in general does offer a more accessible, networked, participatory and democratic model of archive creation and consumption. For a start, digital media means that it is no longer the sole prerogative of a lone archivist to record history for posterity, instead it can be multiauthored by summoning a peer-to-peer approach of 'prosumers' in its curation and dissemination. Everybody with administrative access can upload news, events and photographs and anybody with an interest in amateur theatre can, with the aid of a search engine, find themselves accessing material on different societies around the world. In turn, the relatively horizontal model of the digital is having an effect on the type of material that is preserved. As Hoskins asserts, 'digital media introduce different equations of ephemera into our remembering processes and capacities as well as new means to preserve, restore and represent the past' (2009: 31). Whereas the MHDS archive discussed above compiles items produced for public consumption—photos, programmes and local newspaper reviews—which are inevitably distanced from the activities of making theatre or the day-to-day minutiae of being involved with a company, digital media facilitates the inclusion of material that is immediate, random, personal and discursive.

An example of this more personal and discursive material can be found in the growth of the amateur production blog, 'an online collection of information describing and personalising moments to be revisited at some point in the near future' (Wilson 2009: 187–8). In contrast to digital writer and entrepreneur Andrew Keen's vociferous arguments in *The Cult of the Amateur* against the growth and potentially negative consequences of what he refers to as 'digital narcissism' whereby 'bloggers can post their amateurish creations at will', the digital might instead open up a multiperspectival network of knowledge creators who offer access into worlds that have largely remained uncharted (2008: xiii, 19). The processes of production engaged in by amateur theatre-makers have traditionally remained hidden from view as discussed in Chapter 6, but a production blog facilitates access to working processes as they arise, it enables immediate reflection that can be accessed at a later date to trigger a memory of what occurred and was significant from the perspective of the blogger. As Garde-Hansen et al. argue, 'what digital media brings to this representation of the past is a greater personalisation of events, narratives and testimonies' (2009: 17).

A particularly resonant example of this new form of archiving in the amateur theatre context could be found at the jollylion.com website where numerous reviews could be accessed of amateur theatre productions that have taken place in the southwest of England alongside detailed rehearsal and production diaries. The blog, written by Jolyon Tuck, who self-defines as 'knocking about the South Devon AmDram scene for the best part of ten years', features his image in a banner of photographs at the top of the screen in various theatrical guises from pantomime to Shakespeare to contemporary classics.[20] His rehearsal diary of a TOADS Theatre Company production of *Miss Julie* staged 9th–16th February 2013 at The Little Theatre, Torquay is highly revealing with twenty-three entries running from 19th November 2012 to the dress rehearsal held on 7th February 2013. Documenting his time rehearsing the character of Jean, the blog charts reluctantly, but gainfully, participating in a movement workshop; a long-running battle with learning lines; approaches to character development and attempts to inject sexual tension into the scenes, which descend into fits of giggles. Amidst the self-deprecating humour and countdown to the performance run, Jolyon Tuck explores the benefits of various rehearsal techniques such as speed reads and what is hailed as 'a magical rehearsal' when the director invited different people to read in for Miss Julie and Jean:

> Suddenly we're hearing the last scene of the play as if for the first time. Unfamiliar voices saying words I'm trying to learn, putting emphasis in different places, giving a new perspective, offering a reality check – this ending is very moving. There are tears. There is silence.

There is something very interesting going on here as ultimately this version of the 'social network memory' allows access to forms of thick description and emotionality that may be lost if not captured in the immediate and informal language of blogging. Indeed, the immediacy of the blog format facilities a deep and rich encounter with the particular nuances of human activity and social interaction that occurs during amateur rehearsal processes.

Of course, this form of digital dissemination cannot be addressed without caution. Its health is reliant on the goodwill of those who build and populate the sites for no monetary reward. Also, Garde-Hansen notes that whilst social networking sites 'project a space of disinhibitions it would be naïve to think that users were not acutely aware of their self projections' and hence she refers to digital memories being 'practiced and performed

---

[20] www.thejollylion.com. Accessed 30 August 2016.

rather simply recorded and shared' (2009: 142). Equally, like human memory, the digital is not infallible, as Wilson notes, 'If we consider the presence of embedded memory (and its narrativity) in digital media then the loss of history can occur when, for example, blogs are deleted from servers… Deletion thus becomes a factor in the loss of memories and histories (2009: 195). The fragility of the digital was brought home to me when I returned to look at the jollylion site a year or so after I had first encountered it. With the domain registration expired, the site had disappeared and been replaced by a Facebook page that Jolyon Tuck had painstakingly populated with some of the material from the previous site, but it was impossible to ascertain what had been lost.[21] As de Groot suggests, there is a need to be mindful of how sustainable the digital record might be in the future (2009: 93).

Nonetheless, it is clear that the exponential growth of the digital is having a marked impact on the ways in which amateur theatre-makers, researchers and interested individuals can access different amateur theatre histories and heritage that exists across the UK and beyond. It is also evident that the digital is influencing the working practices of specific amateur theatre companies in the twenty-first century as many use the facilities at their disposal to communicate, disseminate information and access material that they need. In turn, the unprecedented access to information afforded by the digital is having an impact on the wider amateur theatre ecology, particularly the national organisations that support amateur theatre. Whereas organisations such as NODA were once the repositories of knowledge on important issues such as securing rights, public liability insurance and safeguarding, this information is now available at the click of a mouse. This situation is leading some companies to question the value of paying the fees incurred for being a member organisation and a rise of non-affiliated groups. Jo Matthews, Vice Chair of LTG in 2018, is alert to this issue:

> There is no difference between amateur and professional theatre companies in terms of health and safety and safeguarding legislation. We all must comply to the same rules, and you can find these out quite easily on-line. This means that the organisations have to offer something in addition to advice,

---

[21] https://en-gb.facebook.com/The-Jolly-Lion-218283294899373/. Accessed 18 December 2017.

and so far this has been training and skill sharing at conferences and so on. But if professional companies like the RSC are offering this kind of thing, there is reason to reassess what LTG and others offer.[22]

Jo Matthews advocates an increased role for LTG as a campaigning organisation, perhaps signalling a new confidence in the status of the amateur and the rise of interest in amateur creativity that is increasingly evident in the twenty-first century. It is to this cultural shift that we now turn.

REFERENCES

Appadurai, Arjun. 1986. Introduction: Commodities and the Politics of Value. In *The Social Life of Things: Commodities in Cultural Perspective*, ed. Arjun Appadurai, 3–63. Cambridge: Cambridge University Press.

Bennett, Andy, Jodie Taylor, and Ian Woodward. 2014. *The Festivalization of Culture*. Abingdon: Routledge.

Billig, Michael. 1995. *Banal Nationalism*. London: Sage.

Bratton, Jacky. 2003. *New Readings in Theatre History*. Cambridge: Cambridge University Press.

Burgess, Jean, and Joshua Green. 2009. *YouTube*. Cambridge: Polity.

de Groot, Jerome. 2009. *Consuming History: Historians and Heritage in Contemporary Popular Culture*. Abingdon: Routledge.

Delanty, Gerard. 2011. Conclusion: On the Cultural Significance of Arts Festivals. In *Festivals and the Cultural Public Sphere*, ed. Liana Giorgi, Monica Sassatelli, and Gerard Delanty, 190–198. Abingdon: Routledge.

Dolley, Colin. 1989. We're Only Here to Help. *The Stage and Television Today*, July 27: 23.

English, James F. 2005. *The Economy of Prestige*. Cambridge, MA: University of Harvard Press.

Frey, Bruno S. 2006. Giving and Receiving Awards. *Perspectives on Psychological Science* 1 (4): 377–388.

Garde-Hansen, Joanne. 2009. My Memories?: Personal Digital Archive Fever and Facebook. In *Save As...Digital Memories*, ed. Joanne Garde-Hansen, Andrew Hoskins, and Anna Reading, 135–150. Basingstoke: Palgrave Macmillan.

Garde-Hansen, Joanne, Andrew Hoskins, and Anna Reading, eds. 2009. *Save As...Digital Memories*. Basingstoke: Palgrave Macmillan.

---

[22] Interview Jo Matthews with Helen Nicholson, The Globe Theatre, London. 22 November 2015.

Gauntlett, David. 2011. *Making Is Connecting: The Social Meaning of Creativity, Form DIY and Knitting to YouTube and Web 2.0*. Cambridge: Polity Press.

Harrison, Rodney. 2013. *Heritage: Critical Approaches*. London: Routledge.

Harrison, Rodney, and Deborah Rose. 2010. Intangible Heritage. In *Understanding Heritage and Memory*, ed. Tim Benton, 238–276. Manchester: Manchester University Press.

Hewison, Robert. 1987. *The Heritage Industry: Britain in a Climate of Decline*. London: Methuen.

Hobsbawm, Eric. 1983. Introduction: Inventing Traditions. In *The Invention of Tradition*, ed. Eric Hobsbawm and Terence Ranger, 1–14. Cambridge: Cambridge University Press.

Holland, Patricia. 1991. Introduction: History, Memory and the Family Album. In *Family Snaps: The Meanings of Domestic Photography*, ed. Jo Spence and Patricia Holland, 1–14. London: Virago Press.

Horton, John, and Peter Kraftl. 2012. Clearing Out a Cupboard: Memory, Materiality and Transitions. In *Geography and Memory*, ed. Owain Jones and Joanne Garde-Hansen, 25–44. Basingstoke: Palgrave Macmillan.

Hoskins, Andrew. 2009. The Mediatisation of Memory. In *Save As…Digital Memories*, ed. Joanne Garde-Hansen, Andrew Hoskins, and Anna Reading, 27–43. Basingstoke: Palgrave Macmillan.

Jones, Henry Arthur. 2008. *Stage by Stage: 75 Years of Theatre in Market Harborough*. 2nd ed. Leicester: Matador.

Jones, Jonathan. 2014. British Folk Art Review – Welcome to the Old Weird Britain. *Guardian*, June 9. https://www.theguardian.com/artand-design/2014/jun/09/british-folk-art-review-tate-britain. Accessed 21 Sept 2016.

Keen, Andrew. 2008. *The Cult of the Amateur*. Revised ed. London: Nicholas Brealey Publishing.

Kopytoff, Igor. 1986. The Cultural Biography of Things: Commoditization as Process. In *The Social Life of Things: Commodities in Cultural Perspective*, ed. Arjun Appadurai, 64–92. Cambridge: Cambridge University Press.

Ritchie, Richard. 2015. *The Old Stagers: Canterbury, Cricket and Theatricals*. Canterbury: OS Publishing.

Roberts, Elizabeth. 2012. Family Photographs: Memories, Narrative, Place. In *Geography and Memory*, ed. Owain Jones and Joanne Garde-Hansen, 91–108. Basingstoke: Palgrave Macmillan.

Schneider, Rebecca. 2001. Archives: Performance Remains. *Performance Research* 6 (2): 100–108. https://doi.org/10.1080/13528165.2001.10871792.

Shipley, Michael. 2006. *Bolton Little Theatre: 75 Years of Drama*. Leeds: Millnet Financial Services.

Shirley, Rosemary. 2015. *Rural Modernity, Everyday Life and Visual Culture*. Abingdon: Routledge.

Smith, Laurajane. 2006. *Uses of Heritage*. Abingdon: Routledge.

———. 2011. The "Doing" of Heritage: Heritage as Performance. In *Performing Heritage: Research, Practice and Innovation in Museum Theatre and Live Interpretation*, ed. Anthony Jackson and Jenny Kidd, 69–81. Manchester: Manchester University Press.

Smith, Laurajane, and Emma Waterton. 2009. The Envy of the World: Intangible Heritage in England. In *Intangible Heritage*, ed. Laurajane Smith and Natsuko Akagawa, 289–302. Abingdon: Routledge.

Taylor, Diana. 2003. *The Archive and the Repertoire*. Durham: Duke University Press.

Turkle, Sherry, ed. 2007. *Evocative Objects: Things We Think With*. Cambridge, MA: MIT Press.

Wilson, Shaun. 2009. Remixing Memory in Digital Media. In *Save As…Digital Memories*, ed. Joanne Garde-Hansen, Andrew Hoskins, and Anna Reading, 187–197. Basingstoke: Palgrave Macmillan.

Winchester Dramatic Society. 2014. *A History of the Winchester Dramatic Society*. Winchester: Sarsen Press.

CHAPTER 8

Theatre and the Amateur Turn: Future Ecologies

In May 2017 the following notice appeared in the local press and on the Facebook page of The Forum Players, an amateur theatre company in Bourne End, a Buckinghamshire village on the river Thames about 25 miles outside London.

> Over the past couple of years the Forum have suffered from declining membership and active participation. The result of this is that we have only really been doing panto for 3 years and we have struggled to cast each time.
>
> The lack of participation / interest in an autumn show, followed by not a great take up on the spring show, has now brought this to a head. Especially as there is considerable doubt about whether we can cast a panto for 2018, and as yet have had no-one showing any interest in putting forward a script to direct.
>
> Given this the committee have decided that we need to hold an emergency members' meeting for the club on Monday 5th June in the small hall... I hope that I don't need to point out that if we cannot put on a panto in 2018 then the Forum Players will fold.[1]

The Forum Player's repertoire is typical of many small amateur drama groups, marking the village calendar with annual pantomimes, reviews and whodunits since its foundation in 1968. Their call-to-arms was heeded, and the well-attended meeting resulted in enthusiasm for new projects,

---

[1] Bourne End Forum Players Facebook page. Accessed 30 May 2017.

© The Author(s) 2018
H. Nicholson et al., *The Ecologies of Amateur Theatre*,
https://doi.org/10.1057/978-1-137-50810-2_8

averting the company's decline, at least for now. It does, however, illustrate some of the challenges of running an amateur theatre company in the twenty-first century, where competing demands on time, changing theatrical tastes and a fluctuating demographic means that some smaller companies are struggling to engage new members that represent the local community. Yet, as this book testifies, amateur theatre is also resilient; it is the distinctive power of making theatre that has ensured its continued popularity, providing creative opportunities for participants as well as companionship, friendship and feelings of belonging.

One of the key features of amateur theatre companies is their longevity, with many boasting unbroken histories since the heyday of amateur theatre in the 1920s and 1930s, when every village, town, city and many workplaces enjoyed an active amateur theatre scene. Regarded as a social movement with egalitarian intent, amateur theatre was reformist rather than revolutionary. Often supported by cultural leaders and policy-makers in the early twentieth century, amateur theatre was harnessed to an ideal of community that was sustained, in different ways, throughout the century. It is testament to the ability of amateur theatre companies to adapt to new circumstances that it has survived in different cultural climates; in the process of our research we were contacted by many enthusiastic amateur theatre-makers whose companies balance a repertoire of cutting-edge plays and popular favourites that would not be unrecognisable to their predecessors. It would be misleading, however, to imply that all amateur theatre companies are thriving, and we have also learnt about companies who are struggling or dying. The Newcastle Players in Staffordshire, for example, disbanded after eighty-one years of local successful theatre-making in 2015. Its history is well documented in a series of self-published books by Geoff Price, a company member who had been involved for many years. The company lacked new and younger members to take it forward, and in 2013 the committee took the painful decision to close. The sale of their workshop premises, props, costumes and other equipment raised over £60,000, as Geoff Price puts it, the company was 'cash rich'.[2] How they chose to distribute the money illustrates the relationship between amateur theatre companies and the wider community. After donating £6000 to charity, *Newcastle Players Bulletin* notes that the committee offered £5000 to Audley Players, a small local company who had

---

[2] Geoff Price, email correspondence with Helen Nicholson. 22 February 2015.

given the Newcastle Players a surprise gift of £250 in the early 1980s when they were short of funds, a gesture that shows that company-members have long memories. £25,000 went to another amateur company, Porthill Players (established in 1911), whom the Chairman (sic) described as 'an innovative and progressive society with strong and committed members' (2015: 2). Two large sums of money, interestingly, were given to local professional theatres, both of whom were credited with supporting The Newcastle Players through loans of props and use of performance spaces. The New Vic Theatre received £12,000 to extend their community pro-gramme, and a further £15,000 went to the Stoke Repertory Theatre to upgrade their backstage areas. The penultimate *Newcastle Players Bulletin* documented the decisions, capturing the Chairman's comment on the legacy of the Players:

> In this way the Newcastle Players will not only be remembered in archives and in personal records but by making a tangible difference to a cause we all hold dear: local theatre. (2015: 4)

The way in which The Newcastle Players distributed its resources illus-trates how amateur theatre operates as part of a wider ecology of commu-nity interests and local theatres that includes both amateur and professional companies. It also recognises that its legacy and heritage are both mate-rial—in terms of the company's assets and archives—and immaterial, found in memory, feelings of affection and shared values. As part of an ecosystem, however, amateur theatre is inevitably vulnerable to variations in habitat and changes to the wider social and cultural climate.

The story of the Newcastle Players' closure sheds light on some of the ways in which amateur theatre is related to the wider creative economy, and in particular its relationship with local professional theatres. As we pointed out in Chapter 2, the rise of subsidised theatre after World War Two cemented the division between amateur and professional theatres, with professionally-led community theatre and theatre-in-education occu-pying a third space in the cultural ecosystem during the second half of the twentieth century. As Taryn Storey notes, the newly formed Arts Council 'undermined its own egalitarian and artistic aims' by marginalising ama-teur artists in its policies, with the Drama Panel, significantly, making derogatory comments about amateurs (2017: 78–80). This legacy endures, but we have also found that in practice many regional theatres—including Stoke Repertory Theatre, The New Vic in Stoke-on-Trent and

The Swan at Worcester—have sustained good relations with amateurs that are mutually beneficial. Chris Jaegar, artistic director of The Swan, commented that amateurs are key to the financial viability of the theatre, and that the audiences that they bring in are fundamental to the theatre's success.[3] Yet some attitudes are harder to shift, and we have also heard numerous accounts of pejorative or judgmental views about the amateur theatre sector; Jo Matthews and Anne Gilmour, members of The Questors Theatre in London and leading figures in the Little Theatre Guild and the International Amateur Theatre Association (AITA/ IATA), observed that some major conservatoires forbid trainee actors from acknowledging their amateur performances in their biographies, despite productions being 'every bit as good as those at drama school'.[4] We have still found jokes circulating about 'am-drams' from theatre-insiders who would otherwise regard themselves as egalitarian.

In this final chapter we argue that hierarchical divisions between the different sectors belong squarely in the past, a legacy of twentieth century divisions of labour, cultural values and social attitudes. The chapter will chart some of the ways in which amateur theatre is responding to twenty-first century challenges, and assesses its contribution to the wider cultural ecology. We will also consider how the renewed interest in amateur creativity is influencing amateur theatre, and how the culture of participation is beginning to redefine its relationship with professional theatre. We are particularly interested in clarifying what is distinctive about amateur *theatre*—what distinguishes it from other forms of creative practice—and understanding how it might be sustained in a changing social climate, and what the barriers to participation might be. In so doing, we aim to close this book with some thoughts about the future, and how amateur theatre, as a craft, creative practice and community resource, might take its place alongside other forms of artistic activities.

---

[3] Interview Chris Jaegar with Erin Walcon, The Swan Theatre, Worcester, 8 March 2014.
[4] Interview Jo Matthews and Anne Gilmore with Helen Nicholson, Ealing 23 January 2015.

Amateurs, Creativity and the Creative Economy

As we have demonstrated, amateur theatre has long been responsive to the prevailing social and cultural landscape, and amateurs in the twenty-first century are no exception. In the twenty-first century, there is renewed focus on the creative industries as an important economic resource, bringing with it a cultural shift that has also inspired new ways of working and living. In *The New Spirit of Capitalism*, Luc Boltanski and Eve Chiapello offer a detailed analysis of how the artistic ideals of creativity and self-expression have contributed to social and cultural change. Dissatisfaction with the conformity imposed by the early twentieth-century industrial era led, they suggest, to a mid-twentieth century interest in personal fulfilment and self-liberation. They describe this as an 'artistic critique' of capitalist society, which valued 'autonomy in personal and emotional life, but also in work: creativity, unbridled self-fulfilment; the authenticity of a personal life against hypocritical, old-fashioned social conventions' (2007: 419). By the late 1990s and into the new millennium, they suggest, this way of thinking had become absorbed into systems of management; the new spirit of capitalism inverted the idea that paid labour is inherently alienating, replacing it with a new cultural ideal that the workplace might be a site of self-expression. The creative industries have developed unconventional working practices built on these principles, where 'creatives', though often on short-term contracts and working long hours, are encouraged to express their individuality and embrace playfulness. Although this way of working lies outside most people's daily lives, it has nonetheless placed creativity more firmly in contemporary life, both as a profitable commodity and as a route to self-fulfilment.

If, as Boltanski and Chiapello and others argue, creativity has become recognised as an important aspect of the twenty-first century economy, it exerts pressure on the ways in which creative practices – including amateur theatre – are perceived and understood. In her book *Creativity*, Harriet Hawkins argues that creativity 'promises much': economic regeneration, material prosperity, identity formation, well-being, connected communities, subject transformation, social cohesion, knowledge production, place shaping, environmental engagements, world-making (2017: 335).

The ubiquity of creativity places it in a politically ambiguous position, Hawkins suggests, harnessed both to the 'neoliberal production of urban spaces and economies' and also associated with 'avant-garde creative practices as practices of activism and resistance' (2017: 336). In response, Hawkins argues for an expanded notion of creativity as a 'distributed phenomenon' that is related to the arts, but not confined to them. She acknowledges that its qualities are threefold: an attribute of the specialist artist; a skilful practice developed over time, and an unconscious part of improvising everyday life (2017: 338). Creativity inhabits a paradoxical place in the twenty-first century, therefore, with consequences for how amateurs are perceived, and how amateur creativity is understood.

One response to the commodification of creativity, particularly in post-industrial societies, is a renewed focus on the amateur. There are four ways in which the amateur and amateur creativity have entered the contemporary cultural landscape that relate to this study. First, the amateur has been championed as a counter-cultural figure who, in opposing professionalism, raises challenging social questions. This is the position adopted by Andy Merrifield in his polemical book *The Amateur: The Pleasure of Doing What You Love*, in which he argues that professionalisation 'spoils everything' by 'transforming a labour of love into a loathing of labour' (2017: 158). He advocates an 'amateur revolution' in which free-thinking amateurs will oppose the authority of professionals, cast off convention and live by 'affirming your authentic self' (2017: 203). Despite his indebtedness to Marx, this aspect of Merrifield's position has much in common with the ideal of creative self-actualisation that Boltanski and Chiapello identified as a feature of twenty-first century neoliberalism. It is also an idea of amateurism that echoes the past; as we argued in Chapter 5, amateur activities were regularly seen as an antidote to the routine of nineteenth and twentieth century industrial labour, whereas Merrifield's amateur seeks to avoid the constraints of twenty-first century professionalisation. Yet the figure of the amateur, in this conceptualisation, is an imagined political symbol that represents an alternative way of living, and it is not easy to see its relationship to amateur theatre as lived, creative practices.

More rooted in the material world is the second, and related, idea of amateur creativity as a route to self-fulfilment and personal happiness. Often described as 'everyday creativity' by professional artists and cultural policy-makers, the aim is often to extend the emotional benefits of creative practice to a wider public. Advocates of everyday creativity often champion its impact on individual well-being, locating it squarely in the contemporary imperative to promote health and happiness. This apparently well-intentioned ambition has been critiqued in different ways by Carl Cederstrom and André Spicer in their book *The Wellness Syndrome* and by

William Davies in *The Happiness Industry: How the Government and Big Business Sold Us Well-Being* (2015). Cederstrom and Spicer cite Laura Berlant's phrase 'good-life fantasies' to describe the contemporary climate in which cultivating self-expression and happiness has become a moral duty that rests, they argue, on 'traditional middle-class dreams' (2015: 83). Davies is similarly critical of government sanctioned initiatives to promote well-being, arguing that both work and leisure have become increasingly regulated and managed, with participants' levels of happiness, activity levels, quality of life and well-being measured to enable public resources to be targeted and to demonstrate value-for-money to funders. Both analyses of well-being argue that the contemporary climate shifts attention away from material inequalities or systemic problems, placing the emphasis firmly on individuals to create their own happiness. This emphasis on creativity as self-cultivation recycles the idea of self-improvement which, as we noted in Chapter 2, was central to the development of amateur theatre in the early twentieth century. And as we observed in the introduction, initiatives that encourage everyday creativity are often designed to address a perceived deficit in people's lives, and thus have largely ignored the work of established amateur theatre companies.

Thirdly, the digital age is strengthening the cultural influence of amateurs. New online platforms, streaming, social media and so on have opened new opportunities for amateurs to find innovative ways to reach wide audiences. In his book *The Cult of the Amateur: How blogs, MySpace, YouTube and the rest of today's user-generated media are killing our culture and economy* Andrew Keen sees this trend in apocalyptic terms, arguing that it heralds the demise of 'cultural standards and moral values', further suggesting that 'the very traditions that have helped foster and create our news, our music, our literature, our television shows, and our movies are under assault' (2007: 2). Keen's polemical attack describes this apparent democratisation of knowledge and creativity as 'the great seduction', arguing long before the world came to read President Trump's late-night Tweets that the digital revolution is 'undermining truth, souring civic discourse, and belittling expertise, experience, and talent' (2007: 15). Keen is, however, mistaken in his assumption that amateur creativity equates with a lack of experience and expertise; as we have argued throughout this book there are many amateurs who hold considerable craft knowledge and practical skills honed over a life-time of theatre-making. Indeed, amateur theatre-makers make good use of YouTube to share craft skills as prop-makers and expertise as set-builders. But this social climate is re-shaping the significance of amateurs, and in Keen's analysis, it is not the amateur, but the professional gatekeepers and experts that are vulnerable in this changing cultural habitat.

A fourth response to the commodification of creativity is offered by cultural geographers Tim Edensor and his co-authors, and it is perhaps this idea of amateur creativity as a material practice that has most influenced this study. As we observed in Chapter 4, Edensor et al. are critical of the idea of the creative class and the instrumental use of creativity to support urban regeneration, arguing that it privileges certain kinds of creativity, located in fashionable creative cities, in ways that are socially divisive. They use the term 'vernacular creativity' to capture 'alternative, marginal and quotidian practices' that have been overlooked by creative city strategies (2010: 1). Their response is to recognise creativity that happens in diverse settings—in community gardens and suburban sheds, in displays of Christmas lights and in the witty rearrangement of discarded garden gnomes at a local council tip. The idea of vernacular creativity straddles Hawkins' taxonomy of creativity as integral to the improvisation of everyday life and as a skilful practice. Although vernacular and amateur creativity are not synonymous—vernacular creativity is not necessarily associated with an extended passion for craftwork or artistic practice—it is significant to our study of amateur theatre because it is not built on a deficit model; it does not assess what people are *not* doing, but rather seeks to value creative activity in all its myriad of forms, and without imposing judgements of taste. By looking critically at what is happening outside the privileged spaces occupied by the creative class, Edensor et al. offer an alternative to the prevailing view that some places and people are more creative than others and, by implication, that they are in need professional intervention.

Inspired by Edensor et al., this study was initially motivated by an interest in amateur theatre in non-metropolitan places—in towns, villages and suburbia—that are often outside the gaze and experience of city-based arts professionals. We have, however, also investigated amateur theatre in cities, where perhaps unsurprisingly, the diversity of contemporary life is most fully represented; as we have documented, diasporic companies such as Philippine Theatre UK in central London perform stories from their Filipino heritage, and Acting Out, the LGBTQ amateur theatre company in Birmingham celebrate and represent the city's gay communities in their repertoire and casting. In Manchester The Jewish Theatre Company has been performing since 1975, with the primary objective of entertaining the Jewish community. It was established, company member Marilyn Blank pointed out, because Jewish religious practices on Friday nights precluded them from performing in other amateur companies.[5] The fact that companies founded to serve communities of identities flourish in cities reflects an urban demographic, where there is a critical mass of diverse communities that are less likely to be found in the smaller populations of towns and villages where amateur theatre often takes place. If, as Hawkins argues, creativity is a 'material, embodied and "placed" practice' rather than a disposition of the mind, it follows that creative practices not only respond to their environments, they are also 'socially-spatially productive' of communities and identities (2017: 336). This suggests, as we noted in Chapter 4, that amateur theatre companies can shape communities and give new meanings to place. Whether amateur theatre exists in the margins or in the centre, therefore, depends on your vantage point; to many thousands of people, as we have demonstrated, amateur theatre is not a peripheral activity, but lies at the heart of a creative life.

Throughout our research we have observed the contribution amateur theatre makes to maintaining a diverse cultural economy; as we pointed out in Chapter 2, it plays a significant role in an economy that exists beyond market forces, including gifting, volunteer labour, communal assets and in-kind support and care. As John Holden rightly points out, there are porous boundaries between the three spheres he describes as 'homemade, subsidised and commercial' which, he notes, 'operate as mixed-economy models' (2015: 10). Citing Voluntary Arts director Robin Simpson, he further suggests that 'a play written professionally by Alan Ayckbourn could be performed by a mixed cast of amateur and professional actors in a volunteer-run company production taking place in a hired theatre space' (2015: 11). In this mixed-economy amateur theatre companies make a material contribution to their communities, making a significant impact not only on cultural and community life, but also contributing to their local economies. Some amateur productions have large budgets, and money spent on craft and building materials, social activities and so on supports local businesses. Amateur theatre has long benefitted commercial and subsidised theatre, both economically and as a space to nurture talent, though acknowledgement has generally been one-way; as we have pointed out, there are many professional playwrights, choreographers, lighting

---

[5] Telephone conversation Marilyn Blank with Helen Nicholson 27 May 2015.

technicians, musicians and publishers who are beneficiaries of the amateur market. As such, amateur theatre does not exist outside the contemporary creative economy, it is integral to its survival and vitality.

THE AMATEUR TURN: ECOLOGIES OF AMATEUR AND PROFESSIONAL THEATRES

Amateur theatre exists in the context of a twenty-first century cultural shift in which the amateur is no longer a marginal figure, and amateur creativity is re-emerging to take centre stage. On one hand, Keen's cult of the amateur appears remote from amateur productions in church halls, community centres and local theatres. Amateur theatre, as live performance with local people, is often seen as a marker of community stability and rootedness rather than susceptible to fluctuating trends of the digital age. On the other, the current zeitgeist is influencing the relationship between amateurs and professionals across the cultural sector, and beginning to shape new forms of interactivity between amateur and professional theatres. Of course, in the current economic climate in which work in the arts is becoming increasingly precarious, there is an understandable concern that professional theatres are using volunteer or unpaid labour in their productions, thereby denying jobs to those with professional training who seek to make a living in the theatre. As Paul Jepson, the artistic director of the Northcott Theatre in Exeter, points out: 'the phrase "community cast" is quite often used...because the regional producer doesn't want to have an out-and-out row with Equity.'[6]

Yet the amateur turn in contemporary life has inspired professionals to extend access to creative activities to adults, regarded by egalitarian professionals as a way of democratising the arts. This is a view advocated in a report published by Kings College London in 2017, *Towards cultural democracy: Promoting Cultural capabilities for everyone.* To illustrate the benefits of such provision, the report cites the work of The Old Vic Community Company in London, who use their 'relatively substantial budget' to create a new 'community' theatre company drawn by audition from London's diverse adult population (2017: 39). In 2018 the National Theatre launched an ambitious new programme, Public Acts, a nationwide

---

[6] Interview Paul Jepson with Erin Walcon, The Northcott Theatre, Exeter, 6 November 2015.

initiative designed to 'create extraordinary acts of theatre and community'.[7] The first production, an adaptation of Shakespeare's *Pericles* by Chris Bush and directed by Emily Lim, featured a small cast of professional actors with over two hundred non-professional actors, many cast from the National's community partner organisations. To encourage engagement, National Theatre associate artists led a series of workshops in community settings over several months, often working with participants who had accessed support from the community organisation at vulnerable points in their lives. The cast of *Pericles* developed from these workshops, building a company for a performance on the vast Olivier Stage with people with little or no prior experience of theatre-making. Seeing the diversity of London represented in the National Theatre's rehearsal room in Spring 2018 was a moving experience, and one in which the atmosphere and enthusiasm was contagious. I had also witnessed the special qualities of non-professional performers at the Young Vic in late 2017, where David Greig's version of Aeschylus' *The Suppliant Women* performed by a chorus of local women from London brought the play into the twenty-first century. Critically acclaimed and powerful, the 'community chorus' was diverse and energetic, capturing the raw authenticity of women's social roles and raising powerful and contemporary questions about belonging. These initiatives are culturally significant, I think, because they represent a new openness in professional theatres to push their doors wide open. However important they may be, however, the focus is on non-professional or 'community' performers in casts newly formed by professional theatres rather than established amateur theatre companies, and therefore lie outside the parameters of this study.

For some, particularly those with a professional interest in the arts, this renewed interest in the creativity of local people means that the term 'amateur' is redundant, with many preferring to use words such as 'non-professional', 'community' or 'everyday' as descriptive categories. The *Towards cultural democracy report* goes further, regarding the term 'amateur' as 'problematic':

> To promote cultural capability and to facilitate cultural democracy, the arts and creative industries requires a rejection of any false dichotomy between

[7] https://www.nationaltheatre.org.uk/sites/default/files/pericles_press_release_final.pdf. Accessed 21 June 2018.

amateur and professional. At the same time, opportunity for new participants to work with experienced practitioners… is one important way in which people can be enabled to create versions of culture together. (2017: 40)

Of course, this way of thinking is highly relevant to The Old Vic Community Company, the case study for the report, which was designed to reach people who were new to theatre-making in central London. This valuable activity is appropriately not called amateur theatre; the company was formed from a group of individuals brought together and 'enabled' by professionals. Gathering participants from 'hard-to-reach' populations or those who rarely participate in the arts or access major cultural organisations is often a key criterion for funding, and this further precludes collaboration with existing amateur theatre companies. But to imply that word amateur is redundant (or even anti-democratic) is to miss the special attributes we have found in amateur theatre companies. As we argue throughout this book, amateur theatre has qualities that differentiate it from other forms of theatre—its relationship with the audience, the longevity of companies, the life-long commitment of amateur theatre-makers, the opportunity for amateur actors to be seen differently in their communities, their heritage, craft skills and repertoiring—all of which warrant recognition. Furthermore, the theatre companies we have encountered in this research themselves self-identify as amateur, suggesting that the democratic problem lies not in the terminology itself, but in who uses it, for what reason and why. It is important to question hierarchical divisions between professional and amateur, but we maintain that in a pluralist democracy using the term 'amateur' is an act of cultural recognition for a sector that has been systematically overlooked, particularly by those who inhabit positions of cultural privilege. As Stephen Knott argues in relation to craft, amateur creativity occupies a differential space for many amateurs that is distinctive (Knott 2015: 124).

The distinctive qualities of amateur theatre were recognised, however, in the RSC's Open Stages Programme. This nationwide programme was unusual, if not unique, in that it involved major professional theatres collaborating with existing amateur theatre companies, with a primary focus on the craft of making theatre rather than on the social, communitarian or emotional benefits of the participants. Ian Wainwright, the RSC producer who led the programme, described the context in which Open Stages took place:

What I was seeing was the very middle-class world of theatre working with young people and social disadvantaged groups, and that's fantastic, but there wasn't much happening in between, giving the message that you have to be young or disadvantaged to get our attention... There's also a zeitgeisty thing... there is a new respect for people's participation, and ordinary people taking part... Theatre belongs to everyone. It doesn't belong to the tiny super-elite of theatre athletes on stage, it doesn't just belong to education, it belongs to everyone, including amateurs. It is good for theatre that we have this eclectic approach, it would become a museum piece without it. As many people as want to watch, there has to be these amateur guys who want to make theatre.[8]

Wainwright observed that although it is now commonplace for professional theatres to work with young people, there has been very little professional interest in working with the same people who wish to carry on making theatre into adulthood. As soon as young people 'become amateurs', Wainwright suggested, attitudes towards them shift as many professionals regard amateurs as 'foolish'. Michael Boyd, artistic director at RSC from 2002 to 2012, recognised both the power of amateurs and a gap in its provision, and his vision for Open Stages was counter-cultural. It led the RSC to invite amateur theatre companies to participate in a programme of skills-sharing workshops, mentoring for directors and performances of Shakespeare's plays. The criteria for participation was that applicants must self-identify as amateur theatre companies for adults, organised, led and run by amateurs (rather than community theatre companies or youth groups already associated with professional theatres). This, Wainwright observed, brought the RSC into contact with a social demographic that was often different from the 'bubble of left-wing, university educated, middle-class world found in professional theatre'.

Key to the programme's success was mutual respect, and the openness of people from both the RSC and amateur companies to learn from each other. At first, as Anne Gilmour and Jo Matthews of The Questors Theatre observed, some amateurs felt that their existing skills were not recognised by young professional directors, but as the programme evolved, respect

---

[8] Interview Ian Wainwright with Molly Flynn, 4 April 2016, Stratford upon Avon. All other quotations taken from this interview.

and reciprocity between the two sectors became more marked.[9] Michael Corbidge, a highly respected Senior Voice and Text Associate with the RSC, was a particularly popular and successful workshop leader in the Open Stages Programme. In an interview with Molly Flynn, he described his experience of working with amateurs on the Open Stages Programme as 'the most profound thing I have ever done, in my entire career', and summarised his experience of amateur performers:

> They really want to do it. They have the incredible passion, and heart – you know, amateur, it's what it means. And they commit, they just inhabit... Their devotion comes across. There's a different quality to amateurs, and you can't help but revel in their own joy. It's very powerful.[10]

The amateur performers have specific qualities on stage, Corbidge suggests, that can be strengthened when the RSC voice coaches, directors and fights directors share their skills. He pointed out that it is often the older amateur actors, who have honed their skills over many years, who would not be out of place on the professional stage. He regarded his role as opening people's eyes to the creative potential of theatre-making, and moving directors away from blocking scenes to a more fluid, workshop-based approach to rehearsal.

For the amateurs themselves, the Open Stages programme provided an opportunity to learn, extend their cultural horizons and to be recognised for the quality of their work. One Open Stages company came from Pirton, a village of around 1200 people in Hertfordshire. Anton Jungreuthmayer, director of the Pirton Player's production of *Julius Caesar* in 2015, described the significance of the process:

> For a little village in Hertfordshire to get to a nationwide programme was very exciting. The first thing was the directors' weekend... I was quite nervous going up there, thinking that there would be loads of people who would be really, really good, but everyone was just as excited and interested as everyone else. The practitioners all took us seriously. They never for a moment made it feel like them and us, like 'we're going to show you how

---

[9] Interview Anne Gilmour and Jo Matthews with Helen Nicholson, 22 Nov 2015 The Globe Theatre, London.

[10] Interview Michael Corbidge with Molly Flynn, 6 April 2017, The Crescent Theatre, Birmingham.

it's done'. It wasn't like that at all – it was very collaborative, right from the start.[11]

The Open Stages workshops whetted the amateurs' appetite to learn more, and many companies discovered to their surprise that many RSC practitioners are freelance, and available for hire for further workshops for a fee they could muster. The Pirton Players booked Corbidge for several visits, and Tom Jordon, who ran stage combat workshops for Open Stages, also spent time with the company. Tom Jordon commented that he had learnt a lot about his own practice by working with amateurs, not least because his assumptions about levels of skill and ability were often challenged.[12] Perhaps equally important as learning new skills was the respect that the Open Stages Programme afforded amateurs in their own locations, neatly summarised by Anton Jungreuthmayer's comment on Jordon's workshop: 'He's one of the top fight directors for top shows – and he's in our village hall!'.

The RSC's Open Stages programme was a cultural experiment that succeeded in demonstrating the potential for amateur and professional theatre companies to work together. As the Open Stages programme testifies, there is much talent in the amateur sector and, reciprocally, the RSC benefitted from an increased connection with local audiences and amateur theatre-makers. Although it was not without its detractors, Open Stages shed light on what it means to be an amateur, giving greater visibility for amateur performers and raising the status of amateur theatre companies. As Molly Flynn has pointed out, the association with RSC increased the cultural capital of amateur companies leading to greater confidence in their abilities (2017: 288). Some companies, such as Shakespeare at The George in Huntingdon, Cambridgeshire, had an established reputation for staging Shakespeare before the RSC's involvement with them, but for others the experience of performing Shakespeare was a new challenge.

Beyond the performance of Shakespeare, there is growing evidence that fellow professionals are beginning to follow the RSC's lead; Nick Hern Books, who are known for publishing cutting-edge contemporary plays, mounted its first *Amateur Theatre Fest* in 2018, featuring talks by Simon

---

[11] Interview Anton Jungreuthmayer with Molly Flynn, 2 March 2016, Pirton.
[12] Interview Tom Jordan with Molly Flynn, 27 June 2016, Cheltenham.

Fig. 8.1 Richard Brown and Liz Barka in *The Tempest* directed by John Shippey. Shakespeare at The George, Huntingdon, 2016. (By kind permission of photographer, Antonia Brown)

Callow, Mike Bartlett, Amanda Whittington and Jez Butterworth as well as a range of workshops. This marks a change in amateur theatre, observed by playwright Jessica Swale:

> The quality of the work is now very high in amateur theatre... My opinion of amateurs has changed, partly because when I was at university I worked with many fantastic performers, either those who were studying drama with me or in the Exeter equivalent of Footlights. Many of them went on to have jobs outside theatre, but continued to perform with amateur companies, and I knew how good they were.[13]

Swale (also published by Nick Hern Books) writes strong parts for women, and this is one of the reasons why her plays are popular with

---

[13] Interview Jessica Swale with Molly Flynn, 13 December 2016, London. All other quotations taken from this interview.

amateur theatre companies. She observed that there is 'an accessible land-scape' of professional productions through live streaming (she cites the work of the National Theatre and RSC) that can be seen anywhere in the country, and this, she argues, demonstrates to audiences what the potential of theatre can be. Where professional theatre-makers become vocal about the high production values found in some amateur companies, there is potential to increase the diversity of amateur theatre; we have found that one of the barriers to participation amongst black British and British Asian communities and other visible minority groups lies is its image and reputation with professionals as 'second best'. If a range of professional theatre companies were to raise the profile of amateurs by working partnership with them, it could make a long-term difference to amateur theatre as a socially inclusive practice.

All this suggests that there is significant potential for professionals and amateurs to develop new models of collaboration, and for amateur and professional partnerships to address areas of mutual concern, working together to achieve new artistic heights and lift some of the barriers to participation in the cultural sector. In an article in *The Stage*, Lyn Gardner mused on the potential for professional theatre to work more closely with their local communities in their programming:

> A real problem of working and running a theatre is people can very quickly become institutionalised. I'm often surprised that many theatres, who may be highly creative in the work they produce on stage, are often highly uncreative in the way they operate and very set in their ways. Often they operate on hierarchal structures too... For too long theatres have made work for audiences and not with audiences. They have made and programmed theatre that reflects the artistic tastes of those at the very top of those institutions...
>
> One way of ensuring that it does is to be bold, brave and generous enough to hand over decision-making to others, to actively try to make space rather than taking space, and to constantly ask not what the local community can do for the theatre but what the theatre might do for them.[14]

[14] Lyn Gardner: More theatres should follow York and involve the community in programming. The Stage, https://www.thestage.co.uk/opinion/2017/lyn-gardner-more-theatres-should-follow-york-and-involve-the-community-in-programming/?utm_source=newsletter1&utm_medium=email&utm_campaign=newsletter1. Accessed 3 August 2017.

Gardner recognises that there are millions of people who simply never go to the theatre (by which she means the professional theatre), and 'think it's not for them'. But the same people may well see their friends and neighbours in amateur productions, where theatre is made by, with and for their local communities. Greater collaboration between the sectors would go some way to acknowledge the strengths in the amateur sector, recognising that creativity is developed over a life-time, breathing new life into a valued and valuable part of the cultural ecology.

Sustainability, Professionalisation and Entrepreneurship

Many amateur theatre companies have longer histories than their professional counterparts, but it is also the case that the long-term sustainability and health of amateur theatre depends on its ability to adapt to twenty-first century challenges. The future of amateur theatre depends on capturing the imagination of the next generation, and most larger amateur theatres run youth theatres that are increasingly filling the gap left by declining local authority investment in the arts. The challenge amateur theatre companies face is how to maintain the interest and commitment of these young people in adulthood, many of whom want to maintain their creativity without the pressure to make a living from theatre-making. Equally important to the future of amateur theatre is places to perform; maintaining theatre buildings is a continual challenge for members of the Little Theatre Guild, many of whom run their own beautiful theatres on sound commercial footings. We have often heard concerns about funding, but Arts Council money comes with strings, and we have found that although amateur companies have appreciated Arts Council grants to improve disabled access to their buildings for example, they often value their artistic and creative autonomy above subsidy. In this section, we shall turn our attention to the ways in which some of the larger and most professionalised amateur theatres are addressing the challenge to create a sustainable future.

The Questors in Ealing is a large and forward-looking theatre that serves its London suburb and beyond. For Ealing, The Questors is a cultural hub, providing creative opportunities for its membership as well as other community organisations. Founded in 1929 by Alfred Emmet, The Questors has a long history of supporting high quality local amateur theatre as well as maintaining a vision for theatre across international boundaries. Now working in a large theatre building, The Questors stages around eighteen shows each year by their own membership, and provides a venue for other local companies. It has a 370-seat theatre, a ninety-seat Studio theatre as well as technical and workshop facilities, wardrobes and three rehearsal rooms. Unlike many amateur theatres, the Chief Executive, Andrea Bath, is a paid employee of the Trustees. With a background in professional theatre, she described the freedom she has found from working in the amateur sector:

> The balance is how do you work with volunteers to achieve something that is professional in outlook, in appearance and ethos. We call them volunteers, whether they are the talent who work on stage and backstage or those who volunteer front-of house to sell programmes. I look at my bottom line, and I think – what would I have to pay for that? £750 perhaps? And that's all taken out of my budget... But we are not restricted by a big stakeholder, like the Arts Council, like the local authority and we can spin on a sixpence and try things out. The Questors is adaptable because it doesn't have anyone saying 'tick these boxes'.[15]

One of the many distinctive features of The Questors is that, as an organisation, it is heavily committed to providing training in theatre; it is part of its culture and generates around a third of its income. The Questors Academy offers skill-sharing and training in a range of acting classes, all taught by practitioners with professional experience. It also offers a range of courses on technical theatre in partnership with Further Education and Higher Education Institutions that lead to formal qualifications. In 2018, they were working with the University of West London to provide a full-time BA (Hons) in Theatre Production, and with Kingston College to provide a BTEC Level 3 Extended Diploma in Production Arts. In common with many larger amateur theatres, The Questors has a thriving Youth Theatre for ages six to eighteen, and a Young Studio provides acting courses for seventeen to twenty-year olds. In addition to the formal courses offered, young people learn from experienced members through the kind of mentorship, informal training and apprenticeships we have

---

[15] Interview Andrea Bath with Helen Nicholson, The Questors, Ealing. 3 March 2016. All quotations are taken from this interview.

witnessed elsewhere. Andrea Bath commented on the importance of mentorship to the future of The Questors:

> Within the organisation there's an awful lot of mentoring going on. We're not talking about youth theatres, we're talking about the twenty-five-age group upwards, who are able to learn from people with thirty or forty years' experience. That's fantastic, but it's not in a classroom environment. It keeps people involved, as they feel they are learning.

This reciprocity ensures that the older Questors members are valued for their experience, both in the rehearsal period and backstage. The Questors has a commitment to one hundred hours rehearsal, unlike many other theatres, and this is a significant time-commitment. Yet time is often limited for young people in work, and The Questors have adapted to offer more short-term events, such as overnight plays, that are particularly attractive to young adults with busy lives.

London and other major cities are often a magnet for young professionals, and in common with other city-based companies, The Questors seeks to maintain links with local young people who choose not to move away from home and seeks to attract those who return after university. Each time I have visited the theatre, I have been struck by how many young people are evident, using the fashionable vintage-styled café in the day and mingling with older members and local audiences in the bar in the evening. Andrea Bath describes how this is changing the demographic of The Questors:

> Its changing the look of The Questors. People talk about theatre being white and middle-class, but look at the young people at The Questors, and the diversity of young people. They are going to have a big impact on The Questors over the next five years.

In the same conversation, Jo Matthews observed that keeping young people involved in The Questors sometimes meant supporting their own theatre companies and giving free space to rehearse. These young people are often catalysts for new ways of working, and future leaders of theatre-making that may well be defined less by the hierarchies associated with the amateur-professional divide.

Amateur theatre still brings together people from all educational backgrounds and across generations, but there are also young amateur theatre-makers who are moving the sector forward, many of whom hold qualifications in drama and theatre or are former members of youth theatres. Gail Bishop, for example, holds a degree in theatre and has been an enthusiastic member of The Miller Centre Theatre Company in Caterham, Surrey since her early teens. On returning to her hometown after university and working in London, Gail Bishop rejoined her local amateur theatre company, and by 2018 she was serving as artistic director. Bishop also reviews theatre on her blog, where she reveals her theatrical tastes:

> My Theatre degree focused more on the extremes of weirdness in contemporary performance (Franko B, Orlan, Jordan McKenzie.). It has reaffirmed my love of the traditional 'well written play'.[16]

In 2017 Gail Bishop satisfied her appetite for performing in scripted plays by taking the role of Queen Catherine in Jessica Swale's play *Nell Gwynn*. The production also toured to the Minack Theatre in Cornwall, an open-air theatre held in much affection by many amateurs, and which she describes as 'her favourite theatre in the whole world'. Gail Bishop's progression from youth theatre to a university drama degree and back to become artistic director of her theatre serves as an example of future leadership, and her lively presence at the Little Theatre Guild conferences offers fresh perspectives on how young people might be retained in the sector. Some companies—particularly those without buildings to run—are altering their operational structures to accommodate contemporary ways of life, and work on a project-by-project basis rather than as membership societies. Bev Clark, artistic director of the highly successful Hand-in-Hand Theatre Company in Birkenhead, re-forms the company for each production, with actors coming together through friendship, word-of-mouth and social media.

For those companies with buildings to maintain and run, however, membership is central to their business model, and it has led them to diversify their cultural offer. Activities at The Miller Centre Theatre, for example, are not confined to theatre-making, and their membership is served by an eclectic range of clubs and events:

[16] https://gailebishop.wordpress.com/. Accessed 4 May 2016.

Activities, available to Club members only, include two Book Clubs, Bridge, Miller Moviemakers, Crafts, Quilting, Painting (oil and watercolour), Scrabble, Folk Dancing, Table Tennis, Pilates, Tai Chi and Yoga. The Film Club shows films in the theatre each month and the Miller Centre Outings Club arranges frequent excursions to places of interest. Weekly, our Lunch Club offers delicious home-cooked meals and our Coffee Mornings provide excellent coffee with lively conversation.[17]

This approach reflects that entrepreneurial spirit of amateur theatre, where buildings need to pay their way by being used and filled on a regular basis. Cost-cutting is also important, and careful use and reuse of resources amongst amateur theatre-makers to enable them to spend wisely. As Cara Gray has pointed out, the aesthetic of amateur theatre is often defined by its attitude to recycling and re-use of materials, where she sees making and 'un-making as an important process of repair, where the lives of the materials are allowed to be reused in future productions' (2017: 225). The ingenuity of amateur theatre companies is often shown, Gray observes, on small acts of recycling and re-making; each nail and screw is carefully removed and saved as a set is struck, ready for the next production. On a grander scale, theatre buildings are also carefully restored and cared-for through entrepreneurial activities; The People's Theatre in Newcastle-upon-Tyne raised over £1.5 million towards environmentally-friendly restorations, receiving grants from twenty-seven Trusts and Foundations, including the Arts Council, and many smaller donations from local people. Its cutting-edge theatre facilities and the stylish post-industrial design of the bar and foyer is enhanced by regular contemporary art exhibitions, a far cry from the stuffy imaginary of amateur theatre.[18] Entrepreneurial companies also make profit from marketing their cultural assets: The Oasthouse Theatre in Kent, for example, raised over £100,000 to fund an extension to their buildings through costume hire.

There are many examples of companies rising to the challenges posed by the twenty-first century, but the Titchfield Festival Theatre in the south of England has tackled sustainability head-on. Led by chairperson and artistic director Kevin Fraser, the company took over a cavernous disused industrial unit as its base in 2010 and, with significant financial investment

---

[17] https://www.millercentretheatre.org/index.php/about-us. Accessed 21 June 2018.
[18] https://www.peoplestheatre.co.uk/about/support-us. Accessed 12 June 2018.

in its physical infrastructure, have transformed it to meet ambitions to be the first fully sustainable carbon neutral amateur theatre. It has installed a huge bio mass boiler, which generates heat for the building. The cement and asbestos roof has been replaced and fitted with state-of-the-art solar aerovoltic panels that provide electricity. Rainwater harvested from the roof is screened and filtered for use in laundering costumes and toilet facilities. The environmental credentials of this approach are clear, but there is an entrepreneurial aspect to this endeavour too, which has sought to introduce a new fleet-footed business model. After floating his own business on the stock exchange, Kevin Fraser has dedicated himself to Titchfield Festival Theatre and has proved remarkably adept at accessing and benefitting from subsidies designed to encourage the adoption of environmentally sustainable products. According to Kevin Fraser, the Government's Renewal Heat Incentive (RHI) scheme has helped to sub-sidise the rent on the theatre and 'pays for the pellets [for the boiler] and for the interest on the money that we've borrowed to pay the boiler back'.[19] Excess energy from the solar panels is sold back to the national grid as part of a further diversification of income streams. Fraser's ambi-tions are high, as he explained in a press release promoting his 'green theatre':

> Titchfield Festival theatre can optimise its future economic resource through shows, energy production and fuel savings so that it is economically sustain-able. The use of the sustainable energy resource makes this site a flagship in demonstrating the use of environmentally sustainable products … with almost a zero-carbon footprint. It will inspire other theatres and community areas to look at their own carbon footprint.[20]

Future plans include the purchase of four electric minibuses, fuelled by the existing solar panels, which will be used to collect and transport audi-ences, an initiative that will take polluting cars off the road and hopefully increase bar sales. Kevin Fraser also found ways to use empty offices, stor-age space and shops for rehearsals temporarily whilst earning further income. Working with a surveyor who locates appropriate premises, Titchfield Festival Theatre move in and as a registered charity, the owners

---

[19] Interview Kevin Fraser with Nadine Holdsworth, Titchfield Festival Theatre. 27 September 2016.
[20] http://titchfieldfestivaltheatre.com/green/. Accessed 20 June 2018.

of the premises are no longer liable to pay local rates. In one deal, Fraser claimed the company 'ended up getting back forty percent of the savings the owner was making as well as occupying the shop'. In addition, Titchfield Festival Theatre owns the lease and manages a medieval Great Barn situated close to Titchfield Abbey, which dates from 1410. The space is run as a very profitable wedding venue, as well as playing host to the company's annual Bard at the Barn Shakespeare Festival. Titchfield Festival Theatre currently produces twenty-seven shows a year, with new writing and adaptation making up 30% of its output.

Perhaps the scale and scope of Titchfield Festival Theatre is unusual, but, as we have seen, The People's Theatre in Newcastle is similarly making its theatre buildings fit for the twenty-first century, turning its long and radical history into a sustainable future. Together with many other theatres who are working on a smaller scale, they provide excellent examples of how amateur theatres can take on ambitious and forward-thinking projects that engage with issues of financial and environmental sustainability in an age in which resources are declining.

AMATEUR THEATRE, PARTICIPATION AND THE PUBLIC SPHERE

Within a five-mile radius of the community centre in Bourne End where the Forum Players rehearse and where we began this chapter, there are a remarkable eighteen amateur theatre companies that were active at the time of writing this book. There may be more that we have yet to find, but this list (in order of the dates in which they were founded) hints at the scale and range of amateur theatre today:

> Beaconsfield Music and Operatic Society (1910), John Lewis Partnership Society (1929), Maidenhead Drama Guild (1947), Marlow Amateur Operatic Society (1955), Masque Players (1956), Marlow Entertainers (1960s), Stoke Poges Players (1963), Maidenhead Musical Comedy Society (1966), The Grimm Players (1966), Fourways (1966), The Forum Players (1968), The Chiltern Shakespeare Company (1986), The Tarrystone Players (1990s), Beaconsfield Theatre Group (1995), Wycombe Society for the Performing Arts (2007), The Garden Players (2008), Renegade Theatre Company (2013), The Mavericks Drama Group (2015)

Most of these companies stage at least two productions a year, their repertoire ranging from musical theatre, Shakespeare, popular comedies, reviews, TV adaptations, pantomimes and contemporary plays. Some companies are members of national umbrella organisations such as NODA, but many are unaffiliated and thus fall outside national measures of cultural participation. These eighteen companies are all self-governing and run by adult amateur theatre-makers, but there are almost certainly many additional ad hoc performances staged by faith groups, the young farmers, the Women's Institute and other community groups within the same five-mile area. It is an extraordinary range of creative activity that, if replicated across the country (there is growing evidence to suggest that this is not unusual) demonstrates that amateur theatre is very much alive and well in the twenty-first century.

As our research testifies, amateur theatre is rehearsed and performed in village halls, community centres, schools, memorial halls, on ships, military bases, open-air venues, stately homes, in converted buildings and purpose built theatres. These places are often multipurpose and have a wider communitarian or civic function, giving amateur theatre a unique role in the public sphere. In his book *The Theatrical Public Sphere*, Christopher B. Balme comments on the political significance of the buildings in which theatre takes place:

> A town hall meeting curated by a theatre is on the one hand an idea that challenges the central preconceptions of what a theatre can and should be. On the other, it harks back to times when the town hall and the theatre were one and the same building. (2014: 3)

For amateurs, of course, using town halls and other civic buildings for performances does not 'hark back' to a previous era. It is primarily through amateur theatre that the theatre is still situated at the centre of community and civic life, both literally and metaphorically, and especially in areas outside metropolitan city centres. The culture of participation found in towns and villages lends amateur performance a particular place in the public sphere.

The relationship between civic responsibility, communitarianism and amateur theatre runs deep, with long historical roots. As we have evidenced, contributing to local charities and good causes is centrally important to many amateur companies and there is a strong impulse to serve their communities. Yet one of the complexities of undertaking this research is that, by definition, communities are exclusionary, and in the post-Brexit environment currently experienced in the UK, we remain alert to how the limits of amateur theatre's communitarianism might be perceived. Amateur theatre remains part of the civic calendar, but it was striking that the only non-white face in the audience for the All England Festival Theatre Finals in Maidenhead in 2017 belonged to the Mayor, Sayonara Luxton. This is an indication, perhaps, that civic participation is ahead of amateur theatre in terms of widening its demographic. Reciprocally, however, amateur theatre-makers have sometimes felt excluded or overlooked by those in the public sphere, and particularly by those working in subsidised arts. A conversation with long-standing members of Rhyl Little Theatre in North Wales illustrates this issue. The National Theatre of Wales had visited their seaside town, booked their theatre and, they recounted, did 'something on a beach, walked about and went away again'. Unimpressed by the short engagement with local people, they observed the contrast between this and their own theatre with its unbroken seventy-five year history.[21] The National Theatre of Wales *Lifted by Beauty: Adventures in Dreaming* (2017) may be more to the taste of arty professionals than some of the local productions, but Rhyl Little Theatre's ongoing place in the public sphere is secured by offering a lively and eclectic mix of comedy nights, live streaming of theatre and opera and amateur productions. More generally, if amateur theatre-makers are overlooked by cultural policy-makers and creative professionals because of time restrictions, or because their theatrical tastes are unaligned, there is a risk that sectors become increasingly remote from each other. Feelings of isolation from the cultural mainstream has social consequences. Given the evidence from the Brexit vote in 2016 that some social demographic groups felt overlooked and ignored by the establishment, this is a situation that policy-makers ignore at their peril. Of course, were professional artists and policy-makers to engage with the amateur theatre sector, they would find that it is neither culturally or politically homogenous, nor a singular entity; it contributes to the public sphere through its eclecticism, its mixed ecology and the diverse theatrical tastes and interests of its many participants and enthusiasts.

---

[21] Rhyl Little Theatre delegates in conversation at The Little Theatre Guild Conference, 21 April 2018, The People's Theatre, Newcastle-upon-Tyne. 2018.

Despite the many contemporary challenges, all the evidence suggests that the twenty-first century amateur turn is opening new possibilities for amateur theatre. The fashion for everything vintage, post-industrial and home-made suggests that there is a yearning for rootedness and a sense of belonging, and in this cultural landscape amateur theatre offers one way for people to connect. Unlike many other art forms, amateur theatre is distinctive in that it provides creative opportunities for people with a range of interests and talents, whether this is design, the technical aspects of theatre, acting or directing. It is the act of bringing together a production and working towards a shared project, under pressure of time, that creates community and a sense of common purpose. Our role is not to advocate a particular kind of amateur theatre, nor to seek to advocate the radical or cutting edge within it. Rather, in writing this book we have sought to pay attention to amateur theatre as a cultural field, as a craft and creative practice that makes a difference to people's lives.

REFERENCES

Balme, Christopher B. 2014. *The Theatrical Public Sphere*. Cambridge: Cambridge University Press.

Boltanski, Luc, and Eve Chiapello. 2007. *The New Spirit of Capitalism*. Trans. G. Elliott. London: Verso

Cederstrom, Carl, and André Spicer. 2015. *The Wellness Syndrome*. London: Polity Press.

Davies, William. 2015. *The Happiness Industry: How the Government and Big Business Sold Us Well-Being*. London: Verso.

Edensor, T., D. Leslie, S. Millington, and N.M. Rantisi, eds. 2010. *Spaces of Vernacular Creativity: Re-thinking the Cultural Economy*. London: Routledge.

Flynn, Molly. 2017. Amateur Hour: Culture, Capital, and the Royal Shakespeare Company's Open Stages Initiative. *RiDE: The Journal of Applied Theatre and Performance*. 22 (4): 482–499. https://doi.org/10.1080/13569783.2017.1358082.

Gray, Cara. 2017. *A Study of Amateur Theatre: Making and Making-Do*. Unpublished PhD Thesis, Royal Holloway, University of London.

Hawkins, Harriet. 2017. *Creativity*. London: Routledge.

Holden, John. 2015. *The Ecology of Culture: A Report Commissioned by the Arts and Humanities Research Council's Cultural Value Project*. Swindon: AHRC.

Keen, Andrew. 2007. *The Cult of the Amateur: How Blogs, MySpace, YouTube and the Rest of Today's User-Generated Media Are Killing our Culture and Economy*. London: Nicholas Brealey Books.

Kings College London. 2017. *Towards Cultural Democracy: Promoting Cultural Capabilities for Everyone*. London: KCL.

Knott, Stephen. 2015. *Amateur Craft: History and Theory*. London: Bloomsbury Academic.

Merrifield, Andy. 2017. *The Amateur: The Pleasure of Doing What You Love*. London: Verso.

Newcastle Players Bulletin. 2015. No. 523, March.

Price, Geoff. 2009. *150 Years of a Hartshill Institution*. Newcastle: Geoffrey H. Price.

REFERENCES

Adamson, Glenn. 2007. *Thinking Through Craft*. London: Berg Publishers.
———. 2013. *The Invention of Craft*. London: Bloomsbury Academic.
Adorno, T.W. 1991. Free Time. In *The Culture Industry: Selected Essays on Mass Culture*, 162–170. London: Routledge [1969].
Ahmed, Sara. 2000. *Strange Encounters: Embodied Others in Post-Coloniality*. London: Routledge.
———. 2014. *Willful Subjects*. Durham/London: Duke University Press.
Alexander, Anthony. 2009. *Britain's New Towns: Garden Cities to Sustainable Communities*. London: Routledge.
Alexander, Isabella. 2010. 'Neither Bolt Nor Chain, Iron Safe Nor Watchman Can Prevent the Theft of Words': The Birth of the Performing Right in Britain. In *Privilege and Property: Essays on the History of Copyright*, ed. Ronan Deazley, Martin Kretschmer, and Lionel Bently, 321–346. Cambridge: Open Book.
Allain, Paul. 2016. Thick Description/Thin Lines: Writing About Contemporary Performance. *Contemporary Theatre Review* 26 (4): 485–495.
Allnut, Peter. 1957. East and Central Africa. In *A Handbook for the Amateur Theatre*, ed. Peter Cotes, 329–335. London: Oldbourne Press.
Altieri, Charles. 1983. An Idea and Ideal of a Literary Canon. *Critical Inquiry* 10: 37–60.
Angelaki, Vicky. 2013. *Contemporary British Theatre: Breaking New Ground*. London: Palgrave.
Anheier, Helmut, and Yudhishthir Raj Isar, eds. 2008. *The Cultures and Globalization Series 2: The Cultural Economy*. London: SAGE.

© The Author(s) 2018
H. Nicholson et al., *The Ecologies of Amateur Theatre*,
https://doi.org/10.1057/978-1-137-50810-2

Appadurai, Arjun. 1986. Introduction: Commodities and the Politics of Value. In *The Social Life of Things: Commodities in Cultural Perspective*, ed. Arjun Appadurai, 3–63. Cambridge: Cambridge University Press.

Archer, William. 1923. *The Old Drama and the New*. London: W. Heinemann.

Archer, William, and Harley Granville Barker. 1907. *A National Theatre: Schemes and Estimates*. London: Duckworth.

Arendt, Hannah. 1958. *The Human Condition*. Chicago/London: The University of Chicago Press.

Arts Council England. 2000. *The Next Stage: Towards a National Policy for Theatre in England*. London: Arts Council England.

Arts Council of Great Britain. 1960. *Fifteenth Annual Report 1959–1960*. London: Arts Council of Great Britain.

———. 1970. *The Theatre Today in England and Wales*. London: Arts Council of Great Britain.

Aston, Elaine, and Elin Diamond, eds. 2009. *The Cambridge Companion to Caryl Churchill*. Cambridge: Cambridge University Press.

Aston, Elaine, and Geraldine Harris. 2012. *A Good Night Out for the Girls*. London: Palgrave.

Balme, Christopher B. 2014. *The Theatrical Public Sphere*. Cambridge: Cambridge University Press.

Barrett, Daniel. 1999. Play Publication, Readers, and the 'Decline' of Victorian Drama. *Book History* 2: 173–187.

Bauman, Zigmunt. 2003. *Liquid Love: On the Frailty of Human Bonds*. Cambridge: Polity Press.

———. 2005. *Liquid Life*. Cambridge: Polity Press.

Bazalgette, Peter. 2014. *The Value of Arts and Culture to People and Society*. London: Arts Council England.

Bennett, Andy, Jodie Taylor, and Ian Woodward. 2014. *The Festivalization of Culture*. Abingdon: Routledge.

Billig, Michael. 1995. *Banal Nationalism*. London: Sage.

Billington, Michael. 1996. *Harold Pinter*. London: Faber and Faber.

Bishop, George W., ed. 1929. *The Amateur Dramatic Yearbook and Community Theatre Handbook 1928–9*. London: A&C Black.

Bishop, Claire. 2012. *Artificial Hells: Participatory Art and the Politics of Spectatorship*. London: Verso.

Boltanski, Luc, and Eve Chiapello. 2007. *The New Spirit of Capitalism*. Trans. G. Elliott. London: Verso.

Bolton, Jacqueline. 2012. Capitalizing (on) New Writing: New Play Development in 1990s. *Studies in Theatre and Performance* 32 (2): 209–225.

Boyden, Peter. 2000. *Roles and Functions of the English Regional Producing Theatres: Final Report to the Arts Council England*. Bristol: Peter Boyden Associates.

Bradley, Ian. 2005. *Oh Joy! Oh Rapture! The Enduring Phenomenon of Gilbert and Sullivan*. New York: Oxford University Press.

Bratton, Jacky. 2003. *New Readings in Theatre History*. Cambridge: Cambridge University Press.

British Drama League. 1945. *Twenty-Five Years of the British Drama League*. Oxford: Alden Press.

Brown, Ian, and Rob Brannen. 1996. When Theatre Was for All: The Cork Report, After Ten Years. *New Theatre Quarterly* 12: 367–387.

Brownlee, David, David Edgar, Wendy Haines, Clare Ollerhead, and Dan Rebellato. 2015. *British Theatre Repertoire 2013*. London: Arts Council England.

Brunt, A.W. 1942. *The Pageant of Letchworth*. Letchworth: Letchworth Printers.

Burgess, Jean, and Joshua Green. 2009. *YouTube*. Cambridge: Polity Press.

Burton, Sarah. 2011. *How to Put on a Community Play*. London: Aurora Metro.

Canning, Charlotte. 2015. *On the Performance Front: US Theatre and Internationalism*. London: Palgrave Macmillan.

Casey, Edward. 1996. How to Get from Space to Place in a Fairly Short Stretch of Time. In *Senses of Place*, ed. S. Feld and K.H. Basso, 13–52. Santa Fe: School of American Research.

———. 1997. *The Fate of Place: A Philosophical History*. Berkeley: University of California Press.

Castells, Manuel. 2009. *The Rise of the Network Society*. 2nd Revised ed. Oxford: Wiley Blackwell.

Cederstrom, Carl, and André Spicer. 2015. *The Wellness Syndrome*. Cambridge: Polity Press.

Cellier, François, and Cunningham Bridgeman. 1914. *Gilbert and Sullivan and Their Operas*. Boston: Little, Brown and Company.

Chambers, Colin. 1989. *The Story of Unity Theatre*. Basingstoke: Macmillan.

———, ed. 2002. *The Continuum Companion to Twentieth-Century Theatre*. London: Continuum.

Chan, Tak Wing, and John H. Goldthorpe. 2005. The Social Stratification of Theatre, Dance and Cinema Attendance. *Cultural Trends* 14 (3): 193–212.

Channel 4 TV. 2012. All in the Best Possible Taste with Grayson Perry. June 5.

Chansky, Dorothy. 2005. *Composing Ourselves: The Little Theatre Movement and the American Audience*. Carbondale: Southern Illinois University Press.

Churchill, Caryl. 1985. Introduction. In *Plays 1*. London: Methuen.

Churchward, Sally. 2013. Is It the Final Curtain for Amateur Theatre in Hampshire? *Southern Daily Echo*, August 12. http://www.dailyecho.co.uk/news/10605815.Is_it_the_final_curtain_for_amateur_theatre_in_Hampshire. Accessed 18 Dec 2017.

Clifford, James. 1994. Diasporas. *Cultural Anthropology* 9 (3): 302–338.

Coates, David. 2017. A Whistle-Stop Tour of Amateur Theatricals in Nineteenth Century Britain. www.youtube.com/watch?v=eRFMxKn5oR8. Accessed 27 Dec 2017.

———. 2018. *The Development of Amateur Theatre in Britain in the Long Nineteenth Century 1789–1914.* Unpublished PhD Thesis, University of Warwick.

Cochrane, Claire. 2001. 'The Pervasiveness of the Commonplace': The Historian and Amateur Theatre. *Theatre Research International* 26 (3): 233–242.

———. 2011. *Twentieth Century British Theatre Industry, Art and Empire.* Cambridge: Cambridge University Press.

Cockin, Katharine. 1998. *Edith Craig (1869–1847): Dramatic Lives.* London: Cassell.

Cocoa Works Magazine. 1935. York: Rowntree.

Cohen Cruz, Jan. 2005. *Local Acts: Community-Based Performance in the United States.* New Brunswick/London: Rutgers University Press.

———. 2010. *Engaging Performance: Theatre as Call and Response.* London: Routledge.

Cork, Kenneth. 1986. *Theatre IS for All: Report of the Inquiry into Professional Theatre in England Under the Chairmanship of Sir Kenneth Cork.* London: Arts Council of Great Britain.

Corman, Brian. 1992. What Is the Canon of English Drama, 1660–1737? *Eighteenth-Century Studies* 26 (2): 307–321.

Cotes, Peter. 1949. *No Star Nonsense: A Challenging Declaration of Faith in the Essentials of Tomorrow's Theatre.* London: Theatre Book Club.

———. 1957. *A Handbook for the Amateur Theatre.* London: Oldbourne Press.

Cresswell, Tim. 2004. *Place: A Short Introduction.* Oxford: Basil Blackwell.

———. 2006. *On the Move: Mobility in the Modern Western World.* London: Routledge.

Crossick, Geoffrey, and Patrycja Kaszynska. 2016. *Understanding the Value of Arts and Culture: The AHRC Cultural Value Project.* Swindon: Arts and Humanities Research Council.

D'Monte, Rebecca. 2015. *British Theatre and Performance 1900–1950.* London: Bloomsbury.

Davies, William. 2015. *The Happiness Industry: How the Government and Big Business Sold Us Well-Being.* London: Verso.

Davis, Tracy C. 2009. Nineteenth Century Repertoires. *Nineteenth Century Theatre and Film* 36 (2): 6–28.

Davis, Tracy C., and Christopher B. Balme. 2015. A Cultural History of Theatre: A Prospectus. *Theatre Survey* 56 (3): 402–421.

Day, Graham. 2006. *Community and Everyday Life.* Abingdon: Routledge.

DCMS. 2016. The Culture White Paper. https://www.gov.uk/government/uploads/system/uploads/attachment_data/file/510798/DCMS_The_Culture_White_Paper__3_.pdf. Accessed 12 Nov 2016.

de Groot, Jerome. 2009. *Consuming History: Historians and Heritage in Contemporary Popular Culture*. Abingdon: Routledge.

Delanty, Gerard. 2011. Conclusion: On the Cultural Significance of Arts Festivals. In *Festivals and the Cultural Public Sphere*, ed. Liana Giorgi, Monica Sassatelli, and Gerard Delanty, 190–198. Abingdon: Routledge.

DiMaggio, Paul. 1992. Cultural Boundaries and Structural Change: The Extension of the High Culture Model to Opera, Theater and Dance, 1900–1940. In *Cultivating Differences: Symbolic Boundaries and the Making of Inequality*, ed. Michèle Lamont and Marcel Fournier, 21–57. Chicago: University of Chicago Press.

Dobson, Michael. 2011. *Shakespeare and Amateur Performance: A Cultural History*. Cambridge: Cambridge University Press.

Dodd, Fiona, Andrew Graves, and Karen Taws. 2008. *Our Creative Talent: The Voluntary and Amateur Arts in England*. London: DCMS.

Dolley, Colin. 1989. We're Only Here to Help. *The Stage and Television Today*, July 27, p. 23

Dorney, Kate, ed. 2013. *Played in Britain: Modern Theatre in 100 Plays*. London: Methuen.

Downs, Harold. 1926. *Theatre and Stage*. London: Pitman.

Edensor, Tim, Deborah Leslie, Steve Millington, and Norma M. Rantisi, eds. 2010. *Spaces of Vernacular Creativity: Rethinking the Cultural Economy*. Abingdon: Routledge.

Edgar, David. 2013. Playwriting Studies: Twenty Years On. *Contemporary Theatre Review* 23 (2): 99–106.

Edgar, David, Dan Rebellato, Janelle Reinelt, Steve Waters, and Julie Wilkinson. 2009. *Writ Large: New Writing on the English Stage 2003–09*. London: British Theatre Consortium.

Elsam, Paul. 2010. Harold Pinter's the Birthday Party: The 'Lost' Second Production. *Studies in Theatre and Performance* 30 (3): 257–266.

———. 2013. *Stephen Joseph, Theatre Pioneer and Provocateur*. London: Bloomsbury Methuen.

Emmet, Alfred. 1976. The Long Prehistory of the National Theatre. *Theatre Quarterly* 6 (21): 55–62.

———. 2002. Amateur Theatre. In *The Continuum Companion to Twentieth-Century Theatre*, ed. Colin Chambers. London: Continuum.

English, James F. 2005. *The Economy of Prestige*. Cambridge, MA: University of Harvard Press.

Exemption from Entertainments Duty of Amateur Entertainments. 1949. *Hansard* HC Deb vol 466 col 2192. July 6. http://hansard.millbanksystems.com/commons/1949/jul/06/new-clause-exemption-from-enter. Accessed 7 July 2017.

Filewod, Alan. 2004. Named in Passing: Canadian Theatre History. In *Writing and Re-writing National Theatre Histories*, ed. Stephen E. Wilmer, 106–126. Iowa City: University of Iowa Press.

Finnegan, Ruth. 2007. *The Hidden Musicians: Music-Making in an English Town*. Middletown: Wesleyan University Press.

Florida, Richard. 2002. *The Rise of the Creative Class*. New York: Basic Books.

Flynn, Molly. 2017. Amateur Hour: Culture, Capital, and the Royal Shakespeare Company's Open Stages Initiative. *RiDE: The Journal of Applied Theatre and Performance* 22 (4): 482–499. https://doi.org/10.1080/13569783.2017.13 58082.

Frayling, Christopher. 2011. *On Craftsmanship*. London: Oberon Books.

Frey, Bruno S. 2006. Giving and Receiving Awards. *Perspectives on Psychological Science* 1 (4): 377–388.

Garde-Hansen, Joanne. 2009. My Memories? Personal Digital Archive Fever and Facebook. In *Save As...Digital Memories*, ed. Joanne Garde-Hansen, Andrew Hoskins, and Anna Reading, 135–150. Basingstoke: Palgrave Macmillan.

Garde-Hansen, Joanne, Andrew Hoskins, and Anna Reading, eds. 2009. *Save As...Digital Memories*. Basingstoke: Palgrave Macmillan.

Gauntlett, David. 2011. *Making Is Connecting: The Social Meaning of Creativity, form DIY and Knitting to YouTube and Web 2.0*. Cambridge: Polity Press.

Geoghegan, Hilary. 2013. Emotional Geographies of Enthusiasm: Belonging to the Telecommunications Heritage Group. *Area* 45: 40–46. https://doi.org/10.1111/j.1475-4762.2012.01128.x.

Gibson-Graham, J.K. 2008. Diverse Economies: Performative Practices for 'Other Worlds'. *Progress in Human Geography* 32 (5): 613–632.

Giesekam, Greg. 2000. *Luvvies and Rude Mechanicals? Amateur and Community Theatre in Scotland*. Glasgow: Scottish Arts Council.

Gilmore, Abigail. 2013. Cold Spots, Crap Towns and Cultural Deserts: The Role of Place and Geography in Cultural Participation and Creative Placemaking. *Cultural Trends* 22 (2): 86–96.

Gilroy, Paul. 2004. *After Empire: Melancholia or Convivial Culture?* Abingdon: Routledge.

Goulding, Chris. 1991. *The Story of the People's*. Newcastle: Newcastle upon Tyne City Libraries & Arts.

Granville Barker, Harley. 1930. *A National Theatre*. London: Simon Schuster.

Gray, Cara. 2017. *A Study of Amateur Theatre: Making and Making-Do*. Unpublished PhD Thesis, Royal Holloway, University of London

Green, Michael. 1964. *The Art of Coarse Acting*. London: Hutchinson.

Gregg, Melissa. 2011. *Work's Intimacy*. London: Polity Press.

Grossmith, George, and Weedon Grossmith. 2010. *Diary of a Nobody*. London: Vintage.

Guillory, John. 2013. *Cultural Capital: The Problem of Literary Canon Formation*. Chicago: University of Chicago Press.

Gunn, John, and Barbara Bingham. 1957. *Acting for You.* London: Lutterworth Press.

Hammerton, James. 1999. Pooterism or Partnership? Marriage and Masculine Identity in the Lower Middle Class, 1870–1920. *Journal of British Studies* 38 (3): 291–321.

Harrison, Rodney. 2013. *Heritage: Critical Approaches.* London: Routledge.

Harrison, Rodney, and Deborah Rose. 2010. Intangible Heritage. In *Understanding Heritage and Memory,* ed. Tim Benton, 238–276. Manchester: Manchester University Press.

Harvie, Jen, and Andy Lavender, eds. 2010. *Making Contemporary Theatre: International Rehearsal Processes.* Manchester: Manchester University Press.

Hawkins, Harriet. 2017. *Creativity.* London: Routledge.

Hawley, Judith. 2012. What Signifies a Theatre?': Private Theatricals and Amateur Dramatics in Britain and Abroad. Conference Paper, University of Notre Dame in London, July 7.

Hawley, Judith, and Mary Isbell, eds. 2012. Amateur Theatre Studies. *Nineteenth Century Theatre and Film.* Manchester: Manchester University Press.

Heckenberg, Pamela, and Philip Parsons. 1984. The Struggle for an Australian Theatre. In *The Australian Stage,* ed. Harold Love, 118–134. Kensington: New South Wales University Press.

Heinrich, Anselm. 2010. Theatre in Britain During the Second World War. *New Theatre Quarterly* 26 (1): 61–70.

Hewison, Robert. 1987. *The Heritage Industry: Britain in a Climate of Decline.* London: Methuen.

———. 2014. *Cultural Capital: The Rise and Fall of Creative Britain.* London: Verso.

Hirschfield, Claire. 1985. The Actresses Franchise League and the Campaign for Women's Suffrage, 1908–1914. *Theatre Research International* 10: 129–151.

Hobsbawm, Eric. 1983. Introduction: Inventing Traditions. In *The Invention of Tradition,* ed. Eric Hobsbawm and Terence Ranger, 1–14. Cambridge: Cambridge University Press.

Hochschild, Arlie Russell. 2002. *The Managed Heart: Commercialization of Human Feeling.* Berkeley: University of California Press.

Hodder, Ian. 2012. *Entangled: An Archaeology of the Relationships between Humans and Things.* Oxford: Wiley-Blackwell.

Hoggart, Richard. 1976. *The Uses of Literacy.* London: Pelican Books [1957].

Holden, John. 2015. *The Ecology of Culture: A Report Commissioned by the Arts and Humanities Research Council's Cultural Value Project.* Swindon: AHRC.

Holdsworth, Nadine, Jane Milling, and Helen Nicholson. 2017. Theatre, Performance, and the Amateur Turn. *Contemporary Theatre Review* 27 (1): 4–17. https://doi.org/10.1080/10486801.2017.1266229.

Holland, Patricia. 1991. Introduction: History, Memory and the Family Album. In *Family Snaps: The Meanings of Domestic Photography*, ed. Jo Spence and Patricia Holland, 1–14. London: Virago Press.

Horton, John, and Peter Kraftl. 2012. Clearing out a Cupboard: Memory, Materiality and Transitions. In *Geography and Memory*, ed. Owain Jones and Joanne Garde-Hansen, 25–44. Basingstoke: Palgrave Macmillan.

Hoskins, Andrew. 2009. The Mediatisation of Memory. In *Save As...Digital Memories*, ed. Joanne Garde-Hansen, Andrew Hoskins, and Anna Reading, 27–43. Basingstoke: Palgrave Macmillan.

Howard, Ebenezer. 1902. *Garden Cities of Tomorrow*. London: Sonnenschein & Co.

Howard, Pamela. 2009. *What Is Scenography?* 2nd ed. London: Routledge.

Howell, Patrick. 2016. *Consistently Brilliant on a Breezy Hilltop: A History of the Cotswold Players: The First Hundred Years*. n.p.: Quicksilver Publications.

Howkins, Alun. 2003. *The Death of Rural England: A Social History of the Countryside*. London: Routledge.

Hughes, Jenny. 2016. A Pre-history of Applied Theatre: Work, House, Perform. In *Critical Perspectives on Applied Theatre*, ed. Jenny Hughes and Helen Nicholson, 40–60. Cambridge: Cambridge University Press.

Hunt, Tristram. 2004. *Building Jerusalem: The Rise and Fall of the Victorian City*. London: Phoenix Paperback.

Huq, Rupa. 2013. *On the Edge: The Contested Cultures of English Suburbia*. London: Lawrence and Wishart.

Hurley, Erin. 2010. *Theatre & Feeling*. Basingstoke: Palgrave Macmillan.

Ingold, Tim. 2013. *Making: Anthropology, Archaeology, Art and Architecture*. Abingdon: Routledge.

Ingold, Tim, and Elizabeth Hallam, eds. 2007. *Creativity and Cultural Improvisation*. Oxford: Berg.

Jackson, Shannon. 2001. *Lines of Activity: Performance, Historiography, Hull-House Domesticity*. Ann Arbor: University of Michigan Press.

———. 2011. *Social Works: Performing Art, Supporting Publics*. London: Routledge.

Jeffers, Alison, and Gerri Moriarty. 2017. *Culture, Democracy and the Right to Make Art: The British Community Arts Movement*. London: Methuen.

Jeyifo, Biodun. 1990. The Reinvention of Theatrical Tradition. In *The Dramatic Touch of Difference: Theatre, Own and Foreign*, ed. Erika Fischer-Lichte, Josephine Riley, and Michael Gissenwehrer, 239–252. Tübingen: Gunter Narr Verlag Tübingen.

Jones, Henry Arthur. 2008. *Stage by Stage: 75 Years of Theatre in Market Harborough*. 2nd ed. Leicester: Matador.

Jones, Jonathan. 2014. British Folk Art Review – Welcome to the Old Weird Britain. *Guardian*, June 9. https://www.theguardian.com/artanddesign/2014/jun/09/british-folk-art-review-tate-britain. Accessed 21 Sept 2016.

Joseph, Tony. 1994. *D'Oyly Carte Opera Company, 1875–1982: An Unofficial History*. London: Bunthorne Books.

Keen, Andrew. 2007. *The Cult of the Amateur: How Blogs, MySpace, YouTube and the Rest of today's User-Generated Media Are Killing our Culture and Economy*. London: Nicholas Brealey Publishing.

———. 2008. *The Cult of the Amateur*. Revised ed. London: Nicholas Brealey Publishing.

Kelly, Mary. 1939. *Village Theatre*. London: Thomas Nelson.

———. 1948. *Group Play-Making*. London: G.G. Harrap.

Kerman, Joseph. 1983. A Few Canonic Variations. *Critical Inquiry* 10: 107–125.

Kershaw, Baz. 1992. *The Politics of Performance: Radical Theatre as Cultural Intervention*. London: Routledge.

———. 2007. *Theatre Ecologies: Environments and Performance Events*. Cambridge: Cambridge University Press.

Khan, Naseem. 1976. *The Arts Britain Ignores: The Arts of Ethnic Minorities in Britain*. London: Community Relations Commission.

Kings College London. 2017. Towards Cultural Democracy: Promoting Cultural Capabilities for Everyone. https://www.kcl.ac.uk/Cultural/-/Projects/Towards-cultural-democracy.aspx. Accessed 4 Aug 2017.

Knott, Stephen. 2015. *Amateur Craft: History and Theory*. London: Bloomsbury Academic.

Kopytoff, Igor. 1986. The Cultural Biography of Things: Commoditization as Process. In *The Social Life of Things: Commodities in Cultural Perspective*, ed. Arjun Appadurai, 64–92. Cambridge: Cambridge University Press.

Korn, Peter. 2013. *Why We Make Things & Why It Matters: The Education of a Craftsman*. London: Vintage.

Kruger, Loren. 1987. 'Our National House': The Ideology of the National Theatre of Great Britain. *Theatre Journal* 39 (1): 35–50.

Leask, Margaret. 2012. *Lena Ashwell: Actress, Patriot, Pioneer*. Hatfield: University of Hertfordshire Press.

Lee, Jennie. 1965. A Policy for the Arts: The First Steps. http://action.labour.org.uk/page/-/blog%20images/policy_for_the_arts.pdf. Accessed 14 Oct 2016.

Lees, Loretta, ed. 2004. *The Emancipatory City?* London: Sage.

Lefebvre, Henri. 2014. *Toward an Architecture of Enjoyment*. Trans. R. Bononno. Minneapolis: Minneapolis University Press.

Lewis, Henry, Jonathan Sayer, and Henry Shields. 2015. *The Play that Goes Wrong*. London: Bloomsbury.

Leyshon, Andrew, and Roger Lee. 2003. Introduction: Alternative Economic Geographies. In *Alternative Economic Spaces*, ed. Andrew Leyshon, Roger Lee, and Colin C. Williams, 1–26. London: SAGE.

———, eds. 2008. *The Sage Handbook of Economic Geography*. London: SAGE.

Light, Alison. 1991. *Forever England: Femininity, Literature and Conservativism Between the Wars*. London: Routledge.

Lineham, Thomas. 2012. *Modernism and British Socialism*. London: Palgrave.

Lippard, Lucy. 1997. *The Lure of the Local: Senses of Place in a Multicentred Society*. New York: The New Press.

Lowerson, John. 1999. An Outbreak of Allodoxia? Amateur Operatics and Middleclass Musical Taste between the Wars. In *Gender, Civic Culture and Consumption*, ed. Alan Kidd and David Nicholls, 196–211. Manchester: Manchester University Press.

———. 2005. *Amateur Operatics: A Social and Cultural History*. Manchester: Manchester University Press.

Lowrie, Andrew. 2016. Culture, Media and Sports Enquiry. *Little Theatre Guild Newsletter* 30(2): 3. http://littletheatreguild.org/wp-content/uploads/2015/08/Aug-16-LTG-Newsletter.pdf. Accessed 18 Dec 2017.

Luckman, Susan. 2015. *Craft and the Creative Economy*. Basingstoke: Palgrave Macmillan.

Mangan, Michael. 2010. The Theatre in Modern British Culture. In *The Cambridge Companion to Modern British Culture*, ed. Michael Higgins, Clarissa Smith, and John Storey, 154–170. Cambridge: Cambridge University Press.

Marx, Karl. 2007. *Capital: A Critique of Political Economy: The Process of Capitalist Production, Volume 1 Part 11*. New York: Cosimo Classics [1867].

Massey, Doreen. 2005. *For Space*. London: Sage Publications.

Matarasso, Francois. 2012. *Where We Dream: West Bromwich Operatic Society & the Fine Art of Musical Theatre*. West Bromwich: A Multistory Publication.

Matless, David. 1998. *Landscape and Englishness*. London: Reaktion Books.

McAuley, Gay. 2012. *Not Magic But Work: An Ethnographic Account of a Rehearsal Process*. Manchester: Manchester University Press.

McCaffery, Michael. 1988. *Directing a Play*. London: Phaidon.

Meacham, Standish. 1999. *Regaining Paradise: Englishness and the Early Garden City Movement*. New Haven/London: Yale University Press.

Merrifield, Andy. 2017. *The Amateur: The Pleasure of Doing What You Love*. London: Verso.

Meth, Jonathan. 2004. *Commissioning New Work: A Good Practice Guide for Amateur Theatre Companies and Playwrights*. London: Arts Council England.

Miles, Andrew. 1999. *Social Mobility in Nineteenth and Early Twentieth-Century England*. Basingstoke: Macmillan.

Modood, Tariq. 2007. *Multiculturalism*. Cambridge: Polity Press.

Moran, James. 2013. Pound, Yeats and the Regional Repertory Theatre. In *Regional Modernisms*, ed. James Moran and Neal Alexander, 83–103. Edinburgh: Edinburgh University Press.

Mouffe, Chantal, ed. 1992. *Dimensions of Radical Democracy*. London: Verso.

National Operatic and Dramatic Association. 2013. It Isn't Always Black and White. 4th version. http://www.NODA.org.uk/writeable/editor_uploads/files/NODAfacts/It%20isn't%20always%20black%20and%20white%20V4%20July%202013.pdf. Accessed 16 May 2017.

Naylor, Richard, Bethany Lewis, Caterina Branzanti, Graham Devlin, and Alan Dix. 2016. *Analysis of Theatre in England.* London: Arts Council England.

Newcastle Players Bulletin 2015. No. 523, March.

Newey, Kate. 2005. *Women's Theatre Writing in Victorian Britain.* Basingstoke: Palgrave Macmillan.

Newton, Robert. 1967. *A Creative Approach to Amateur Theatre.* London: J. Garnett Miller.

Nicoll, Allardyce. 1973. *English Drama 1900–1930.* Cambridge: Cambridge University Press.

Nicholls, Tony. 2013. *Theatre West Four: So Far As I Can Remember, Three Volumes.* London: Into Print.

Nicholson, Helen. 2014. *Applied Drama: The Gift of Theatre.* 2nd ed. Basingstoke: Palgrave Macmillan.

———. 2015. Absent Amateurs. *RiDE: The Journal of Applied Theatre and Performance* 20 (3): 263–266. https://doi.org/10.1080/13569783.2015.1059262.

Nititham, Diane Sabenacio. 2017. *Making Home in Diasporic Communities: Transnational Belonging Amongst Filipina Migrants.* London: Routledge.

O'Brien, Dave and Kate Oakley. 2015. *Cultural Value and Inequality: A Critical Literature Review.* London: Arts and Humanities Research Council.

Patterson, Eric J. 1919. Beginnings. *Drama* 1 (1): 5.

Pellecchia, Diego. 2017. Noh Creativity? The Role of Amateurs in Japanese Noh Theatre. *Contemporary Theatre Review* 27 (1): 34–45. https://doi.org/10.1080/10486801.2016.1262848.

Penny, Sarah. 2016. Crossing the Line. *Performance Research* 21 (2): 32–37. https://doi.org/10.1080/13528165.2016.1162524.

Penny, Sarah, and Cara Gray. 2017. The Materialities of Amateur Theatre. *Contemporary Theatre Review* 27 (1): 104–123. https://doi.org/10.1080/10486801.2016.1262850.

Pink, Sarah. 2009. *Doing Sensory Ethnography.* London: Sage Publications.

Pirsig, Robert M. 1974. *Zen and the Art of Motorcycle Maintenance.* New York: Quill Publications.

Portelli, Alessandro. 1998. What Makes Oral History Different. In *The Oral History Reader,* ed. Robert Perks and Alistair Thomson, 63–74. London: Routledge.

Postlewait, Thomas. 1986. *Prophet of the New Drama: William Archer and the Ibsen Campaign.* Westport: Greenwood Press.

Powell, David. 1996. *The Edwardian Crisis: Britain 1901–1914.* Basingstoke: Macmillan.

Price, Geoff. 2009. *150 Years of a Hartshill Institution.* Newcastle: Geoffrey H. Price.

Priestley, J.B. 1934. *English Journey.* London: Victor Gollanz.

Purdom, C.B. 1908. *Letchworth Dramatic Society: The First Annual Report (1907–1908).* London: J.M. Dent.

Purdom, C.B. 1930. *Producing Plays: A Handbook for Producers and Players.* New York: E.P. Dutton.

Purdom, C.B. 1951. *Life Over Again.* London: J.M. Dent and Sons.

Purdom, C.B., and Charles Lee. 1910. *The Second Garden City Pantomime.* Letchworth: Dent Publishers.

Putnam, Robert. 2000. *Bowling Alone: The Collapse and Revival of American Community.* New York: Simon and Schuster.

Radosavljević, Duska. 2013. *Theatre-Making: The Interplay Between Text and Performance in the 21st Century.* Basingstoke: Palgrave Macmillan.

Rebellato, Dan. 1999. *1956 and All That.* London: Routledge.

Reinelt, Janelle. 2011. The Performance of Political Correctness. *Theatre Research International* 36 (2): 134–147. https://doi.org/10.1017/S03078833110 00216.

Ridout, Nicholas. 2013. *Passionate Amateurs: Theatre, Communism, and Love.* Ann Arbor: University of Michigan Press.

Ritchie, Richard. 2015. *The Old Stagers: Canterbury, Cricket and Theatricals.* Canterbury: OS Publishing.

Roach, Joseph. 1996. *Cities of the Dead.* New York: Columbia University Press.

Roberts, Elizabeth. 2012. Family Photographs: Memories, Narrative, Place. In *Geography and Memory,* ed. Owain Jones and Joanne Garde-Hansen, 91–108. Basingstoke: Palgrave Macmillan.

Rose, Jonathan. 1986. *The Edwardian Temperament 1895–1919.* Ohio: Ohio University Press.

———. 2001. *The Intellectual Life of the British Working Classes.* New Haven: Yale University Press.

Rosenthal, Daniel. 2013. *The National Theatre Story.* London: Oberon.

Rowell, George, and Anthony Jackson. 1984. *The Repertory Movement: A History of Regional Theatre in Britain.* Cambridge: Cambridge University Press.

Rowntree, Seebohm. 1901. *Poverty: A Study of Town Life.* London: Macmillan Publishers.

Rugoff, Ralph. 2008. Other Experts. In *Amateurs,* 9–14. San Francisco: California College of the Arts.

Rural Extension Scheme (Devon). 1938. *Drama* 16 (5): 68.

Russell, Dave. 2004. *Looking North: Northern England and the National Imagination.* Manchester: Manchester University Press.

Samuel, Raphael. 1994. *Theatres of Memory Vol. 1 Past and Present in Contemporary Culture*. London: Verso.

Samuel, R., E. MacColl, and S. Cosgrove. 1985. *Theatres of the Left 1880–1935 Workers' Theatre Movements in Britain and America*. London: Routledge Kegan Paul.

Saunders, Graham. 2012. Prizes for Modernity in the Provinces: The Arts Council's 1950–1951 Regional Playwriting Competition. *History Research* 2 (2): 73–109.

Schneider, Rebecca. 2001. Archives: Performance Remains. *Performance Research* 6 (2): 100–108. https://doi.org/10.1080/13528165.2001.10871792.

Schoch, Richard. 2016. *Writing the History of the British Stage*. Cambridge: Cambridge University Press.

Sennett, Richard. 1998. *The Corrosion of Character: The Personal Consequences of Work in the New Capitalism*. New York: Norton Books.

———. 2008. *The Craftsman*. London: Penguin Books.

———. 2013. *Together: The Rituals, Pleasures and Politics of Cooperation*. London: Penguin Books.

Seton, Marie. 1937. Theatre in Berlin. *Drama* 15 (4): 50–52.

Sharma, Sarah. 2014. *In the Meantime: Temporality and Cultural Politics*. London: Duke University Press.

Sharman, Helen E. 2004. *Directing Amateur Theatre*. London: A&C Black.

Shaughnessy, Nicola. 2012. *Applying Performance: Live Art, Socially Engaged Theatre and Affective Practice*. Basingstoke: Palgrave Macmillan.

Shepherd, Simon, and Mick Wallis. 2004. *Drama/Theatre/Performance*. London: Routledge.

Shipley, Michael. 2006. *Bolton Little Theatre: 75 Years of Drama*. Leeds: Millnet Financial Services.

———. 2015. New Writing. *Little Theatre Guild Newsletter*, November 9.

Shirley, Rosemary. 2015. *Rural Modernity, Everyday Life and Visual Culture*. Abingdon: Routledge.

Sladen-Smith, Francis. 1933. *The Amateur Producer's Handbook*. London: Thomas Nelson.

Smedley, Constance. 1937. The Story of the Cotswold Players. *Drama* 16 (1): 4–6.

Smith, Laurajane. 2006. *Uses of Heritage*. Abingdon: Routledge.

———. 2011. The 'Doing' of Heritage: Heritage as Performance. In *Performing Heritage: Research, Practice and Innovation in Museum Theatre and Live Interpretation*, ed. Anthony Jackson and Jenny Kidd, 69–81. Manchester: Manchester University Press.

Smith, Laurajane, and Emma Waterton. 2009. The Envy of the World: Intangible Heritage in England. In *Intangible Heritage*, ed. Laurajane Smith and Natsuko Akagawa, 289–302. Abingdon: Routledge.

Stebbins, Robert A. 1979. *Amateurs: On the Margin Between Work and Leisure.* London: Sage Publications.

———. 1992. *Amateurs, Professionals and Serious Leisure.* Montreal: McGill and Queen's University Press.

———. 2007. *Serious Leisure.* New Brunswick: Transaction Publishers.

Stengers, Isabel. 2005. Introductory Notes on an Ecology of Practices. *Cultural Studies Review* 11 (1): 183–196.

Storey, Taryn. 2017. 'Village Hall Work Can Never Be Theatre': Amateur Theatre and the Arts Council of Great Britain, 1945–56. *Contemporary Theatre Review* 27 (1): 76–91.

Taylor, George. 1976. *History of the Amateur Theatre.* Melksham: Colin Venton White Horse Library.

Taylor, Charles. 2002. Modern Social Imaginaries. *Public Culture* 14 (1): 91–124.

Taylor, Diana. 2003. *The Archive and the Repertoire.* Durham: Duke University Press.

The Fabian Society. 1894. *The Parish Council's Act: What It Is and How to Work It*, Fabian Society Tract. Vol. 53. London: The Fabian Society.

The Office for National Statistics, Taking Part. www.gov.uk/government/collections/sat%2D%2D2. Accessed 13 Oct 2016.

Thompson, E.P. 1967. Time, Work-Discipline and Industrial Capitalism. *Past & Present* 38: 56–97.

Thompson, Paul. 1992. *The Edwardians: The Remaking of British Society.* London: Routledge.

Thompson, James. 2009. *Performance Affects: Applied Theatre and the End of Effect.* Basingstoke: Palgrave Macmillan.

Throsby, David. 2003. Determining the Value of Cultural Goods: How Much (or How Little) Does Contingent Valuation Tell Us? *Journal of Cultural Economics* 27: 275–285.

Tomlin, Liz. 2015. *British Theatre Companies 1995–2014.* London: Bloomsbury.

Turkle, Sherry, ed. 2007. *Evocative Objects: Things We Think With.* Cambridge, MA: MIT Press.

Turner, Cathy. 2015. *Dramaturgy and Architecture: Theatre, Utopia and the Built Environment.* Basingstoke: Palgrave Macmillan.

Turner, Cathy, and Synne Behrndt. 2007. *Dramaturgy and Performance.* Basingstoke: Palgrave.

Twydell, Dave. 2011. *Mr. Fothergill to Lark Rise: Harefield Amateur Dramatic Society 1951–2011.* Harefield: Harefield Amateur Dramatic Society.

Veitch, Norman. 1950. *The People's: Being a History of the People's Theatre, Newcastle upon Tyne, 1911–1939.* Gateshead upon Tyne: Northumberland Press.

Voluntary Arts. 2016. Open Conversations: Developing Strong, Effective Connections to Black, Asian and Minority Ethnic Communities. https://www.voluntaryarts.org/Handlers/Download.ashx?IDMF=03810465-0337-4f49-a1d6-5ac97b06b349. Accessed 9 May 2017.

Wagner, Anton. 1999. Becoming Actively Creative: Dr. Lawrence Mason the Globe's Critic 1924–1939. In *Establishing our Boundaries: English-Canadian Theatre Criticism*, ed. Anton Wagner, 119–214. Toronto: University of Toronto Press.

Walcon, Erin, and Helen Nicholson. 2017. The Sociable Aesthetics of Amateur Theatre. *Contemporary Theatre Review* 27 (1): 18–33. https://doi.org/10.10 80/10486801.2016.1262851.

Wallis, Mick. 2000. Unlocking the Secret Soul: Mary Kelly Pioneer of Village Theatre. *New Theatre Quarterly* 16 (4): 347–358.

———. 2006. Drama in the Villages: Three Pioneers. In *The English Countryside 1918–39: Regeneration or Decline?* ed. Paul Brassley, Jeremy Burchardt, and Lynne Thompson, 102–115. Woodbridge: Boydell and Brewer.

Warden, Claire. 2016. *Migrating Modernist Performance*. London: Palgrave Macmillan.

Weingärtner, Jörn. 2012. *Arts as a Weapon of War*. London: I. B. Tauris.

Wetherell, Margaret. 2012. *Affect and Emotion*. London: Sage.

Whiting, James, and Kevin Hannam. 2015. Creativity, Self-Expression and Leisure. *Leisure Studies* 34 (3): 372–384.

Whitworth, Geoffrey. 1919. The British Drama League. *Drama* 1 (1): 5.

———. 1937. The British Council. *Drama* 15 (4): 57.

———. 1951. *The Making of a National Theatre*. London: Faber and Faber.

Wickham, Glynne. 1977. A Revolution in Attitudes to the Dramatic Arts in British Universities 1880–1980. *Oxford Review of Education* 3 (2): 115–121.

Williams, Paul. 2013. *Paul Gilroy*. Abingdon: Routledge.

Williams, Raymond. 1971. *The Long Revolution*. London: Penguin.

Wilson, Shaun. 2009. Remixing Memory in Digital Media. In *Save As…Digital Memories*, ed. Joanne Garde-Hansen, Andrew Hoskins, and Anna Reading, 187–197. Basingstoke: Palgrave Macmillan.

Wilson, Nick. 2010. Social Creativity: Re-qualifying the Creative Economy. *International Journal of Cultural Policy* 16 (3): 367–381. https://doi.org/10.1080/10286630903111621.

Winchester Dramatic Society. 2014. *A History of the Winchester Dramatic Society*. Winchester: Sarsen Press.

Wolf, Stacy. 2017. 'The Hills Are Alive with the Sound of Music': Musical Theatre at Girls' Jewish Summer Camps in Maine, USA. *Contemporary Theatre Review* 27 (1): 46–60. https://doi.org/10.1080/10486801.2016.1262853.

Worthen, William B. 2010. *Drama: Between Poetry and Performance*. Oxford: Wiley-Blackwell.

Young, John N. 1999. *A Century of Service: The Story of the National Operatic and Dramatic Association*. London: NODA.

Zarhy-Levo, Yael. 2008. *Making of Theatrical Reputations*. Iowa City: Iowa University Press.

INDEX[1]

[1] Note: Page numbers followed by 'n' refer to notes.

© The Author(s) 2018
H. Nicholson et al., *The Ecologies of Amateur Theatre*,
https://doi.org/10.1057/978-1-137-50810-2

Progressive Players, Gateshead, 86
Progressive Theatre, 48
Prop-making, 2, 7
Proscenium arch, 140
Public subsidy, 52
Publicly subsidised arts, 28
Publicly subsidised culture, 27
Pugh, David, *see* Firth, Tim
Purdom, Charles B., 45, 92, 122–128,
    130, 131, 133, 134, 136, 149,
    150
  socialist principles, 122
Putnam, David, 218

Q
Quakers, 166
The Questors Academy, 297
The Questors, Ealing, 53, 72, 93–95,
    98, 99, 101, 137, 140, 194, 219,
    241, 252, 282, 291, 296–298
Quinn, Beverly, 101

R
Racial stereotyping, 222
Racism, 223
Radius (the Religious Drama Society
    of Great Britain), 59
Radosavljević, Duska, 98
Rahilly, Les, 209, 211, 214
Rattigan, Terence, 83
RBS Theatre Company, 171
Reality TV shows, 4
Rebellato, Dan, 71, 82
Rees, Roger, 94
Regional culture, 47
Regional identity, 45
Regional theatre, 13, 23, 25, 30, 35, 42,
    46, 49, 50, 59, 68, 79, 80, 281
Rehearsal/rehearsals, 1, 15, 16, 72,
    141, 158, 168, 179–181, 201,
    204, 208–218, 231

Reid, Georgina
  Ladies of Spirit, 86
Reilly, Alan, 132
Reinelt, Janelle, 224
Renegade Theatre Company, High
    Wycombe, 302
Repertoire, 6, 8, 9, 13, 15, 31, 36, 40,
    43–45, 52, 54, 59, 67–71, 73,
    78–80, 82, 85–89, 91, 93, 94,
    96, 98, 103, 104, 114, 124, 125,
    139–141, 151, 195, 204, 206,
    213, 220, 226, 229, 241, 243,
    245, 248, 255, 279, 303
  everyday repertoire, 88
  national repertoire, 67, 70, 79, 89,
      104
  as performance modes, 87
  performance repertoire, 82
  repertoire formation, 71
  repertoiring, 13, 69, 79, 80, 88, 89,
      103, 290
Repertory theatre, 23, 43–45
Repertory theatre movement, 42, 43,
    68, 70
Research process, 15, 16
Reuben-Travers, Leitina, 222, 223
Revolutionary Road, 117
Rhyl Little Theatre, 304
Richardson, Ralph, 94
Rickmansworth Players, 139
Ridout, Nicholas, 5, 161, 163
Ritchie, Richard, 255
Rix, Brian, 95
Roach, Joseph, 88
Roberts, Elizabeth, 245
Robeson, Paul, 36
Robins, Gertrude, 34
Robson, Flora, 126, 174
Rogers, Dafydd, *see* Firth, Tim
Roots/rootedness, 151, 288, 305
Rose, Deborah, 250
Rose, Jonathan, 34, 171
Rose Bruford Drama School, 94

Printed in Great Britain
by Amazon